SECOND LANGUAGE ACQUISITION PROCESSES IN THE CLASSROOM

LEARNING JAPANESE

Second Language Acquisition Research
Theoretical and Methodological Issues
Susan Gass and Jacquelyn Schachter, Editors

Tarone/Gass/Cohen • Research Methodology
in Second Language Acquisition

Schachter/Gass • Second Language Classroom
Research: Issues and Opportunities

Birdsong • Second Language Acquisition
and the Critical Period Hypothesis

Monographs on Research Methodology

Gass/Mackey • Stimulated Recall Methodology
in Second Language Research

Yule • Referential Communication Tasks

Markee • Conversation Analysis

SECOND LANGUAGE ACQUISITION PROCESSES IN THE CLASSROOM LEARNING JAPANESE

Amy Snyder Ohta
University of Washington

LEA
LAWRENCE ERLBAUM ASSOCIATES, PUBLISHERS
2001   Mahwah, New Jersey   London

Lawrence Erlbaum Associates, Inc., Publishers
10 Industrial Avenue
Mahwah, New Jersey 07430

Cover design by Kathryn Houghtaling Lacey

Library of Congress Cataloging-in-Publication Data

Ohta, Amy Snyder.
    Second language acquisition processes in the classroom :
learning Japansese / Amy Snyder Ohta.
        p.   cm. — (Second language acquisition research)
    Includes bibliographical references and index.
    ISBN 0-8058-3800-7 (cloth : alk. paper) — ISBN 0-8058-3801-5 (pbk. :
alk paper)
        1. Japanese language—Acquisition.   2. Second language acquisition.
    3. Language and languages—Study and teaching—Psychological aspects.
    I. Title.   II. Series.
PL524.85.O39   2001
495.6′8′0071—dc21   00-056163
                                                                        CIP

Books published by Lawrence Erlbaum Associates are printed on acid-free paper,
and their bindings are chosen for strength and durability.

Printed in the United States of America
10 9 8 7 6 5 4 3 2

To Kaoru

Contents

PREFACE xiii

1 FROM SOCIAL TOOL TO COGNITIVE RESOURCE:
  FOREIGN LANGUAGE DEVELOPMENT AS A
  PROCESS OF DYNAMIC INTERNALIZATION 1

  The Learner and the Social/Interactive Environment 2
    SLA as Process 3
    Functional Systems and SLA 4

  Interactional Routines and Language Acquisition 5
    The Role of Interactional Routines in Adult L2
      Acquisition Contexts 6

  Language Acquisition as Assisted Performance 9
  Language Acquisition as a Process of Internalizing
    Social Interaction 11
    The Role of Private Speech in Internalization 12
    Definitions of Private Speech 14
    Functions of Private Speech 17

  Development of Inner Speech 18
  Second Language Acquisition: A Sociocognitive
    Perspective 21
  The Data 21
    The Language Program and Pedagogical Approach 22

The Learners *23*
The Teachers *24*
Audio/Video Recording Procedure *25*
Transcription of Data *26*
Transcription Conventions *26*
English Translations of Excerpts and Examples *26*
Data Analysis *28*

Overview of the Book: A Study of Classroom Language
Learning *28*

**2   PRIVATE SPEECH: A WINDOW ON
    CLASSROOM FOREIGN LANGUAGE ACQUISITION**   **30**

The Role of Private Speech in Language Acquisition:
Previous Research *31*

L1 Studies of the Private Speech of Children *31*
Studies of the Private Speech of Children Learning
    a Second Language *32*
Studies of the Adult L2 Learner *33*
Private Speech and Regulation *34*
Studies of Learning Strategies That Relate to L2
    Private Speech *34*

The Present Study: Private Speech in the Foreign
Language Classroom *37*

The Data *37*
Identifying Private Speech in the Transcripts *37*
Results of Analysis: Frequency of Private Speech *38*
Types of L2 Private Speech Found in the Data *39*
Vicarious Response *39*
Repetition *54*
Manipulation *61*

Classroom Private Speech and the Development
of Language Proficiency *64*

Private Speech and the Structure of Classroom
    Events *66*
The Role of Oral Rehearsal in Learning *67*
Individual Differences in Participation in Private
    Speech *68*
Private Speech and Hypothesis Testing *69*
Private Speech as a "Simulative Mode" of Functioning *69*
Private Speech and Assimilation/Expansion
    Processes *70*
The Active Learner *71*

**3   PEER INTERACTIVE TASKS AND ASSISTED
      PERFORMANCE IN CLASSROOM LANGUAGE
      LEARNING   73**

The Theoretical Basis of Peer Learning:
   From the Social to the Individual   *73*
      Research Questions   *74*

Working Memory and Selective Attention
   in Learner–Learner Interaction   *75*
      The Demands of Production for Beginning Learners   *77*
      The Active Listener   *77*
      Evidence From the Classroom Corpus   *79*

Assisted Performance in Action   *88*
      Assistance to a Struggling Peer   *88*
      Waiting   *89*
      Prompting and Co-construction   *91*
      Assistance When a Peer Makes a Linguistic Error   *96*
      Asking for One's Partner   *100*
      Explaining   *102*
      Other Means of Support   *104*
      Overhearing as a Resource for Learner Performance   *104*
      Language Play: Another Source of Support   *106*

Do Learners Pick up Each Other's Errors?   *113*
Conclusion   *124*

**4   A LEARNER-CENTERED ANALYSIS
      OF CORRECTIVE FEEDBACK AS A RESOURCE
      IN FOREIGN LANGUAGE DEVELOPMENT   128**

Corrective Feedback in the L2 Classroom   *134*
Definitions and Methodology of Analysis   *135*
      Defining "Corrective Feedback"   *135*
      Considering Audience Design   *136*
      Classifying Corrective Feedback   *138*
      The Consequences of Corrective Feedback   *138*

Results   *139*
      Corrective Feedback in L2 Classrooms   *139*
      Types of Corrective Feedback   *140*
      Recasts   *143*
      Recasts and Their Use   *145*
      Incidental Recasts   *152*
      Incidental Recasts in the Teacher-Fronted Setting   *153*
      Private Speech and Incidental Recasts   *160*
      Incidental Recasts in the Peer Learning Context   *165*

Noticing Corrective Feedback Addressed to Others   *172*
Self-Correction   *173*

Summary and Discussion   *175*

Corrective Feedback—Is It Effective?   *177*

**5   THE DEVELOPMENT OF INTERACTIONAL
     STYLE IN THE FIRST-YEAR CLASSROOM:
     LEARNING TO LISTEN IN JAPANESE**   **179**

Being a "Good Listener" in Japanese   *181*
What Is *ne* and Why Is It Critical in Spoken
   Japanese?   *186*
Analysis of Listener Responses in the First-Year
   Classrooms   *187*

Listener Responses and the Interactional Routines
   of the Classroom   *187*
The IRF Routine   *188*
Teacher Use of Listener Responses   *189*
Teacher Guidance in the Use of Listener Responses   *194*
Student Development in the Use of Listener Responses   *197*
The Four Learners   *198*
Rob and Kuo-ming   *199*
Using *Aa soo desu ka*   *203*
Development of Kuo-ming and Rob's Use of *ne*   *204*
Candace and Sara   *212*
Using *Aa soo desu ka*   *213*
Using *ne* in Listener Responses   *213*
Candace and Sara? Rob and Kuo-ming?
   Who Is Typical?   *225*

From Acknowledgment to Alignment:
   Proposing a Developmental Sequence   *228*

**6   FROM TASK TO ACTIVITY: RELATING TASK
     DESIGN AND IMPLEMENTATION TO
     LANGUAGE USE IN PEER INTERACTION**   **232**

Learner Use of English: The Relationship Between
   Task Design, Task Implementation, and Individual
   Differences   *235*

Measures of English Language Use   *237*
Understanding the Numbers: English Use in
   Peer Interaction   *240*
Individual Differences in L1 Use   *242*

Task Type, Pre-task Instruction, and Quality
of L2 Use   *249*
Task Design   *252*
Implementation of Tasks   *261*
Considering Available Support   *265*
Post-task Follow-Up   *267*
Conclusion   *268*

REFERENCES   **272**

APPENDIX   **282**
Transcription Conventions   282
Abbreviations Used to Gloss Japanese   283

AUTHOR INDEX   **285**

SUBJECT INDEX   **289**

Preface

The purpose of this book is to provide a view of classroom second language acquisition[1] (SLA) processes through a longitudinal case study of seven adult learners of Japanese. The book is designed both for researchers interested in second or foreign language (L2) development, as well as for those who work to promote L2 learning—language teachers. In particular, what I hope to accomplish here is, through data that was collected by the miking of individual learners, to amplify the voices of classroom learners loudly enough that all of us who are interested in adult SLA can hear these voices and what they have to show us. In writing this book, I have again and again been impressed by what learners do in classrooms, and how they take what is offered by teachers and curricula and work to make it their own. These voices have volumes to tell us about how social interaction builds into second language development. It is my hope that the readers of this book will hear the voices of these learners and will, as a result, take a more learner centered view in their own work.

Another goal of this book is to show readers the benefits of looking at old problems in a new way. The question of how L2 development proceeds through social interaction is not a new one, but here I work to illuminate classroom SLA processes by using a theoretical framework that may be new to many readers, and by taking a longitudinal approach to classroom

---

[1]In this book, I use the terms *acquisition* and *learning* to talk about the process of L2 development.

interactive data. It is my hope that the lenses provided with this framework and data set will inspire others to be innovative in their development and use of different approaches to L2 research.

The foreign language classroom has been an under-investigated arena in the field of SLA research. The impossibility of controlling the dizzying range of variables has discouraged experimentalists from doing research in actual classrooms. For qualitative researchers, although great strides have been made in understanding classroom interactional processes, there have been many methodological hurdles to overcome. In addition, lack of longitudinal studies of classroom learners has made it difficult to make connections between learning processes and L2 development. Despite these problems besetting the classroom as a research space, SLA researchers and language learning specialists have continued to call for classroom research. There have also been calls for increased attention to longitudinal work, where one might be able to find evidence of the processes that lead to SLA.

This book is my response to these repeated calls for a new kind of classroom research—a kind of classroom research that speaks to the situated language development of real language learners. In order to do this, the project was designed as longitudinal in nature, and student-centered in approach. Data collection focused on a group of individuals by using individual microphones to capture student voices. In addition, the voices collected are from a group of students who agreed to have their interactions periodically collected over an entire academic year. The resulting longitudinal corpus allows examination not only of processes that occur in a single class period, but of the development of individuals over time. This book is the story of the Japanese language development of seven individuals—Candace, Rob, Kuo-ming, Sara, Katie, Andrea and Bryce[2]—as they proceeded through a year in their lives as classroom language learners.

The role of theory in any analysis of classroom SLA processes is an important one. Theory provides, in a sense, a viewer for data analysis. Where a theory lacks concepts or terminology, the researcher's vision may be clouded. And, the particular concepts or terminology used by a particular framework, in turn, focus the researcher's attention on those phenomena as most worthy of interest. In that regard, it is very important that the framework chosen be appropriate for the nature of the data selected, as well as flexible enough to allow the researcher to see and highlight key processes that occur in the data. In my analysis, I have made use of a sociocognitive framework based on the theoretical work of the sociohistorical school of psychology, particularly the work of Vygotsky and those inspired by his work. Use of this framework provides a starting point for under-

---

[2]All names of learners and teachers are pseudonyms.

standing the processes that occur in the corpus, bringing a new perspective to the analysis of longitudinal classroom data.

Chapter 1 provides an overview of the conceptual framework adopted for analysis of the data. The chapter aims to provide an accessible introduction that can be used by those interested in L2 development, whether researchers, teachers, or graduate students. This aim is accomplished by setting out the key constructs that are useful in considering developmental discourse data. This includes the concepts of functional systems, interactional routines, the zone of proximal development (ZPD), assisted performance, and the internalization processes evidenced through learner use of private speech (self-addressed speech). Chapter 1 also provides an overview of the setting and methodology of data collection and a description of the process of analysis. Discussion of the data begins in chapter 2 with an intimate look into the mental processes of language learners—an investigation of private speech and its role in foreign language development. After providing an overview of previous work on private speech and its role in cognitive development, the chapter moves to an investigation of how the seven learners used private speech in the corpus. Results provide a window into the mental activity of learners as they work out problems in L2 internalization and production, moment by moment, as they interact in the classroom environment. These results show the individual learner to be more active than previous research has suggested, even in situations where the learner may appear to be quite passive.

Chapter 3 takes a step away from the individual and into the interactive space that is created when learners work with each other on language learning tasks. In this investigation of the role of peer interaction in classroom language learning, the concept of assisted performance is highlighted. Analysis examines assistance from two different points of view. First, the ways that learners assist each other are examined. Secondly, from the perspective of the learners, what actually functions as "assistance" is considered. The results of this examination show how learners act upon the various affordances of the classroom setting. In considering interactional processes, it is particularly interesting to see how peers with differential abilities are able to, through collaborative talk, accomplish what they could not have accomplished without assistance. Findings, in addition, show that even peers with less knowledge are able to help a more proficient peer. In addition, the question of learner errors is raised, with the corpus examined to determine whether or not the seven learners pick up errors used by their interlocutors. The role of collaboration in providing the building blocks to the individual's linguistic growth is considered through evidence of how collaboration builds into the learners' growing abilities to use the L2. These results speak to the importance of social cognition in learning. In particular, the nature of working memory and selective attention underscore the importance of collaborative processes, and allow for an understanding of the effectiveness of assisted performance in promoting development.

Chapter 4 continues the investigation into the role of interaction in L2 development by targeting the question of corrective feedback. Although corrective feedback has, in the previous research literature, been considered from a teacher centered perspective, in chapter 4, corrective feedback is defined from a learner centered perspective. The word "corrective" is taken to mean not what a teacher does in attempt to correct, but what actually functions as corrective for the seven learners. Classroom learners take on various roles as they participate in the language learning process. They act as addressees who interact with the teacher, auditors who are privy to the interaction of the teacher with others, and also overhearers of the interactions of students in other groups during peer learning tasks. These roles interact with each setting and each learner's cognitive capacity to make them more or less able to take advantage of the corrective information that is available in the interactive setting. Results show how learners make use of this corrective information, particularly of recasts, both recasts directed to the learner and what I have termed *incidental recasts* (Ohta, 2000b), which are utterances that incidentally contrast with a learner's own utterance during classroom interaction. These results provide new evidence of the effectiveness of recasts, while broadening our conception of what constitutes corrective feedback from a learner's perspective.

Chapter 5 continues the book's focus on interactional processes, but more specifically tackles the question of language development by utilizing the longitudinal corpus to investigate the development of interactional competence of the four first-year learners of Japanese. There are many facets of interactional competence that could be investigated. Chapter 5 looks at the question of interactional style, focusing on how the learners develop the ability to use listener response expressions in Japanese. Japanese differs from English in the verbosity of listener response behavior; listeners give frequent verbal signals of attention and interest. The chapter first looks at the occurrence of listener responses in the corpus, considering the linguistic environment in which learners participate, and the role of interactional routines in socializing interactional style. Then, the development of each of the four first-year learners is examined. Results show that the learners both develop increased proficiency with listener response expressions and that they follow a similar developmental sequence, moving from expressions of acknowledgement to the use of aligning expressions. The chapter ends by proposing a developmental sequence for acquisition of listener response expressions.

The focus of chapter 6 is different from the previous chapters. Although each of the previous chapters tackles a particular area of inquiry, whether private speech, assisted performance, corrective feedback, or the development of interactional competence, chapter 6 steps back from the data as a whole to ask about the relationship between "task" and "activity." That is, how is what students are asked to do in the classroom (the "task"), related to what students actually do in their interaction with each other (the "activity")? The use of English by these learners of Japanese is examined with the question of how task design and individual differences impact the use of English as they learn Japanese in the classroom setting. Then, a set of questions about how tasks are designed and implemented is presented. These questions were developed through reflection on issues that came up during analysis of the corpus. The questions work to provide a bridge to the realities of classroom practice in the increasingly task-based world of language teaching methodology.

Throughout the chapters of this book, the reader is invited to look at SLA processes from a perspective that is grounded in an understanding of social interaction as a key locus of language development for the beginning adult learner. It is my hope that the examination of learning processes provided here will inspire further socially situated, longitudinal studies. In order to understand how adults learn Japanese or any other foreign language, researchers must study adult learners in the settings in which they grapple with the language. This book presents one step forward by allowing us to join learners in the classroom as they meet the challenges of learning a new language quite different from English. This book does not begin to answer all of the questions we have about the L2 development of adult learners, but it provides a view into a particular slice of the developmental processes of seven learners of Japanese. The work that remains undone here is left for future projects. It is my hope that this book will raise questions in the minds of readers, and will inspire its readers to take up those questions in their own research as they work to achieve a robust understanding of how adults learn foreign languages.

In writing this book, I have been fortunate to have the assistance and support of many people. It was a pleasure to work with the teachers and students whose voices constitute my data. Without them, this book would not exist. In addition, this book has its intellectual roots in the research of many others who have preceded me. These are too numerous to name, but their work is cited throughout the book.

I am grateful to a large number of colleagues, former teachers, graduate students, and family and friends for their support during this project. I cannot possibly list everyone, but I would specifically like to thank Jim Lantolf, Michael Shapiro, Hiroshi Nara, Ruth Kanagy, Elinor Ochs, Kaoru Ohta, Joan Kelly Hall, Lorrie Verplaeste, Ken Rose, Tomoko Nakaone, Anne Yue-Hashimoto, Suzanne Snyder, Daniel Snyder, Gabriele Kasper, Merrill Swain, Isabel Genger, Hesson Genger, Yetta Snyder, Dina Rudolph

Yoshimi, Izumi Matsuda, Michio Tsutsui, Ruth Kanagy, Eri Yasuhara, Yoshiko Matsumoto, Susan Gass, Pauline Foster, Margaret D. Smith, and Elizabeth Platt. I would also like to thank the University of Washington's Japan Studies Program for financial support and student assistants, especially Stephanie Box, Jennifer Hallmon, and Naomi Kawabata.

I am particularly grateful to Judith Amsel, my acquisitions editor at Lawrence Erlbaum Associates, for listening to my book idea at the American Association of Applied Linguistics Conference held in Chicago in 1995. Judi's interest and encouragement have been of tremendous help. Not only did she give me useful feedback during our discussions, but email contact and annual breakfast meetings allowed me to monitor my own progress during this lengthy project.

Finally, I am grateful for the discussion that this book will generate between me and others interested in L2 development. As this book is being published, I am prodded by its limitations; I have already begun a new project prompted by what I have left undone here. It is my hope that this book will stimulate further research by others both in response to what I have written, and as well as to what I have neglected to say. I am grateful for the opportunity to participate in this ongoing dialogue, and look forward to learning more as we work together to construct a better understanding of SLA processes.

Chapter 1

From Social Tool to Cognitive Resource: Foreign Language Development as a Process of Dynamic Internalization

Language is acquired through social interaction—through the use of language in settings of daily life.[1] Foreign and second language (L2) classrooms are a key daily life setting in which language acquisition occurs. This book provides an intimate view of language learning in the foreign language classroom setting by taking a longitudinal case study approach. The interactive data that inform this study were gathered from a group of adult learners of Japanese who were followed through the academic year as they participated in their foreign language classes. The processes revealed in this book will be of interest to teachers and researchers who work with any second or foreign language, and also contribute to the little-researched area of Japanese L2 development. This book provides an opportunity to better understand how learners develop facility in a foreign language through the classroom learning experience. The data show us how learners grapple with problems ranging from the difficulties of pronunciation and sentence structure to problems of interactional style. We learn how interactional processes build into a growing L2 proficiency over time. The Japanese language is typologically distant from English; observing the Japanese language development of English speakers provides an excellent opportunity to understand how learners construct new understandings of a language very different from their own. A discourse-based case-study approach gathers the voices of the teachers and learners to provide an excel-

---

[1]A portion of this chapter was previously presented at the 1999 Second Language Research Forum held at the University of Minnesota. Some of the material on language play discussed in this chapter was presented in Ohta (1998).

1

lent view of developmental processes as they occur moment by moment in the classroom. Careful collection, transcription, and analysis of classroom interactive data provide results that show how classroom interaction provides the building blocks for language acquisition. The approach taken is learner centered; priority is given to understanding how learner use of language impacts L2 development. Through excerpts of classroom interaction, the reader is invited to listen to the interaction of teachers and students, and gains an intimate view of language learning processes. The chapters of this book provide various perspectives on classroom language learning processes, looking at private speech, assisted performance, corrective feedback, interactional style, and the relationship between task design and implementation features and L1 and L2 use. Each provides a unique vantage point on the day-to-day foreign language classroom.

This chapter presents a perspective of language acquisition as an integrated, interactive process, providing an appropriate foundational framework for this book on classroom language learning. The chapter, like language learning itself, begins with the environment of the classroom, moving to understanding the nature of the learner's interface with that environment, and finally considering how internalization processes function to transform social interactive processes into the individual cognitive processes that we recognize as what it means for a person to "know" a language.

First, the importance of the learner's environment in language development processes is discussed. Second, the specifics of that environment in terms of its regularity is considered, focusing on the role of interactional routines in language acquisition. Third, the chapter considers how learners respond to the interactive classroom environment as they grapple with the language being learned, in particular looking at the role of peer interaction in language learning. Finally, the chapter more specifically addresses issues of internalization. The mechanisms are considered through which social language becomes a tool of thought. More specifically, the process of how inner speech develops through the transformation of social speech to private speech is outlined. The chapter concludes by presenting an overview of the corpus that forms the database for the book, including a discussion of the context and methodological orientation of the language program in which the data were gathered.

THE LEARNER AND THE SOCIAL/INTERACTIVE ENVIRONMENT

There has been a tendency in second language acquisition (SLA) research to consider linguistic development as distinct from learners' interactional histories. Van Lier (2000) challenged SLA researchers to approach language development as a complex process that is situated in sociocultural settings; van Lier calls for an ecological model of language acquisition that views acquisition processes as part of the dynamic interrelationships between persons in social interaction. This voice is one of a growing chorus in the field of SLA research calling for a richer understanding of second language acquisition processes (Brooks, 1992b; Coughlan, 1995; Coughlan & Duff, 1994; DiCamilla & Lantolf, 1994; Donato, 1994; Dunn & Lantolf, 1997; Guerrero, 1994; Hall, 1995a, 1995b; Kramsch, 1992; Lantolf, 1997; Lantolf & Ahmed, 1989; Lantolf & Appel, 1994; Ohta, 1995a, 1999; Platt, 1995; Swain, 1997; Swain & Lapkin, 1998; Tarone & Liu, 1995; van Lier, 2000). These researchers have begun to think seriously about how language learning results from the internalization of processes that are visible in social interaction, resulting in a useful and growing body of research that examines processes of situated language learning and use.

SLA as Process

This book investigates SLA as interactive process. *Process*, here, does not mean a sequence of products. Process is a dynamic interaction of person-in-environment, including the interactions of the person with the social and physical environment that eventually resulted in a particular product. The same product can be a result of a variety of different processes. In the SLA context, to say that something is *acquired*—that a learner has full control of a particular structure or idiom—tells us little about acquisition processes. Processes are sociocognitive events that occur along the road from novice to expert. Process involves transformative interactions that are different for each individual in each social setting, and that result in *products* that may, on the surface, look similar, but are produced though variable paths in different individuals.

As social beings, our ability to use language emerges from our social interactions. What L2 students learn, even in the same classroom with the same teacher, is as variable as the different backgrounds and goals each brings to the classroom, as well as the different interactive processes in which each participates. Levels of language learning are dependent on the level of learner participation in the learning activities around them (Wong Fillmore, 1989). Two learners in the same classroom will learn different things depending on, among other things, how they engage with the affordances of the classroom setting. Teachers can capitalize on strategies that work to maintain joint attention and work to arrange classroom activities to promote engagement in language learning activities, but learners are in control of their own engagement and learning (Nelson, 1989).

Learner production is a rich source of information about SLA processes, but that production should always be considered in its context.

Because each learner's oral participation is embedded in context, and produced in collaboration with other persons and with artifacts of the classroom setting, learner utterances are intimately dependent on these factors. *Other persons* include the classmates and the classroom teacher with whom the learner interacts during learning activities, as well as those seated around the learner in the classroom, whose utterances and interactions the learner can overhear and appropriate. *Artifacts* of the classroom setting include the teacher's jottings on the blackboard, overhead transparencies, worksheets and other handouts, and textbook pages. In this view, language is not a unique product of just the learner's individual brain, but of a mind that actively draws on the interactive environment of the setting in which language is used. This book views the learner within the L2 classroom setting, and looks at development within that setting, analyzing processes as they occur in particular contexts of classroom interaction. Other settings with other interactive features would have different implications for the learner's use of the L2, with resulting implications for the processes by which the language is acquired.

Functional Systems and SLA

Within this holistic view of processes of learning in interaction, the language learners whose interactions form the heart of this book are not considered as isolated individuals. Rather, learner development is analyzed by examining the tasks learners are working to accomplish and the role of the learner, the support of interlocutors and features of the physical environment in accomplishing these tasks. Before, I said that the same product can result from different processes. To use Luria's (1973) terminology, the same product can result from different functional systems. In Luria's words, "the presence of a constant (invariant) task, performed by variable (variative) mechanisms, bringing the process to a constant (invariant) result, is one of the basic features distinguishing the work of every 'functional system' " (Luria, 1973, p. 28). A *functional system*, therefore specifies different complements of mechanisms that may work together to produce a particular end result. Luria draws his examples from human physiology, most notably considering how respiration is possible through the application of different functional systems. If certain muscles are paralyzed, for example, breathing is still possible through employment of other muscles not traditionally used for that purpose. In applying this idea to the context of language use and acquisition, we can consider that production of language for a particular purpose may be accomplished by different functional systems at different times. The functional system needed to accomplish a particular linguistic task is different for the beginning learner than it is for the native speaker, and is different at different stages of development. For the learner performing a task, the collaboration of peer or teacher may be part of the functional system needed for task performance. As competence grows, the components of the functional system will change, with the learner independently accomplishing functions that were only possible collaboratively at earlier stages. In the same way, the learner harnesses the tool of speech in certain ways at early phases that are discarded later, using oral repetition, for example, as part of the functional system for a particular task. Each language learner is part of a plurality of functional systems that includes the individual as well as the local environment (including the utterances of other persons and classroom artifacts). These various components are drawn on as resources in the learner's interactive and developmental processes. Language acquisition is not only a process of internalizing the language of the interactive environment, but also involves the development of the skills needed for learners to utilize the language and appropriate it for the their own purposes.

INTERACTIONAL ROUTINES AND LANGUAGE ACQUISITION

The predictable patterning of language use in the social environment facilitates learner participation in social interaction. From the earliest mother–child echoic facial play, interactions that become a joyful routine between mother and child, *interactional routines* may constitute the basic social experience through which links between speech perception and production are formed (Bjorklund, 1987). These interactional routines form a predictable interactive environment not only for infants, but for adult L2 learners as well. Whether in the classroom or in nonpedagogical settings, language learners are exposed to routines involving language that are frequently repeated in the learner's experience (Johnson, 1995; Nelson, 1986; Ochs, 1988; Schieffelin, 1990; Snow, Perlmann, & Nathan, 1987; van Lier, 1988, 1996). Linguistic anthropologists Peters and Boggs (1986) defined an interactional routine as "a sequence of exchanges in which one speaker's utterance, accompanied by appropriate nonverbal behavior, calls forth one of a limited set of responses by one or more other participants" (p. 81). Interactional routines are meaningful, culturally formulated modes of expression. These routines serve important functions in the communities in which they are used. Because of their repetitive nature, they also structure the interactive environment in predictable ways; this facilitates language acquisition by promoting the acquisition of relationships between language structure and social meaning. Because these routines are embedded in the rich social fabric of everyday life, they carry not only linguistic information, but also key cultural concepts (Schieffelin & Ochs, 1986).

Interactional routines fall along a continuum of formulaicity (Peters & Boggs, 1986). The content of the most formulaic routines does not vary. Greeting routines are typical of formulaic routines. Less formulaic routines vary widely in terms of content, but are predictable because the activity involved is consistent from routine to routine. The classroom Initiation, Response, and Follow-up (IRF) routine, which will be discussed further, is a good example of a less formulaic routine. Wherever routines fall on the continuum of formulaicity, their predictability allows the transmission of cultural and linguistic knowledge that results as learners gradually develop facility with these routines.

The Role of Interactional Routines in Adult L2 Acquisition Contexts

SLA researchers have begun to show interest in the power of interactional routines to shape L2 development. Hall and Brooks (1995) outlined how adult L2 learners may acquire interactional routines. Following this work, I proposed that adults acquire interactional routines similar to the way children do (Ohta, 1999). This occurs through a process of participation that is, at first, peripheral, becoming gradually more active as the learner develops facility with the routine (see Fig. 1.1).

Initially, participation in the routine is only possible via limited peripheral participation (Lave & Wenger, 1991). Here, the learner is included as a ratified observer, gradually becoming able to participate, at first only minimally. This minimal participation is enabled through scaffolding (Wood, Bruner, & Ross, 1976) by participants who already are expert in the routine. Even at these earliest stages, learning is taking place. The learner learns the meaning of the routine, what its purpose is, and how to participate appropriately. Through repeated participation, the learner becomes more actively involved while getting a better sense of how the routine is likely to develop. This ability to anticipate is a prerequisite to expanded participation and to participation in a wider range of contexts. Figure 1.1 shows the results of this increased participation: knowledge of the routines' deeper meaning, of the variable roles of participants, and of cultural values and concepts. Finally, the learner can use the routine for his or her own purposes, becoming a creative, full participant in the cultural practice. Full participation includes the ability to customize the routine as needed. Through the process of internalizing the interactional routine, the learner develops new cognitive structures (Vygotsky, 1978; Wertsch, 1985). I propose that this acquisition process applies to interactional routines learned in naturalistic settings as well as classrooms, and in first as well as SLA contexts. Language learning is a fundamentally social process, and the internalization processes involved in the acquisition

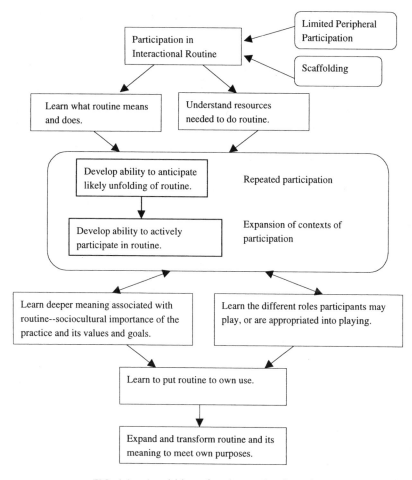

FIG. 1.1.   Acquisition of an interactional routine.

of international routines provide a foundation for further internalization of linguistic knowledge.

Language teachers commonly exploit interactional routines in their teaching. Newly introduced language is routinized through classroom practice so that students have a clear model for how new structures and vocabulary can be used in conversational contexts. Ideally, even beginning learners are given a degree of freedom to use what is being taught in guided interaction with one another. As they move from the more controlled "teacher-fronted" setting to the relatively freer environment of pair or group-practice activities, they begin to use language more flexibly and more creatively. Through this creative process learners work to apply what is being taught to the particular language learning task at hand, while also interjecting their own interests, goals, and personalities into the interaction. In this way, learners develop the ability to apply the language being taught to their own expressive needs, and to use the routines of the classroom to find their own voices in the language being learned.

In general, previous research has suggested that socialization into the routines of classroom language use may misguide learners by socializing ways of interaction that are effective in the classroom but not in the real world of target language use (Hall, 1995b; Hall & Brooks, 1995; Ohta, 1993, 1994). The L2 may be used to translate L1 concepts and ideas so that learners are given a mistaken impression of how the L2 is to be used. For example, when teaching *joozu* 'good at' and *heta* 'bad at', Japanese language teachers might guide students to ask each other what they are good at, or whether they are good at this sport or that subject in school. While answering that one is good at something may not be a problem in the learner's native culture, this task promotes behavior that is likely to be inappropriate in Japanese, where people tend to avoid touting their own strengths. Of greatest concern to researcher and pedagogue alike is the observation that the very structure of foreign language lessons, which tends to follow initiation, response, follow-up (IRF) structure may be the source of interactional problems for students, particularly if students' participation is limited to the response turn of the routine, as has been found in teacher-fronted contexts (Consolo, 1996; Ohta, 1993, 1994). Previous studies, however, did not examine how learners used language in pair and group work, where they might be free to apply the routines of the classroom to their own needs. More recent work (Ohta, 1995a, 1995b, 1997b, 1999, 2000a, 2000b, in press-a, in press-b), which examined how learners use language in peer interactive contexts, found that the power of peripheral participation may be stronger than previously supposed; in the peer learning context, learners develop the ability to use language that they were exposed to in the context of peripheral participation in teacher-fronted interaction. For example, Ohta (1997b) found that a learner, Becky, used teacher talk during interaction with peers. While practicing a semiscripted dialogue and adjusting the content of the dialogue to their own interests, Becky helped her partner with a linguistic problem, using teacher talk to indicate to her partner that his utterance was correct. Although at first glance, her use of teacher talk seemed inappropriate, in fact, it was part of a repair sequence (an insertion sequence). While using teacher talk in the insertion sequence, Becky also used the L2 appropriately in the role play being practiced. Her use of Japanese teacher talk to assist her partner suggests that classroom interactional routines have a positive role as well. The results of this case study also suggest the importance of examining how learners appropriate classroom language in functionally meaningful ways. Further work with a broader range of learners is needed to help us better understand the role of interactional routines, in general, and the role of the IRF routine, in particular, in socializing L2 interactional style.

LANGUAGE ACQUISITION AS ASSISTED PERFORMANCE

The socializing role of interactional routines is evident not only in teacher-fronted settings, but also in peer learning contexts. Just as Becky used teacher talk in a repair sequence, subsequent studies illustrated how classroom language learners use the interactional routines of the classroom in appropriate interaction with one another (Ohta, 1999). Through collaborative interaction with peers, learners apply the tools at hand to linguistic and interactive problems as they work to do assigned tasks, learning the language as they use it for particular purposes. Language is acquired as learners interact in the *zone of proximal development* (ZPD). Vygotsky (1978) defined the ZPD as "the distance between the actual developmental level as determined by independent problem solving and the level of potential development as determined through problem solving under adult guidance or in collaboration with more capable peers" (p. 86). This enabling process is referred to as *assisted performance* (Tharp & Gallimore, 1991), or *scaffolding* (Wood et al., 1976). For the purposes of considering SLA, I worked to develop a definition of the ZPD suitable for the context of classroom SLA. For the L2 learner, the ZPD is the distance between the actual developmental level as determined by individual linguistic production, and the level of potential development as determined through language produced collaboratively with a teacher or peer (Ohta, 1995a).[2] Vygotsky's notion of the ZPD required the one providing the assistance to be a teacher or more capable peer. However, true peers are also able to assist each other through interactive processes. Assistance from peer interlocutors is possible for two reasons: Assistance may be enabled by differential abilities—even true peers have different strengths and different weaknesses. And, the nature of differential interactive roles enables peer listeners to provide assistance to their interlocutors. This is discussed

---

[2]The ZPD is a social interactive construct designed to understand how linguistic and cognitive development occur through social interaction. The ZPD as realized in interaction between people is not the only place where L2 development occurs. Learners also develop facility with the L2 through experiences that do not involve talking with another person, such as listening and reading. Social interaction is, however, relevant to the reading and listening situation in that the developmental roots of cognition are found in social interaction (see Roebuck, 1998, on reading comprehension processes). Examination of the role of literacy or listening comprehension activities in language development is beyond the scope of this book.

in detail in chapter 3. The result is that appropriate assistance enables learners to successfully accomplish interactive tasks pitched just above their independent ability. Through this collaborative process, the helper becomes a part of the functional system used by the learner to accomplish the task. This accomplishment constitutes a building block that works toward growing independence. Vygotsky (1981) outlined this process in his general genetic law of cultural development:

> Any function in the child's cultural development appears twice, or on two planes. First it appears on the social plane, and then on the psychological plane. First it appears between people as an interpsychological category, and then within the child as an intrapsychological category. This is equally true with regard to voluntary attention, logical memory, the formation of concepts, and the development of volition. . . . [I]t goes without saying that internalization transforms the process itself and changes its structure and functions. Social relations or relations among people genetically underlie all higher functions and their relationships. (p. 163)

Vygotsky's developmental law may be applied to L2 learning settings; this construct aptly describes interactive processes whereby what was initially social becomes a resource for the individual through the process of meaningful social interaction. This occurs through various participation structures, including peripheral participation, which was discussed in the previous section. Here, we specifically consider the locus of peer interaction and how interacting with a language learning peer promotes language acquisition.

In this framework, language acquisition occurs through the meaning making process, a process that is visible in peer interaction. Previous research examined many interactive learning settings, including tutor–tutee interactions (Lantolf & Aljaafreh, 1996), group work (Donato, 1994), and pair work (Brooks, 1992a, 1992b; Ohta, 1995a, 1997a, 1997b, 1999, 2000a, 2000b, in press-a; Swain & Lapkin, 1998). In each of these studies, language acquisition processes were found in the interactions. As Donato (1994) stated regarding his data, "the speakers are at the same time individually novices and collectively experts, sources of new orientations for each other, and guides through this complex linguistic problem solving" (p. 46). In a previous study (Ohta, 2000a), I documented specific mechanisms of language development in an investigation of the interactive processes of a peer interactive task, showing microgenesis (Wertsch, 1985). For assistance to be developmentally appropriate, it can be neither too much nor too little. The question I addressed was how these learners were able to discern the amount of assistance the interlocutor needed, or when assistance should be withheld. I found that subtle peer assistance mechanisms were used by the pair as they worked through a grammar task. Learner assistance was finely tuned and appropriate because of mutual attention to these mechanisms, including attention to subtleties such as glottal stops and vowel elongation. Through attention to these mechanisms, the learners provided assistance just when needed, and also withheld assistance when appropriate. Analysis revealed how peers may be well equipped to provide developmentally appropriate assistance. When the broader classroom setting provides appropriate preparation and support for completion of a task, peer collaboration works to promote mutual comprehension and appropriate assistance as the interaction is tailored to the needs of the interlocutors moment by moment. It is through this process that peer interaction promotes language development.

It is important to underscore that collaboration, alone, does not guarantee that learning will occur. In and of itself, collaboration is not sufficient to promote development for L2 learners. The construct of the ZPD includes the need to accomplish something beyond the current level of development as a necessary ingredient. Research investigating the results of learner interaction during tasks that lack any sort of challenge comfirms this (Olsher, 1999). Along with collaboration, a developmentally appropriate challenge is necessary to stimulate development in the ZPD.

LANGUAGE ACQUISITION AS A PROCESS
OF INTERNALIZING SOCIAL INTERACTION

Through classroom interaction in teacher-fronted and peer interactive settings, learners go through a process of incorporating the L2 into their interactive and cognitive processes as they use the L2 with others. This process is not a simple, linear one, but is parallel and dynamic. The word *internalization* implies movement of language from environment to brain. However, a better conceptualization is to understand internalization as the process by which the foreign language gradually becomes an interactive and cognitive resource for the learner. At first the L2 is alien and quite "external," such that even comprehension is impossible. Through social interaction, learners take steps toward adopting that language for themselves. Internalization occurs through the process of social interaction.[3] To the extent that learners have internalized the L2, they can participate more independently in interactive settings. Although no one is ever totally independent of his or her social and physical environment, internalization

---

[3]Social interaction is not the only place where internalization of language occurs. For children learning their first language, social interaction is historically the earliest locus of internalization. L2 learners, adults who already have an internalized language, are able to use their already developed cognitive skills (including literacy skills) to access the L2 outside of the social interactive setting through, for example, L2 reading or listening opportunities.

involves a growing level of control, or the ability to regulate interaction in the L2, and a growing ability to use the L2 itself as a tool of thought.

The Role of Private Speech in Internalization

Private speech is a component of the internalization process for both children and for adult L2 learners. From the babbling and word play of young children, to the self-directed mutterings of adult language learners, people talk to themselves when acquiring language. The ready availability of child private speech data has provided a rich source of analysis for linguists interested in language acquisition, as shown by Weir's (1962) classic study of crib speech, and by those inspired by her work. L2 researchers have found private speech to be a rich resource for the study of second language acquisition. Private speech has particular potential as a data source because it provides a window into the mind as it works on the cognitive, intimately social interactive problems presented by learning language. And adult language learners not only report engaging in private speech in the L2, but a number of studies documented L2 private speech. Regarding the importance of private speech as a data source for SLA research, Saville-Troike (1988) stated that:

> [T]he now-dominant conception of language learning as critically involving social/interpersonal interaction has left potentially important *noninteractive* phenomena generally out of researchers' awareness. Further, there has been a tendency in the second language learning field to equate overt production with active learning, and lack of overt production with passivity and disengagement. These conceptual perspectives, together with the more obvious character of socially interactive speech and the difficulties of observing intrapersonal speech, have led to an unconscious assumption that nothing of significance was happening unless learners were talking to others. (p. 569, italics added)

Although Saville-Troike (1988) used the word "noninteractive" to describe private speech phenomena, this is only in the sense that private speech is addressed to the self rather than to another individual. Private speech is highly interactive, working in the ongoing interface between the individual and the social setting, in mediating thought through the use of social language. In studies of foreign language learning, private speech data show that the seemingly silent learner is neither passive nor disengaged (Ohta, in press-b), but is involved in an intrapersonal interactive process. In order to understand SLA processes, data from both interpersonal communicative contexts as well as from individual intrapersonal language use contexts needs to be examined. In private speech, what learners attend to and how this relates to their subsequent language use in interpersonal interaction is made explicit; private speech data are therefore useful for the analyst seeking to understand language acquisition processes.

For children, private speech plays an important role in development. Private speech functions as a regulatory tool as the child proceeds through a developmental continuum of regulation from object regulation, to other regulation, to self-regulation (Wertsch, 1985), a process through which the language of social interaction becomes a tool for the child's own thought. When a child is *object regulated*, he or she is primarily responsive to whatever draws attention in the physical environment. Next on the developmental continuum is *other regulation*; the other-regulated child is responsive to the direction of other people. The highest developmental level is that of *self-regulation*. Self-regulated individuals have full control of their own activity, having internalized the cognitive tools needed to direct their own behavior, and having the ability to focus without being distracted by objects or by others. Development of self-regulation is not an all-or-nothing event, but represents a continuum that is present throughout the life cycle. These terms, which are normally used to describe the cognitive development of children, can also be applied to consideration of language development by cognitively mature adults who are working to acquire a new set of linguistic tools.

Developmental psychologists have studied the role private speech plays in cognitive development, as just described, through its use to regulate the development of self-controlled cognitive processes and behavior. *Private speech* is oral language uttered not for communicative interaction with another, but for dialogue with the self. Through the developmental process, speech that originally serves an interpersonal function, comes to be internalized as an intrapersonal cognitive tool. Thus, in addition to being mediator of interpersonal relationships, language comes to be a mediator of thought. In first language development, children use oral language, not only to talk with others, but also in dialogue with the self, both in play and during problem-solving tasks. This *egocentric speech* seems to disappear as the child matures. Piaget (1923/1962) theorized that the private speech of young children, which he termed egocentric speech, was a precursor of social speech that disappeared when children were fully socialized. In Vygotsky's view, egocentric speech does not disappear, but is transformed into inner speech, or verbal thought (Vygotsky, 1987). Transformation of social speech from inner speech to thought involves a process of reduction, with private speech forming an audible link between the individual's social and inner worlds. From this perspective, private speech is the meeting point between the social and the individual, a site of verbal cognition. Rather than being a presocial form of speech, Vygotsky proposed that private speech was social in origin. He posited a developmental process through which the child internalized the language of social interaction for cognitive purposes. As the child increases in capacity for mental thought, private speech becomes increasingly abbreviated. Ultimately, the linguistic mediation of thought occurs primarily internally, without need for oral verbalization. For adult learners, repetition to the self may occur in inner speech, though in cognitively demanding situations inner speech re-emerges as private speech.

Even though developmental psychologists have focused on the regulatory functions of private speech as the child develops increasing cognitive control, private speech is not only uttered by children or the cognitively immature. Private speech is also a part of the internalization processes of adults. Private speech is a tool that adults make use of in cognitively demanding situations (John-Steiner, 1992). L1 and L2 private speech has been documented in adult foreign language learners (e.g., Frawley & Lantolf, 1984, 1985, 1986; Lantolf, 1997; McCafferty, 1992, 1994a, 1994b; Ohta, 1998; van Lier, 1988). Rather than indicating cognitive immaturity, this use of private speech is a part of the internalization process as the social interactive resources of the L2 are adopted for the learner's own use. As learners become gradually more involved in the L2 routines of their environments, they begin to draw on linguistic resources that enable delayed access to the language tools being acquired. *Private speech*, which can be used for imitation and repetition, is one of these tools. Through private speech, the learner may prolong the availability of the language he or she is working to learn. Private speech, which begins from the seeds of imitation of others, or repetition of what others say, is a cognitive resource for the adult learner.

Definitions of Private Speech

In this chapter, private speech has already been defined as oral language uttered not for communicative interaction with another, but for dialogue with the self. However, there are various definitions of private speech in the research literature. In this section, definitions of private speech will be explored, both those that define private speech by its form, and those that define its function. Researchers working with spoken discourse needed to distinguish private speech from social utterances in order to study its significance. Therefore, definitions that permit identification of private speech in oral discourse were developed. Most commonly used definitions focus on the form of private speech as oral language not addressed to another. Private speech has been defined as "speech spoken out loud that is addressed either to the self or to no one in particular" (Bivens & Berk, 1990, p. 443) or as speech which is "not adapted to a listener or not clearly and definitely addressed to another" (Berk & Garvin, 1984, p. 276). In practice, without multicamera video recordings that capture the eye gaze of all parties involved in interaction, it can be difficult to determine whether or not speech is addressed to another, or to whom speech is addressed, and these definitions reflect this difficulty. Smolucha (1992) took care of the problem of addressivity of an utterance by defining private speech "as discourse with the self that is spoken out loud and that does not require a response from another person" (p. 128).

Private speech has also been examined as a part of research on *language play*. Kuczaj (1983) identified three types of language play in his study of a child's language development, two of which would be considered private speech according to the definitions just given. Kuczaj's three categories of language play are solitary play, social context play, and social play. Kuczaj uses the term language play to describe verbal manipulation or rehearsal of the language being acquired. Kuczaj's solitary language play and social context language play are both private speech—language directed to the self. Solitary language play refers to self-addressed speech when the individual is alone. This speech has been of interest to linguists studying the language development of young children. Social context language play is private speech produced when the individual is in the presence of others. Kuczaj's third type of language play, social play, does not involve private speech; in social language play, the language is manipulated in interaction with another person. A fourth type of language play not examined by Kuczaj, and not fitting most definitions of private speech was discussed by Lantolf (1997), who used a questionnaire to study the role of language play in the acquisition of adults, adding the category *mental rehearsal*, or mental manipulation of language.

The definitions considered so far have defined private speech by its self-addressed form. Private speech has also been defined by its function. Appel and Lantolf (1994), for example, define private speech as "speaking to understand" (p. 437). In other words, they define a function of private speech as aiding the speaker's comprehension—as speech used as a tool for thought. For Appel and Lantolf (1994), the defining feature of private speech is that it represents "the externalization of what otherwise would remain as covert mental processes" (p. 439). In this vein, several studies of L2 private speech have looked at externalization of mental processes that occurs in the retelling of a story, or in writing, identifying these externalizations, even when they have a clear social purpose, as private speech or private writing. In studies like these, private speech is identified not by any self-addressed nature, but by its cognitive function, by the use of language as "speaking to understand" or "writing to understand."

Differing uses of terminology for private speech phenomena have complicated matters for those investigating these phenomena and their role in language learning. For the purpose of considering the role of private speech in classroom language learning, a straightforward definition is needed. This can be accomplished by distinguishing private speech, inner speech, and social speech according to (a) whether or not there is an addressee, and (b) whether or not the speech is articulated audibly. Because social utterances may all be considered as having a cognitive function, a functional definition of private speech as "speaking to understand" is unwieldy for examination of learner language in the classroom. However, if we consider private speech as audible speech not adapted to an addressee, it can be distinguished from both social speech and inner speech. This does not preclude examination of the cognitive functions of social speech or the use of other definitions for other research purposes, but tightens up what is being referred to when the term *private speech* is used here. By defining terms based upon modalities of language use, it is possible to lay out a range of terminology and clarify what they mean. Figure 1.2 presents a classification of terminology used in research on private speech, with terms shown relating to private speech, inner speech, or social speech. The lines separating the three areas are dotted to indicated that although they are characterized by differences in modality and context, it is not always possible to make a discrete separation. Overlapping areas show how these different types of speech may share functions, and occur in different modalities.

In this way, the different phenomena that have been identified under the rubric of language play or private speech may be loosely classified ac-

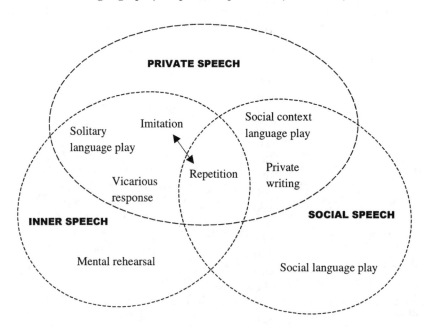

FIG. 1.2. Terminology related to private speech.

cording to the modalities in which they predominantly occur. Although some terms, like *mental rehearsal*, only refer to one modality of speech, others may occur in differing modalities. Solitary language play, if audible, is private speech, but can also occur as a mental, unarticulated phenomenon. In the same way, *vicarious response*, a process by which learners in a classroom setting formulate their own answers to a question the teacher has addressed to another (Ohta, 1998; chap. 2 this volume), may occur as an interior, inner response, or in private speech. Repetition serves a function in social speech, but also occurs in private and inner speech. Imitation, distinguished from repetition in its lacking of a social function, is placed in the overlapping area between inner and private speech. Social context language play and private writing occur in private and social speech modalities, depending on the extent to which they are adapted for an audience. Figure 1.2 is intended as a conceptual aid to consideration of relationships between the terminology related to private, inner, and social speech, but should not be taken as a final solution to understanding the relationships between these various terms.

Functions of Private Speech

Private speech has been noted to have a range of functions. Frawley and Lantolf (1986), argued that the "sole function of private speech is self-regulation" (p. 707). Diaz (1992), stated that private speech is "speech addressed to the self (not to others) for the purpose of self-regulation (rather than communication)" (p. 62). Other researchers defined a broader range of private speech functions. For example, Zivin (1979) listed the functions of guiding cognitive performance and regulating social behavior (as cited in Frauenglass & Diaz, 1985). Additional private speech functions noted in the research literature are emotional/expressive functions (Fuson, 1979; Rubin, 1979) fantasy/role-play functions (Olszewski, 1987), attentional functions (Berk, 1986; Bivens & Berk, 1990), and language acquisition functions (Berk, 1992; Saville-Troike, 1988; Weir, 1962). Berk (1992) posited that disagreement about the function of private speech may be rooted in the differing definitions of self-regulation, resulting from different interpretations of what Vygotsky considered to be regulatory functions. According to Berk, those who propose a single self-regulatory function for private speech (Diaz, 1992; Frawley & Lantolf, 1986) are operating under very broad definition of what *regulation* means. Berk (1992) uses a narrower definition, stating that the term regulation should refer only to the "intentional channeling of behavior in the service of learning goals" (p. 42). I will not work to solve this problem here. Private speech can be seen to have a range of functions, whether they are considered as falling under the regulatory umbrella, or considered as standing alongside regulatory private speech as other independent functions. In chapter 2, when the role of private speech and classroom language learning are examined, additional studies of private speech and its relationship to language learning are discussed. Other studies that relate to private speech phenomena, such as learning strategy studies, are explored.

DEVELOPMENT OF INNER SPEECH

Private speech in the L2 is evidence of language development in process and occurs as a precursor of inner speech. Vygotsky (1987), Luria (1982), and Wertsch (1985) discuss how inner speech develops and the relationship between private speech and inner speech. For adults speaking their first language, it is thought that private speech generally emerges from inner speech. But, for a learner who has yet to develop a useful command of a language, at first private speech cannot emerge from inner speech, because inner speech has not yet developed. Inner speech is not primary but must be formed through social interaction. Ontogenetically, the initial source of private speech is the interpsychological plane; private speech initially emerges from social interaction. At this stage, the learner is, in a sense, "borrowing" words, phrases and sentences picked up from social interaction. These bits of language are recycled and manipulated in private speech for use as cognitive tools. At the early stages of language learning they do not emerge from the learner's own verbal thought. Inner speech begins to develop through the process of social interaction, and through verbal interaction that includes private speech. Analysis of the development of children's private speech show that it becomes increasingly abbreviated, mirroring the expansion of the child's developing capacity for inner speech. This undergrounding of private speech is the emergence of inner speech. Luria (1982) proposed a range of stages for inner speech development that follows the abbreviation of external speech into inner speech, as shown in Fig. 1.3. This figure graphically represents Luria's statement that inner speech develops from "external speech, fragmented external speech, whispered speech, and finally abbreviated speech for oneself" (p. 153), resulting ultimately in the formation of true verbal thought. In my drawing, the overlapping circles recognize that these are not discrete stages, but are part of a dynamic continuum, with cycling between stages, and moving back and forth among them, as inner speech develops. As previously mentioned, from this theoretic perspective, language production emerges initially not from inner speech but from the dialogic context of language use; here we see a cycling between external speech and fragmented external speech, where inner speech is not yet formed, but verbal interaction is present. As inner speech develops, pri-

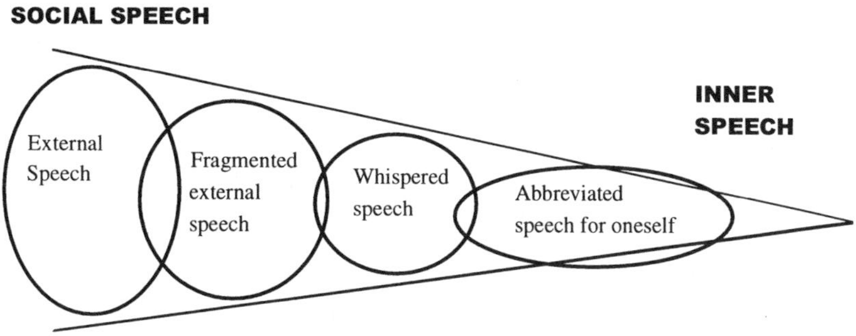

SOCIAL SPEECH

FIG. 1.3.   The dynamic process of inner speech development.

vate speech becomes increasingly abbreviated, as what is assimilated need no longer be stated. Inner speech, once formed, continues to develop in complexity, resulting in the child's ability to perform progressively more complex cognitive operations.

Once inner speech is established, it is available to serve as a basis for language production. To produce an utterance, the speaker must expand inner speech into a social utterance that can be understood by others. The research of Luria (1982) and his colleagues "indicate[s] that children's speech production begins with isolated words and proceeds to isolated sentences. Only in the last stage is speech production characterized by complex expanded texts" (p. 156). Language production thus reflects the stage of development of inner speech. One might imagine the developmental process reversed in the case of production, as inner speech is expanded into private speech, where language is rehearsed for use in a social context. Private speech, therefore, functions in the whole assimilation/expansion process.

Luria's conceptualization of the assimilation/expansion process can be readily applied to the L2 acquisition context. Although the adult L2 learner already has fully developed inner speech capacity, this capacity is in the L1. L2 capacity for inner speech also may develop through interactive processes. These interactive processes are visible in oral data. Private speech is a psychological process by which new vocabulary, morphology, or syntactic structures from the interpsychological plane may move to the intrapsychological plane. When the language is not yet incorporated into the adult's inner speech, the learner may pluck bits of language from the interpsychological context for further manipulation and practice. At first, the language from the immediate aural context may be manipulated without recourse to L2 inner speech. Rote memorization of unprocessed "chunks" of language is a good example of what may result from this surface level repetition if further analysis is not accomplished, either because the form cannot yet be analyzed, or because the learner fails to analyze the form due to, for example, lack of interest in doing so. Manipulation of the language being repeated is evidence of analysis in progress. Learners break down and build up chunks of language, chewing apart pieces for analysis. Through inner speech, further practice and processing may occur, along with analysis of the L2 accomplished through use of the L1, which forms the learner's developed cognitive capacity for thought.

Evidence for the role of speech in the development of cognitive processes emerged from studies of speech perception. There is a growing body of research showing the intimate involvement of covert speech production in the process of the speech perception of adults; in this view, inner speech that occurs prior to the production of utterances produces both kinesthetic and auditory representations. Smith, Reisberg, and Wilson (1992) found that adult subjects were able to perceive information in their inner voice that they could not perceive when subvocalization was blocked by chewing candy, or when phonological processing was blocked through receipt of irrelevant auditory messages. They conclude that "the inner voice provides an actual (kinesthetic) stimulus for the subject . . . 'raw material' to be interpreted and . . . reinterpreted" (p. 100). Imitation, therefore, is not a trivial or rote process, but interactive processes of inner imitation are part of comprehension processes themselves. The development of an inner voice is a complex process that begins with imitation, through which the inner voice works not only to formulate utterances, but is involved at the earliest stages of speech comprehension as well.

Once the learner is able to imitate orally, the stage is set for the use of speech as a tool for learning, including the use of both oral and inner speech. MacKay's (1992) work on imitation and oral rehearsal provide a bridge between consideration of the oral and inner voices and their role in thought. MacKay found that that the ability to imitate and do inner rehearsal, an ability taken for granted by the adult native speaker, is dependent on language proficiency. In other words, without a certain ability in the L2, inner rehearsal isn't possible: "Sentences heard in a foreign language are unrehearsable even if the phonology of these sentences is compatible with [L1] phonology" (MacKay, 1992, p. 142). MacKay found that prior oral practice was prerequisite to the ability to do inner rehearsal. MacKay's results both support the complexity of the imitative act, and demonstrate that language-specific articulatory skill is tied to the ability to use the inner voice. For inner speech to function in the comprehension processes, muscle movements must first be learned. In addition, MacKay (1992) also found that inner rehearsal was not effective without sufficient prior experience with a particular language task. MacKay's most important finding is that both comprehension and motor skills are necessary components of the ability to use one's inner voice. For the language learner, then, the ability to use inner speech is not automatic, but is indicative of a level of mastery of L2 form and meaning, of internalization of private speech that is intimately connected with social interaction.

SECOND LANGUAGE ACQUISITION: A SOCIOCOGNITIVE PERSPECTIVE

There is a need in SLA research today for a more holistic view of language learning processes, for viewing these processes as emergent from relationships between individuals and their sociointeractive environments. *Social* and *cognitive* are all too often considered to be discrete categories, separated and isolated in an attempt to better understand their nature. If considered developmentally, however, the dialogic origins of cognition are evident because cognition itself is formed through social interaction. Thus, one way to consider the social and the cognitive are as interpenetrated elements that cannot be isolated from the environments in which the learner finds him or herself. To avoid oversimplification and to understand the nature of SLA processes as they occur in real life settings, researchers need to push beyond discrete separation of the social and the cognitive to consideration of SLA as a dynamic, sociocognitive process, in which the social and cognitive interpenetrate one another. From peripheral participation in interactional routines to creative application of those routines for individual purposes, from the social interactions of others to the whispers of private speech and back to social interaction again, language use and acquisition are dynamic and interwoven. The challenge is how to deal with such complexity in a principled way that moves toward a deeper understanding of SLA processes. This book works toward such a goal in its presentation of the results of a study of SLA processes of seven learners of Japanese, considering these processes as not only extant in the productions of the individual students, but as residing in the sociocognitive milieu of each student. Analysis prioritizes examination of learner development in concert with an understanding of the learner as part of a functional system that shifts from moment to moment. Throughout this book, the learner is the centerpiece of analysis. In the following section, the data are presented. The chapter concludes with a brief overview of the book.

THE DATA

This section first presents a description of the setting in which data were collected, describing the language program, teaching methodology, and other factors that impact what happens in the classroom on a day-to-day basis. Then, the method of data collection is described. Finally, methodology of analysis is briefly discussed. Subsequent chapters also present more detailed information about analytic procedures as appropriate.

The Language Program and Pedagogical Approach

The learners whose interactions form the database for this book participated in the everyday environment of Japanese-as-a-foreign-language classrooms at a large university. The program had recently implemented a more task-based approach to language teaching. Task-based instruction has been defined differently by different writers. Some use the term *task-based language teaching* to indicate a curriculum that uses tasks, a task being defined in real-world terms as something learners must do with language in the setting in which the L2 is to be used, as the unit for syllabus construction (Long & Crookes, 1992). Tasks are ideally selected via a needs analysis of the language that learners will actually need in the L2 settings they find themselves in. Grammatical syllabi have no place in this realization of task-based teaching; rather, focus on language emerges as the teacher adjusts content to learner difficulties that emerge as tasks are introduced and implemented (Long & Robinson, 1998). Skehan (1996), in outlining a framework for task-based instruction, noted that there are strong and weak versions of the task-based approach. The version just described is the strong form. It elevates task above all other matters and sees "the need to transact tasks . . . as adequate to drive forward language development" (Skehan, 1996, p. 39). Weaker forms of task-based instruction

> claim that tasks are a vital part of language instruction, but that they are embedded in a more complex pedagogic context. They are necessary, but may be preceded by focused instruction, and, after use, may be followed by focused instruction which is contingent on task performance. (Skehan, 1996, p. 39)

Skehan noted that the weak form of task-based instruction "is clearly very close to general communicative language teaching" (p. 39).

The task-based instruction implemented in the foreign language program where these data were collected is a weak form of task-based language teaching. The setting of the program is a true foreign language setting, in which few learners have any immediate real-world need for the language. Most learners will never go abroad or use the L2 outside of the classroom. The curriculum instituted in the program creates the need for L2 language use within the classroom and language program setting. As is usual in settings where Japanese is taught to English speakers, a grammatical syllabus forms the core of curricular organization. The purpose for this organization is to provide foundational L2 knowledge in an environment in which grammatical principles are clear and easy to understand. Simpler structures are taught before more complex ones. With an agglutinative language like Japanese, simpler morphological paradigms (that are both structurally and conceptually simpler), are taught earliest. This grammatical syllabus was overlaid by a theme-based one, involving chapter units organized around real-life topics. Rather than serving to drive the syllabus, in this program, tasks, along with the chapter topic and grammatical patterns to be introduced, were used to organize lessons. The methodology, therefore, was task-based in the sense that collaborative tasks involving speaking, understanding, reading, and writing the L2 were used as a focus of lesson planning and instruction. Tasks that were congruent with the lesson's theme and grammatical content were selected, with lesson planning organized around these tasks. In the first-year program, the textbook presented a range of tasks teachers could use in the classroom. The first-year instructional team also developed a variety of instructional materials to increase opportunities for creative language use.

The task-based curriculum was in its first year at the time data were collected for this study. The language program was in transition, having introduced new curricular materials in the first year only, although still using older materials with a different orientation for the second year. In the second year program, the textbook, which promoted a teacher-centered approach to mastery and drill of model dialogues, did not contain any peer collaborative tasks. Second-year instructors individually and collaboratively developed their own tasks to go along with the material taught in this text.

The Learners

The data were collected over an academic year, by miking and audio recording the interactions of student volunteers as they participated in their language classes. This process began with ten learners—six enrolled in first-year Japanese, and four enrolled in second-year Japanese—whose interactions were to be recorded. The ten volunteers were selected from a larger group who expressed a willingness to have their interactions taped. They met the following criteria: In the first-year classes, only students without previous formal or informal Japanese language learning opportunities were selected. For second-year Japanese, learners all had completed the first-year course at the same university, and none had studied abroad. The original group of ten volunteers shrunk to seven through attrition, with four first-year and three second-year students completing the academic year. The learners (with pseudonyms) are described in Table 1.1. One of the second-year learners, Andrea, had lived in Japan on a military

TABLE 1.1
The Learners

Name	Level	Previous Japanese Instruction	Native Language
Sara	First year	None prior to fall quarter	English
Candace	First year	None prior to fall quarter	English
Rob	First year	None prior to fall quarter	English
Kuo-ming	First year	None prior to fall quarter	Mandarin Chinese
Katie	Second year	First year program at the same university	English
Andrea	Second year	First year program at the same university	English
Bryce	Second year	First year program at the same university	English

base, but spent most of her time on the base and did not learn the Japanese language. Sara, a first-year learner, is Japanese-American, but her parents were native speakers of English who used English in the home. The language courses these students were enrolled in were quite large, so the volunteers were not all enrolled in the same class sections. Occasionally two students were enrolled in the same class. In addition to this small group of learner volunteers, all other students as well as the teachers involved in the classes consented to data collection by signing informed consent forms.

The Teachers

The teachers in the program were both full-time lecturers and teaching assistants. As the researcher, I was not involved in any aspect of the courses, and did not exercise any control over the content of lessons. Teachers were not specifically selected for participation, but the data collection procedure followed the same students over the academic year, meaning that data were collected in the classes of many different instructors. All teachers involved in data collection sessions signed informed consent forms. The pedagogical backgrounds of the teachers varied. Table 1.2 shows their names (pseudonyms), educational backgrounds, experience in teaching Japanese as a foreign language (TJFL), and the level of the program in which they taught (first year or second year). This is not a complete list of instructors and graduate students involved in these courses, but lists only those who taught the classes in which the targeted learners were enrolled. Both courses were quite large and there were other graduate students employed, as well as other full-time instructors. Graduate students who worked as teaching assistants all completed one or more language teaching orientation seminars, scheduled each fall prior to the start of classes. Non-native speakers were screened via an oral proficiency interview prior to being employed, and were highly proficient in

TABLE 1.2
The Teachers and Their Backgrounds

Name	Education	TJFL Experience	Native Language	Program Level
Yasuda	M.A. in TJFL	5+ years	Japanese	Instructor in charge of first year level
Kikuchi	M.A. in TJFL	2+ years	Japanese	First year course
Jones	Graduate student	no prior	English	First year course
Nakata	Graduate student	3 years	English	First year course
Morita	Graduate student	no prior	Japanese	First year course
Otani	Graduate student	no prior	Japanese	First year course
Iida	Graduate student	1 year	Japanese	Second year course
Endoh	Graduate student	2 years	Japanese	Second year course
Suzuki	Graduate student	2 years	Japanese	Second year course

the L2. Graduate student majors were related to Japan studies (usually Japanese literature or linguistics) or language teaching. Some of the graduate students had also taken a foreign language teacher-training course. The staff for each level had weekly meetings where the goals of each week and approaches for reaching pedagogical goals were discussed.

Audio/Video Recording Procedure

Data were collected by video and audio taping the classes of these learners about three times each quarter. Data collection dates were set with the consent of the teachers involved, and according to the schedules of the targeted learners and data collection assistants. Individual learners wore clip-on microphones attached to individual tape recorders. All students and teachers were notified of the data collection schedule in advance, and targeted learners were advised to wear clothing with loose pockets that would accommodate the small recording units. A video camera monitored classroom activities on a grosser level, but was not connected to any of the individual students' microphones. A research assistant took detailed field notes on what transpired in the classes, including writing down what appeared on the blackboard and overhead projector. Classroom materials used (handouts and copies of transparencies) were also collected from the teachers. Large classes (23 to 25 students per class) in small classrooms (many designed for a student capacity of 18 to 20), and frequent reconfiguration of students for different activities made data collection a difficult task, resulting in occasional technical difficulties including disconnected microphones and recorder buttons being accidentally bumped, causing recorders to turn off during class. Jamming of recorders into too-small pockets resulted in other technical problems.

Transcription of Data

Thirty-four classroom hours of data were transcribed for analysis using conventions from Conversation Analysis (CA). Table 1.3 shows the learners' pseudonyms, class level, and the classes transcribed for each: These data were selected for transcription based on the following: (a) 4–6 classes per student were transcribed, (b) tapes selected had good sound quality and were complete, and (c) classes were selected from fall, winter and spring quarters. Transcription included careful attention to details such as learner pronunciation, overlap, pauses, false starts, stuttering, whispering, and repair. All of the chapters except one (chap. 5), use the entire data set. Chapter 5 specifically looks at the development of interactional style in first-year learners, and thus uses the first-year data only.

Transcription Conventions

Transcription conventions are listed in Table 1.4. The conventions, adapted from Conversation Analysis (CA), are used to show a variety of features. Punctuation marks are used to show intonation, not as they are conventionally used in English or in Japanese. There are also notations used to show pauses, false starts, speaker emphasis, and volume. The conventions also show how turns are uttered in relationship to one another—overlap is indicated with square brackets. Finally, arrows and underlining are used to draw the reader's attention to particular portions of excerpts, with transcriber's comments listed in double parentheses.

English Translations of Excerpts and Examples

Through the use of English translations of the excerpts and examples, every attempt is made to make the data accessible to the reader unfamiliar with Japanese. Sometimes translation is provided line by line, and some-

TABLE 1.3
Data Transcribed

Name	Level	Classes Transcribed
Sara	First year	10/23/96, 12/4/96, 2/7/97, 3/3/97, 5/22/97
Kuo-ming	First year	11/18/96, 1/30/97, 2/27/97, 5/22/97
Candace	First year	11/27/96, 1/24/97, 2/28/97, 4/24/97, 5/22/97
Rob	First year	11/13/96, 11/27/96, 12/2/96, 1/24/97, 2/28/97, 4/21/97
Andrea	Second year	11/21/96, 1/22/97, 2/5/97, 4/18/97, 5/16/97
Bryce	Second year	11/21/96, 1/27/97, 2/10/97, 4/17/97, 5/16/97
Katie	Second year	10/24/96, 11/21/96, 2/6/97, 6/2/97

TABLE 1.4
Transcription Conventions

?	Rising intonation
,	Slight rise in intonation
.	Falling intonation
:	Elongation of a syllable
(.)	Brief pause
(#)	Timed pause
-	False start
CAPS	Small caps in the discourse are used to show the speaker's emphasis.
° °	Reduced volume—soft voice
°° °°	Reduced volume—whispered
°°° °°°	Reduced volume—very soft whisper, with consonant sounds articulated and certain vowel sounds difficult to determine.
[	Indicates overlap with portion in the next turn that is similarly bracketed.
[[	Indicates overlap with portion in the next turn that is similarly bracketed. Used when the single bracket is used in the previous line and or turn so that there will not be confusion regarding what brackets correspond to.
→	Line to be discussed in the text.
__	Portion of special note to the current analysis is underlined.
(( ))	Comments enclosed in double parentheses.
T:	The teacher in the particular excerpt; the identity of "T" may differ across excerpts.
S1:, S2:	Unidentified student

times turn by turn, depending on what will make the excerpt clearest to the reader unfamiliar with Japanese. Because of this, excerpt *line numbers* sometimes indicate a line, and sometimes indicate a turn. Most often, colloquial translations are provided. Because of differences between English and Japanese word order (English sentences are ordered subject–verb–object, whereas Japanese word order is subject–object–verb), incomplete sentences often cannot be translated adequately in English. In these sorts of cases, a word-for-word translation is used. Word-for-word translation is also used where needed to illuminate a particular excerpt or line of an excerpt. The abbreviations in Table 1.5 are used in English word-for-word translations to indicate Japanese function words and affixes. Another ramification of the differing word order between Japanese and English that impacts translations is that the location of pauses cannot be accurately rendered in the English glosses. Finally, most of the learners' Japanese errors are noted in the English translations of the glosses in double parentheses. Again, because of differences between English and Japanese, the errors learners make often cannot be conveyed in the English translation. These errors may or may not be relevant to the particular point highlighted by an excerpt, but such errors are noted to avoid giving the reader unfamiliar with Japanese a false impression of what learners are able to do in Japanese.

TABLE 1.5
Abbreviations Used in Word-for-Word Translations

ACC	Accusative case marker *(o)*
NOM	Nominative marker *(ga)*
TOP	Topic marker *(wa)*
DAT	Dative marker *(ni)*
GEN	Genitive marker *(no)*
INT	Interrogative marker *(ka)*
adv	Adverbial affix *(-ku)*
CMP	Complementizer *(to)*
CONJ	Conjunction *(soshite, de, etc.)*
COP	Copula *(da/desu, etc.)*
nom	Nominalizer *(no, koto)*

Data Analysis

Methods of discourse and Conversation Analysis (CA) were used to analyze the data. CA, in particular, has attracted recent attention as a tool for SLA research (Markee, 1995, 2000). Classroom interaction is structured differently from ordinary conversation, not only in its turn-taking conventions (McHoul, 1978), but also in interactional structure, which has been shown to be dominated by a three-turn question/answer/follow-up sequence called the initiation–response–follow-up (IRF) sequence (Bellack et al., 1966; Mehan, 1985; Ohta, 1993, 1994; Sinclair & Coulthard, 1975). Analyses were informed by an understanding of the structure of classroom discourse in general, and were tailored to the questions under investigation in each chapter. More specific procedures are described in each chapter as appropriate.

OVERVIEW OF THE BOOK:
A STUDY OF CLASSROOM LANGUAGE LEARNING

This first chapter of this book presented a theoretical foundation for examination of learner discourse. This foundation will illuminate analysis of the data in order to better understand the language learning process. Language learning, according to this framework, is a process of internalization. This book explores that process from a range of different entry points. Chapter 2 presents an analysis of private speech and its role in classroom learning. As explained in chapter 1, private speech is a form of speech that is intermediary between social and inner speech. Private speech illuminates language learning in process. Chapter 3 considers the role of social interaction in language learning, and how interaction in the

ZPD leads to development. This is done by examining the role of assisted performance in the development of language proficiency. Chapter 4 examines corrective feedback, a key element of interactive processes of language learners. In chapter 4, errors are examined from the learner's perspective, considering the variety of ways learners receive meaningful feedback in the classroom learning setting. The first four chapters all look at the developmental processes that are part of language learning. Chapter 5 continues this process focus in its examination of language development. Specifically, the chapter presents a study of how first-year learners acquire facility with listener response expressions. Finally, in chapter 6, the relationship between task and activity—between how assigned interactive tasks relate to what learners actually do in the peer learning setting—is probed. With the recent attention to and interest in tasks as language learning tools, a data-based understanding of how tasks are realized in learner discourse—the discourse that forms the foundation for internalization of social interaction—is essential to understanding how languages are learned in the classroom.

Chapter 2

Private Speech: A Window on Classroom Foreign Language Acquisition

This chapter examines the role of private speech in the interactions of the seven first- and second-year learners which make up the classroom corpus.[1] This analysis of private speech allows us to better understand the role of attentional processes in second language acquisition. The various analyses also illustrate how speech is used, not only for social interaction, but also as a cognitive tool that is key to the process of language development. The findings show private speech to be a creative locus of linguistic manipulation and hypothesis testing, a covert social space in which learners actively involve themselves in language lessons when they are not the focus of teacher attention. The data show how even when the teacher is addressing another, all learners are tacitly invited to formulate their own responses as legitimate, peripheral participants (Lave & Wenger, 1991) in the interaction. These findings reveal learners to be proactive and learner centered in their activity, even when instruction is focused on the needs of other learners. Private speech was found to be a vehicle for hypothesis testing, where learners try out new language prior to using it in a social situation; this is a precursor to *interactive hypothesis testing*, which occurs when the learner uses the language in social interaction. Analysis reveals the extent to which covert learner activity is a centerpiece of learning processes, deepening our understanding of how learners appropriate language through interactive processes. Analysis here focuses on the question of

---

[1]A portion of this research was previous presented at the 1998 annual meeting of the American Association for Applied Linguistics (Ohta, 1998) and at the Linguistics Society of American Linguistics Institute (Ohta, 1997a).

how private speech reveals acquisition in process. Results suggest the power of engagement as a factor in L2 acquisition, as the data reveal instances in which linguistic affordances acted on by the learner in private speech are incorporated into the learner's developing linguistic system.

THE ROLE OF PRIVATE SPEECH IN LANGUAGE ACQUISITION: PREVIOUS RESEARCH

L1 Studies of the Private Speech of Children

Most studies of children's private speech are studies of cognitive development, not studies of language acquisition. In these studies, the private speech of children doing visual/spatial puzzles (Behrend, Rosengren, & Perlmutter, 1988), pretend play (Smolucha, 1992), and classroom seatwork (Berk, 1986, Berk & Garvin, 1984), was examined in order to understand the development of higher mental functions. This line of research explores the regulatory continuum described in chapter 1, and prioritizes an understanding of the role of private speech in the regulation of children's behavior, not in language development. The very characteristics of private speech of most interest to linguists—word play, repetition, and play with linguistic structure—were classified as "task irrelevant" or "immature" in these studies (Kohlberg, Yaeger & Hjertholm, 1968). What may appear to be irrelevant to the child psychologist (word play, for example), is of high relevance to the linguist. Berk (1992), in her review of the literature on children's private speech, noted this oversight in the developmental psychology research, and makes a plea for research that examines "the relationship of playful and linguistically oriented private speech to socioemotional and *language* outcomes" (p. 43, italics added).

Toddlers learning their first language and children of all ages learning second/foreign languages actively engage in manipulation of language in the context of private speech. Toddlers prolifically engage in private speech when playing or when alone, producing language that is of tremendous interest to linguists. Child first language acquisition researchers extensively used this kind of data in their studies, whether or not they use the term *private speech* to describe the data collected. Cazden (1976) posited that in communicative situations where the focus is on meaning, language forms are normally "transparent." By manipulating the language, these transparent forms are made "opaque" for analysis by the child.

> Children may shift more easily than adults between using language forms transparently in inter-personal communication, and treating them as opaque objects in play. In other words, when the child's intention is to communicate, he—like the adult—can "hear through" his language to that end;

but it is hypothesized that the child can also intend to play with the elements of language for the very delight of self-expression and mastery, and does so more easily than the adult unless the latter is a poet. (Cazden, 1976, pp. 604–605)

Children learning their native languages manipulate linguistic patterning (whether phonetic, morphological, or syntactic) in both private and social contexts. Manipulating the language being learned is a part of the process by which children make the language their own. The "crib speech" studies provide rich evidence of this phenomenon. Weir (1976), in her study of a 2½-year-old child, found that her child's private speech contained "sense in nonsense," being "structured so that it serves as a systematic linguistic exercise" (p. 610). The child manipulated language freely in a manner different from the way he used language in interpersonal interactive settings. Kuczaj (1983) concluded that *what* children manipulate is indicative of their progress in acquiring the language. Children do not play with language structure that is far beyond their current capacity, but spend the most time manipulating what they are currently working to acquire.

Studies of the Private Speech of Children Learning a Second Language

Peck (1980) studied the private speech of a Spanish native speaking child who was learning English as a second language. She found the same types of phenomena that Weir and Kuczaj documented in work with children learning their native languages. Saville-Troike (1988) studied the private speech of six children who exhibited a "silent period" during which they engaged in little interpersonal interaction in English, the language being acquired. Saville-Troike hypothesized that the children "were not merely passively assimilating second language input, but were using private speech in an active process of engagement with the input data" (p. 568). By collecting the naturally occurring speech of these children, she found that they were not silent, but were using private speech in both their first and second languages. The children engaged in L2 sound play and repetition. Most of what the children repeated was meaningful. But, they also repeated function words "many weeks before there was any indication they could understand or use them appropriately" (Saville-Troike, 1988, p. 582), and repeated other utterances that were clearly incomprehensible to them. In private speech, learners may act on language that is not yet understood because of sound, frequency, or other features of interest to the learner. Perhaps even incomprehensibility may highlight a particular item for further attention. Krashen's (1985) conceptualization of a path from input to comprehension to intake does not capture how learners attend to or comprehend language in the first place. First, language must be apperceived because it is "noticed in some way" due to "some particular recognizable features" (Gass, 1997, p. 4), a process that may or may not involve comprehension. The children studied by Saville-Troike (1988) used private speech to attend to language form, as shown in (a) through (d) below:

(a) Walking, walking, walk. Walking, walking, walk.
(b) Quick. Quick, quick. Quickly. Quick
(c) Bathroom. Bath.
(d) Out, Outside
(Excerpted from Saville-Troike's 1988 examples 50–53, p. 584)

The children also manipulated sentence patterns and did substitutions and expansions of their own and others' English utterances. Their private speech contained both L1 and L2, with L1 an integral part of L2 oral play as children did translation exercises, and produced utterances mixing the L1 and L2. When manipulating the L2, older children tended to focus on linguistic form more than younger children did. Saville-Troike (1988) also found that the children rehearsed privately prior to using the L2 in social interaction. One child, for example, "responded privately to the teacher's daily question about the weather for at least a week before he raised his hand and first volunteered an answer. When he finally did, his voice was loud and self-assured" (p. 575). The L2 produced in private speech was of a higher level than the children used in the social situations in which they spoke the second language. Private speech was found to provide an accurate forecast of where the children were headed in language acquisition.

In summary, in studies that have tapped into the private speech of children, similar results have been found. Kuczaj's (1983) and Weir's (1976) studies of L1 acquisition, and Peck's (1980) and Saville-Troike's (1988) studies of children learning an L2 noted that the children engaged in private speech in the L2, including repetition, manipulation of language on phonological, morphological, lexical and syntactic forms, recombination and substitution, and expansion of utterances. Saville-Troike, Kuczaj and Weir concur that private speech shows us where the child is headed in terms of language development. Private speech is a tangible enactment of the child's ZPD—a measure of the distance between the child's actual developmental level, and level of potential development.

Studies of the Adult L2 Learner

For the adult as well as for the child, private speech activity should provide a useful environment for examination of language development. I propose that just as the private speech of the child forecasts the child's language de-

velopment, for the adult as well, private speech should provide a picture of
the developmental path of language acquisition. For adults as well as children, private speech in the language being learned should reveal internalization processes. The private speech of adults, however, has been little
examined. If, as for children, private speech data reveals where the adult is
headed in acquisition of the language—if such data provides a snapshot of
the ZPD—then private speech is important as a barometer of language acquisition. Private speech data may constitute a moving picture of language
acquisition in process. In this section, the role of private speech for the adult
learner is examined, considering its regulatory functions, and looking at
the role of private speech as a tool for language learning.

Private Speech and Regulation

There are a growing number of studies of the private speech of adult language learners. Most of these studies have focused on the regulatory function of private speech. As noted in studies of children, for adults as well,
private speech emerges when the adult encounters difficulty in solving a
problem (John-Steiner, 1992). In such situations, the adult may use private speech to gain control of the problem. This has been found to be true
of L2 learners as well, who have been found to use L2 private speech when
encountering difficulties in picture-sequencing tasks (Ahmed, 1994;
Lantolf & Frawley, 1985; McCafferty, 1994a), or the recall of narrative and
expository texts (Appel & Lantolf, 1994). The learners who participated in
these studies, however, were all ESL learners or advanced foreign language learners. The performance of lower level learners has been little examined. For learners in the early stages of acquiring a second language,
the language used for the planning of action, or mediation of thought is
likely the L1 rather than the L2. Efforts to master the L2 itself—as seen in
rehearsal processes—may occur in the L2 (Brooks, Donato, & McGlone,
1997). As learners increase in L2 proficiency, they may then gradually become able to use the L2 not only as a tool for its own acquisition, but also
as a tool to regulate higher cognitive processes. Studying the private
speech of lower level learners, therefore, should yield results that differ
from the findings of studies of advanced learners. How learners use private speech in the language classroom or as a tool for L2 acquisition has
been little examined.

**Studies of Learning Strategies That Relate
to L2 Private Speech**

Some studies of learning strategies, although not using the term *private
speech* nor considering its role in language development, have documented the use of L2 private speech by learners. Ramsey (1980), studied

how monolinguals and multilinguals approached learning the language Euskera, looking at the relationship between level of success and learning strategies used. Ramsey found oral rehearsal to be one factor distinguishing successful from unsuccessful learners. Successful learners also did better than unsuccessful learners on a lexical memory pre-test, were more willing to produce L2 phonemes, and were better at imitating L2 words presented visually. Lexical memory and the ability to imitate target language sounds may be related to the use of L2 private speech. All of the successful learners engaged in solitary oral rehearsal in the L2 (and in private speech in English), while learning the target language. Ramsey (1980) described this as follows:

> The SLs [successful learners] (some immediately, some after a few moments) evinced no inhibition at all about practicing aloud; they also verbalized freely on the mental processes they were going through. The outstanding P [participant] spent the entire time in vocal TL [target language] activity . . . often cutting off the tape in mid-phrase and continuing the dialogue by himself. . . . and kinetic involvement in the learning process was the rule. Walking around, spatially arranging cards, gesturing while vocalizing were conspicuous activities among SLs and notably absent among USLs [unsuccessful learners]. SLs spotted their errors often . . . *They were totally absorbed in the ongoing TL task.* . . . They used vocabulary creatively or in sentence frames. (pp. 88–89, emphasis added)

Ramsey's successful learners were totally absorbed in the learning task as evidenced by their L1 and L2 private speech. Unfortunately, Ramsey says nothing more about the content of the private speech of these learners. From the quotation cited, however, we can infer that the L2 private speech included both mechanical and expressive sorts of L2 activities: imitation, completion of utterances, creative vocabulary use, use of sentence structures as expressive "frames," and self-correction of errors.

J. Rubin (1981) investigated cognitive strategies in second language acquisition through observation of classes and tutoring sessions, and through learner self-report diaries. Students reported *monitoring*, through which they corrected their own or another learner's error, and *practice*, which involved experimentation with new sounds, words, and structures. Both of these entail involvement in either L2 private speech or mental rehearsal. O'Malley, Chamot, Stewner-Manzanares, Kupper, and Russo (1985) conducted interviews concerning use of learning strategies by beginning and intermediate high-school ESL students from a variety of L1 backgrounds. Students reported engaging in private speech in the L2, including repetition, note-taking, recombination, contextualization, transfer, and self-monitoring.

Reiss (1985) used questionnaires to study the learning strategies of successful language learners. She found that: 97.3% of good language learners reported "listening closely in class and mentally answering questions whether called upon or not," 76.3% reported "listening to other students in class and mentally correcting their errors," 76.3% reported "applying new material mentally while silently speaking to oneself" (p. 515). Unfortunately, for our purposes here, Reiss did not ask the learners whether not they used language orally as they covertly answered questions, corrected errors, or applied new material in speaking to themselves; her questions reflect her assumption that such a strategy would involve mental, not oral, language use. And, although students "were encouraged to mention any strategies they employed which had not been listed" (p. 516), Reiss' supplementary list of strategies mentioned by the students does not include any reference to L2 private speech. Reiss (1985) concluded that

> Above all, the good language learner is an ACTIVE participant in the conscious learning process. The word "active" is of great significance because the successful language learner is constantly processing information whether called upon or not. Even when silent he is active mentally and thus becomes a *silent speaker* . . . he may not volunteer nor take chances on errors "aloud" but this does not stop him from practicing silently. . . . Once a student is "speaking silently" he is ipso facto practicing, inferencing, looking for meaning, etc. . . . the good language learner is a *silent speaker*. He is an active participant in the language learning process. He is watchful and alert to sound, meaning, and form of the language. He answers questions mentally whether called upon or not. He enjoys manipulating the language for its own sake. (p. 518)

It is possible that these good learners were not just "silent speakers," but were also using audible private speech as part of the language learning process.

There is one study that explicitly investigates engagement in private speech by adult foreign and L2 learners. Lantolf (1997) used questionnaires to investigate how and when adult learners engage in *language play*, a term he uses to encompass L2 private speech and mental rehearsal. In the questionnaire, Lantolf gives examples of language play as "talking out loud to yourself in Spanish; repeating to yourself silently; making up sentences or words in Spanish; imitating to yourself sounds in Spanish; having random snatches of Spanish pop into your head" (p. 9). Through these processes, language learners engage in manipulation of the L2 to differing degrees, whether deliberately or spontaneously, orally or mentally. Lantolf (1997) found that 90% of the advanced Spanish students reported engaging in language play "often" or "very often." Since this study did not separately examine private speech, it is not clear whether learners are aware of their own private speech.

THE PRESENT STUDY: PRIVATE SPEECH
IN THE FOREIGN LANGUAGE CLASSROOM

Previous studies of private speech have not looked at how private speech is used by classroom learners, or considered the role of private speech in the classroom acquisition of foreign language. Investigation of naturally emerging private speech will clarify the characteristics of private speech, deepening our understanding of its role and function in SLA. This chapter investigates private speech as it occurred in the classroom language of the seven learners, in order to document the characteristics of private speech as uttered by learners, considering the functions of private speech in L2 acquisition processes.

The Data

The data were described in chapter 1. In order to prepare the transcripts for analysis of private speech, all transcripts and tapes were reviewed with careful attention to the potential occurrence of private speech. Through this process, transcripts were refined, with details regarding the volume of learner utterances added. This process did not involve making judgments about what was, or was not, potentially private speech, but simply involved comparing utterances of reduced volume with the loudness of preceding utterances by the same learners and making judgments of how reduced the volume was. A three-scale system of noting reduced volume was developed, as follows:

TABLE 2.1
Symbols for Transcribing Reduced Speech Volume

°	Utterance at a lower volume than usual, but not in a whisper
°°	Very soft voice or whispered speech
°°°	Soft whisper. Consonant sounds clearly heard, with vowel sounds difficult to discern

All transcripts were thus reviewed, with reduced volume marked as appropriate. When it was difficult to decide which level of loudness should be used, notation indicating the louder of the two levels under consideration was selected.

Identifying Private Speech in the Transcripts

Following refinement of transcripts to include indications of reduced volume, transcripts were reviewed for evidence of private speech—language addressed to the self, but uttered in the presence of others to whom it is

TABLE 2.2
Incidences of Private Speech Per Class

Level	Name	Number of Private Speech Episodes Per Class	Avg.
First year	Kuo-ming	(11/18) 39, (1/30) 64, (2/27) 77, (5/22) 36	54
	Candace	(11/27) 13, (1/24) 24, (2/28) 8, (4/24) 15, (5/22) 27	17.4
	Sara	(10/23) 26, (12/4) 12, (2/7) 15, (3/3) 1, (5/22), 27	16.2
	Rob	(11/13) 6, (11/27) 11, (12/2) 2, (1/24) 4, (2/28) 14, (4/21) 1	6.33
Second year	Bryce	(11/21) 23, (1/27) 11, (2/10) 11, (4/17) 3, (5/16) 21	13.8
	Andrea	(11/21) 2, (1/22) 0, (2/5) 0, (4/18) 11, (5/16) 4	3.4
	Katie	(10/24) 2, (11/21) 3, (2/6) 3, (6/2) 2	2.5

not addressed. The definition of private speech used is based on Smo-lucha's (1992) definition, combined with an understanding of private speech as language directed to the self, whether or not an overhearer or potential interlocutor may be present. In the present data, private speech was clearly identifiable by its (a) reduced volume, (b) because it was not in response to a question/comment directed specifically to the individual by the teacher or another student, and (c) because it did not receive a response by the teacher or a classmate.[2] Ambiguous utterances—which might have been addressed to another learner, for example—are not included in the analysis.

Results of Analysis: Frequency of Private Speech

Preliminary review of the transcripts revealed dramatic variability in the frequency of private speech across students: Two of the students, Andrea and Katie, hardly ever engaged in private speech. The other five engaged in private speech more often. As Table 2.2 shows, Kuo-ming evidenced the most private speech, with an average of 54 instances of private speech per class; Kuo-ming engaged in private speech much more frequently than any of the other learners. The next most frequent user of private speech was Candace, with an average of 17.4 episodes per class. The individuals also varied widely in how much private speech each used from class to class. Candace, for example shows a range of 13–27 episodes of private speech over the classes in the corpus. To provide an idea of the variability, however, consider Table 2.2. Almost all of this private speech was in Japanese, not English. Beyond these counts of the number of episodes of private speech per learner per class, further quantitative analysis

---

[2]See chapter 1 for a more extensive discussion of the various definitions of private speech used in the research literature.

was not conducted. The numbers in Table 2.2 are dependent not only on differences between learners, but on a number of other factors, such as (a) the structure of classroom lessons, (b) the types of tasks learners did during each class period, and (c) the configuration of learners as they worked on peer interactive tasks. Classroom activities naturally varied from class to class, and private speech occurred more or less frequently in different settings and tasks, rendering any quantitative comparison of private speech frequency meaningless. For example, private speech was much more frequent during teacher-fronted practice than during peer learning tasks. And, even with peer learning tasks, the number of students in each group has relevance for private speech production. Variability across the same student from class to class, therefore, cannot be used to make any claims regarding changes in the learner over time. These numbers are mostly useful as a demonstration of individual differences in the gross amount of private speech used.

Types of L2 Private Speech Found in the Data

The data provide significant documentation of engagement in L2 private speech by adult language learners. As shown in Table 2.2, the extent of L2 private speech clearly varies widely from learner to learner. Analysis reveals that learners used L2 private speech to take a "private turn" (van Lier, 1988) during the class in a variety of ways. The private speech in these data may be categorized into the three broad categories of private turns, as shown in Table 2.3. These categories are not completely discrete, but overlap somewhat as will be shown in the following analysis. In this section, each type of L2 private speech is examined in more detail, considering how each functions in classroom L2 acquisition.

Vicarious Response

Ramsey (1980) found that successful learners would orally "cut off" the dialogue tape and finish sentences themselves. Reiss' (1985) subjects reported "mentally answering questions whether called upon or not," and "mentally correcting [other students'] errors" (p. 515). In the present study, learners used L2 private speech in similar ways—particularly to covertly respond during another learner's turn. I have termed this use of language *vicarious response*. Through vicarious response, the learner covertly answers questions directed to another student or to the class, completes the utterance of another, or provides an alternative to the utterance of another. The response is vicarious because it is uttered "in place of" another. But, the response is for the self, not for an audience, as indicated by the covert nature of the vicarious response; it is low in volume, and often

TABLE 2.3
Types of L2 Private Speech

Vicarious response	Learner covertly answers a question addressed to another student or to the class, completes the utterance of another, or repairs another's error.
Repetition	Learner repeats words, phrases, and sentences, in whole or in part. Material repeated may or may not be in the immediately preceding context. The learner may repeat after another or after him or herself. Repetition as part of choral drill is excluded from consideration here.
Manipulation	Learner manipulates sentence structure, morphology, or sounds.

overlaps the response of another. Vicarious responses differ from ordinary choral responses in that they are not addressed to the teacher—the low volume makes response from the teacher or a classmate impossible. Vicarious responses occur in three different contexts: First, the student may answer or begin to answer prior to the answer of the student nominated to answer, or of the class, if the question was directed to the class. Second, the student may complete an answer or utterance left incomplete by the nominated student or the teacher, or complete an utterance during a pause. Third, the student may correct the nominated student's utterance. Finally, these responses often overlap that of another classmate or classmates. The student producing the vicarious response, therefore, is neither being individually addressed by the teacher, nor is the response likely to be noticed. The audience for private speech utterances is, as already mentioned, the self. In the corpus, there are no ambiguous cases in which another person seems to respond to a student's vicarious response.

Vicarious response is difficult to observe without using individual microphones to collect learner utterances. Rubin's (1981) and O'Malley et al's (1985) studies, although using trained observers to identify learning strategies used in ESL classes, did not identify the use of private speech. Learners themselves may not be aware of these sorts of responses; in Reiss' (1985) questionnaire study, although students reported "mentally answering," "mentally correcting," and "applying new material mentally," none of the students mentioned using private speech responses. It appears that the use of private turns occurs largely outside of the awareness of teachers, researchers, and language learners themselves. In fact, in an informal survey conducted via email at the end of the data collection period while the learners were still taking Japanese classes, I asked the seven learners whether or not they whispered responses to themselves in class. The learners responded that they seldom or never did so. Kuo-ming, the student who used vicarious responses most prolifically, said that he rarely uses covert responses in Japanese class.

Despite the fact that vicarious responses may not be noticed by teachers or even by learners themselves when asked about them retrospectively, vicarious responses are a significant mode of participation that provides evidence of a learner's high level of engagement in classroom activity. Although today there is a tendency to consider students as active during pair or group work, but passive during teacher-fronted, lock-step classroom activities, these vicarious responses are evidence of engagement. Vicarious responses show learners to be active in using the L2, even in settings that have been considered less interactive, such as teacher-fronted instruction. These students are actively engaged, even though they are not directly nominated as participants. The occurrence of vicarious response reveals an unspoken contract that may exist in language classrooms—while the teacher may be addressing one student, all other students are tacitly invited to formulate their own responses. Vicarious responses are a form of legitimate, peripheral participation (Lave & Wenger, 1991) in classroom activity.

Vicarious response provides a safe context for L2 use and experimentation. Through vicarious response, learners formulate their own responses, and then have the opportunity to gage the appropriateness of their response based on the ongoing discourse. An example is shown in Excerpt 1. In this class, the teacher is guiding students in practicing locative expressions by talking about the features of various cities. In Japanese, the same word order is used for questions and statements, as follows:

Question: Pari ni nani ga arimasu ka.
                  Paris DAT what NOM exist INT.
                  What is there in Paris?
Statement: Pari ni (noun) ga arimasu.
                  Paris DAT (noun) NOM EXIST.
                  There's a (noun) in Paris.

As is evident from the Japanese question, statement, and their translations, the word order in the colloquial English gloss differs radically from the Japanese. In reading Excerpt 1, the reader unfamiliar with Japanese may find it useful to refer to the above structures for reference. A word-for-word gloss will be used for incomplete sentences, because these cannot be appropriately translated into English due to differences in word order. When the entire sentence is uttered, a colloquial English translation is provided. Note Kuo-ming's use of vicarious response in lines 8 and 14.

(1)   1 T: Pari un Pari wakarimasu ka?
              "Pari" yeah do you understand "Pari" ((Paris))?
     2 Ss: Hai. Paris
              Yes. Paris

```
    3   T:    Paris. (.) wa Pari.  hai [ (.) jaa Pari:::
              Paris. (.) is "Pari." Yes. (.) Okay Paris:::
    4   Km:                           [Oh hehehehe ((laughter))
    5   Ss:   N[ani ga arimasu ka? [
              W[hat NOM exists INT? ((here, students are completing the
              question the teacher started in line 3, by adding "what is
              there?"))
    6   T:    [Ni?              [Hai ii desu ne,³ kore wa?
              DAT?               Yes, that's good. What about this?
    7   S4:   [[Chuugoku nani ga arimasu ka?
              China ((error: dative particle missing)) what NOM exist INT?
→   8   Km:   [[°°Chuu:goku (.) ni:: (.) nani ga    nani [ga arima-°°
              °°China       (.) DAT (.) what  NOM what  NOM exis-°°
    9   T:                                         [Soo desu ne?
                                                    Yes that's it.
   10         Chuugoku ni nani ga arimasu ka? jaa kore ne pea
              de: (.) chotto kiite kudasai.
              What is there in China? Okay in pairs (.) please ask.
   11         ((Teacher matching up pairs of students—students
              all get up to find their partners—task begins))
   12   Km:   So what are we supposed to do? (.) haha
   13   M:    I guess we ((sic)) supposed to (.)
→  14   Km:   Heh Nyuu Yoorku ni nani ga arimasu ka? ((Laughs
              while saying this))
              Heh what is there in New York?
   15   M:    E:h o::h. (3) Statue of Liberty::: ga arimasu.
              E:h o::h. (3) There's the Statue of Liberty.
                                              (Kuo-ming, 11/18)
```

In line 8, Kuo-ming overlaps S4 and formulates his own response in private speech. Then, when pair practice begins, he initiates questions (line 14), using the same pattern he just rehearsed privately.

Rehearsal in the vicarious response context can be quite elaborate, as students try out different forms. Excerpts 2 and 2.1, present just such an example. The teacher has the students respond to the comment "You're tired aren't you?" Candace, who is not nominated, orally formulates her

---

³There are many ways to translate *ne*, depending upon the context. Here, the particle is not translated in the English gloss, because there is not a good English equivalent for *ne* here. *Ne* may often be translated as a tag question, such as "isn't it?" or "right," though often these English translations often do not do a very good job of conveying the sense of the original Japanese. When there is not an appropriate English translation of *ne*, the particle will not be translated. Exceptions to this will occur if *ne* is the focus of analysis in a particular excerpt, in which it may be left in the original Japanese, with *ne* appearing in the English gloss.

TABLE 2.4
Morphological Structure of *dekaketakatta* and *dekaketa*

"Dekaketakatta"	**dekake-**	**-ta-**	**katta**
Meaning: "Wanted to go out"	stem of *dekakeru*	stem of desiderative affix (adjective stem)	past tense marker (for adjectives)
"Dekaketa"	**dekake-**	**-ta**	
Meaning: "Went out"	stem of *dekakeru*	past tense marker (for verbs)	

own answer. To do this, she works to conjugate the verb *dekakeru* 'to go out' into its past tense form. In Excerpt 2, Candace tries to produce the past form of *dekakeru* 'to go out', first coming up with the past desiderative form *dekaketakatta* 'I wanted to go out'. The desiderative inflection adds the meaning "want to" to the verb stem—this is not the form Candace needs for this context. Rather, what is appropriate is just the past tense, not the past tense of the desiderative. For reference of the reader unfamiliar with Japanese, the segmentation of *dekaketakatta* and *dekaketa* are shown in Table 2.4. Excerpt 2 shows how Candace uses vicarious response to work on this morphological problem. She works with the verb through vicarious response and finally settles on the correct form in line 14:

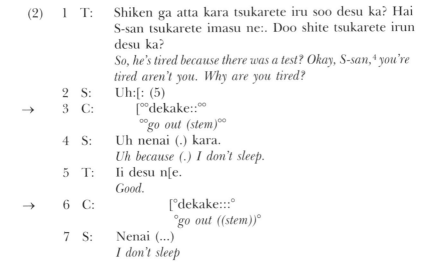

(2)	1	T:	Shiken ga atta kara tsukarete iru soo desu ka? Hai S-san tsukarete imasu ne:. Doo shite tsukarete irun desu ka?
			So, he's tired because there was a test? Okay, S-san,[4] you're tired aren't you. Why are you tired?
	2	S:	Uh:[: (5)
→	3	C:	[°°dekake::°°
			°°*go out (stem)*°°
	4	S:	Uh nenai (.) kara.
			Uh because (.) I don't sleep.
	5	T:	Ii desu n[e.
			Good.
→	6	C:	[°dekake:::°
			°*go out ((stem))*°
	7	S:	Nenai (...)
			I don't sleep

---

[4]The Japanese title *-san*, is translated as "Mr." or "Ms." The title *-san* is used in Japanese with first or last names. In general, these teachers used students' last names. Student pseudonyms, however, are most often first names. In the English translation, when a pseudonym is a last name, *-san* is retained.

        8 T: [Past tense. Ne:,

→   9 C: [°Takatta (.) dekakke::°
                °wanted to ((past tense desiderative affix)) (.) go out ((stem))°

     10 S: Nennakunai. Uh:: ya ne- (.) nakatta (.) kara tsukarete
                iru.
                Didn't sleep ((error)). Uh:: ya sle- (.) since I didn't sleep, I'm
                tired.

     11 T: Ii desu ne didn't sleep. Nenakatta kara tsukarete irun
                desu. Ne? Nenakatta kara tsukarete irun desu. Ja doo
                shite atama ga itain desu ka? Doo shite kaze o hiitan
                desu ka? Doo shite kenkoo nan desu ka? Kenkoo tte
                nan desu ka? Genki desu.=
                Good, didn't sleep. He's tired because he didn't sleep. Okay?
                Tired because he didn't sleep. Okay, so why do you have a
                headache? Why did you catch a cold? Why are you well?
                What does "kenkoo" mean? To be healthy=

→   12 C: °°Dekake:°°
                °Go out (stem)°

     13 T: =Healthy ne. Doo shite kenkoo nan desu ka? Doo shite
                karada no chooshi ga ii n desu ka?
                =Healthy. Why are you well? Why are you in good physical
                health?

→   14 C: °°De (.) ka (.) ke (.) ta ((overlapped with T's turn above))
                °Went out° ((uttered syllable by syllable, with pauses))
                                            (Candace, 5/22)

In line 3, Candace begins working with the stem of *dekakeru*, elongating the final vowel. She is working to formulate her own answer to the question, "Why are you tired?" Candace tries the past desiderative form (which means "wanted to go out") in line 9, which is not correct for this context. She continues working with the stem in lines 9 and 12 until she comes up with the appropriate form in line 14.

In Excerpt 2, just shown, it seems as if Candace has resolved her problem—by the end of the excerpt she has made the correct choice. However, in the interactive task that immediately follows Candace's vicarious response, shown in Excerpt 2.1, she replays the same forms again as she works to formulate the answer "Because I went out with a friend." In Excerpt 2.1, Candace goes through the same manipulations of *dekakeru* she did in teacher-fronted practice:

(2.1) 1 T: Karada no chooshi ga ii n desu ka? Wakarimasu ka?
                  Ne? Ja tonari no hito ni mata kiite kudasai.
                  So, are you in good physical health? Do you understand?
                  Okay? So, ask your neighbor.

2　C:　Nn.
　　　　Uh huh.

3　T:　Doo shite?
　　　　Why?

4　C:　Anoo sumimasen. Doo shite:: (.5) u::m dooshite
　　　　tsukarete irun desu ka?
　　　　Um excuse me. Why::: (.5) u::m why are you tired?

5　S:　Uh nenakatta kara (.5) tsukarete irun desu.
　　　　Uh I'm tired because (.) I didn't sleep.

6　C:　Ah soo desu ka?
　　　　Oh really?

7　S:　Uh doo shite tsukarete irun desu ka?
　　　　Uh why are you tired.

→　8　C:　(2) Hmm (2) tsu- ah um:: tomodachi to::
　　　　dekake:ta::katta::: desu. °deka-° Wait. Tomodachi to::
　　　　dekak- [(.) deka:ke:[: (.) ta:katta right?
　　　　(2) Hmm (2) tir- ah um:: because I <u>wanted to go out</u> with a
　　　　friend. °go o° Wait. <u>Go out</u> with a friend (.) <u>go out</u> (.) <u>wanted</u>
　　　　<u>to go out</u> right? ((Error: Candace mistakenly uses the
　　　　past-tense desiderative rather than the plain past)).

9　S:　　　　　　[keru　　　　[ru
　　　　　　　　　((these are verb endings))

→　10　S:　Uh I think its taka- uh::

→　11　C:　Hehe (.) D[[ekake::ru? Dekake::ta? [[
　　　　Hehe (.) go ou:t?　　　Went ou::t?

12　S:　　　　　　[[dekakeru?　　　　　　[[dekake<u>TA</u>. eh:
　　　　　　　　　go out?　　　　　　　　　　*Went out. Eh:*
　　　　　　　　　　　　　　　　　　　　　　((past marker
　　　　　　　　　　　　　　　　　　　　　　emphasized))

13　C:　And: to make it past?

14　S:　Yeah dekakeru (.) dekakete kudasai is go out please go
　　　　out?

15　C:　Hm

16　S:　Dekake<u>TA</u>.
　　　　went out ((past marker emphasized))

17　C:　Dekaketa
　　　　went out

18　S:　Dekaketa kara aa soo desu ka. (.) Doo shite atama ga
　　　　itain desu ka?
　　　　Because you went out, oh really. (.) Why do you have a
　　　　headache?

19　C:　Um (.) uh takusan ben- benkyoo:: shita kara
　　　　Um (.) uh because I stu- studi:::::ed a lot

　　　　　　　　　　　　　　　　　　　　　　　(Candace, 5/22)

In line 8, Candace gives the past desiderative form of *dekakeru* in her answer—this is the wrong choice she tried out before. Her realization of the error is evident in her manner of production. First, her production of *dekaketakatta* in line 8 has significant lengthening of the vowel after *ta*. If she had stopped there, she would have been correct. Instead of stopping, however, she drags out that vowel, evidence that she is considering her options. Her choice is to use *ta* as the stem of the desiderative affix, which she continues to conjugate, producing *dekaketakatta*.

Candace's recognition of her mistake is evident from her private speech in line 8. Both the partial repetition of the stem in reduced volume and her use of "wait" in English reflect her cognitive processing. She repeats her answer, again producing the past desiderative, again lengthening *ta*. Uncertainty is revealed both by this lengthening, and by her appeal for confirmation, "Right?" Her partner helps her, as she struggles in line 8. Note how he provides the citation form endings for her, as she hesitates. She says *dekak-*, and he provides *keru*. When she says *deka:ke:*, he says *ru*. This is the base form that Candace needs in order to make the simple past form. Finally, Candace produces the correct conjugation in line 11, *dekaketa*. Again, she lengthens the vowel before the choice point. She considers her options, and chooses the past morpheme *ta*, rather than the past desiderative *takatta*. Candace's partner repeats her answer in line 12, and Candace asks again for confirmation in line 13. Her partner goes through the paradigm from *dekakeru*, to the gerund (*te*-form) *dekakete*, providing an analogy with *dekaketa*, which he utters to complete the paradigm in line 16. After Candace repeats the verb, her partner finishes the sentence, and asks Candace another question, which she answers appropriately using the simple past form.

Excerpts 2 and 2.1 show how L2 private speech functions in hypothesis testing, in this case, helping Candace test hypotheses about the verb form. More importantly, this data allows us a snapshot of what is in the ZPD. Candace is grappling with a linguistic problem that she cannot yet resolve without assistance. This is a picture of what Candace is working to acquire. In the teacher-fronted setting, Candace actively formulates her own response to a question the teacher asked another student. Here, Candace engages in a sort of "parallel" practice, working to formulate her own response, even as she listens to the teacher interacting with the nominated students. She works on the problem in an intrapsychological context. Although in her private speech she seems to solve the problem, ultimately coming up with the correct form, the problem remains unresolved. The data show this. Working with a peer, Candace initially produces the same wrong conjugation she did covertly. She struggles with the two possibilities. Her partner, even though evidencing some uncertainty himself, does not accept the incorrect response. In addition, as noted, he provides her with the plain present endings, which she can use to form the past tense. Candace's partner is just one step ahead of Candace. He shows his own uncertainty in line 10, as he considers Candace's answer. Candace comes up with the correct conjugation in line 11, *dekaketa*, which she also rehearsed covertly. Candace's partner confirms this correct choice by saying "dekake_TA_" in line 12, emphasizing the past morpheme *ta*. Then, Candace's partner runs through a strategy to use to check her answer—recitation of the paradigm *dekakeru, dekakete, dekaketa* (roughly equivalent to the English "go out, going out, went out," but useful in this case because the simple past form is derived in the same way as the *te* form, the second form in the paradigm he recites), in lines 14 and 16. Private speech and subsequent peer interaction reveal Candace's ZPD—a problem she is unable to resolve without assistance in covert rehearsal, she solves with the support of her partner during a peer language learning task.

Two metaphors are useful for understanding what is occurring. First, I have already discussed how this data shows Candace's ZPD. Second, the data also provides an intimate view of hypothesis testing in process. Hypothesis testing is one of the processes that occurs in the ZPD. Swain (1993) proposed that there are three options a learner has when faced with a gap in knowledge of the L2 during production. The learner can:

(1) Ignore the problem.
(2) Work to solve the problem using individual knowledge and resources.
(3) Tag the problem for attention when the form occurs in input, using input for hypothesis testing.

A fourth, interpsychological option, is evidenced in peer interactive data, and would be appropriate to add here. This option involves interactive hypothesis testing:

(4) Test the candidate form or forms in social interaction.

This option moves beyond option 2 (to work to solve the problem using individual knowledge and resources), and presents a collaborative option (Swain 1997). In testing the form in social interaction, the learner moves beyond individual resources to draw on collective resources to solve the problem.

Let us look at Excerpts 2 and 2.1 in terms of these four options. Candace never uses option 1—she does not ignore the problem. Faced with a gap in her knowledge, she first works with the form intrapsychologically during teacher-fronted practice (Excerpt 2, lines 3, 6, 9, 12, and 14). This is Swain's option 2. She applies her own knowledge and resources to the problem at hand. At the same time, Candace is exposed to the grammatical form she needs—the plain past tense form—as it is produced by the student in line 10 and the teacher in line 11. The student produces a plain past negative form however, *nenakatta* 'didn't sleep'. The plain past affirmative form, which might have been more helpful to Candace, was *neta* 'slept'. Whether Candace makes use of this form or not is not clear. Attending to this form would constitute Swain's option 3. Candace might have noticed this form. However, because her private speech remains fixed on the problem she is working to solve, one could argue that she does not compare *nenakatta* with the form she is working to produce. She does, however, tentatively produce the correct form, *dekaketa*, in line 14. Candace is not yet finished with her hypothesis testing, though. She engages in interactive hypothesis testing, shown in Excerpt 2.1. She actively uses the candidate form, *dekaketakatta*, her first choice during private speech, in social interaction. When her use of *dekaketakatta* is unsuccessful, she then tests her other alternative, finding success. Option 4 reveals the power of the ZPD, an interpsychologically defined space in which hypothesis testing occurs through social interaction.

Candace's vicarious responses in Excerpt 2 provide us with an insider's view of her hypothesis testing in process. Each incidence of vicarious response is an instance relevant to the process of hypothesis testing, whether the hypothesis being tested is morphosyntactic in nature, as we saw, or whether the learner is simply projecting what might come next, with the vicarious response then available to be compared with what actually transpires. Learners test their understandings by providing their own answers, working to see whether their answers match up with those of others. Candace and most of the other students engage in this process. Vicarious response also shows how students work to anticipate what is coming next, as we see in Excerpt 3, an example from one of Kuo-ming's classes:

(3) 1 T: Ne jaa review shimasu ne? (.) hai ii? jaa (.) supeesu
              niidoru wakarimasu ne:, space needle.
              Let's review, okay (.) Okay ready? Okay (.) Do you
              understand "supeesu niidoru?" Space needle.
     2 Km: °°°Seattle°°°
     3 T: Supeesu niidoru wa doko ni arimasu ka?
              Where is the Space Needle?
     4 Km: Seatoru ni (.) arimasu.
              It is (.) in Seattle.

                                                        (Kuo-ming, 11/18)

In line 2, Kuo-ming anticipates that the teacher is going to ask where the Space Needle is located. The predictability of the classroom discourse structure allows him to anticipate this. When the teacher does ask this ques-

tion in line 3, he is ready to answer appropriately. Kuo-ming consistently
engages in vicarious response throughout the year. Excerpt 4 is an example
from the end of the academic year. Here, the teacher asks what one does
when one has a stomach ache (line 1), nominating S2 to respond. S2 responds in line 6. Kuo-ming's vicarious response occurs in lines 7 and 11:

(4)   1   T: Onaka ga itai toki doo shimasu ka? dare ka? Onaka ga
                 itai toki doo shimasu ka?
                 What do you do when you have a stomach ache? Anyone?
                 What do you do when you have a stomach ache?

      2   (5)
      3   T: Eh? Doo shitan desu ka? (Onaka) desu ka?
                 (   ) S2-san.
                 Hm? What happened to you? Is it your (stomach)?
                 (   ) S2.

      4   S2:   Uh?
      5   T/Ss: ((all laugh))
      6   S2:   Ehto:: takusan[[kusuri o:: nondari:
                 Uh:: I took   *a lot of medicine: and*
→   7   Km: [°°°Nomanakatta:: [°°° ((whispering))
                                    °°°*Didn't drink*°°°
      8   T: Kusuri ?
                 Medicine?
      9   S2:   Kusuri?
                 medicine?
      10 T: Kusuri nondari: takusan netari kusuri o nondari
                 shimasu. Soo desu ka? Hoka ni? Onaka ga itai toki ni
                 doo shimasu ka?
                 You took medicine, and slept a lot and took medicine. Oh
                 really? Anything else? What do you do when you have a
                 stomach ache?
→   11 Km: °°Osake o n::::ak- nomanak- (.) attari°°°°°
                 °*I don't drink alcohol.*°°°°((*false starts, pause, as Kuo-ming*
                 works to formulate the verb))
      12 T: Kusuri o nondari netari shimasu. Ja nodo ga itai toki
                 doo shimasu ka?
                 You take medicine and sleep. Okay what do you do when you
                 have a sore throat?

                                                        (Kuo-ming, 5/22)

In line 7, Kuo-ming provides his own response, producing only the verb,
in a very soft whisper that moves into a decrescendo. In line 11, Kuo-ming
elaborates his response, adding what it is that he does not drink when he

has a stomach ache—alcohol. In line 11, Kuo-ming again begins with a soft whisper, and decreases volume until by the time he utters the morpheme *tari*, only the consonants are audible. The teacher repeats S2's response, and moves on to another question. Kuo-ming consistently produces these sorts of covert responses. In one particularly striking instance, Kuo-ming whispers the correct answer repeatedly, yet he never raises his hand. When none of the students provides an audible answer, the teacher finally provides the correct answer herself. Kuo-ming laughs in response. Kuo-ming is his own audience, using the L2 in class for his own learning. His answers are appropriate, but he does not volunteer to use Japanese in front of others, even when the teacher seems to beg for a response. And, he is rarely nominated by the teacher in this large class. Even so, Kuo-ming is not a passive observer of classroom activities; during teacher-fronted lockstep instruction, he is an active participant, clearly engaged in the activity of learning Japanese, testing his own hypotheses about the L2.

Vicarious response also gives students the opportunity to compare their responses to the language of the teacher or other students, and to notice and correct their own errors. This process of noticing (Schmidt, 1990; Swain, 1985), is integral to SLA. In Excerpt 4 from a second year class, the teacher is going over a grammar exercise students did as homework, writing sentences on the board. Bryce, a second year student, does vicarious responses in lines 4, 6, and 8:

(4)	1	T:	Denwa shite okimasu. ((writing)) (.) Denwa shite okimasu (.) Hoka ni wa?
			To telephone in advance. ((writing)) (.) telephone in advance(.) Others?
	2	F:	Sunakku to sarada o sunakku to sarada o shite oku
			To do ((error—verb choice)) snacks and a salad in advance
	3	T:	Sunakku to sarada o:,
			Snacks and salads:: ACC:, ((T prompts by providing the beginning of the sentence))
→	4	B:	°°Tsukete::°°
			°°*Attach*°° ((likely a mispronunciation of *tsukutte* 'make'))
	5	S:	Oh tsukutte
			Oh to make
→	6	B:	°°°Oku°°°
			°°°*In advance*°°°
	7	T:	Tsukutte okimasu
			make in advance.
→	8	B:	°°°Tsukutte oku°°°
			°°°*Make in advance*°°°

(Bryce, 1/27)

Bryce corrects F's line 2 error (using *shite* 'do' instead of *tsukutte* 'make') in line 4 when the teacher prompts for a correction by repeating the part of the sentence before the verb. However, Bryan's correction is wrong. Another student chimes in with the correct choice in line 5, but does not provide the entire verb phrase. Bryan completes the verb phrase, whispering in line 6. The teacher then states the whole verb phrase in line 7, which Bryan whispers in line 8. Bryan's candidate response in line 4 allows him to immediately compare his response with the response of another, thus learning whether or not he made the right choice, without suffering the embarrassment of an overt correction from the teacher. In this way, he tests his hypothesized pronunciation, and gets immediate feedback. Kuoming also self-corrects in Excerpt 5 after comparing his vicarious response with the language the teacher uses:

(5) 1 T: Eto jaa kanji no kuizu arimashita ne::. (.) arimashi<u>ta.</u>
              (.) ne arimashita ne, muzukashikatta desu ka?
              Um well there was a kanji quiz wasn't there. (.) there was
              (.) right? There was, was it difficult?

     2 Km: °Um°

     3 Ss: Iie
              No

     4 Km: °E::h yasashi desu°
              °E::h it is easy°((error: should be in the past tense))

     5 T: Yasa[shikatta desu um
              It was easy um

     6 Km: [°°Yasashikatta desu°°
                   °°It was easy°°

     7 T: Ii desu ne::. jaa kanji ii desu ka?
              That's good. Is everyone okay with the kanji?

                                                      (Kuo-ming, 2/27)

The teacher's line 5 utterance is not a correction of Kuo-ming, but is actually an expansion of the students' choral "No" in line 3. After the students say "No," Kuo-ming expands this into *Yasashii desu* 'it is easy', which contrasts with the teacher's subsequent expansion *Yasashikatta desu* 'it was easy'. Kuo-ming then self-corrects in line 6.

Students also insert words and grammatical particles into their teachers' utterances during teacher pauses. Candace inserts grammatical particles and verbs and also appropriately completes her teacher's utterances; she does this in each of the classes in the corpus. The hypothesis testing function of vicarious response is satisfied when the teacher produces the utterance as expected. One example from early in the school year is shown in Excerpt 6:

(6)   1   T: Hai ja: ginkoo, (.)[[ni ⌃, ikimasu ii desu ne, (.) hai
                 Yes well go, (.)   to, the bank good, (.) okay
→   2   C: [°Ni° [
                                     °To°

                                                    (Candace, 11/27)

Here, Candace softly inserts the particle *ni*, when the teacher pauses. The
vicarious response is not only correct, but immediate confirmation is available as the teacher completes her own utterance with the same particle
Candace chose. By completing the teacher's utterances, students readily
test hypotheses about how the language is structured. In Excerpt 7, Sara
finishes sentences not yet completed by another student. Here, the
teacher asks one student, Nellie, to ask another student, John, what his
room is like. Because the student puts together her utterance phrase by
phrase, translation into colloquial English is difficult, and a word-for-word
gloss is used. The structure of the question is as follows:

Question: John-san no heya wa donna   heya desu ka.
              John   GEN room TOP what-sort-of room COP INT.
              What is your room like, John?

In line 1, the teacher prompts Nellie by providing her with the question:

(7)   1   T: Hai. Soshite, John-san no: (.) John-san no heya wa?
                 (.) donna heya desu ka? (.)
                 Yes. And, John GEN (.) John GEN room TOP? (.) What
                 type room COP INT?
                 Yes. So then, John, what is your room like? (.)
      2   N: John-san no:: (.)
                 John GEN
→   3   Sr: °Heya wa°
                 °*Room TOP*°
      4   N: He[ya wa
                 Room TOP
→   5   Sr: [°Heya wa (.) donna (.)°
                      °*Room TOP (.) what type*°
      6   N: Donna
                 what type
→   7   Sr: °Donna heya desu ka.°
                 what type room COP INT?
      8   T: Donna heya desu ka? Ookii heya?
                 what type room COP INT? Big room?
                 What kind of room is it? A big room?

                                                    (Sara, 10/23)

In line 2, as Nellie begins to formulate the question, she elongates the possessive marker *no*, and stops. Sara whispers the next phrase in line 3. Just as Nellie begins the next phrase in line 4, Sara also does, whispering in overlap with Nellie. Finally, she whispers completion of the question in line 7, which Nellie never does. The teacher completes the question for Nellie in line 8. Although Sara is not the one who the teacher called on, she formulates the question covertly in private speech. In the same way, Rob, in Excerpt 8, completes fellow student Hank's utterance in whispered vicarious response, as Hank works to answer the teacher's question about what he eats for Thanksgiving dinner. The question and answer are as follows:

Question: Hank-san nani o tabemasu ka.
            Hank, what ACC eat INT.
            Hank, what do you eat?
Answer: Wain o nomimasu.
            Wine ACC drink.
            I drink wine.

The teacher begins by asking Hank what he eats:

(8) 1 T: Hank-san nani o tabemasu ka?
             Hank, what do you eat?
     2 H: (.) Oh uh um wine wi or wine (.) o
             (.) Oh uh um wine wi or wine (.) ACC
     3 T: Wain o,
             Wine ACC,
     4 H: Wain o
             Wine ACC
→   5 R: °Nomimasu (...) no (.) mimasu°
             Drink (.) dr (.) ink
     6 T: Wain o nan [desu ka?
             Wain ACC what COP INT?
             What do you do with the wine?
→   7 R: [°Nomimasu°
                         Drink
     8 Ss: Nomimasu
             Drink

(Rob, 11/27)

Hank starts his answer in line 2, but stops the sentence *wain o nomimasu* 'I drink wine' after the accusative marker *o*. The teacher prompts him in line 3, Hank starts again in line 4, and then Rob comes in with his own vicarious response. In line 6, the teacher prompts Hank, who remains silent. Rob again whispers *nomimasu* 'drink', and the other students chime in in chorus.

Students who participate in vicarious response show that they not only understand what is going on around them, but that they are actively engaged to the point that they accurately anticipate what is coming next. Using vicarious responses, the students (a) pick up where a speaker left off, (b) covertly correct classmates, (c) fill in words during the pauses, and (d) make their own, unique responses. Of the seven students whose classes are transcribed in the corpus, five do vicarious responses.

Repetition

Repetition is the most common type of L2 private speech found in the corpus. I am not speaking of the repetition that accompanies choral drill, but rather of covert repetition; in covert repetition, a learner repeats after the teacher, another student, or him or herself in a soft voice or whisper.

Language learners do not repeat everything they hear. What they repeat may be indicative of what they are working to acquire, as noted by Kuczaj (1983) and Saville-Troike (1988). In Japanese, verbs and adjectives are conjugated using a variety of bound affixes. These affixes are one target of repetition, as shown in Excerpt 9, where the teacher guides students to answer questions using the affix *-tari*, which is used when making a list of activities:

(9) 1 T: De shiken no ato (.) nani o shimashita ka? Hai hai.
              Tari tari ne. Clark-san kinoo shiken no ato nani o
              shimashita ka?
              *And after the test (.) what did you do? Okay okay. Use
              'tari tari' okay. Clark what did you do yesterday after the
              test?*

     2 C: Eh::to (3) (suugaku) no jugyoo:: (.) ni (.) ikimashita.
              U::h (3) I went (.) to (.) (math) class.

     3 T: Uh:: tari (.) [tari ((*prompts student to use 'tari'*))
→   4 Km: [°tari°

     5 C: Itta[ri::::: u:::n hiru gohan o (.) tabetari shima(shita).
              Go ((tari form)) U::n lunch ACC eat ((tari form)) did.
              did things like going (to math class) and eating lunch.

     6 Km: [°°°tari°°° ((only consonants audible))

                                             (Kuo-ming, 5/22)

Although this exercise involves the teacher asking students about events in their real lives, the pedagogical focus of the task is the use of *-tari*, an affix which expresses that the person did "things like," in this student's case, things like going to class and eating lunch. In line 4, Kuo-ming whispers -*tari*, when the teacher prompts Clark to rephrase using -*tari*. When Clark does, Kuo-ming again repeats -*tari* in line 6, this time so softly as to be almost inaudible. Kuo-ming's use of private speech evidences his focus on the grammatical form. Even though he is not addressed by the teacher in this teacher-fronted, question–answer grammatical practice activity, he is engaged in the activity. He zeroes in on the affix being taught as he acts as a coparticipant in this activity.

Excerpt 10 provides an additional example, this one involving Bryce, a second year student. Bryce repeats after another student as his small group works on grammar exercises. In this exercise, they are practicing the structure "Verb stem + -*te aru*," which is used to talk about how things have been arranged by someone else. The degree of Bryce's engagement increases from repetition of the affix and the verb *aru* 'exist' in line 5, to vicarious response in line 7.

(10) 1 F: Mado ga:: shimete arimasu.
          The window is::: closed.
   2 G: Denki ga: [tsuite arimasu.
          The lights are on ((G uses the wrong verb, the
          intransitive verb *tsuku* 'to turn on.'))
   3 B: [Ahem. ((clears throat))
   4 F: Tsukete aru. hikidai ga (.) hiki- hikidashi? hikidashi?
          Left on. ((F repeats G's verb phrase, but substitutes the
          correct verb, the transitive verb tsukeru *'to turn on'))* the
          draw is (.) dr- drawer? drawer?
→ 5 B: °°°te aru°°° ((Bryce repeats the affix -*te* and the verb
          aru)
   6 F: O- (.) o- ku ku. (.) Oite.
          ((*F repeats the verb stem*[5] *'o', adding the citation for ending
          'ku,' before making the te-form 'oite' which is needed for
          this structure*))
→ 7 B: °°°Oite aru°°°
          °°°*Is left there*°°°

(Bryce, 1/27)

In line 4, Frieda corrects Greg's mistake (*tsuite arimasu*) from line 2, saying *tsukete aru*, as appropriate. Bryce repeats *te aru*. Bryce's repetition does not

---

[5]Actually, the stem of the verb oku is *ok-*. However, because Japanese does not permit final stops (except for *n*), and the Japanese syllabary represents the verb as *o-ku*, the speaker says *o* rather than *ok-* for the stem.

function as help for Frieda. His utterance is clearly not relevant to Frieda's difficulty in completing her sentence in line 4, where she is struggling with the word *hikidashi* 'drawer'; in addition, Bryce's utterance is so soft as to make it highly unlikely that Frieda could even hear him. As she completes her sentence in line 6, she uses the verb *oku* 'put' (instead of *akeru* 'open', which would be correct here), conjugating it correctly as *oite*. Bryce repeats *oite*, expanding to include the entire structure *oite aru*, as a vicarious response. At this point the teacher begins showing signs of moving on to another activity, returning to the front of the room and writing on the board. Frieda never completes her sentence. Even though it is not his turn to provide a sentence, Bryce is actively engaged in the activity, working with the new form.

The most frequent type of repetition that the learners engage in is repetition of words and expressions uttered by the teacher during teacher-fronted presentations or teacher-fronted oral practice. In Excerpt 11, the teacher introduces the game "20 Questions," in which students are to ask yes/no questions to determine what celebrity she is thinking of:

(11) 1 T: Soshite sensei ni shitsumon shite kudasai. Ne. Amerikajin desu ka? Nihonjin desu ka? Onna no hito desu ka? Otoko no hito desu ka? Se wa takai desu ka? Se wa hikui desu ka? Kami wa shiroi desu ka? (.) Kami ga kinpatsu desu ka. Kinpatsu desu ka? Wakarimasu ne.
   And ask me questions. Okay. Am I American? Japanese? A woman? A man? Am I tall? Short? Is my hair white? (.) am I blond? Am I blond? Got it?

→ 2 C: °°Kinpatsu desu ka°°.
   °°Are you blond?°°

3 T: Sore kara (.) hai haiyuu desu ka? Ne sono hito wa (.) haiyuu desu ka? Joyuu desu ka?
   Then (.) okay am I an actor? Is that person an actor? An actress?

(Candace, 4/24)

Review of the transcripts and curricular materials confirms that the items repeated are often those that are new to the learner. Andrea, a second year student who almost never engages in private speech, does repeat an expression that is new to her, as shown in Excerpt 12:

(12) 1 T: Ainiku nan desu ka? (..) Unfortunately. Kirashite orimashite wa?
   So what does 'ainiku' mean? (..) Unfortunately. What does it mean to run out of?

| | 2 | T: | We don't feel have- we are running out of cheesecake Unfortunately. |

    2   T: We don't feel have- we are running out of cheesecake Unfortunately.

    3   A: What is it? Kaiwa?

    4   T: Ainiku kirashite orimashite.
               Unfortunately we are out

→   5   A: °°Kirash ^ (.) kashite°°

    6   T: Chiizukeeki wa ainiku (.) kirashite orimashite.
               Unfortunately (.) we are out of cheesecake.

                                                (Andrea, 4/18)

Andrea's unfamiliarity with the expression is evident from her line 3 question. She attempts to pronounce the expression covertly in line 5, where she is unable to repeat the first word correctly. Andrea continues working with this expression as class proceeds. Later, when the teacher performs the dialogue with another student, Paul, Andrea successfully repeats the first part of the new expression. This is shown in Excerpt 13:

    (13)   1   T: Ah mooshiwake gozaimasen ga matchakeeki wa ainiku kirashite orimashite.
                     Oh, I am very sorry but unfortunately we are out of green-tea cake.

→   2   A: °°Kirashite°°

        3   P: Ah soo ka? Sore ja (.) chiizukeeki (.) ga
                     Oh really. That being the case (.) cheesecake (.) ACC

                                                    (Andrea, 4/18)

Repetition reveals Andrea's focus on the new expression. Successful repetition is evidence of her progress. Out of the four classes of Andrea's in the corpus, these are her two only episodes of private speech in the L2.

Word repetition often occurs when the teacher is introducing new vocabulary, or after the presentation of new vocabulary when that vocabulary is being practiced. In Excerpt 14, the teacher has introduced new vocabulary for items of clothing, and asks students to identify items that would be sold in the men's section of a department store. Rob, a first year student, zeroes in on the word *nekutai* 'tie'.

    (14)   1   T: Ja shinshifuku uriba ni nani ga arimasu ka?
                     So, what is there in the men's department?

        2   S9:   Kutsushita ga arimasu.
                     There are socks.

        3   T: Kutsushita ga arimasu.
                     There are socks.

        4   S10: Jaketto
                     Jackets.

    5   S11:   Nekutai
               Ties.
    6   T: Jaketto ga arima:su. Un S12-san? Nekutai ga
               arimasu. S12-san?
               There are jackets. Uh S12? There are ties. S12?
    7   S12:   Uh [kutsushita ga arimasu
               Uh there are socks.
→   8   R: [°°Nekutai nekutai°° (.) °nekutai nekutai°
                     °°Tie tie°° (.) °tie tie°

                                                               (Rob, 2/28)

In line 5, S11 says *nekutai* 'tie', which the teacher expands into a sentence
in line 6. Then, Rob repeats the word in line 8.

In sum, these students have a marked tendency to repeat new material.
Kuo-ming and Bryce repeat grammatical morphemes or markers, as does
Katie. Often, repetition evidences difficulty in forming the new words, as
we saw in Excerpts 12 and 13, where Andrea struggled to repeat the word
kirashite. Whether the repeated item is new is not always clear from the
context, but the evidence points to students' use of repetition with items
that are, if not novel, not yet well learned or acquired. This private speech
data provides evidence of the salience of these items to the learners who
manipulate them.

Salience may also be highlighted by contrast between an item used incorrectly, and then correctly. In the next example, shown in Excerpt 15,
even though Candace is not the one who produced the error, she repeats
the teacher's correction of a classmate's grammatical error. The focus of
practice in the next example is adjectival negation. There are two grammatical types of adjectivals which negate differently, as shown in Table
2.5: These two types of Japanese adjectivals are called *adjectives* and *adjectival nouns*. Adjectives are verb-like in that they are formed of a stem and inflect to show negation and tense. Adjectival nouns are like nouns in that
they do not take inflections. Adjectives are negated by adding the affix *-ku*
to the adjective's stem, and the adding the negative form *nai* or *arimasen*.
Adjectival nouns are negated by adding *ja* (or *dewa*) to the adjectival noun,
along with the negative form *nai* or *arimasen*. This is what is being prac-

TABLE 2.5
Adjectival Negation in Japanese

Adjectival Type	Negation Rule		Example
Adjective	Drop *-i*, add *-ku*	add *nai* or *arimasen*	*oishii* → *oishiku arimasen*
Adjectival noun	Add *ja*		*kirei* → *kirei ja arimasen*

ticed here. Excerpt 15 shows how learners are sensitive to contrasts in form, even when they do not involve their own responses or vicarious responses.

(15) 1 T: Kon shuumatsu hima desu ka? Hyun-san
            Hyun, are you free this weekend?
→   2 H: Um (..) iie (.) um (.) uh:: (.) hima- (.) hima: (.) hima
            nai,
            Um (.) no (.) um (.) uh:: (.) free- (.) free: (.) free-NEG,
            ((*negator 'nai' is incorrect.*))
→   3 T: Hima ja⌃ arimasen
            You're not free ((T uses the correct negative form))
     4 H: Oh ja arim[asen=
            Oh not free=
→   5 C: [°°hima ja⌃ arimasen°°
                    °°not free°°
     6 T: =Hima ja arimasen (.) ii desu ne (.) Eh:to ja S-san
            kon shuumatsu hima desu ka?
            *=You're not free (.) well done (.) Uh so S, are you free
            this weekend?*

                                            (Candace, 1/24)

In line 1, the teacher asks Hyun whether he is free this weekend. In line 2 Hyun leaves out *ja*. The teacher provides the correct response in line 3, which Hyun repeats in line 4, and Candace covertly repeats in line 5, in overlap with both Hyun and the teacher. Then, in line 6, the teacher repeats the response, moving on to ask another student the same question. Although Candace is not called on during this particular oral practice session, she is engaged as a peripheral participant in the interaction. The results of this engagement are evident later in the class when she uses the form correctly in peer interaction, as well as when, in subsequent teacher-fronted practice, she covertly corrects classmates who use the wrong form.

Repetition not only occurs immediately following what is repeated, but students may continue to play with a word, repeating after themselves, even as the topic being discussed changes. An example of this is given in Excerpt 16. I have numbered the first line of Excerpt 16 as line 26, because the word *kutsushita* 'socks' has been a focus for the previous (though not shown) 25 lines of transcript. During these lines, the teacher has students repeat chorally (as she again in line 26), and also nominates individual students to repeat the word *kutsushita*, which is difficult to pronounce. The teacher never calls on Kuo-ming, but in private speech he repeats the word *kutsushita* six times prior to line 26. Kuo-ming continues

repeating the word in Excerpt 16, even after the teacher changes the topic
to *kutsu* 'shoes' in line 28:

(16) 26 T: Hai ii desu ne minna de itte kudasai kutsushita
                        Okay good everyone please say "socks"

→   27 Ss/Km: Kutsushita
                        Socks (literally "under-shoes")

      28 T: Um hai [taihen desu ne::.
                        Hai jaa kore nan desu ka?
                        Um yeah it is difficult isn't it.
                        Okay so what are these? ((T shows a pair of shoes))

→   29 Km: [°Kutsushita°
                              °*socks*°

      30 Km: Uh
      31 s8:   [Kutsu
                   Shoes

      32 T: [Kutsu (   ) kutsu [[ii desu ne demo ano: eto:
                      suniikaa demo ii desu
                      Shoes (   ) shoes good, but uh: u::m you can also say
                      sneakers.

→   33 Km: [[°Kutsu ohh ano: shita°
                                  shoes o::h uh: under

      34 Km: [°Suniika°
                   Sneakers

      35 T: [Ne suniikaa kore suniikaa kore kutsu (.) Ne?
                      Right sneakers these are sneakers, these shoes (.) right?

      36 Km: °Kutsu:: (.) [[kutsu°
                   °*Shoes:: (.) shoes*°°

      37 T: [[Ii desu ka? hai jaa kore wa nan deshoo
                          kore
                        Okay? Yeah so these, what are these?

      38 s7:   [Sandaru
                   Sandals

      39 Km: [°Kutsu?°
                   °*Shoes*°?

      40 T: Hai sandaru (.) ne sandaru
                      Yes sandals (.) right sandals

→   41 Km: °Kutsushita°
                   °*Socks*°

      42 T: Hai (.) soshite kaban (.) ii desu ne (.) kaban sore kara,
                      Yeah (.) and bag (.) good (.) (this is a) bag and,

→   43 Km: °Kutsu kutsushita°
                   °*Shoes socks*°

                                          (Kuo-ming, 2/27)

After the teacher introduces the word for shoes, *kutsu* (line 32), Kuo-ming repeats it, but repeatedly returns to saying *kutsushita* 'socks' also, even performing a self-imposed expansion drill in line 43. Private speech constitutes a rich resource for linguistic practice for students who exploit it. It is here where we see how the resource of repetition builds into language manipulation, the next category of private speech to be considered.

Manipulation

Students not only repeat morphemes, grammatical markers, words, and sentences or phrases verbatim, but also use repetition as an opportunity to manipulate grammatical and morphological structures, to break down or build up compound words, or to play with the sounds of particular words. The simplest form of this seems to be the breaking down of compound words, as just we saw Kuo-ming do with *kutsu kutsushita* 'shoes socks'. Excerpt 17 presents an example from one of Rob's classes:

(17) 1 T: Shokuryoohin shokuryoohin. (.)
              Foodstuffs foodstuffs (.)
→   2 R: °Shokuryoo (.) shokuryoohin°
              °Food (.) foodstuffs°
      3 T: Hai. Ne? Shokuryoohin. Ja minna de moo ichido
              shokuryoohin-uriba.
              Yes. Okay? Foodstuffs. Okay everyone, once again,
              foodstuffs-counter
      4 R/Ss: Shokuryoohin-uriba
              Foodstuffs counter
      5 T: Un. Ii desu ne. Sore kara: (.) hai kore ne? stationary
              ne:? Bunboogu-uriba
              Yep. Good. And (.) what about this? Stationary, right?
              Stationary supplies counter
      6 R/Ss: Bunboogu (.) uriba
              Stationary (.) counter
→   7 R: (.) °Bunboogu (.) bunboogu uriba°
              (.) °Stationary supplies (.) Stationary supplies counter°
                                                      (Rob, 2/28)

In line 2, Rob breaks down *shokuryoohin* 'foodstuffs' into its component parts, and in line 7, he breaks up the compound *bunboogu-uriba* 'stationary supplies counter'. In Excerpt 18, Bryce manipulates verb conjugations:

(18) 1 T: Ah: ja onaka suite inai n desu ka:. Onaka?
              Okay isn't your stomach empty: Stomach? ((this means,
              "Aren't you hungry?"))

        2   E: (Onaka ga)
                 (Stomach NOM)
        3   T: Suite imasen.
                 Isn't empty
        4   E: (Suite imasen.)
                 Isn't empty
  →   5   B: °°Suite inai? (.) Suite imase::n.°°
                 °°Isn't empty? ((uses informal negator 'nai')) (.) isn't empty
                 ((uses formal negator 'masen'))°°
                                                            (Bryce, 11/21)

In line 5, he repeats *suite imasen* 'isn't empty' in the informal and formal
forms, saying *'suite inai'* and *'suite imasen'*. Katie, another second year student, manipulates the adjectival conjugation in answering a question during pair practice, shown in Excerpt 19:

  (19) 1   S6: Katie-san wa kodomo no toki nani ni naritakatta
                 desu ka?
                 Katie, what did you want to become when you were a
                 child?
  →   2   K: Uh, kagakusha. (.) ni naritakatta. (.) °taka taka°
                 takatta.
                 Uh, scientist (.) DAT want to become-past (.) °taka taka°
                 takatta.
                 Uh I wanted to become (.) a scientist. ((conjugation
                 practice with the past desiderative affix))
                                                            (Katie, 2/6)

Although this cannot be adequately translated, in her line 2 answer, Katie
manipulates the past tense affix *-katta*. The past tense form of the
desiderative *naritai* 'want to become' is *naritakatta* 'wanted to become'. In
line 2, Candace manipulates the adjectival ending, saying *'taka taka takatta'*.

Manipulation can also be carried out over multiple turns, as Candace
shows in Excerpt 20, where she builds up an expression in her private
speech, in a self-imposed "expansion drill." Here the students are practicing how to say sentences and phrases that describe physical appearance.
The English glosses represent a fairly literal translation, which is necessary
to better capture what Candace is saying. The two most frequently used
Japanese phrases in this excerpt are:

Kao iro ga warui. (Literally "face color is bad." This means "pale.")
Kibun ga warui. (Literally "feeling is bad." This means "to feel ill.")

The expressions are best translated as "I am pale," "You are pale," "He/she is pale," or "They are pale," depending on the context, but here a more literal gloss is used for illustrative purposes, even though the English sounds unnatural (the Japanese, on the other hand, is quite natural). Candace's expansion of these expressions occurs in the indicated lines.

(20) 1 T: Kore (.) kao iro ga warui desu. Kao ne (.) iro (.) warui not good. Ii desu ka? Pale ne hai. Kao iro ga warui desu. Ne?
This (.) face color is bad. Face (.) color (.) is bad not good. Okay? This means pale okay? Face color is bad. Okay?

        2 T: [Kao iro ga warui, soshite:: hai. [Kibun ga warui desu, (.)
Face color is bad, and:: okay.   Feeling is bad,

→   3 C: [°°Kao°°   [°°kao iro warui°°
°°Face°°   °°face color is bad°°

        4 T: Ii desu n[e. Kibun ga warui desu.
Good.   Feeling is bad.

→   5 C: [Kibun: [°Kibun ga //warui°
Feeling   °Feeling is //bad°

        6 T: Kao iro ga warui desu sono hito wa kibun ga warui. Minna de kibun ga warui.
Face color is bad. This person is feeling is bad. Together, his feeling is bad.

        7 C/Ss: Kibun ga warui
Feeling is bad.

        8 T: Kao iro ga warui
Face color is bad.

        9 Ss: Kao iro ga warui
Face color is bad.

→ 10 C: °Kao°
Face°

   11 T: Nn ii desu ne. Soshite[nodo ga itai ha ga itai hai sore[kara kore hai netsu ga aru
Okay good.   And   he has a sore throat and a toothache, and okay he has a fever.

→ 12 C: [°°Kao iro ga warui°°
°°Face color is bad °°

          [kao iro
face color

   13 C/Ss: Netsu ga aru
Has a fever

   14 T: Netsu ga arimasu
Has a fever

15   C/Ss: Netsu ga arimasu
            Has a fever

                                                    (Candace, 5/22)

Candace begins by repeating the word *kao* 'face' in line 3. She attempts to repeat the entire sentence, but leaves out the subject marker *ga* in the same line. In line 5, she takes the same strategy, saying first the noun *kibun* 'feeling', and then placing it in the phrase *kibun ga warui* 'feeling is bad'. Then, she comes back to repetition of the word *kao* in line 10, after the class repeats the entire sentence *kao iro ga warui* 'you look pale'—literally "face color is bad," meaning "pale," in line 9. Then, after the teacher moves on to the expressions, *nodo ga itai* 'have a sore throat' and *netsu ga aru* 'have a fever' in line 11, Candace repeats the entire sentence *Kao iro ga warui* in line 12. Through this practice, she seems to have gained a new understanding of the components of the sentence, as evidenced by her repetition of *kao iro* 'face color', the subject of the sentence, also in line 12. And she does this while selectively participating in choral drilling (in line 7 she repeats with the class, but does not repeat with the class in line 9, instead practicing on her own in lines 10 and 12). Through the use of L2 private speech, Candace takes this new sentence, breaks it into its components, and reassembles it, as she repeats the sentence and parts of the sentence during the teacher's introduction of new vocabulary.

Although all of the students participate in manipulation in some way or another, Candace does more than the other students. Earlier the same day, as her teacher began class, she practiced with the adjective *warui* 'bad'. This is shown in Excerpt 21.

(21)   1   C: °°waru- waruku°° (.) °°waru::ku°° (.) °°ku warui::°°

                                                    (Candace, 5/22)

In Excerpt 21, Candace is repeating after herself, not after the teacher or another student. She breaks the adjective *warui* down into its stem *waru-*, builds the adverbial form *waruku*, then returns to the nonpast form of the adjective, *warui*. As pointed out in discussion of Candace's use of vicarious response, she often focuses on the manipulation of linguistic form in her private speech.

CLASSROOM PRIVATE SPEECH AND THE DEVELOPMENT OF LANGUAGE PROFICIENCY

This chapter provides an overview of private speech as it occurred in a corpus of classroom interaction. The purpose of this section is to summarize the findings of this chapter, and to consider how these findings can be integrated into a dynamic theory of L2 development. The paramount understanding is that private speech is not only a frequent feature of L2 classroom activity, but evidences SLA in process.

Although completely discrete categories cannot be created, private speech fell broadly into three types of language use: repetition, vicarious response, and manipulation. Repetition however, may occur in vicarious response and during manipulation. In addition, manipulation of language occurs during vicarious responses. This overlap between categories is natural when we consider the nature of the categories themselves. While vicarious response is defined as turns taken as "for another," and are thus tied to particular contexts where the teacher has addressed a question or utterance to another student or to the class, repetition and manipulation may occur in any context. Most of the private speech in the classroom corpus involved repetition, which has also been found to be a frequent feature of the private speech of children learning second languages (Peck, 1980; Saville-Troike, 1988). Adult learners repeated words, phrases, and sentences, morphemes and grammatical particles. Learners repeated after the teacher, after other learners, and after themselves. Learners seemed, in particular, to repeat newly introduced lexical items, as well as phrases and sentences that were the focus of teacher-fronted language practice. Analysis also demonstrated that, as found in studies of children learning their L1 or L2, the private speech of adults involves not merely repetition, but also creation with language. Learners creatively used the L2 in vicarious response and oral manipulation. During teacher-fronted or group presentations, question–answer or role-play activities, learners create their own individual responses, uttering them in the modality of private speech. They covertly answer questions addressed to others, complete the incomplete utterances of others, and even fill in words and grammatical particles during pauses in the talk of the teacher or of classmates. Vicarious response not only evidences a high degree of engagement, but also the learners' growing linguistic abilities as they use the L2 to create their own responses and successfully anticipate what is coming next. Vicarious response is a key context for interactive hypothesis testing—before using forms in social interaction, learners try them out in the covert social space of private speech. Here they create utterances or complete the utterances of others in a safe environment where useful feedback is immediately available. This prepares learners to use the foreign language with an interlocutor in social interaction. Finally, in the modality of private speech, learners orally manipulate grammatical paradigms, build up and break down words, and engage in sound play. Manipulation functions as part of the process through which learners work to analyze bits of the L2 being learned.

Private Speech and the Structure of Classroom Events

The present data also yield insight into how the structure of classroom events impacts the use of private speech. A certain amount of privacy seems necessary for the emergence of private speech; private speech occurred primarily in teacher-fronted, lock-step instructional settings, less often in group work settings, and rarely occurred during peer learning tasks. This explains some of the variation in private speech. As lessons differ in their structure, opportunities for private speech increase or decrease. For example, the day that Kuo-ming produced 77 episodes of private speech (2/27), there was no pair or group work. The teacher-fronted setting, which focuses learner attention on the teacher or on the activities of performing classmates, allows a private space to emerge for each learner who is not receiving individualized teacher attention. In this private space, which is private because it is free from explicit focus of teacher or peer, learners are free to engage in their own, private interactive activity. This is a unique space in which learners can focus on their own language use, working to create with language without the pressures of ordinary social interaction. Analysis of the classroom corpus shows that learners who are not being addressed in the teacher-fronted setting may be quite active. A parallel may be drawn with the relationship of a reader and a text. Just as reading is an interactive process, so are the processes that individual learners engage in during developmentally appropriate teacher-fronted activity. Private spaces also occur at other points in the lessons observed, such as prior to the beginning of class, or during transitions from teacher-fronted to pair or group activity; private speech, particularly manipulation of the L2, was found in these contexts as well. In contrast, L2 private speech rarely occurred during peer learning tasks, where use of the L1 (English) was incorporated into the learner's private speech when learners encountered difficulty. Students whispered or muttered, for example, expressions such as "Wait" (Excerpt 2.1, line 8) or "Where am I going?" "What's that word?" in reduced volume. In the present corpus, these sorts of expressions were sometimes combined with whispered reformulation in the L2 (also in Excerpt 2.1, line 8). In general, interacting with peers limits the possibility of a private turn. Therefore, instead of vicarious response, learners overtly complete each other's utterances, or insert words when a partner pauses. This is done not as covert private speech, but in normal volume. In teacher-fronted or group work settings, learners do some of the same participatory activities—completing utterances, inserting words, correcting errors—that occur in peer interactive tasks. But in the group context, these activities are performed covertly. The present data suggest that private speech works together with social speech in resolving L2 problems; the next step is to use the L2 on the public stage of dialogic interaction.

The Role of Oral Rehearsal in Learning

Much of the private speech in the present data consisted of *repetition*, when learners repeat words used by the teacher or other learners in covert oral rehearsal. Private speech data can help us to better understand the role of spontaneous oral rehearsal in learning, and how oral rehearsal might be related to inner rehearsal. Although much of the psychological research has conflated oral and inner rehearsal processes, the role of oral and inner rehearsal may be fundamentally different for an individual depending on the extent to which the language has been internalized as a cognitive resource. For the adult learning L1 material, either oral or inner rehearsal may equally facilitate learning, whereas for the foreign language learner, the physical utterance of the language being learned may be a necessary component. Involvement of the articulators is likely to be necessary for efficient development of phonological analysis and processing.

American psychologists have long noted the facilitative effect that oral rehearsal has on memory. These researchers have attempted to determine why oral rehearsal results in better retention. It was hypothesized that oral rehearsal involves either an "articulatory loop" or an "auditory loop." Researchers (see Baddeley, 1990, and the references cited therein) attempted to determine whether the facilitative effect of oral rehearsal was auditory or articulatory by having subjects do repetitive tasks under various conditions, including the condition of "articulatory suppression." Recall was greatly impeded if the subject was required to suppress articulation by uttering another syllable like "ta-ta-ta." From results like these, it was concluded that the facilitative effect of oral rehearsal was due to articulatory mechanisms; because the articulators were occupied with the nonsense syllables, they could not be used for the rehearsal task, and retention was reduced. However, Gupta and MacWhinney (1995) noted that these sorts of studies suffer a key confound. The uttering of a nonsense syllable creates not only articulatory interference, but auditory interference as well. They found that if vigorous gum chewing was substituted for the uttering of a nonsense syllable, rehearsal regained its facilitative effect. They conclude that the power of rehearsal springs from both auditory and articulatory components, and that the two cannot be separated.

Gupta and MacWhinney's (1995) finding implied that oral and inner rehearsal are functionally identical for adults, both involving an articulatory/auditory loop whether or not actual articulation was involved. But, is this true for foreign language learners? If language acquisition is a process of internalizing speech from the social (interpsychological) plane to become an inner (intrapsychological) resource, then would not actual articulatory processes be necessary? MacKay (1992), whose research was discussed in chapter 1, felt that the identity of inner and oral rehearsal found in the literature was only possible because subjects were all functioning in their native language. MacKay investigated the role of oral and inner rehearsal in the ability to recall foreign language expressions. For adult language learners, the ability to do inner rehearsal was found to be dependent on prior oral practice. This is an important finding. Inner rehearsal was not possible unless adult learners already had significant L2 articulatory experience. MacKay found that motor skills are a key component in comprehension and thought processes; for an inner voice to develop, there must be a foundation of articulatory skill. This finding underscores the importance of private speech for foreign language learners, because along with social interaction, private speech is a modality in which oral skills develop. In private speech, adults engage in oral manipulation of the language being acquired, whether words, structures, phrases or sentences. Private speech results from the cognitive demand of language learning; it helps the learner to actively engage in solving L2 problems, whether resolving pronunciation or grammatical difficulties. MacKay's (1992) findings are congruent with Luria's (1982) theory of the development of thought. Oral work with new or problematic language is foundational for further rehearsal in the modality of inner speech.

Individual Differences in Participation in Private Speech

What, then, of learners who rarely engage in private speech? One possibility is that the classes were not as challenging to these learners as they were to those who engaged in private speech more frequently. Another possibility is that the learners were not paying attention, or were not working to participate in the classroom learning environment. The individual differences in frequency of private speech may also result from differences in learning styles. Oral practice can take place through private speech or more public venues, such as participation in speaking activities in the foreign language class. Adults may suppress private speech out of concern for behaving in a socially appropriate manner. With a foundation of oral practice in whatever modality, some adult learners may transition to inner rehearsal quite rapidly, while others may continue to exploit private speech. Questionnaire studies, in fact, documented that students do use inner rehearsal in their language learning processes (Lantolf, 1997; Reiss, 1985). It is also possible that learners who produced less private speech were engaged in a more covert articulatory process, soundlessly articulating L2 words and phrases using more subtle movements of the articulatory mechanism. It has long been noted that speech includes "soundless, individual, reduced . . . movements of the speech mechanism" (English & English, 1958, p. 272). Subvocal rehearsal, which involves articulatory processes, may be an important resource for many adult learners. However, other data collection methods besides audio- and videotaping are clearly necessary to further investigate subvocal rehearsal.

Private Speech and Hypothesis Testing

The private speech data examined here provide behavioral evidence that learners are actively involved in making comparisons between their own utterances and the language used by others. Learners reveal their uncertainties in private speech. They produce different candidate forms, which they then test in social interaction. Learners correct their private speech based on what they hear used by others, and also notice the errors of others and provide corrections. Lantolf (1997) proposed that by manipulating the language in oral or inner rehearsal, the learner compares the developing linguistic system with newly encountered L2 data; when the learner's hypothesis is compared to differing linguistic data, private speech is one modality through which learners work toward resolution of the problem. My data confirm the importance of understanding hypothesis testing as a dynamic process in order to capture what occurs in language acquisition. Private speech does not constitute the final step of resolution to problems with L2 form, but it is one modality in which the language acquirer may work toward a solution. Ultimately, solutions must be reworked on the public stage of social interaction.

Private Speech as a "Simulative Mode" of Functioning

Hypothesis testing can also occur in social interaction, but private speech is a particularly suitable modality for testing the language being learned in a context that simulates social interaction but is designed only for one's own ears. Private speech allows the learner to covertly participate in interactive events without being constrained by the requirements of interpersonal interaction. Private speech may constitute what Reynolds (1976) called a simulative mode of functioning:

> The essential feature of the simulative mode is that the system, while functioning normally, is uncoupled from its normal consequences vis-à-vis the other systems. However, the feedback consequences within the acting system are unimpaired. It is to this feedback capability that simulation owes its current popularity in modern technology. A simulated space mission, for example, should give evidence of any unforeseen consequences deriving from the system's operation, yet at the same time it should not actually result in those consequences (p. 621).

In L2 private speech, the interlocutor may be the self or an imaginary or idealized other; social speech is exploited for use in dialogue with the self, for consideration and evaluation by the self, not by another. For example, for the children studied by Saville-Troike (1988), private speech provided an environment in which they practiced the language freely, using the L2 more creatively, and at a more advanced level than they did in social speech. In the same way, Olszewski (1987) found that fantasy play allowed children to practice interpersonal skills with their imaginary partners in play. Analysis of the present data show how, in private speech, adults may also be released from social concerns. In adults as for children, the freedom to indulge in exploratory language use via private speech may be a particularly powerful vehicle for language learning; by using private speech, learners are free to experiment with the language in a situation where there is ample time to try different forms or modes of expression, and "hear" how they sound. The uncoupling of language from immediate interpersonal social consequences allows for a freedom of language use in the private speech setting that may be particularly powerful for language learning.

Private Speech and Assimilation/Expansion Processes

Private speech, particularly the use of repetition, has an assimilative function for these beginning learners, as they work to incorporate new language data into the developing L2 interactive system. For beginning learners, private speech is part of the process of understanding a language's linguistic structure. Through private speech, the learner focuses on a particular string of sounds or a particular word or phrase. Through oral manipulation, the learner examines meaning as well as its sound. The segmentation problem for the classroom learner is arguably not as complex as that which faces the naturalistic learner, who may not encounter as much simplified language data (Peters, 1985). The highly structured linguistic environment of these adult learners shapes private speech; teachers isolate words for learners to practice, and repetition is the most frequently occurring private speech of these adult learners. Learners repeat, not only entire words, but also parts of words. As learners notice candidate segments during lexical or morphological practice, these segments are worked over in private speech, as we saw in Excerpt 16, where the teacher teaches the word *kutsu* 'shoes', after working with students on the word *kutsushita* 'socks'—literally, "under-shoes." A few lines after the teacher introduces first the word *kutsu* 'shoes' and then moves on to the word *suniikaa* 'sneakers', Kuo-ming shows through private speech that he is still working on the segmentation of *kutsushita* in line 43 when he says *"kutsushita kutsu."* And, although repetition is the most common type of practice, learners do not repeat all words highlighted for their attention by the teacher. In addition, other learners work on segmentation problems themselves; we saw Candace manipulate conjugations of the adjective *warui* in Excerpt 21. Further studies, particularly longitudinal case studies of learners as they use the L2 in settings inside and outside of the classroom, are needed to explore the significance of what learners choose to repeat, and how this reveals their developing linguistic abilities. The data suggest that learners repeat what they are working to acquire, as evidenced by oral rehearsal prior to social use of language.

In addition to repetition and manipulation, vicarious response also evidences the assimilation processes involved in L2 acquisition. Vicarious response represents a part of the process that is cognitively more complex than repetition, because, like manipulation, it evidences analysis in process. What is uttered is not available in the immediate speech context, but is provided by the learner. At early stages, this represents recycling of interpsychological voices in vicarious response, as when the learner provides a word or phrase recently practiced in class. As the learner develops expressive capacity through the process of assimilation, vicarious responses begin to emerge from the learner's own developing L2 inner speech, showing movement from assimilation to expansion. Vicarious response evidences the learner's growing ability to produce thoughts in the L2; the L2 becomes more and more personally meaningful as the learner works to flesh out ideas in the L2. In situations where the learner must speak the language, preparatory rehearsal in private speech may function to internalize language so inner speech can then be expanded to social speech. As inner speech develops, the learner can expand it into an utterance for social use. The analyst can observe this process in vicarious response. The learner is not yet using language socially, but is preparing to do so in the future. The gradual elaboration of vicarious response is evidence of internalization and expansion from the intrapsychological to interpsychological planes of linguistic functioning. Manipulation of language structures, already mentioned as having an assimilative function, also has a productive function when the learner elaborates language from inner speech, playing with or testing the item for its feel and sound in a covert context.

The Active Learner

Private speech data provide one way of learning the extent to which learners are active during classroom language learning, even in settings during which they may seem rather passive because they are not involved in overt conversational exchange. Van Lier (2000), in his ecological model of SLA, envisions an *active learner* availing herself of linguistic affordances. This term evokes a rich social context in which the learner is an explorer, engaging with the environment, and selecting items of interest for further discovery. Van Lier's (2000) scheme emphasizes the importance of learner engagement in the process through which language from the social milieu is acted on and internalized. The use of private speech in the classroom corpus supports this view. Learners grab onto bits of language for their own personal manipulation and use. The data reveal the power of teacher modeling of L2 use. As evident in private speech data, each learner is potentially very active, actively repeating, manipulating, monitoring, correcting, and expanding the language of others such that he or she may actually be able to "jump in" to answer, fill in blanks, finish sentences, or correct other participants. In private speech, the learner actively rehearses language to be used in subsequent pair or group practice. The learner works to grasp how words and utterances are constructed, actively finding patterns and manipulating them. The learner finds structure, and expands application of that structure to other words she or he knows. The learner actively repeats not everything he or she hears, but that which is important at each particular developmental level. The learner, through private speech, tailors the language class or social situation to personal learning needs. Even during "teacher-centered" lessons, private speech provides evidence that students are "learner-centered" in their activity. As teachers build toward appropriate peer interactive tasks, the covert rehearsal that occurred in the teacher-fronted context finds ready application to language use in the social context, allowing the learner to take language use one step further into a meaningful context of use. The results of this study raise many additional questions. Regarding teaching methodology, when peer learning tasks frequently follow relevant teacher-fronted practice and are anticipated by students, one wonders whether this may have a washback effect increasing student orientation toward teacher-fronted activities as personally relevant rehearsal opportunities, possibly increasing the use of private speech. This should inspire us both as teachers and researchers to further investigate the role of private speech in foreign language acquisition and to study the characteristics of the classroom settings in which private speech emerges. Then we may learn more about how participation in private speech impacts language use in subsequent interactive tasks. Further investigations into the private speech of classroom learners are needed to deepen our understanding of classroom SLA processes, and how the structure and relevance of classroom events impacts the use of private speech by language learners.

Chapter 3

Peer Interactive Tasks and Assisted Performance in Classroom Language Learning

In chapter 2, we considered the role of private speech in the development of the seven learners. In this chapter, we move "outward" from private speech, an intrapsychological speech form, to *interpsychological speech*—social interaction as it occurs in the context of peer interactive tasks. It is through social interaction that the ZPD is formed. In particular, we consider how peer interactive tasks promote the provision of help from learner to learner that results in assisted performance (Tharp & Gallimore, 1991), which forms building blocks for language development.

THE THEORETICAL BASIS OF PEER LEARNING: FROM THE SOCIAL TO THE INDIVIDUAL

In chapter 1, a sociocognitive framework for understanding classroom language development was presented. In this framework, two key constructs that illuminate developmental processes were presented, the ZPD and the general genetic law of cultural development. The general genetic law of development outlines how assistance in the ZPD leads to learning and how social interaction forms the basis of the development of thought (Vygotsky, 1981). Through the enabling process that occurs in the ZPD, and continued use of what the learner is working to acquire, internalization occurs as the learner becomes less dependent on assistance, and more able to individually control language as a tool of thought. In other words, the learner moves from *other regulation*—from being dependent on the guidance of others, to *self-regulation*, in which the learner is able to control language use effectively (Wertsch, 1985). The dialogic process of interaction in the L2 works to form the conceptual structure of the L2; meta-cognitive skills related to language development are formed through this process (Donato & Lantolf, 1990).

While the ZPD was initially conceptualized as an interactional space in which a child's activity is supported by an adult or more capable peer, the ZPD has been found to be alive and well in peer learning settings where there is no unequivocal expert. Because no two learners have the same complement of strengths and weaknesses, peer learning has the potential of allowing learners to share their strengths with one another, together producing performance that is of a higher level than that of any individual involved. This finding has been repeatedly noted in qualitative L2 research with small numbers of participants (Brooks, 1992a, 1992b; Donato, 1988; Ohta, 1995a, 1997b, 1999). The ZPD is visible in classroom language learning in instances where support enables a learner to reach a level higher than that which could have been reached without that assistance. Assistance is not only provided by teacher or peers, but by instructional materials acting as supportive structures that learners may turn to for assistance. Learning occurs as the learner takes on increasing autonomy. Increasing autonomy is evidence of increasing internalization. As the learner acts more independently, support is reduced accordingly. This process of development that occurs moment-by-moment through social interaction is called *microgenesis*. In this chapter, we observe microgenesis in progress in the interaction of learners with each other and with the teacher in the peer learning setting. Though previous research has noted the positive effects of peer learning in foreign language classrooms, the mechanisms of learner assistance have been little examined. In addition, the nature of interactive tasks and how the processes and roles involved in interaction contribute to peer assistance have been insufficiently considered. This study allows examination of the processes that occur in actual classrooms; rather than utilizing a laboratory setting or researcher-designed tasks, the classroom corpus provides a naturalistic data set. Compared to the data used in previous studies of language learner interaction, the classroom corpus provides the opportunity to observe a greater diversity of learners across a broader range of classroom language learning tasks. This data base should be useful for examining questions regarding peer learning and assisted performance as they occur in actual classrooms.

Research Questions

This chapter builds on previous findings from studies of learner–learner interaction by further examining the mechanisms of peer assistance. The questions examined in this chapter are as follows:

(1) How is it possible for a "weaker" peer to assist a "stronger" one? Is this a result of differential expertise, as has been discussed in previous studies, or are other factors involved? How does the nature of interaction impact peer ability to provide assistance? In particular, how do differential roles, and the focus of learners in these roles impact the provision of assistance in the ZPD?

(2) How do peers provide assistance to one another? Is this scaffolding beneficial?

(3) Is there a downside to peer interactive tasks in the classroom corpus? What happens when learners make linguistic errors or provide each other with erroneous L2 forms? Do the learners in the classroom corpus use such forms in their own speech?

In addressing these questions, this chapter is structured as follows. First, the role of social interaction in facilitating peer assistance is examined, with a focus on how social roles impact the availability of working memory and the channeling of selective attention. Excerpts from the corpus are presented, which show how peer listeners are enabled by natural conversational processes to provide appropriate assistance that is even a bit beyond what a helper might have been able to do if she or he were in the role of speaker. Secondly, mechanisms of assistance are presented, with examples of how peers assist each other. A range of techniques that are tailored to the needs of the peer interlocutor, from more to less explicit forms of assistance, are introduced. In this section, the benefits of the episodes of help for the particular learners assisted are also discussed. Finally, the chapter considers the impact of linguistic errors on the peer interlocutor, as well as what transpires when a learner provides a partner with erroneous assistance.

WORKING MEMORY AND SELECTIVE ATTENTION
IN LEARNER–LEARNER INTERACTION

Analysis of the corpus reveals, time and time again, that peer interaction has a facilitative effect. Although a "novice–expert" scenario resulting from differential expertise, in which the stronger learner helps the weaker learner may seem to provide an explanation, this is not a productive generalization. Previous research provided vivid examples of peers supporting each other in language learning tasks. This research illustrated how, even though stronger peers clearly do help those with weaker skills, the reverse is also true (Brooks, 1992b; Donato, 1994; Ohta 1995a, 1997b, 2000a). In addition, peers assist each other when no one peer clearly has greater expertise; the peer who receives help in one instance provides help in the next. This finding is contrary to Vygotsky's (1978) formulation of the ZPD, which specified that assistance comes from one who is more capable. Certainly there are cases in which a more proficient peer provides more assistance and the weaker peer makes greater gains (Ohta, in press-a), the stronger peer has also been shown to benefit via the assistance of the weaker (Ohta, 1995a). Although the words "expert–novice," "more capable," "more proficient," or "stronger," imply a persistent state of one participant being generally more able than the other participant, in fact, learner abilities are not fixed. Rather, peer assistance is often mutual, with peers helping each other, rather than expert helping novice. Previous studies explained their findings by discussing how peer tasks allow learners to pool differential knowledge, such that learners, though individually novices, together become expert (Donato, 1994). Researchers posited that no learner is universally more or less capable than a peer, but that each learner presents an array of strengths and weaknesses that may be complementary. When learners work together, therefore, these strengths and weaknesses may be pooled, creating a greater expertise for the group than of any of the individuals involved.

Consistent with the findings of previous research, analysis of the classroom corpus reveals that facilitative help is not only ubiquitous in the peer learning tasks found in the corpus, but is overwhelmingly mutual. But how is this pooling of resources possible? The corpus includes examples of learners who provide assistance in one instance, but then are unable to produce the same kind of utterance themselves. How is it possible for a learner to provide help with something he or she cannot even do without assistance? In these cases, is the helper really enabled by a greater expertise, or is the ability to assist another a result of the unique affordances of the helper's role? The answer lies in the nature of the cognitive workspace—in the way working memory and selective attention function during social interaction.

Although the specter of the weaker assisting the stronger, or of two learners doing together what either individual could not have accomplished may seem counterintuitive, analysis of the classroom corpus suggests that the process of assisted performance is enabled by the nature of working memory and how it is harnessed in conversational interaction. Pooling of expertise is possible because of the differential way working memory and selective attention are employed by interlocutors in different interactive roles. Working memory is of severely limited capacity, and attention is, by nature, selective (Baars, 1997; Pashler, 1998). Selective attention makes sense of the barrage of sensory information an individual is exposed to, allowing the learner to capitalize on affordances by focusing on the process of constructing meaning (Osborne & Wittrock, 1983). Interactive tasks are similar to conversation in that learners alternate as "speaker" and "listener," sharing the floor. This means that learners alternate between who must produce an utterance, and who must listen to and monitor the production of another. It is the nature of these social roles of speaker and listener and the differential focus of learners who take on these roles that empowers learners to help one another. The difference in how working memory and selective attention are used in these different roles enables even a struggling learner to be a resource to the peer partner.

The Demands of Production for Beginning Learners

For beginning learners, formulating an utterance in the L2 takes up enormous attentional resources. Depending on the particular task and the language needed to do that task, for learners who are daily being introduced to new linguistic tools, the learner's ability to produce the L2 is not automatized. Rather, the learner must use working memory to consciously form the utterance. Unlike the proficient speaker who can focus on what he or she wants to say, with unconscious processes solving most linguistic problems (such as lexical choice, case marking, verb inflection, etc.), the language learner must consciously work through many of these problems. Simply figuring out which words to use in an utterance, or how to do a particular inflection, may take the learner's full attention, with few resources remaining to figure out what to say next. In the classroom corpus, teachers help to alleviate the burden by preparing students for interactive tasks via pre-task practice activities that help students practice the vocabulary and structures to be used in the task. Even so, when learners construct utterances in the peer setting, they must use working memory not only to formulate the utterance, but also to solve any phonetic, phonological, lexical, morphological, or syntactic problems that emerge. For beginning learners, working at any one of these levels may overwhelm the limited resources available. This is evident in the pauses, false starts, and filled pauses, which characterize the utterances of beginning learners. These are far from being mere disfluencies but are evidence of the learner's cognitive effort. Therefore, when we place the language learner with a peer interlocutor who is jointly engaged in the interactive task, this joint participation has a major impact. This impact results from the nature of the listener's role in social interaction, and the differential use of working memory and selected attention afforded to the person in the listener's role.

The Active Listener

While the L2 speaker is tied up with the task of production, the listener, who may seem passive, is actively involved, working collaboratively with the speaker. Conversation analysis research has shown in great detail the work that listeners do, repeatedly demonstrating how attentional processes are realized in conversation. Although a lay understanding of listening and of comprehension processes is that the listener focuses on decoding what he or she has heard, in actuality, listeners are not merely parsers. The listener not only works to understand what has been said, but mentally maps along with the utterance in progress while moving beyond to consider what may follow in a process called *projection* (Levinson, 1983). In this process, which is common to all conversational interaction, the listener anticipates what might come next in the speaker's production, making predictions about how the utterance may continue. This is a process of selective attention. The projection process is a constant in conversation—it is what makes turn taking, the most ordinary and ubiquitous of conversational processes, possible (Sacks, Schegloff, & Jefferson, 1974). Projection is also the mechanism underlying the precise placement of overlap (Jefferson, 1986) and the frequent occurrence of *co-construction*—the collaborative construction of sentences in conversation through which different persons become co-creators of a turn at talk (Goodwin, 1979). These basic conversational processes are demonstrations of the attention that conversationalists employ as they engage in interactive talk. Conversationalists are attuned not only to what is just being said, but are actively involved in a process of both analyzing what has occurred and projecting what might come next.

The way attention is harnessed in the everyday conversational process of projection is naturally applied by learners as budding conversationalists in the L2 as they work on L2 interactive tasks in the language classroom, even when learners' L2 skills are still rudimentary. Projection enables peer interlocutors in the listener's role to do two things that their partners in the immediate speaking role are less able to do: to notice errors the speaker may not notice, and to anticipate and mentally formulate what might come next. Learners notice discrepancies between their own knowledge or production and that of others via the process of selective attention (Gass, 1991). This noticing results from the predictive process that is a part of projection. And, learners do more than just notice when a well-formed utterance does not match with their own incomplete grammatical knowledge. Learners also do the opposite—they apply their developing knowledge to notice when deviant utterances do not match up to what the learner believes to be true about the L2. Through this whole process, the learner in the listener role does more than map along with the utterance in progress while projecting what is to come; the learner also has available working memory to collaborate with the speaker to handle any discrepancies that emerge. The enablement of noticing, active involvement in projection, and a "free hand" to provide help using available working memory, work together to allow the listener to provide assistance when the speaker has difficulty. Conversation analysis research has shown the ubiquity of repair in L1 conversational contexts. Repair includes both self-initiated repair, as well as other-initiated repair, which involves, among other things, noticing errors produced by the interlocutor (Schegloff, Jefferson, & Sacks, 1977). Because the ability to project what is coming next in an interaction is basic to any conversational interaction, collaborative construction of utterances is a common occurrence not only for classroom learners, but even in native–native conversation. This whole process is integral to second language acquisition; conscious noticing is, according to Schmidt (1990), integral to the development of the learner's L2 grammar.

These natural conversational processes that work to facilitate human interaction provide the foundation that allows L2 interactive tasks to facilitate language learning. When a learner is working to formulate an utterance, his or her resources are fully occupied by the local productive task. Meanwhile, the peer partner listens, unencumbered by the demands of production. The peer listener thus has resources available both to think about the immediate production and to think more broadly, beyond the local problem to the larger utterance and the task as a whole. The listener involved in the joint task is naturally attentive as a result of the conversational processes that are being enacted. This complements the heavy burden carried by the L2 speaker who must devote the bulk of cognitive resources to the task of formulating an utterance. Differential application of working memory and selective attention results in a peer listener who contributes a quality of attention that is different in focus from that of the speaker. Even learners who are not fully proficient are able to provide assistance based on the affordances accessed when working jointly on the interactive task. Peer interlocutors may provide assistance even without any capability superior to that of the interlocutor. The most important evidence for this are instances in which peer interlocutors provide assistance with what they cannot yet do themselves.

Evidence From the Classroom Corpus

The data that comprise the classroom corpus provide a range of evidence that supports my proposal that assisted performance is enabled by the differential ways speaker and listeners utilize working memory and selective attention. The following episode, divided into two excerpts (Excerpt 1.1 and Excerpt 1.2), provides a good example of how the same individual, when a listener, notices what he did not notice when he was speaker. Here, we see how Kuo-ming does not appear to notice an error in his own production, but subsequently notices (and repairs in private speech) the same error when it is produced by another. First, in pair practice of a role play, Kuo-ming uses the wrong demonstrative in acting out giving directions (line 2). Instead of *asoko* 'over there', Kuo-ming uses *koko* 'here' (underlined). There is no evidence that Kuo-ming notices his own error:

(1.1)   1   M: Ano sumimasen (.) sakanaya wa (.) doku ni
                 arimasu ka?
                 Um excuse me (.) where ((mispronounced)) is the (.) fish
                 shop?

→   2   Km: (.) Ah sakanaya desu ka:? ah (.) <u>koko</u> ni:: ginkoo (.)
                 ah (.) ga arimasu ne:, heheh ((laughter))
                 (.) Ah the fish shop? Ah (.) <u>here</u> is (.) ah (.) the bank
                 right? heheh

        3   T: Hai ii::::? [ja: demonstration shimashoo.
                 Oka::::?   so: let's have a demonstration.

        4   Km: [Heheh (   ) (.) hehe ((laughter))

Following Kuo-ming's line 2 error, in line 3 the teacher discontinues pair practice, asking for a volunteer pair to demonstrate the role play. As Kuoming, no longer absorbed by the demands of production, observes the performance of another, he notices what he did not notice in his own performance (underlined). Private speech provides a window on this process:

(1.2)   5   T: Hai borantia imasu ka:? (.) borantia:: borantia ah oh
                 jaa Lin-sa:n
                 So are there any volunteers? (.) voluntee::rs volunteers okay
                 Lin.

        6   L: Ano sumimasen
                 Um excuse me

        7   Km: Heheh

        8   L: Eki wa doko ni arimasu ka?
                 Where is the train station?

→   9   s11: Ah eki wa - eki desu ka? (.) <u>koko</u> ni ahh
                 Ah the train station i- the train station? (.) <u>Here</u> is ahh

→   10   Km: °°Asoko°° (.) hmf
                 °°Over there°° (.) hmf

       11   s11: Ah=

→   12   Km: =°°Asoko°°
                 =°°Over there°°

       13   s11: Asaki ni:
                 Over there ((misprounounces 'asoko' as 'asaki'))

→   14   Km: Hehe

       15   S11: (1) Byooin ga arimasu ne:. (.) Um: eki wa byooin no:
                 (.) tonari arimasu yo,
                 (1) Is the hospital right? (.) Um: the train station is (.) next
                 to the hospital. ((error: particle deleted))

16 L: Ahh soo desu ka? [doomo arigatoo gozaimasu
Oh I see? *thank you very much*
17 Km: [°°Hmf°°

(Kuo-ming, 11/18)

In line 9, the learner S11 uses *koko* 'here' just as Kuo-ming did in line 2. In lines 10 and 12, Kuo-ming softly whispers *asoko* 'over there'. In line 10, he not only notices the error in S11's talk, but Kuo-ming also notices S11's line 12 mispronunciation of *asoko* 'over there' as *asaki*, as evidenced by his laughter in line 14, which immediately follows S11's error. Noticing occurs when what is produced contrasts with what is expected via the process of *projection*.

In peer interaction, this capacity for noticing allows partners to provide suggestions that increase the accuracy of the interlocutor's production. The power of peer learning is in the maintenance of the learners' joint attention on the interactive task. Joint attention facilitates learning because working memory available for the task is effectively doubled. This occurs when the nonspeaking partner is able to provide help beyond what he would be able to do if he were the one speaking. The impact of joint attention is magnified for beginning language learners because of the enormous cognitive load required by L2 production.

Another example of Kuo-ming's peer interaction is described to illustrate this point. Kuo-ming's partner notices what Kuo-ming does not— that Kuo-ming is making particle errors. The partner handles the discrepancy by asking the teacher about particle use, resulting in the provision of information that helps Kuo-ming. The episode is much too long to list in its entirety. Rather than listing the entire episode, Table 1 lists only Kuo-ming's questions and answers to his partner's questions. The task here was an interview task, in which learners asked each other what activities they usually did on certain days of the week. The task was designed not only to practice using days of the week and activity verbs, but also to teach particle use. The rule taught was that *ni*, the dative particle, was to be used to mark the day of the week in questions and affirmative statements, with the topic marker *wa* inserted after *ni* in negative statements.

Table 3.1 lists all of Kuo-ming's utterances from the activity. Rather than listing the utterances in order, I listed Kuo-ming's questions, affirmative statements, and negative statements in separate sections of Table 3.1. A pattern in Kuo-ming's production is clear. Kuo-ming uses *ni* in questions and *ni wa* in statements, whether affirmative or negative. This is contrary to the rule taught and practiced, which is to insert *wa* only with negative statements. During the pair interactive task, these sentences were not produced in the order listed in Table 3.1. Rather, Kuo-ming and his partner alternated asking and answering questions, so all of Kuo-ming's state-

TABLE 3.1
Kuo-ming's Questions, Affirmative and Negative Statements
During a Pair Interview Task (Kuo-ming, 1/30)

Kuo-ming's Questions

- Taitei nanyoobi: aru– (.) nanyoobi <u>ni</u> arubaito o shimas::: ka?
  Usually what day of the week do– (.) <u>DAT</u> what day of the week do you work?
- Taitei nanyoobi <u>ni::</u> ah undoo sh– shim undoo shimas:u ka?
  Usually what day <u>DAT</u> uh exercise d– do you exercise?
- Taitei:: nanyoobi <u>ni::</u> (.) supaa ni::: ikimas:u ka?
  Usually what day <u>DAT</u> (.) do you go to the supermarket?

Kuo-ming's Affirmative Statements (should use ni, not ni wa)

- Doyoobi <u>ni wa</u>– eh? doyoobi <u>ni wa</u> shimasu oh– undoo shimasu
  Saturday <u>DAT TOP</u>– eh? Saturday <u>DAT TOP</u> I do oh– I exercise.
- Taitei doyoobi <u>ni wa</u>^ (.) supaa ni: ikimasu.
  Usually Saturday <u>DAT TOP</u>^ (.) I go to the supermarket.
- Taitei nichiyoobi <u>ni wa::</u> (.) ah sooshi o shimash–
  Usually Sunday <u>DAT TOP</u> (.) uh clean ((mispronounced)) ACC do–

Kuo-ming's Negative Statements

- Suiyoobi <u>ni wa:</u> (.) ikimasen.
  Wednesday <u>DAT TOP</u> I don't go.
- Kinyoobi <u>ni:: wa</u> (.) sooshi o - sooji o: shimasen.
  Friday <u>DAT TOP</u> (.) I don't clan- clean ((mispronunciation self-corrected)).

Key: DAT = dative particle *ni*
     TOP = topic particle *wa*

ments occurred in response to his partner's questions. Even so, Kuo-ming's partner F noticed the discrepancy. When the teacher came by, F discontinued the interview task to ask the teacher about which particles should be used. In the first turn of Excerpt 2, F asks the teacher if they should say *suupaa ni wa* (Supermarket DAT TOP) or *suupaa ni* (Supermarket DAT). The word *ikimasu* in line 1 means 'go (affirmative)' Kuo-ming's attentiveness to his partner's question is shown in the lines indicated with arrows. The relevant structures in Japanese are underlined:

(2) 1 F: Sensei ((this means "teacher")) when we're—when
             we're asking to say (.) ah like "<u>supaa ni wa</u>?" or just
             "<u>supaa ni ikimasu</u>."
     2 T: Taitei nanyoobi ni <u>supaa ni ikimasu</u> ka:.
             Usually what day of the week do you go to ((DAT)) the
             supermarket?

→ 3 Km: A:h
4 F: When we answer back do we say "<u>supaa ni ikimasu</u>" and that's it or like "<u>supaa ni wa ikimasen?</u>" ((F contrasts the affirmative and negative statements, using the topic marker *wa* only in the negative statement))
5 T: Sososo
→ 6 Km: A::h.
7 T: <u>Supaa ni wa ikimasen</u> totemo (   ) taitei nanyoobi ni supaa ni ikimasu ka. (.) getsuyoobi ni ikimasu
Supermarket DAT TOP go-neg that's very (   ) usually it's what day of the week do you go to ((DAT)) the supermarket. (.) I go on ((DAT)) Mondays.
8 F: Hai
Yeah
→ 9 Km: Hm[:
10 T: [Getsuyoobi ni <u>supaa ni ikimasu</u> (   )
Monday DAT supermarket DAT go-affirmative (   )
→ 11 Km: Ok (.) I was messing up ((laughs))
12 F: I get confused with these <u>ni wa</u> and [(its so) confusing
13 Km: [Yeah I know
(Kuo-ming, 1/30)

In line 1, the partner pinpoints Kuo-ming's problem by asking the teacher if *ni* or *ni wa* should be used in questions. Although the partner is the one who asks the question, Kuo-ming uses the opportunity to reflect back on his own performance, as seen from his attentive listening shown in lines 3 ("A:h"), 6 ("A::h"), and 9 ("Hm:"), and his acknowledgement of his own error in line 11 ("I was messing up"). Kuo-ming's partner's question functions effectively to help Kuo-ming differentiate between the use of *ni* and *ni wa*. F's diplomacy in line 12, describing her own confusion with *ni wa*, is striking because she did not use *ni wa* with affirmative statements as Kuo-ming did. Rather, Kuo-ming's misuse of the particles raised a question that his partner clarified with the teacher, not only affirming to herself what was correct, but also helping Kuo-ming.

Examples of noticing and other-initiated repair like those just mentioned emerge from natural conversational processes that are applied to the peer foreign language learning task, and result from the resources that the learner who is not occupied with a speaking role has at hand. And the process of projection enables the listener to assist in other ways. While one interlocutor is producing an utterance, the other, who is not burdened by the need for immediate production, maps along, formulating the utterance mentally and projecting what he or she expects to come next. This mental activity of projection allows the nonspeaking interlocutor to be ready to "chime in" with assistance as needed. This seemingly silent partner is active not only in processing what the other says, but stays mentally one step ahead to recall and suggest needed vocabulary and grammatical forms. In Excerpt 3, Bryce, a second-year learner, and his partner Matt, take turns describing what people in magazine pictures are wearing. Each chimes in to help the other in the indicated lines:

(3)   1   B: Un. Hai um kuroi ti-shatsu o kiru, to: um
                 Yeah. Yes um he wears a black T-shirt, a:nd um

→   2   M: Kiteimasu?
                 He's wearing?

       3   B: Kiteimasu? (.) um (.) ahh
                 He's wearing? (.) um (.) ahh

→   4   M: Han::=
                 Ha::lf=

       5   B: =Han- han- han- han-zubon (.) han zubon o um
                 haiteimasu?
                 =Half- half- half- half-slacks (.) he's um wearing half-slacks?
                 ((han-zubon, literally "half-slacks" means "shorts"))

       6   J: Um hm:,

       7   B: Ah kutsu o:: (.) a:::h haiteimasu, (.) s- (.) um socks
                 he//he
                 Ah He's a:::h wearing (.) shoes, (.) s- (.) and socks hehe

→   8   M: Kutsushita
                 Socks ((literally "under-shoes"))

       9   B: Sha uh?

       10 M: Kutsu shita.
                 Under shoes.

       11 B: Kutsushita o:, (.) [o::
                 Socks ACC:, (.) ACC::

→   12 M: [Haite?
                                    Wear-?

       13 B: Haiteimasu un haiteimasu, (.) Ah tokai o um hai um
                 hameteimasu?
                 Wearing yeah wearing, (.) Ah he's um wearing a watch
                 ((mispronounced))?

                                                              (Bryce, 5/16)

In line 1, Bryce uses the citation form of the verb rather than the appropriate form, and Matt initiates repair by providing the right form. Then, when Bryce has difficulty beginning in line 3, Matt chimes in by prompting him with the first syllable of what he expects will come next. When Bryce has difficulty with vocabulary, using the English word "socks" in line 7, Matt provides the appropriate word in line 8. Most striking is the projection process evidenced in lines 11 and 12, in which Matt prompts Bryce by providing the first part of the verb Bryce is reaching for as he pauses, and then repeats the accusative marker *o*. Matt provides the first part of the verb, which Bryce then picks up and completes, going on to finish his description. Because of the projection process, Matt is available to provide appropriate assistance to Bryce when he struggles. The helpfulness of this episode is visible in Bryce's continued manipulation of the word *kutsushita* 'socks' in private speech. In addition, in subsequent practice Bryce uses the verbs *kiru* 'wear' (on torso) and *haku* 'wear' (on lower body), using the correct inflections.

Even learners who are unable to produce a particular grammatical structure on their own are able to assist a partner with the same task when they are afforded the abundant attentional resources of the listener's role. In Excerpt 4, a group of learners has been formed with members of other groups who have just completed a decision-making task. Each person must report the decision that was made in his or her previous group, using a new grammatical structure:

Miru koto ni natte iru
Watch nom. DAT become AU
"It has been decided that we will watch"

In this example, *miru* 'watch' can be replaced by any verb. *Koto* is a nominalizer. The verb combined with *koto ni natte iru* means there is a standing decision regarding a particular course of action that has been previously settled on. The comparison of the Japanese with the English colloquial translation shows how very different Japanese and English word order are. In the following excerpt where there are many elliptical utterances, a word-for-word translation with a colloquial translation is provided wherever possible. Andrea helps her partner to form a question using this structure when her partner has difficulty completing the verb phrase *suru koto ni natte* 'it has been decided that we will do'. Even though Andrea is able to chime in and co-construct the sentence with her partner, when it is her turn to formulate the whole statement and report her group's decision, she cannot make a similar sentence herself without assistance:

(4) 1 N: Andrea-san no gruupu wa: (.) ah:: (.) ah yube:: (.) yube::: ah:: (.) nani o suru:: koto:: (.)
Andrea's group TOP: (.) ah:: (.) ah last night (.) last night ah:: (.) what ACC do thing:: (.) ((N does not provide the main verb))

→   2   A: Ni natte
               DAT become ((this is the missing verb))

      3   N: Ni natteiru n desu ka desu ka?
               DAT become-AUX NOM COP INT COP INT?
               ((The question, here completed means: Andrea, what did
               your group decide to do last night? N's line 1 utterance
               can't be given a colloquial English translation because
               the main verb is missing until Andrea provides it in line 2))

      4   A: Ah (.) hai. (4). So, it's basically like (.) what-
               [what did we decide on?

      5   N: [Yeah, what did you decide on? What to do or what to
               eat or what?

→   6   A: Oh (.) um:: (.) Simpsons o hoho::: (.) uh: Simpsons o:
               (.) mimasu.
               Oh (.) Um:: (.) Simpsons ACC hoho::: ((laughs)) (.) uh:
               Simpsons ACC: (.) watch. ((This means: We will watch
               The Simpsons. Andrea does not use the form "V+koto
               ni natte"))

      7   N: O:h, terebi o:?
               O:h, Television ACC:?

      8   A: Terebi
               Television

      9   N: Oh. You just ask (.) you just go and ask somebody else.

→   10   A: Yeah, how do I say that though? I mean, how do I say
               like- (.)

     11   H: Simpson o::
               Simpson ACC::

     12   A: Simpson o::
               Simpson ACC::

→   13   H: It's sort of [like miru koto [
               [ni [[ni natteiru

→   14   A: [[miru koto
               [[ni [natteiru n desu yo

     15   N: [Terebi de simpsons o miru: miru
               [koto ni natteiru and then you go on
               ((Meaning: We've decided to watch The Simpsons on TV.))

     16   A: Okay Ming-san wa?
               Okay, what about you, Ming-san?

     17   M: Watashi no guruupu wa: (.) itari no resutoran ni, (.)
               tabe- taberu:: koto ni na:: teiru (.) um:: uh::
               Hoshi- Hoshino-san wa?

My group (.) decided to go and eat at ((error: particle choice)) (.) an Italian restaurant. What about your group, Hoshino-san?

(Andrea, 11/21)

When Andrea's partner struggles (line 1), Andrea provides appropriate assistance in line 2. However, we see in line 6 that Andrea cannot form the sentence herself without help. When it is Andrea's turn to report, she not only uses a much simpler sentence without using the structure " *ni natteiru*," but persists in asking for help in line 10, even after one group member, N, suggests that Andrea just ask questions and not answer them. Andrea, then, receives help with the structure from H in line 13 (and, from N in line 15 also). In line 14, Andrea follows along with H, at first lagging behind and repeating after H. She anticipates the verb *miru* 'watch', providing it slightly ahead of H. Andrea does have an idea of what she should say, but interlocutor support enables her to produce the utterance. Andrea then goes on in line 16 to ask other group members what their decisions were. What is most interesting about this episode is that Andrea provided assistance in line 2 with the formulation of a grammatical structure that she could not produce independently as shown in lines 6, 10, and 14. The resources available to Andrea as a listener allow her to provide such assistance. She has some knowledge, but cannot yet produce the whole sentence without help. Even so, the projection process enables Andrea to use what she does know to help another learner.

In sum, although previous research has analyzed the phenomena of peer assistance as having its source in the pooled expertise of collaborators, analysis of the classroom corpus reveals that the source of assistance is not merely expertise. Rather, three key factors combine to make assisted performance possible in the peer language learning setting. These factors are learner knowledge, the attentional resources needed to apply that knowledge, and the conversational process of projection, which keeps the listener one step ahead of the speaker. Superior knowledge is not prerequisite for a learner to be a sensitive and appropriate support to a peer interlocutor. Even rudimentary knowledge is helpful when the learner is enabled by the abundant resources afforded the listener's role to capitalize on the projection process in order to step in to provide assistance. When learners work together on a peer learning task, available cognitive resources are effectively doubled—what one student cannot notice, the interlocutor is often able to notice. While demands of production occupy the speaker, the partner is not similarly encumbered, but is free to map along mentally and to project what might be coming next, and thus to provide assistance as needed. This process is powerful because it enables learners who are still developing themselves to provide developmentally appropriate assistance to their peers. And, through provision and receipt of such assistance, the students use the language being learned for interaction in a way that supports their own linguistic development.

ASSISTED PERFORMANCE IN ACTION

As we have just seen, application of natural conversational processes enable the "assistance" aspect of assisted performance to occur. In addition, for assistance to be provided by a peer partner, that partner must become aware of the interlocutor's need for assistance. This section considers the way the learners in the corpus provided scaffolding to one another and when they provided that assistance. Finally, the impact of assistance on language learning is discussed. Table 3.2 lists an array of mechanisms learners use to assist one another. These are divided into two contexts: when the peer interlocutor is struggling, and when the peer interlocutor produces an error. Next to each mechanism, the level of explicitness is noted in the column labeled *E*, with level 1 indicating the least explicit, and level 4 indicating the most explicit forms of assistance. The level of explicitness is determined by how much information the assistance provides to the interlocutor. As shown in Table 3.2, learners provide assistance not only as corrective feedback when a peer interlocutor makes an error, but also when the peer is struggling. Peers are only one source of corrective feedback; the sources and the impact of corrective feedback will be considered in greater depth in chapter 4. This section considers the different types of assistance that learners provide to one another and the way that the learners benefit from the assistance they receive.

Assistance to a Struggling Peer

Qualitative review of assisted performance in the classroom corpus reveals that assistance of struggling interlocutors is very common, occurring in virtually all peer learning tasks, whether or not the learners produce linguistic errors. This assistance takes three major forms. The least explicit form of assistance is waiting—the interlocutor simply waits while the peer formulates an utterance. More explicit is prompting—when an interlocutor helps the partner to continue by repeating a word or syllable just uttered. Alternatively, peers may assist via co-construction, which even more explicitly provides assistance, as the peer chimes in with a syllable, inflection, word, or phrase, or completes an utterance started by the peer. Co-construction sometimes results in vertical constructions, in which peers collaborate to produce an utterance, alternately providing words or

TABLE 3.2
Some Methods of Assistance Occurring
During Classroom Peer Interaction

Methods	E	Description
(1) When the peer interlocutor is struggling		
Waiting	1	One partner gives the other, even when struggling, time to complete an utterance without making any contribution.
Prompting	2	Partner repeats the syllable or word just uttered, helping the interlocutor to continue.
Co-construction	2–3	Partner contributes a syllable, word, phrase, or grammatical particle that completes or works toward completion of the utterance. This includes prompts that occur in the absence of an error, when the learner stops speaking, or produces false starts.
Explaining	4	Partner explains in English.
(2) When the peer interlocutor makes an error, partners use the above methods (waiting, co-construction and prompting) as well as the methods listed below.		
NTRI (w/o repair)	1–2	Partner indicates that the preceding utterance is somehow problematic (for example, by saying "huh?" or *nani?* 'what'.) When the NTRI is in the form of a prompt, it more explicitly targets the error. The NTRI provides an opportunity for the interlocutor to consider the utterance and self-correct. This is the case even when the NTRI is triggered by comprehension difficulties rather than by a linguistic error.
NTRI (provide)	3	Partner initiates and carries out repair (either fully or partially by providing a syllable, word, or phrase to the interlocutor. These may be in the form of recasts, which build semantically on the learner's utterance but change or expand it.)
Asking	4	Peer partner notices their interlocutor's error and asks the teacher about it.

Key: E = level of explicitness from least explicit (1) to most explicit (4)
NTRI = Next Turn Repair Initiator

phrases to the growing utterance. Finally peers also provide explanations to one another to help their interlocutors.

Waiting

One striking feature of peer interaction is the ubiquity of waiting as a technique of assisted performance. Peer interlocutors tend to provide their partners with ample wait time. Wait time allows the student who is speaking to do what he or she is able to do without assistance. This is important, because assistance is only helpful when it is needed, not when it is redundant with the learner's established abilities. In Excerpt 5, Kuo-ming's partner, P, waits as Kuo-ming completes his utterance in turn 1:

(5)   1   Km: Um (1) um (1) suteki <u>no::</u> (.) um ske-suteki <u>na</u> sofa desu
                   <u>ka?</u> (2) Desu <u>ne</u> or desu <u>k-</u> (.) haha desu <u>ne:,</u> (.)
                   Um (1) um (1) is it the (.) nice ((wrong particle)) um ni- nice
                   ((correct particle)) sofa ((wrong final particle))? (.) ((re-states
                   copula with corrected final particle and wrong final particle))
                   (.) ((chooses correct final particle))
        2   P: Ah donna sofa desu? (2)
                   Ah which sofa do you mean? (2)
        3   Km: Suteki na ha ((laugh)) sofa desu, hehehe (.)
                   The nice ((correct particle)) ha ((laugh)) sofa hehehe (.)
        4   P: Soo desu ka?
                   Oh really?

                                                         (Kuo-ming, 10/24)

As P waits, Kuo-ming completes his utterance. While doing so, Kuo-ming
notices and self-corrects all of his own errors. He corrects a particle choice
error in the first line of turn 1, moving from using the genitive *no* following the adjectival noun *suteki* 'nice', which is incorrect, to using the copular
form *na*, which is the appropriate choice. Kuo-ming also tries different final particles, first using the question marker *ka*, then the tag *ne*, and finally
settling on *ne*, which is the correct choice. Because partners tend to wait
for one another, the peer interactive setting allows students to work as independently as they are able to in a supportive environment where they
can produce their own utterances and work out many of their own problems. In this way, students learn to monitor and correct their own performance rather than relying on others to initiate the repair process. This
experience not only builds confidence as learners successfully produce
and self-correct their utterances, but also promotes the ability to self-
correct. In the peer learning tasks of the classroom corpus, self-correction
is not triggered by teacher cues, but by each learner's developing capacity
to self-monitor. In fact, premature cues would, according to Vygotsky's
(1978) theory of the zone of proximal development, impede development
by providing assistance with what a learner is able to notice and remedy
unaided. Waiting, on the other hand, promotes an environment where
learners do for themselves what they are able to do, with assistance provided as needed. When a learner waits for another to continue an utterance, the skill of self-monitoring and self-correction is acquired as the
learner uses the developing language and tests growing skills. In Excerpt
5, the interaction benefits Kuo-ming because he is able to draw on his own
resources to accomplish what he is able to do independently. More direc-
tive assistance is helpful only when it is *developmentally appropriate*—that is,
when it is not premature, but works to support a learner in what he or she
is unable to do independently.

Prompting and Co-construction

When a learner pauses in mid-utterance, partners may wait for the speaker to continue, as just discussed, or may help their interlocutor to continue by prompting or co-construction. In a prompt, the helper repeats a word or syllable just uttered, elongating the final syllable, to help the struggling partner to continue without providing any additional language. In co-construction, the listener chimes in with the next syllable, word, or phrase when the speaker is having difficulty. Difficulty is evidenced by false starts and pauses. In the next example (Excerpt 6), Sara's partner provides assistance by prompting. Sara knows the answer to her partner's question, but says it in English and leaves a pause. Instead of accepting an English answer or translating Sara's answer, Sara's partner repeats the partial answer (from line 4) in line 7, elongating the final vowel in a prompt for Sara to continue:

(6)	1	Pf:	Anoo sumimasen.
			Um excuse me.
	2	Sr:	Hai
			Yes
	3	Pf:	Ima nanji desu ka?
			What time is it?
	4	Sr:	Um (2) kuji?
			Um (.) Nine o'clock?
	5	Pf:	Kuji
			Nine o'clock
→	6	Sr:	I guess that's ten after (.)
→	7	Pf:	Kuji:::
			Nine o'clock:::
	8	Sr:	Juppun desu.
			Ten minutes (('kuji juppun,' literally "nine o'clock ten minutes," is the correct way to tell the time)).
	9		(5)
	10	Pf:	Kuji juppun desu ne:?
			It's Nine-ten isn't it? ((literally, "nine o'clock ten minutes"))
	11	Sr:	Soo desu ne.
			Yes it is.

(Sara, 12/4)

When prompted, Sara correctly completes her utterance, and the two move on to continue their activity. Sara's partner pushes her to tell the time in the L2 and not to rely on English.

Prompting is also used when learners do not complete an utterance, as in the following example (Excerpt 7), where Sara prompts her partner

James to continue. When prompting, the helper restarts the utterance by repeating just the word or phrase that the learner was having difficulty with, as shown in line 2:

(7)   1   Jm: Ahm dooshite: (.) dooshite: (.) karada no sh- (.)
                 chosh- (.)
                 Ahm why: (.) why (.) is your physical con- (.) condi- (.)
→   2   Sr: Cho::::[shhi
                 Con::: dition
       3   Jm: [Chooshi ga ii n de[su
                        Condition is good ((this is the the correct ending
              for the sentence Jm started line 1))
       4   Sr: [ga ii n desu
                                            condition is good

                                                            (Sara, 5/22)

Here, instead of saying the entire expression *chooshi ga ii desu* 'condition is good', Sara's partner stops after partially uttering the first word of the expression. Sara's assistance, the prompt in line 2, allows James time to work out the complete expression. Prompting is evidence of the projection process that peer interlocutors apply to their L2 interaction. In order to provide an appropriate prompt, the learner must mentally produce the utterance along with the interlocutor, projecting what is likely to come next. This process allows learners to give timely and helpful prompts to one another. In Excerpt 7, Sara's partner James formulates the word he left incomplete in overlap with Sara's prompt. Prompts serve as a non-invasive way of helping a partner to move forward when she or he hesitates, providing a helpful nudge that assures the partner that everything is going well so far, and supports the partner in completing the utterance-in-progress.

The listener's high level of attention and involvement is even more evident in the phenomenon of co-construction, where, rather than repeating what has just been uttered, the peer moves ahead to what might come next. When one learner encounters difficulty formulating an utterance, or when learners are working together on a common task, such as reading the sentences on a worksheet, co-construction occurs when an interlocutor chimes in to provide a continuation of what the partner has said. The attentional resources of listeners that are focused on understanding the interlocutor and projecting what might come next serve to allow this assistance. When practicing new, difficult material, co-construction is a common practice that enables learners to build competence. Learners do for each other what adult caregivers do for toddlers who are working to acquire the L1 (Moerk, 1992). Interlocutors provide assistance in this way

TABLE 3.3
Three Forms of the Adjective *Yasashii* 'Kind'

Stem	Affirmative Nonpast	Negative Nonpast	Negative Past
yasashi- Kind (stem)	yasashi-i kind-nonpast *is/will be kind*	yasashi-ku arima-sen kind-adv COP-neg *isn't kind*	yasashi-ku arima-sen de-shita Kind-adv COP-neg COP-past *wasn't kind*

when a partner indicates difficulty through false starts, pauses, and, in particular, the use of elongated vowels. Recall how Andrea stepped in to complete the verb phrase her partner needed in Excerpt 4. Sometimes the partner will just contribute a single syllable, as Candace's partner Will does in Excerpt 8. Affirmative nonpast, negative nonpast, and negative past forms of the adjective Candace is working to conjugate are shown in Table 3.3. In Excerpt 8, Candace repeatedly utters part of the stem (underlined) in line 2, and Will steps in (line 3) to provide the rest of the stem, which enables Candace to go on to complete the sentence:

(8) 1 W: Uh (.) kookoo no:: sensei wa doo de (.) shita ka?
            Uh (.) what were your high school (.) teachers like?

→   2 C: Mm (.) Uh:: (.) amari: yasa:^ (.) amari: yas- yasa::
            um (.) amari: yasa::=
            Mm (.) uh:: (.) ((not)) very: kind- ((partial stem))
            ((not))very ki- kind ((partial stem)) very kind ((partial
            stem)) ((that Candace's utterance will be negative is
            implied by her choice of adverbial 'amari', which generally
            occurs in contexts of negative concord))

→   3 W: =shi
            =((completes stem))

     4 C: Yasa:: (.) yasashiku arima-sen (.) desh- (.) desu
            Kin:: (.) kind-adv COP-neg (.) COP- (.) COP ((Meaning:
            not kind)) ((error—copula should be marked for past
            tense))

     5 W: Ee
            Uh huh

     6 C: Yasashiku arimasen?
            Kind-adv COP-neg? ((meaning: Is not kind?))

     7 W: Yasashiku (.) arimasen deshita
            Kind-adv (.) COP-neg COP-past ((meaning: Wasn't kind.))

     8 C: Deshita. (.) hahahaha (..) arigato
            COP-past. (.) hahahaha (..) thanks

     9 W: Koko no kurasu me:to (..) doo: deshita ka?

What were your high school classmates (.) like? ((error: high school 'kookoo' is mispronounced as 'koko'))

(Candace, 1/24)

Candace, who produces her line 2 utterance with filled and unfilled pauses, repeatedly utters a partial stem of the adjective. She stops at the syllable before that which she must commit herself to a particular inflection. With two possibilities for negating adjectivals, depending on whether the lexical item is an adjective (which inflects) or an adjectival noun (which does not inflect), Candace has a decision to make. Will does not prompt by repeating what Candace has already said (a prompt here would be *"yasa::"*), but joins Candace in producing the utterance by providing just the next syllable, the mora right before the inflection in line 3. As shown in Table 3.3, *yasashii* 'kind', is an adjective that inflects by dropping the final mora, *'-i'*, and adding the appropriate inflection (whether negative, past or negative past). The difficulty is that words with adjective-like meanings that end in *-i* are not necessarily adjectives, so Candace has to make a decision. This choice is Candace's problem, as evidenced by her repeated false starts, pauses, and lengthened vowels, underlined in her second turn. When Will contributes the next syllable, Candace continues and produces the appropriate inflection, but uses the wrong tense in line 4. Her confusion is evident when she first says *desh-* the first part of the past tense form *deshita*, before saying *desu*, the affirmative copula. She reconfirms her answer with Will in line 6, and he provides the correct tense. Will's provision of the next syllable guides Candace to move forward and do what she is able to do—to inflect the verb properly—as well as to get assistance with constructing the past tense.

Even when helping to co-construct a partner's turn, learners still take their own turns, as shown in Excerpt 9 from one of Sara's classes. After chiming in with the case particle and verb, Sara goes on to do a follow-up move:

(9) 1 G: Yeah. (.) Uchi no:[chikaku de
             Yeah. (.) near my house

     2 Sr: [O:h uchi no:: chikaku de:
                              O:h near my house:

     3 G: Watashi no uchi:: no uh chikaku de (.) uhh
             booringu:
             *Near my house bowling: ((G's sentence is correct so far,
             but is missing the accusative particle and verb)).*

→   4 Sr: o shimasu?
             ACC do? ((the verb 'to bowl' is 'booringu o shimasu'))

     5 G: Hai.
             Yes.

→   6   Sr: Ahh soo desu ka.
                  Oh really.

                                                    (Sara, 2/7)

Here, Sara helps G to complete the verb phrase, producing a vertical construction in which each interlocutor produces a part of the utterance, but no one repeats the whole utterance. Vertical constructions may facilitate language acquisition by allowing learners to participate in producing and comprehending utterances that are beyond their current level of ability.

Co-construction occurs not only when speaking, but also when reading aloud. In Excerpt 10, Kuo-ming and his partner M are reading a question from a worksheet. They are in the sixth week of instruction, so reading the Japanese syllabaries is still a challenge. The sentence they are reading is the following question:

Konbenshon sentaa no chika-ku ni donna tatemono ga arimasu ka
Convention center GEN near-adv DAT what building NOM exist INT
"What building(s) is (are) near the convention center?"

Excerpt 10 show how Kuo-ming and his partner M work to read the sentence aloud collaboratively:

(10)   1   M: Konbenshiyon sentaa::: no: chika-ku ni
                   Convention center:: GEN near-adv DAT
       2   Km: -taa no chika-ku [ni
                   -ter GEN near-adv DAT
       3   M: [Donna tatemono (.)
                                     what building(s) (.)
       4   Km: Desu ka? (.)[or don—tatemono ga arimas:u ka?
                   cop INT? (.) or wha- building NOM exist INT?
       5   M: [Donna
                               what
       6   M: Donn::a,
                   Wha::t,
       7   Km: Donna tatemono ga arimasu ka?
                   What building(s) NOM exist INT?
                                              (Kuo-ming, 11/18)

Prompting and co-construction are two methods of assistance provided as interlocutors attend to the ongoing interaction in the peer learning setting. As shown, learners use these methods to help the partner move ahead, or to complete what the partner has started. Sometimes co-construction becomes so mutual that a vertical construction is produced as learners work together to formulate sentences in the L2. Finally, partners also help each other by providing explanations—this will be discussed in the next section.

Assistance When a Peer Makes a Linguistic Error

In the classroom corpus, learner assistance occurs frequently during peer interactive tasks as students struggle to produce utterances in the L2. Learners help each other not only by waiting and allowing partners to complete their utterances and solve their own problems, or by providing assistance such as prompts or co-construction when the partner hesitates, but learners also help each other to correct linguistic errors. The least explicit method learners used to help one another with an error is to simply wait, as we saw in Excerpt 5. Learners also use prompting and co-construction to assist peers with linguistic errors, though examples are not shown here. Next turn repair initiators (NTRI) are used specifically to show the learner that something is wrong with the utterance, possibly pinpointing the error. NTRIs may be in the form of recasts, which are based semantically on the erroneous utterance, but expand or change it. Peers also correct their interlocutor's errors by using explanations or requests to the teacher for assistance.

NTRIs were used following peer errors, and were also triggered by the listener's difficulties with comprehension. Whatever triggers an NTRI, because it occurs in the turn subsequent to a learner error, the NTRI allows the learner time to reflect on the misformed utterance. Excerpt 11 is an example of an NTRI that follows an error in adjectival conjugation. Will, Candace's partner, uses the wrong method of marking past tense for an adjective, adding the past copula *deshita* to the adjective *tanoshii* 'fun' instead of inflecting the adjective from *tanoshi-i* 'is fun' to *tanoshi-katta* 'was fun.' Candace responds with an NTRI, and Will reformulates:

(11)	1	C:	Um Will-san uh: (.) Ko:ko: no uh koko no sensei (.) sensei (.) doo um deshita (.) sensei wa doo deshita ka?
			Um Will-san uh: (.) what were your high school teachers (.) teachers (.) like um (.) what were your teachers like?
	2	W:	Um (.) tanoshii deshita.
			Um (.) fun COP-past ((error))
→	3	C:	hm? hm?
→	4	W:	Tanoshi-te? (.) Tanoshi (.) te
			Fun-te? (.) Fun (.) te? ((error—tries to use another form, but is wrong))
	5	C:	Tano:shi-katta.
			Fu:n-past ((this is correct))

6   W: Tanoshi-katta desu
         Fun-past COP
7   C: Tanosh:
         *Fu:: ((Candace elongates the sound right where the past
         ending would be attached))*
8   W: Tanoshi-katta desu
         Fun-past COP

(Candace, 1/24)

Will's reformulation (line 4) is still incorrect, and Candace goes on to provide more explicit assistance in the form of a recast in line 5, a reformulation of Will's incorrect utterance. There is no way to clearly discern
whether Candace's line 3 NTRI is triggered by his linguistic error, or by
her own comprehension difficulties. Whatever the trigger, the NTRI has
an important function for Will because it provides him with an opportunity to reflect on and work to repair his own utterance, as well as to receive
further help from Candace in producing the correct form.

Learners not only initiate repair using NTRIs, but NTRIs may also provide a partial or more complete repair. In Excerpt 12, Candace's partner
S1 provides repair when Candace produces the wrong answer, misinter-
preting the picture on the worksheet. The worksheet shows someone
coughing, and Candace says he has a sore throat. Instead of providing the
entire correct answer initially, Candace's partner prompts her with the
first part of the correct utterance in the line 3 NTRI:

(12) 1   S1:   Doo shitan desu ka?
               What happened?
      2   C: (1) Wakarimasen. Nodo nodo ga itai n desu?
               (1) I don't understand. Throat throat NOM *painful* COP?
               Does he have a sore throat throat?
→   3   S1:   Goban?   [Uh seki ga (..) [
               Number five? uh cough NOM
      4   C: [Hai   [Seki ga?
                           Yes   *cough* NOM?
      5   S1:   Hai
               Yes
      6   C: Doko?
               Where?
      7   S1:   Deru n desu.
               comes out COP *((this completes the sentence seki ga
               derun desu, which means "he's coughing"))*

8   C: Hmm aahhh seki ga   (.) deru n des- deru derun desu.
            Hmm aahhh cough NOM *(.)comes out* COP- *comes out* COP.
                                            (Candace, 5/22)

When Candace can't figure out what S1 is referring to and asks for clarifi-
cation (lines 4 and 6), S1 provides the rest of the sentence in line 7.
Candace's repetition of the utterance in line 8 shows her understanding.
By at first prompting, and then providing further help when asked,
Candace's partner provides just the amount of assistance she needs.

NTRIs may provide repair in the form of a *recast* as well. Recasts, which
will be discussed in much more depth in chapter 4, provide a restatement
of all or part of the learner's utterance that reformulates that utterance,
while maintaining semantic content. Because recasts provide a semantic
bridge to the reformulated utterance, the form-related contrasts they
present are considered to be particularly salient to language learners. This
salience results from the reduced semantic load, which frees the learner's
processing capacity for consideration of linguistic form (see further discussion in chap. 4). Recasts are one type of overt correction that learners provide for each other. In Excerpt 13, Katie's false starts and use of the wrong
form are evidence of her difficulty. One of her group members recasts the
misformulated portion of Katie's utterance. Here, the learners are participating in a discussion task, in which they are to make suggestions about a
weekend activity, and then agree on which activity they would like to do
together. Katie, in line 3, has difficulty in formulating her utterance:

(13) 1   S1:   Tenisu ni shimasen ka?
                Tennis DAT *do-neg* INT
                Do you want to play tennis?
      2   S2:   Tenisu mo ii desu kedo (.) badminton ni shimasen ka?
                Tennis is good but (.) badminton DAT *do-neg* INT
                Tennis is good but (.) do you want to play badminton?
→   3   K: Badminton ii desu kedo::: (.) uh (.) basukettobooru ni
                shi- (.) or (.) basketball shi- shi- shite (   ).
                Badminton is good bu:::t (.) uh (.) Basketball DAT *do-* (.)
                *or (.) basketball do- do- do-*TE *(   ). ((Katie picks the
                wrong verb form))*
      4   S1:   Ni shimasen.
                DAT *do-neg.*
      5   K: Shimasen?
                Do-neg?
      6   S1:   Jaa. (I think we're supposed to pick one).
                Okay. (I think we're supposed to pick one).
                                            (Katie, 11/21)

Katie's partners, S1 and S2, begin the discussion, with S1 suggesting that they play tennis. S2's suggestion in line 2 builds on S1's utterance, adding a contrasting suggestion. This pattern was modeled by the teacher in the pretask activity. In line 3, Katie works to form a similar utterance, but has difficulty with the verb form in her suggestion in line 3. In line 4, S1 recasts the misformulated verb, adding the missing particle. Katie repeats the corrected verb in line 5. In another example, shown in Excerpt 14, Rob's partner says *yoji* 'four o'clock' instead of *yojikan* 'four hours', in line 8. Rob provides a recast in line 9, accompanied by question intonation.

(14) 1 R: Nanji goro nemasu ka?
             What time do you go to bed?

      2 S: Sanji goro desu
             At around 3 o'clock.

      3 R: Sanji goro desu? ((Surprised)) Nanji kan gurai nemasu ka?
             Around 3 o'clock? ((surprised)) How many hours do you sleep?

      4 S: (.) Moo ichi do itte kudasai?
             (.) Would you repeat that?

      5 R: San ji: kan gurai nemasu ka? (2) Na nan jikan gurai?
             Do you sleep about three hours? (2) About ho- how many hours do you sleep?

      6 S: Nan jikan gurai?
             About how many hours?

      7 R: (.) Well you said you're going to bed around three (.) how long are you going to sleep?

→   8 S: (.) Ah. (.) Yo yoji yoji gurai
             (.) Ah. (.) four- about four o'clock.

→   9 R: Yoji kan ha- yoji kan gurai?
             Four hours ha- about four hours?

→   10 S: Yoji kan gurai desu.
             I sleep for about four hours

     11 R: Ah: soo desu ka?
             Oh really?

             (Rob, 1/24)

Rob's line 9 NTRI functions both to initiate and complete repair. Rob's partner does not simply accept Rob's other correction, but incorporates the recast into his own line 10 utterance. Rob then continues by showing interest in his partner's response. Other examples of recasts are shown in chapter 4, which provides a learner-centered perspective on corrective feedback.

Asking for One's Partner

Another way students may handle problems that crop up during class is to ask the teacher for help. When pair and group tasks are used, learners ask for help not only for themselves, but also on behalf of their interlocutors. Learners ask the teacher about discrepancies between their performance and their interlocutor's or about their interlocutor's errors. Asking the teacher results in the provision of explicit explanation or other assistance to the peer. This also helps the learner who notices the problem and receives confirmation that their hunch was correct, as well as receiving further information regarding the item in question. In fact, in each of the cases in the data where a learner asks a teacher about a peer's error, the learner turns out to be correct. A good example of this was shown earlier (Table 3.1 and Excerpt 2), where we saw Kuo-ming's partner, F, ask the teacher about how particles should be used, resulting both in clarification for F and in useful grammatical information for Kuo-ming.

In another example, Andrea notices that her partner, S, is inserting particles where Andrea thinks they might not be necessary. Andrea and S are making sentences following prompts on a worksheet. The lesson contrasts the expressions *dake* and *shika*, both of which mean 'only', but which contrast in that *shika* exhibits negative concord, requiring a negative verb. When working on a task using *shika* 'only', Andrea notices that her partner repeatedly and incorrectly uses the accusative particle *o* along with *shika*. The incorrect case-marking particles are underlined in Excerpt 15. S's line 3 error is one she has made repeatedly. In line 4, Andrea tentatively points out the problem by asking S a question, and in line 5, S responds that she is not sure how she should construct the sentence. In line 6, Andrea declares her intention to ask the teacher:

(15)　1　S:　So doyoobi mo nichiyoobi mo
　　　　　　　So on Saturday and on Sunday also

　　　2　A:　Dekakeru? dekakemasu ka?
　　　　　　　Go out? Do you go out?

　　　3　S:　Anoo nichiyoobi:: (.) nichiyoobi <u>o::</u> <u>shika</u> um dekakemasen.
　　　　　　　Um Sunday:: (.) Sunday <u>ACC only</u> um don't go out.
　　　　　　　I don't go out but on Sunday ((incorrect use of accusative particle))

→　　4　A:　But for not- not for all of them do we use a: (.) particle, right?
　　　　　　　[When you answer it? [

　　　5　S:　[Um- that's- I- (.)　　[I don't know. (.) what we're supposed to do.

→ 6 A: I'm gonna ask.
   7 S: Or do you say "nichiyoobi shika dekimasen".
        Or do you say Sunday only can do
        Or do you say "I can't do it but on Sunday" ((this is correct—
        S does not include the accusative particle))
→ 8 A: Sensei::? ((this means 'teacher')) I was just wondering.
        For each of these when you answer, is there always
        a particle? (.) Is there always a particle when you
        answer like, nichiyoobi <u>o uh shika</u> dekakeraremasen?
              Sunday <u>ACC uh only</u> can go out
        ((A incorrectly includes the accusative particle))?
   9 T: Ah
  10 A: [Dekakemasen.
        Don't go out
  11 T: [nichiyoobi shika dekakemasen. No particle.
        I don't go out but on Sunday. No particle.
  12 A: No particles? 'Cause some of them don't have, don't
        have particles. Okay. (..) Dekake:masen. (..)
              Don't go out.

                                   (Andrea, 4/18)

After saying she is going to ask the teacher in line 6, Andrea's partner proposes another sentence in line 7—one without the accusative particle *o*. This proposal is, in fact, correct. The learner's line 7 reformulation shows her attentiveness to candidate forms. She is already reflecting on her own misformed utterance, and proposes the correct solution. S, then, is well prepared to hear what the teacher has to say in response to Andrea's line 8 question. Andrea also benefits from her question to the teacher. She makes an additional error of her own as she repeats the misformulated utterance, using an unnecessary additional inflection—*rare*- when she conjugates the verb *dekakemasen* 'can't go out'. She catches her error in line 10 just as the teacher begins to reformulate the utterance. In the second line of turn 11, Andrea repeats the verb that she had difficulty with, elongating the vowel at the point where she misinserted the inflection. Andrea's question to the teacher results not only in assistance for her partner, but confirms for Andrea something she was not quite sure of, while giving her an opportunity to try out a verb form and hear confirmation of her reformulation from the teacher.

Although peer interaction stimulates partners to seek help for their interlocutors when they are not sure what is correct, in large classes the teacher is not always readily accessible. Learners are not always able to ask the teacher their questions during the class period. When the teacher is not available, the process of helping another may still enable students who help to gain awareness of the status of their own knowledge, and of what they are uncertain of. Using the L2 in peer learning tasks provides a context for students to confirm their knowledge and discover their deficiencies. The act of providing help to a peer may trigger the helpers' attention to their own language, as shown in Excerpt 16. Mary, in line 2, is working to say "beautiful friend," but is having difficulty. In line 3, Sara steps in with candidate particles and discovers that she herself is not sure which particle to use:

(16) 1 S: Ano: sumimasen M-san no (.) tomodachi:: (.) wa (.)
                 donna: (.) donna hito: desu ka
                 Um: excuse me! What kind (.) of friends (.) do (.) you have?
       2 M: Watashi no tomodachi wa, (.) kirei to, (.) um-
                 My friend is, (.) beautiful ((error: particle)), (.) um-
→   3 S: Kirei no hi-   //Kirei na hito I think.
                 Beautiful GEN per- Beautiful COP person I think.
                 ((error: S first picks the wrong particle, but self-corrects))
       4 M: Kirei na hito   Kirei na hi[to.
                 Beautiful COP person Beautiful COP person
                 Beautiful person   Beautiful person ((correct
                 particle use))
       5 S: [Right.
       6 M: Soshite:,
→   7 S: I'll make sure.

                                                    (Sara, 10/23)

What Mary is reaching for in line 2 is the expression *kirei na hito* 'beautiful COP person'. Sara, in line 3, provides assistance, first saying *kirei no* 'beautiful GEN', which is incorrect, and then self-correcting to *kirei na hito* 'beautiful COP person', which is correct. Sara's self-correction overlaps with Mary's statement of the same phrase, which Mary repeats following the overlap. Sara, however, still is not sure. This is evident from her line 7 utterance, "I'll make sure." Sara does not ask the teacher during the class period, but by helping another, Sara clarifies what she is and is not certain of, providing a way for her to track her progress. This result, that assisting a peer triggers the student's desire to find out for herself, is also seen in the classes of other students. For example, Kuo-ming and Andrea both asked the teacher about discrepancies they noticed between their own and their partners' performance. By asking the teacher about a peer's error, these students both assist their partners and benefit themselves.

Explaining

The students in the classroom corpus also assisted one another by providing explanations when a fellow student was having difficulty. We saw this occur in Excerpt 15. Before Andrea asked the teacher for help, she tried to explain the problem to her partner by asking her partner about the misformulation. Learners provide explanations when an interlocutor makes linguistic errors, including errors in word choice. In Excerpt 17, the learners are playing the roles of secretaries from different companies who are describing their boss's activities that day. This requires use of humble verb forms because the interlocutor is not an employee of the same company. In line 1 of Excerpt 17, Katie chooses an inappropriate word to explain that her "boss" in the role play went to the university. Her partner, P, initiates repair in line 2::

(17) 1 K: Ah kuji (.) ( ) uh:: (.) daigaku (3) eh (.) uh (.) ni: ^
(.) orimashita.
Ah at nine o'clock (.) ( ) uh (.) (3) eh (.) uh (.) he was (.) at the university.

→ 2 P: Orimashita? (3) Orimashita is be located (.) Is it ittekimasu?
(("ittekimasu" means "go and return", and is used to mean "go" in Japanese when the one who goes will return home or to the office afterward))

3 (3)

4 K: Oru?
Be located?

→ 5 P: Mairimasu?
Go? ((humble form))

(Katie, 10/24)

Katie's partner waits through a 3-second pause in Katie's utterance in line 1, as well as through other shorter pauses, allowing Katie to finish her sentence. After Katie finishes, her partner initiates repair with an NTRI, repeating the word *orimashita* with question intonation. Although the word is appropriately humble (*oru* is the humble equivalent of the word *iru*, which means 'to exist'), it sounds a bit odd juxtaposed with other verbs that all describe the boss' activities. When Katie does not respond, her partner explains the meaning of *orimashita* as indicating location. She then suggests an alternative, *ittekimasu*, which means 'to go and return.' This would be an appropriate choice, but it is not a humble verb. Katie counters with the citation form of *orimashita*, which is *oru*. In line 6, Katie's partner then suggests *mairimasu*, which is an humble verb meaning 'go', and is the most appropriate choice yet. In this instance, Katie's partner explains the meaning of a word and suggests more appropriate choices. Learners explain not only the meanings of words, but also grammatical structures. And, they also explain task-related procedures when their partners have difficulty in deciding what a task requires.

Other Means of Support

Learners provide each other with a range of assistance during peer learning tasks, from waiting, thereby allowing their partners to finish their utterances and self-correct, to initiating repair, completing repair, prompting, chiming in with co-construction, and explaining. In addition to giving and receiving assistance from peers, there are other ways that learners receive support during task performance. Learners, as active participants in the classroom setting, capitalize on the affordances available in that setting and find help when they need it. They even manage to obtain help from classmates who may not be intentionally providing assistance. In the next section, the impact of *overhearing* and *language play* will be examined.

Overhearing as a Resource for Learner Performance

Although learners collaborate with one another in pair or group interaction, their pairs or groups function alongside those of other students who are simultaneously doing the same tasks. The participation status (Goffman, 1974) of learners includes not only the roles of speakers and listeners in their own pairs or groups, but also the role of "overhearer" (Bell, 1984) of what occurs in neighboring groups. And, in the process of overhearing, learners may find a source of linguistic support. The corpus contains examples like Excerpt 18, where learners make use of language that is overheard. Student B (which stands for "background") is part of a neighboring pair. B is not working with Sara and her partner John, but her voice was clearly recorded on Sara and John's microphone. These background utterances are shown in boldface type.

(18)	1	Sr:	Ah John-san wa dooshite atama ga itai n desu ka?
			Ah John why do you have a headache?
	2	**B:**	**U::::m ((female student clearly audible in the background))**
	3	J:	Ahh eto
			Ah um
	4	Sr:	Osake:: (.)
			Wine:: (.)
	5	**B:**	**U::::m**
	6	J:	Osake o:
			Wine ACC:
	7	**B:**	**Nenakatta:**
			Didn't slee:p
	8	Sr:	Ahaha (.) nonda::
			Ahaha(.) drank::

→   9 B: **Kara**
             So
→   10 J: Nonda kara. (.) osake o nonda kara nomimasu (.)
             doo shimasu
             drank so. (.) I drank wine so drink (.) what should I do
→   11 Sr: Takusan osake o nonda kara::, hm atama ga itai n desu
             You drank a lot of wine so::, hm you have a headache.
                                                      (Sara, 5/22)

When John has difficulty getting started with his answer in line 3, Sara suggests a vocabulary word, *osake* 'Japanese wine' in line 4. John uses this word in line 6. John does not continue, and in line 8, Sara provides the verb as well. In line 9, the conjunction *kara* 'because' is then uttered by student B, speaking in the background, who is formulating the sentence *nenakatta kara* 'because I didn't sleep'. Then, in line 10, John incorporates *kara* into his utterance. First he completes the verb phrase, and then tries to complete the whole sentence. He has difficulty, though, and asks Sara for help at the end of line 10. In line 11, Sara recasts John's line 10 utterance, appropriately incorporates *kara*, and completes the sentence appropriately. For John, a potential source of *kara* in line 10 is B's line 9 utterance. Excerpt 19 provides an example where overhearing is credited by a learner as a source of language; Andrea explicitly talks about using overheard language. Here, the task is a description and drawing task. One student describes a drawing projected from an overhead projector (a picture of a man wearing a scarf, shirt, jacket, and slacks), while a peer partner, who faces away from to the screen, listens to the description and draws a picture. A is Andrea, and B (background) is a male student sitting by Andrea who is working with a different partner. The repeated elements in the Japanese are underlined.

(19)   **1 B:**   <u>**Sukaafu ga arimasu**</u>
                   There is a scarf
       2 A: Sorekara hehehe <u>sukaafu ga</u> haha <u>arimasu</u>. (.) anoo
                <u>nekutai</u> wa uh
                And then hehehehe there is a scarf. (.) uh necktie TOP *uh*
       3 B: <u>**Sutoraipu no nekutai::**</u>
                   Striped necktie
       4 A: <u>Sutraipu no</u> hehehehe (.) diagonal no stripe ga
                arimasu kedo shiroi to kuroi desu. Sorekara::
                Striped hehehehe (.) There's a diagonal stripe but it's black and white. And then::
       5 B: <u>**Shiroi no shatsu::**</u>
                   White GEN *shirt:: ((error: particle 'no' shouldn't be used))*

6 A: <u>Shiroi no shatsu</u> ga oh ^
         White GEN shirt:: ((error: particle 'no' shouldn't be used))
7 **B: Kiteimasu**
         Is wearing
8 A: Kiteimasu. I'm just saying everything you say.
         Uh sorekara suutsu ga::
         *Is wearing. I'm just saying everything you say. Uh and then
         suit NOM::*
9 **B: Jaketto::**
         Jacket::
10 A: Oh I'll just do that. <u>Jaketto::</u>
         Oh I'll just do that. Jacket::
11 **B: Pantsu:**
         Pants
12 A: <u>Jaketto</u> o ha ^ a <u>kiteimasu</u>. Sorekara <u>pantsu</u> o:: (.)
         pantsu o haiteimasu. Suutsu ga arimasu. Hai. Sorekara
         kutsu wa kutsu o hameteimasu. Kutsu wa kuroi desu.
         *He's wearing a jacket. And then pants ACC (.) he's wearing
         pants. And there's a suit. Yeah. And then shoes TOP he's
         wearing ((error: wrong verb)) shoes. The shoes are black.*
13 **B: Pantsu:: o haiteimasu.**
         He's wearing pants.
                                                        (Andrea, 5/16)

Andrea builds her own utterances by incorporating what she overhears.
She explicitly refers to borrowing B's utterances in lines 8 and 10. When B
falls silent in line 11, Andrea continues unassisted.

Language Play: Another Source of Support

Another source of assistance for learners is language play. In the corpus,
language play occurs as playful manipulation of the L2 during interaction.
Banter in the L2 is not common in the corpus, but has power for language
learning when it occurs. In the next episode, language-related teasing and
laughter resulted in an increased focus on pronunciation that raised Sara's
awareness of her own production in a positive way. In interaction between
Sara and her partner Mary, Sara's habit of lengthening vowels as she mulls
over which adjective ending or particle she should use results in a playful
episode involving deliberate distortion of vowel length, as a result of
Mary's imitation of Sara. This distortion has its origins in the difficulties of
Japanese adjectival conjugation, which have been explained. Japanese
prenominal adjectivals present an "either–or" decision. In prenominal
position, adjectives can be placed directly in front of the noun, a charac-

TABLE 3.4
Prenominal Forms of Adjectives and Adjectival Nouns in Japanese

Adjectival type	Adjectival	Prenominal Use
Adjective	furui 'old'	furui e 'old painting'
Adjectival Noun	yuumei 'famous'	yuumei na e 'famous painting'

teristic they share with verbs. Adjectival nouns are nounlike in that they re-quire that a particle be inserted between the adjectival noun and the noun. While the genitive particle *no* is used when a noun modifies another noun, the copular form *na* is used when an adjectival noun is in prenominal posi-tion. Table 3.4 shows the choices involved. When the adjective *furui* 'old' is placed before the noun *e* 'painting', the particle *na* is not inserted. But *na* must be inserted when an adjectival noun like *yuumei* 'famous' is placed in prenominal position. When faced with a choice such as this, some students lengthen a syllable prior to the *choice point*—a syllable prior to the point where they must make commitment. Sara does this frequently in class when prenominal use of adjectives and adjectival nouns is taught con-nected to the topic of describing rooms in a home. One task presented for both teacher-fronted and peer practice is an interview task. In this task, students must ask for descriptive information about their partner's rooms and belongings. The target structure used in both teacher-fronted and peer interaction is shown:

　name -san no 　　　noun wa donna 　　　noun desu ka?

　name -title GEN 　　noun TOP what-sort-of noun COP INT?

What sort of noun is your noun ?

In Excerpt 20, Sara answers her partner Russ' questions. In this and the related excerpts that follow, the adjectivals used are underlined, as well as the particle *na* where it is inserted after adjectival nouns. Note Sara's elon-gation of vowels (indicated by colons) in the adjectivals she uses in lines 2 and 10:

(20) 　1 　R: 　Uh, Sara-san no e wa donna e desu ka.
　　　　　　　　Uh, Sara, what is your painting like ((literally, "What sort
　　　　　　　　of painting is your painting"))?

→ 　2 　Sr: 　(2) Oh Watashi no e wa: yuumei:: na e desu ka. Uh
　　　　　　　　e desu. Sorry. (2) Russ san no e? (.) Russ-san no e wa:
　　　　　　　　donna e desu ka. Uh
　　　　　　　　(2) Oh! My painting is a fa::mous painting? Uh painting.
　　　　　　　　Sorry. (2) And Russ, your painting? (.) What is your
　　　　　　　　painting like?

      3   R: Boku no e wa <u>furui</u> e desu.
                  My painting is an old painting
      4   Sr: ((laughs)) What
      5   R: <u>Furui.</u>
                  Old?
      6   Sr: <u>Fu-furu:?</u>
                  O- o::l?
      7   R: Furui, old. ((laughs))
      8   S: Hahaha. Well? Could be- (.) could be interesting.
                hmhahm. U:::m
      9   R: Sara-san (.) no tokei wa donna tokei desu ka.
                  Sara (.) What is your watch like?
→   10   Sr: To:kei::. (.) Ah. Watashi no (.) tokei wa (.) <u>sute::ki na</u>
                to- tokei desu.
                  Wa:tch::. (.) Ah. My watch (.) is a (.) <u>ni:::ce</u> wa- watch.
                                                              (Sara, 10/23)

In line 2, Sara lengthens the last syllable of *yuumei* 'famous', and in line 10
she elongates the "e" in *suteki* 'nice', appropriately inserting *na* in both
cases, since these are both adjectival nouns. Sara is not the only student in
this class who lengthens vowels in these adjectival nouns. Another student
in the same class, Kara, does the same thing in teacher-fronted practice, as
shown in Excerpt 21. In this excerpt, the teacher has asked the class to ask
Kara what her desk is like:

      (21) 1   Cls: Kara-san no tsukue wa donna tsukue desu ka?
                         Kara, what is your desk like?
            2   T: Hai.
                         Right.
→   3   K: Watashi no tsukue wa (.) um, (.) <u>kirei</u> tsukue- <u>kirei::</u>
                       <u>na</u> tsukue desu.
                         My desk is a (.) um, (.) pretty des- <u>pre::ty</u> desk.
                                                              (Sara, 10/23)

In line 3, at first Kara does not at first elongate the final vowel in *kirei*, the
adjectival noun, which means "beautiful." But, when she works to self-
correct her error, she elongates the vowel at the choice point, showing the
cognitive effort involved in considering whether or not *na* needs to be inserted.

Sara elongates vowels both overtly, as shown in Excerpt 20, and covertly, in private speech. In Excerpt 22, the teacher has asked Sara to ask
Lee, who is seated across the room from her, what the window in his room
is like. After asking Lee the question, as he struggles, Sara whispers the answer to herself in private speech.

(22)   1   Sr: Lee-san no:: (.) Lee-san no mado wa, (.) uh, donna
                 mado desu ka.
                 Lee-san, (.) What is your window (.) what is your window
                 like?
       2   L: Uh, watashi no-
                 Uh, my-
       3   Sr: ((whispers)) °mado°.
                 °Window°
       4   L: (.)
       5   T: Watashi no mado?
                 My window?
       6   L: Watashi no mado wa?
                 My window TOP?
       7   Sr: Wa?
                 TOP? (topic marker *wa*)
       8   T: Wa.
                 TOP.
       9   L: Wa,
                 TOP,
      10   T: <u>Kirei</u>
                 Beautiful
→   11   Sr: °<u>Kirei</u>:: mado desu.°
                 °Is a <u>beau:::tiful</u> window°° ((Error: the particle 'na' is
                 omitted))
      12: L: (.)
      13   T: <u>Kirei na</u> mado desu. Hai. Hai, watashi no mado? (.)
                 Hai, itte kudasai
                 Is a <u>beautiful</u> window. Okay. Okay, my window? (.)
                 Okay, please repeat ((The teacher includes the particle
                 'na'))
      14   T/L: Watashi no mado: (.) wa kirei na mado desu.
                 My window (.) is a beautiful window.

                                                         (Sara, 10/23/96)

Sara asks the question in line 1. Lee has difficulty forming the sentence,
and receives help from the teacher in lines 4 and 10. Sara, meanwhile,
provides her own vicarious responses in lines 3 and 11. In line 11, she
elongates the final vowel of *kirei*, making the incorrect choice not to insert
na. In line 12, there is a pause—Lee does not respond to the teacher's line
10 prompt. The teacher then provides the correct response in line 13 (underlined), and asks Lee to repeat after her.

Sara lengthens vowels again in Excerpt 23. First, in line 2, she fails to
use *na* where she should, but in line 4, inserts the particle as appropriate
with a different adjectival noun. In line 8, she repeats her line 2 response,

including *na* as appropriate. Vowels in *rippa* 'splendid' are lengthened as shown in the indicated lines.

(23)   1   T: Soshite::: Martin Luther King ga arimasu ka?
                        And:::: ((do you have an adjective for)) Martin Luther
                        King?
→   2   Sr: <u>Ri::pa</u> hito.
                        Sple::ndid person. ((Error: particle 'na' is omitted))
        3   T: Ehto, ma. Yuumei, (.) hai. Yuumei,
                        Well, okay. Famous, (.) yes. Famous,
        4   Sr: <u>Yuumei</u> na hito
                        A famous person! ((Particle 'na' is included))
        5   T: Hai. Clinton-san wa watashi no tomodachi desu.
                        Ja, Watashi no tomodachi wa, donna hito desu ka?
                        Yes. (President) Clinton is my friend. So, what kind of
                        person is my friend?
        6   Ss/Sr: Yuumei na hito desu.
                        He's a famous person.
        7   T: Soshite,
                        And,
→   8   Sr: <u>Ri::pa</u> na hito desu.
                        He's a sple::ndid person.((The particle 'na' is included))
                                                                                  (Sara, 10/23/96)

In both line 2 and line 8, indicated with arrows, Sara elongates a vowel in the word *rippa* 'splendid'. The first time, she makes the wrong choice, failing to insert *na*. The teacher accepts her answer for its meaning, suggesting a different word in line 3 without correcting the grammatical error. When Sara says *rippa* again in line 8, she again lengthens the vowel as she considers her options, this time selecting *na* as appropriate. In confidently exclaiming *"Yuumei na hito"* 'a famous person' in line 4, Sara does not elongate any vowels in *yuumei* 'famous', revealing her certainty.

All of these examples show how Sara, like Kara and other learners in the class, tends to lengthen vowels in the adjectivals she uses, with the lengthening occurring at the point where she must consider whether or not to insert *na*. In pair practice, Sara's partner, Mary, who does not elongate vowels when she uses adjectivals, begins to play with vowel length, a process that raises Sara's awareness of her own language use. Mary's playful teasing of Sara increases the salience of vowel length for Sara. In Excerpt 24, Sara asks Mary about her apartment:

(24)   1   Sr: Mary-san no apaato (.) uh Mary-san no apaato (.)
                        apaato wa uh (.) donna apaato desu ka

Your apartment (.) uh Mary, your apartment (.) what is
your apartment (.) like?

→ 2 M: Watashi no apaato wa <u>semai</u> apaato desu.
My apartment is a <u>small</u> apartment.

(Sara, 10/23/96)

Mary uses the adjective *semai* 'small' in her line 2 answer, and does not lengthen any vowels. This is typical for Mary. In Excerpt 25, when Sara answers Mary's question, she lengthens one of the vowels in *chiisai* 'small', in line 3. When Mary imitates Sara in line 6, laughter and sound play ensues:

(25) 1 M: Sara-san n[o:- (.) Sara san no:: terebi wa donna
terebi desu ka,
Sara,   (.) What is your television like?,

2 Sr: [heee ((laughter))

→ 3 Sr: Watashi no terebi:, (.) Watashi no terebi <u>chiisa::i</u>
terebi desu.
My televison,   (.) My television is a <u>sma:::l</u>
television. ((Errors: leaves out topic marker. Also
exaggerates vowel length))

4 M: Aa soo desu ka.
Oh really

5 Sr: ((laughs)) Mary-san no terebi ((laughter)) donna
terebi desu ka?
((laughs)) Mary, what is your ((laughter)) television like?

→ 6 M: Watashi no terebi wa <u>ookii:::</u> terebi desu.
My television is a <u>bi:::g</u> television. ((M includes the topic
marker, and exaggerates the vowel length of the adjective))

7 S/M: ((laughing))

→ 8 M: Sos[hite, (.) <u>ii::::</u>
An [d,   (.) goo::d

9 Sr: [Hhehehe

→ 10 Sr: <u>Ii::::</u> terebi desu.
it's a <u>goo::::d</u> television.

(Sara, 10/23)

In line 1, Mary asks Sara about her television. Sara's response that her television is small, *chiisai*, contains an elongated vowel *chiisa::i* 'small' (line 3). Then, when Sara asks Mary about her television, Mary describes it as *ookii:::* 'large', with exaggerated lengthening of the final vowel, resulting in mutual laughter by both students in line 7. Mary goes on, in line 8, to describe her television as good, *ii:::::*, making the vowel even longer. Sara imitates Mary's pronunciation in line 10. This play continues for 19 more lines of transcript, with all of the adjectivals similarly distorted. This sound play is accompanied by mutual laughter throughout. Vowel lengthening, previously indicative of Sara's cognitive effort, becomes a focus of sound play. Through this, Sara gains conscious control over vowel length. What was previously unconscious—that she was lengthening vowel sounds in the adjectivals she used—becomes manipulable in play.

After pair practice, the teacher calls on the students to ask them about what they learned from their partners. During this activity, Sara uses adjectivals three times, never elongating vowels. An example is given in Excerpt 26:

> (26) 1 T: Jaa ano:: Sara-san? (.) Sara-san? Mary-san no: (.)
> tomodachi wa donna hito desu ka. Otoko no hito?
> Onna no hito?
> *Jaa uh:: Sara? (.) Sara? What are Mary's (.) friends*
> *like? Are they men? Women?*
>
> 2 Sr: Mary-san no tomodachi wa (.) uh: (.) °forgot.°
> *Mary's friends are (.) uh: (.) °forgot.°((includes topic*
> *marker))*
>
> 3 T: Aa, kikimasen?
> *Aa, you didn't ask?*
>
> → 4 Sr: Hhahe Iie- iie tomodachi (.) ii (.) um ii tomodachi
> desu.
> *No- no her friends (.) are good (.) um good friends.*
> *((Error: topic marker omitted)).*
>
> (Sara, 10/23)

In line 4, she describes Mary's friends as good, *ii*, and does not elongate the vowel. What began as a cognitive strategy of Sara's—to elongate a vowel in a cognitively demanding situation—became the focus of language play in Mary and Sara's pair practice. Mary's teasing changes Sara's use of the lengthened vowel from being a by-product of her cognitive effort, to being a deliberate focus of play. Through this process, Sara's level of control over vowel length increased. Her awareness of how her pronunciation was distorted is evident in the laughter and mutual exaggeration that occurred in play. Sara's increase in control is evident in that, whereas she lengthened vowels prior to the language play episode and exaggerates lengthening during the episode, she stops lengthening vowels following the episode. Mary's participation in this playful teasing process clearly had a facilitative effect, stimulating Sara to focus on her pronunciation of the adjectives. This playful episode engaged Sara in a process through which her attention was focused and channeled, enhancing her awareness and control of her own language production.

DO LEARNERS PICK UP EACH OTHER'S ERRORS?

Qualitative examination of the corpus reveals the benefits of the peer interactive language learning tasks used to far outweigh any problems that emerge.[1] That is the reason that this chapter has, thus far, focused on the benefits of peer assistance. We have looked at how peer interaction during developmentally appropriate tasks in and of itself facilitates language development through a pooling of expertise that is enabled by the way attentional resources are applied in peer learning, and we have examined examples of the different ways learners provide help to one another. Now, let us look at some quantitative evidence.

The focus of this chapter is on the positive role of peer assistance. The question remains as to whether peer interaction might also have negative effects. We see how learners err in their language use—do these errors provide an inappropriate language environment for the peer partner? Do peers pick up each other's errors? In addition, although the assistance provided from learner to learner is overwhelmingly correct and helpful, what about cases in which learners pass along erroneous information? Does assistance from learner to learner ever promote the use of inaccurate L2 forms? These questions are not new. Early studies of peer interaction in the interactionist tradition incidentally claimed that learners, in fact, do not pick up each other's errors (see, e.g., Porter, 1986). However, more recent studies present evidence to the contrary. One classroom case study found that learners may retain erroneous information when they negotiate and settle on an incorrect form (Swain & Lapkin, 1998). And a recent laboratory study found that non-native subjects performing information gap tasks repeated certain types of errors of their non-native interlocutors (Mackey, McDonough, & Kim, 1999).

This question is, however, a difficult one to investigate, and is not resolved by these previous studies. Difficulties are presented because it is impossible to know, even when an error seems to be "picked up" from an interlocutor, whether or not the error was truly caused by the interlocutor's influence, or whether the learner would have made the same error anyway. In addition, these studies, although useful, used intermediate to advanced level learners and tasks that did not provide any linguistic focus. These results, therefore, tell us little about how lower level learners working on more structurally oriented tasks are potentially impacted by an interlocutor's errors.

Mackey et al. (1999) acknowledged the difficulties of this kind of inquiry in their laboratory study of non-native–non-native interaction. In their study, intermediate ESL learners were paired in order to investigate

---

[1]See chapter 6 for a discussion of tasks which were not productive, and of task implementation and design features which may work against language development.

whether or not the subjects would repeat each other's errors. The subjects, eight intermediate ESL learners, performed two tasks—a description task, and an information gap "spot the difference" task. They limited their investigation to just a few types of easily defined errors: indefinite article errors, plural errors, and lexical (vocabulary) errors. They used the term *incorporation* to indicate peer repetition of an interlocutor error. This term implies that the source of the error is the interlocutor. However, the authors emphasized that they could not establish that the source of the repeated errors was the peer interlocutor. For indefinite article and plural use, in fact, it was actually more common for learners to make errors than to use either correctly. The researchers were unable to determine whether these errors were caused by interlocutor error or whether they coincidentally occurred. The clearest cases were those involving lexical errors, which were uncommon in the data. In reporting Mackey et al.'s (1999) results in Table 3.5, therefore, I use the neutral term *repetition* rather than the term *incorporation*. The researchers found that for these types of errors the peer interlocutor subsequently, whether immediately or later in the same task, made the same error 19% to 27% of the time.

These numbers, however, cannot be simply generalized to other settings of L2 use. What about learners who are performing interactive tasks designed to provide learners with an opportunity to use forms and vocabulary practiced previously in class? Peer interactive tasks embedded in the curriculum of a language class might include a linguistic focus that was not part of Mackey et al's (1999) study. And, what about learners at lower levels of language proficiency? Mackey et al.'s ESL learners were highly proficient compared to foreign language learners in the first 2 years of language study. In order to understand the extent to which the seven learners in the classroom corpus repeated the errors of their interlocutors, language use in peer interactive tasks were analyzed. Errors were classified as shown in Table 3.6. Errors by the seven targeted learners and their peer interlocutors were examined. In this process, what happened following each error was noted, and a set of categories was developed. These categories are shown in Table 3.7. Each episode of an error was categorized in

TABLE 3.5
Peer Repetition of Interlocutor Errors With Indefinite Article,
Plural Noun, and Lexicon by Non-Native ESL Learners

	Immediate Repetition	*Subsequent Repetition*	*Both*	*Total*
Indefinite article errors	9%	6%	4%	19%
Plural noun errors	9%	4%	9%	22%
Lexical errors	23%	3%	0	26%

Note. Data from Mackey et al., 1999.

TABLE 3.6
Types of Errors Found in Peer Interaction in the Classroom Corpus

Grammatical particle errors	Errors in grammatical particle choice, omission, or inclusion
Affective particle errors	Errors in affective particle choice, omission, or inclusion
Verb errors	Errors with verb inflection (including negation errors) or tense used
Adjective errors	Errors with adjective inflection, errors resulting from confusion between adjectival nouns, adjectives, and nouns and errors related to adjectival negation and tense
Lexical errors	Word choice errors
Pronunciation errors	Errors in pronunciation
	Use of English in place of the L2 was not counted, but pronunciation of borrowings characterized by a mixture of L2 and English-like phonology was included in this category.
Other	Word order problems, generally garbled syntax, and other errors which did not fit in the other categories.

TABLE 3.7
Results of Learner Errors

Immediate other-repetition of error	In the turn following a peer error, the interlocutor repeats the same error.
Subsequent other-repetition of error	Later during the same task, the interlocutor makes the same error a peer made earlier. (In the instance where immediate repetition had also occurred, the episode was coded as "subsequent").
Self-correction	The learner who made the initial error self-corrects within the next turn or two.
Other-correction	The interlocutor provides corrective feedback (usually a recast) to the learner who made the initial error in the next turn or two. The learner does not self-correct.
Other-correction with self-correction	After other-correction, the learner who made the initial error self-corrects.
Subsequently used correctly, "self"	The learner who made the initial error later uses the form correctly.
Subsequently used correctly, "other"	The interlocutor who witnessed the initial error later uses the form correctly. This includes cases where the interlocutor previously repeated the error.
Correct then incorrect	A learner first uses a form correctly, and then incorrectly.
Error apparently ignored	The error is made, but there is no repetition by the interlocutor, no self/other-correction, and no subsequent use of the error by the learners.

TABLE 3.8
Peer Repetition of Interlocutor Errors During Peer
Interactive Tasks in the Classroom Corpus

| | Total Errors | Other-Repetition | | |
		Immediate	Subsequent	Total
Bryce and peers	24		1	1
Katie and peers	35	2	1	3
Andrea and peers	47	5		5
Candace and peers	58	3		3
Sara and peers	22	1		1
Rob and peers	49	4	1	5
Kuo-ming and peers	10	1		1
Totals	245	16	2	19
Percentages		6.53%	1.22%	7.76%

one of these categories, according to what transpired following the error. The results of this examination were tabulated for two categories—*immediate repetition* and *subsequent repetition*. These results are shown in Table 3.8. Compared to Mackey et al.'s (1999) results, repetition of interlocutor errors was strikingly less frequent in the classroom corpus. These differences may be due to a range of factors. The learners' levels, the setting, and the tasks all differed from those in the earlier study. In addition, most of the tasks in the classroom corpus had some linguistic focus and often included pretask practice with the forms being learned. In addition, supporting materials, whether notes on the blackboard, prepared handouts, or overhead transparencies were used, providing a source from which learners could "mine" language for use in the interactive tasks (Samuda, in press). It appears that, in these classrooms, the potential harm that might be caused by learners "picking up" each other's errors is far outweighed by the benefit of peer interaction.

Swain and Lapkin (1998) brought up another question regarding the repetition of interlocutor errors that occurs in learner–learner interaction. What happens when learners negotiate a form and collaboratively agree on an erroneous form through the negotiation process? Swain and Lapkin (1998) presented what resulted when one pair of middle-school French immersion students did an interactive writing task in class. Swain and Lapkin found that although the vast majority of form-related negotiations resulted in correct French usage, when the pair of learners collaboratively agreed on an incorrect form, the incorrect form was used by the two students on a subsequent post-test. This was a clear case of incorporation. Contrary to Swain and Lapkin's case study, however, in the classroom corpus learners rarely haggled over forms. Swain and Lapkin's two learners were far advanced compared to the learners in the classroom corpus, and worked on a task that did not present a linguistic focus. In addition, the teacher in Swain and Lapkin's study did not intervene while the learners did the task. In contrast to Swain and Lapkin's findings for the pair and task they studied, the 34-hour classroom corpus does not contain any examples of learners collaboratively agreeing on an incorrect form. Rather, when there was uncertainty, learners worked out problems (a) by helping each other, (b) by referring to instructional materials (for example, a verb conjugation pattern on an overhead transparency or a schematic sentence structure on a worksheet), or (c) by asking the teacher for assistance. The form focus of the activities and the ready availability of the teacher may have made an important contribution in preventing learners from using erroneous forms introduced by their peers.

Some examples from the classroom corpus of learner interaction involving errors serves to illustrate the processes involved when a learner uses an incorrect form. In general, rather than providing a model for incorporation, the occurrence of errors in the classroom corpus actually appears to provide an opportunity for language analysis. Perhaps this happens because the forms, vocabulary, and so on, are new to all learners involved and because of the consistent provision of interactive models by the teacher in the form of pretask practice, pretask demonstration, and reference materials. In addition, post-task activities often include the teacher going over the peer learning task by calling on volunteers to perform, or by the teacher taking one part and performing with a nominated student. Post-task instruction, therefore, provides additional models of correct forms and the opportunity to clarify any misunderstandings regarding the introduced structures. Some teachers presented some tasks incrementally, with simpler tasks preceding more complex ones, so that earlier tasks would provide a foundation for later ones. When this was the case, later tasks incorporated review as well as innovation, as new material was practiced along with older material. Through this incremental process, learner questions arose and were resolved smoothly during the process of doing the tasks.

During peer learning tasks, the production of an error, therefore, presents a unique problem for learners—a plurality of ways of producing a particular form or structure. Errors thus provide an occasion for learners to focus more carefully on the teacher's language use and the use of language in instructional materials to resolve the tension between different possibilities.

In Excerpt 27, an example from Rob's class, the students are doing an interview task in which they ask one another for examples of classes that can be described using adjectivals such as *omoshiroi* 'interesting' and *taihen* 'difficult/arduous'. In a question to Rob, Rob's partner, S, pronounces *taihen* 'arduous/difficult' incorrectly. When Rob asks him to repeat the question, S repeats the same pronunciation error. When Rob answers in line 4, however, after first making a different error with the same word, he then pronounces it correctly. The relevant syllables are underlined.

(27)
→   1   S: Taihan desu ka?
                 Is it difficult? ((error in pronunciation of 'taihen'))
    2   R: Mooichi do itte kudasai?
                 Would you please repeat that?
→   3   S: Nihongo: (.) no taihan desu ka?
                 *Is Japanese: (.) difficult? ((error in pronunciation of
                 'taihen' and in particle choice))*
→   4   R: Uhm (.) hhai nihongo wa taihon taihen desu.
                 *Uhm (.) yyes Japanese is difficult difficult. ((error in R's
                 first utterance of 'taihen.' The second is correct))*
                                                            (Rob, 1/24)

In line 4, not only does Rob self-correct to the appropriate pronunciation of *taihen* 'difficult/arduous', but he incidentally also recasts his partner's line 3 error in the use of a grammatical particle, replacing the incorrect *no* (genitive marker) with the correct *wa* (topic marker).

The problem introduced by S in Excerpt 27—different candidate pronunciations of *taihen* 'difficult/arduous', maintains Rob's attention following the episode. The task that Rob and S are working on in Excerpt 26 functions as pretask practice for a more complex task that is coming. The grammatical focus of the lesson is the use of the conjunction *demo* 'but'. After the pair task in Excerpt 27, in teacher-fronted practice shown in Excerpt 28, the teacher guides the students to use the same vocabulary to contrast a class that is *taihen* 'difficult/arduous' with one that is not, introducing the conjunction *demo* 'but' through the teacher-fronted activity. Rob attends to the word *taihen* in his private speech in line 4:

(28) 1   T: Ja: jugyoo (.) ne taihen desu (.) ne taihen na jugyoo
                   (.) ii desu ka? Jaa:: Larry-san?
                   *Okay: class (.) right? A difficult class (.) right a difficult
                   class (.) okay? So:: Larry?*
      2   L: (.) Gengo:gaku:: wa taihen desu
                   (.) Linguistics:: is difficult.
      3   T: Gengogaku wa taihen desu, (.) gengogaku
                   [(..) linguistics desu ne, wa taihen desu?
                   *Linguistics is difficult, (.) gengogaku
                   (..) linguistics right? Linguistics is difficult?*

→   4   R: [°°taihen°°
              °°difficult°°
    5   T: Demo?
              But?
    6   L: Demo anthropology wa: amari (.) taihen (.) taihen
              nai desu
              But anthropology isn't very (.) difficult. ((error: negation))
    7   T: Mm? Amari:, nan desu ka?
              Mm? It what?
    8   Ss: Taihen ja ^ arimasen
              Isn't very difficult ((negation is correct))
    9   T: Taihen ja nai desu taihen ja arimasen ne amari
              taihen ja arimasen (.)
              *It isn't very difficult isn't very difficult right? It isn't very
              difficult.*

(Rob, 1/24)

In line 4, Rob whispers to himself the correct pronunciation, resolving the
problem introduced by S' error in Excerpt 27. Although Rob appeared to
resolve the discrepancy soon after S' initial error, Rob's mental activity
continues beyond that task as he works with the correct form in his private
speech during teacher-fronted practice that followed.

What about cases where learners "help" each other by providing wrong
information? In Excerpt 29.1, Andrea asks for confirmation of the sentence structure that she is having difficulty with in line 1. In line 2, her
partner gives a misleading answer, which confirms Andrea's erroneous utterance as correct. And, in line 3, Andrea uses the wrong structure:

(29.1)
→   1   A: Piza to: (.) sushi to: tempura:: (.) no naka de (.) or
              how do you say it (.) yoku:: (.) <u>tabe::</u> (.) tabe: (.) <u>te,</u>
              *Among pizza and (.) sushi and tempura:: (.) or how do
              you say it (.) which do you often:: (.) ea:: (.) eat ((Error))*
→   2   S: Yeah. <u>Yoku ta//bete</u> (.) something like that
              *Yeah. Often e//at (.) something like that ((agrees with
              error))*
→   3   A: <u>Tabete</u> (.) um (.) dono:(.) dono: (.) ichiban suki desu
              ka?
              Eat ((te-form)) (.) which (.) which (.) do you like best?
    4   S: Um (.) pizza, (.) sono mitsu: tabemono no naka de:
              (.) pizza (.) o ^ (.) yoku (.) <u>tabemasu.</u> Pizza o ichiban
              yoku tabemasu.

> Um (.) pizza, (.) among those three foods: (.) I eat (.)
> pizza (.) the most. I eat pizza the most.

5   A: Okay.
6   S: Sushi to katsudon to: (.) sukiyaki (.) no naka de.(.)
         dore ga ichiban (.) yoku:(.) <u>tabemasu</u> ka?
         Among sushi and cutlet bowl and (.) sukiyaki (.) which do you
         (.) eat ((NOTE—correct verb form)) the most?
7   A: Uh sono mitsu: (.) tabemono: (.) de ^ (.) sushi ga:
         ichiban: yoku: <u>tabemasu</u>. (.) Um
         Ah among those three: (.) foods: (.) I eat sushi the: most
         (.) um
         (3)
8   A: U::h (.) Otomodachi to: oka:san to: oto:san (.) no
         naka de: (.) dochira ga:(.) yoku: ai (.) aimasu k- (.)
         how do you say that.(.) aimasu ka?
         U::h (.) Among your friends, mother and father (.) which
         do you (.) most often mee- (.) meet (.) how do you say that
         (.) meet? ((error: particle <u>ga</u> used for <u>ni</u>))
9   S: Yeah.

                                                    (Andrea, 1/22)

However, after Andrea asks her line 3 question, in line 4, S, the same student who confirmed Andrea's wrong usage, answers using the correct verb form. And, S forms a question correctly using the same structure in line 6. When answering this question in line 7, Andrea also uses the structure correctly, and in line 8 she proceeds to produce her own question using the appropriate verb form.

 This excerpt also provides a good example of learner repetition of interlocutor errors. Andrea and her partner have difficulty with grammatical particles, which is very common among learners of Japanese. S, in line 4, uses the accusative *o* correctly in her statement *pizza o yoku tabemasu* 'I eat pizza often'. However, both Andrea and her partner tend to overuse *ga*, the nominative case marker, for other particles. In line 6, S uses the nominative case marker *ga*, saying *dore ga ichiban yoku tabemasu ka* 'what would you most like to eat?' where she should have used the accusative marker *o*. Andrea follows suit, making the same error line 7. This is an example of repetition of an interlocutor's error. Then, when Andrea asks her own question in line 8, she uses the nominative *ga* rather than the dative *ni*. As with most cases of learner repetition of an interlocutor's error, it is not clear whether Andrea would have made these errors anyway, since these errors are quite common, or whether she was negatively influenced by S. Several lines later, as shown in Excerpt 29.2, S says the following:

(29.2)
1 S: Tomodachi to: oka:san to: oto:san no naka de (..)
u:h (.) otomodachi <u>ni</u> yoku aimasu. (.) ichiban yoku
aimasu.(..) u:h (..)
*Of my friends, mother and father (..) u:h (.) I see my
friends a lot. (.) I see them most. (..) u:h (..)*
2 Ken Griffey Jr. to Michael Jordan to ( ) no naka
de (.) dare <u>ga</u> ichiban aitai desu ka?
*Of Ken Griffey Jr. and Michael Jordan and ( ), who (.)
do you see the most?*

(Andrea, 1/22)

Here, S uses *ni* correctly in line 1, but then returns to an overgeneralized
use of *ga* in line 2. And, in follow-up teacher-fronted practice shown in Excerpt 30, other students make similar errors, overusing *ga*, as well as making errors with other particles. The teacher treats these errors using both
implicit and explicit techniques. Relevant particles are underlined, with
particle errors shown in small caps. The correct particle is explained in
the gloss. Lines in which the teacher treats errors are indicated by arrows.

(30) 1 T: Hai (.) ii desu ne (.) chuuka ryori <u>o</u> ichiban yoku
tabemasu.(.) Hai eh::to (.) Gold-san.
*Yes (.) good (.) you eat Chinese food most often. Yes u:::h
(.) Gold-san.*
2 G: Hong-san. Hawaii to niu:yo:ku to banku:ba dewa (.)
sono mitsu no naka <u>NI</u> (.) dore <u>GA</u> ichiban yoku
ikimasu ka?
*Hong-san. Of Hawaii and New York and Vancouver (.)
among those three DAT ((error: should be LOC)), where do
you go NOM ((error: should be DAT)) most often?*
3 H: Sono mitsu no naka <u>de</u> (.) hawaii <u>WA</u> ichiban(.) yoku
ikimasu.
*Of those three LOC (.) I go to Hawaii TOP ((error: should
be DAT)) (.) the most.*
→ 4 T: Hai^ ii desu ne (.) eh::to:(.) nyu:yo:ku to hawaii to
banku:ba:(.) no^ naka <u>de</u> wa, (.) eh:to(.) doko <u>ni</u>^
(.) ichiban yoku ikimasu ka.
*Yes good (.) U:::h (.) of New York and Hawaii and
Vancouver LOC TOP, (.) u:h (.) where DAT (.) do you go
most often?*
5 Ii desu ka. Doko <u>ni</u>^(.) soo desu ne. Hai. Ki o
tsukete kudasai, (.) Eh::to ja:::(.) Shiden-san.

> *Okay. Where* DAT *(.) that's how it is. Hai. Be careful, (.)*
> *U::h let's see::: (.) Shiden-san.*

6 S: Ellis-san wa (.) uh: (.) gorufu to: suki: to: tennisu
um sono mitsu: (.) no naka de: (.) um (.) ichiban:(..)
uh dochira GA ichiban uh yoku shimasu ka?
Ellis-san TOP *(.) u:h (.) among golf and skiing and tennis,*
among those three LOC *(.) um (.) most (.) uh which*
NOM *(should be* ACC*) do you do the most?*

7 T: Dochira ga futatsu no pair desu.
"Dochira" is used when there are two items.

8 S: Dore GA ichiban uh yoku shimasu ka?
Which NOM *(should be* ACC*) uh do you do the most?*

9 T: Hai kore (.) anoo (.) suru desu ne (.) dore (..)
((writing on board))
Yes here (.) uh (.) you're using 'do' so (.) which (.)
((writing on board))

10 S: Dore o ichiban (.) uh yoku shimasu ka?
Which ACC *(.) do you do most?*

11 E: Mm sono mitsu no naka de: (.) gorufu o ichiban
yoku shimasu.
Mm among those three LOC: *(.) I do golf* ACC *the most.*

(Andrea, 1/22)

In these examples, beginning with Andrea and her partner S's pair learning task, and concluding with teacher-fronted, follow-up practice, we see that although learners do use wrong forms in pair practice, and may repeat the incorrect forms used at times, follow-up, teacher-fronted work allows the teacher to treat errors that emerge and provides learners with the opportunity to again observe use of the correct forms. What impact this has on Andrea is not clear, because she does not use this structure again in the corpus. Certainly erroneous forms, whether their source is internal or external, may be confirmed by the experience of hearing another learner use the wrong form. However, as we see here, learners have the opportunity to hear the correct forms used as well as they, with the teacher's help, work with the L2.

Excerpt 30 shows how difficult it is to determine the source of an error. Errors such as these are very common with beginning and intermediate learners. Excerpt 19 provided another good example of a learner repeating the errors of another. Excerpt 31 repeats the portion of Excerpt 19 that shows how Andrea repeats the particle errors of the student she overhears. The error involves overgeneralized use of the particle *no*. Andrea first imitates a correct use of the particle *no* to connect two nouns—*sutoraipu no nekutai* 'is the structure NOUN *no* NOUN, and means 'striped tie'. However, in line 5, B overgeneralizes the use of *no*, using it to connect an adjective with a noun. This is incorrect. Adjectives do not require insertion of *no*. And, Andrea repeats B's error in line 6:

(31) 3 B: <u>Sutoraipu no nekutai::</u>
            Stripe ((noun)) GEN necktie
            striped necktie

      4 A: <u>Sutraipu no</u> hehehehe (.) diagonal no stripe ga
            arimasu kedo shiroi to kuroi desu. Sorekara::
            Stripe ((noun)) GEN hehehehe (.) There's a diagonal stripe
            but it's black and white. And then::

  →   5 B: <u>Shiroi no shatsu::</u>
            White ((adjective)) GEN ((error: genitive particle should be
            omitted after an adjective)) shirt::

  →   6 A: <u>Shiroi no shatsu</u> ga oh ^
            White ((adjective))GEN ((error)) shirt::

      7 B: <u>Kiteimasu</u>
            Is wearing

      8 A: <u>Kiteimasu.</u>
            Is wearing

                                        (Andrea, 5/16)

As in Excerpt 30, it is important to note that overgeneralization of grammatical particles such as the topic marker *wa* and the genitive marker *no* are very common developmental errors. Children commonly make these kinds of errors. Clancy (1985) noted that "an error which occurs in the speech of many Japanese 2-year-olds is overgeneralization of the genitive particle *no* in prenominal modifiers. . . . Children frequently produce ungrammatical ADJ *no* N constructions" (p. 406). Clancy (1985) also pointed out that some particle errors persist: "substitution of *ga* for *o* can be found not only at the early stages of acquisition, but also in much older children" (p. 390). In the learner data just presented, such errors occurred in Excerpt 29 and Excerpt 30 as well as elsewhere. Clancy (1985) reported children making errors with the particle *ni*, errors which were common in the classroom corpus. L2 acquisition researchers have found that adult L2 learners tend to follow developmental sequences similar to Japanese children (Kanagy, in press). With developmental errors such as these, it is difficult to determine causality when one learner makes a similar mistake after another learner has made the same error. The learners are all making these sorts of errors, and must pass through these sorts of errors through the developmental process (Kanagy 1995, in press). It cannot be expected that learners will master grammatical forms in the order that they are taught. Here, they are gaining practice with these different forms and are developing an awareness of grammatical categories that do not exist in English (like the distinction between adjectival nouns, nouns, and adjectives). However, it will be some time before learners have reached a level where they consistently use the correct forms. It is also useful to reiterate that in the classroom corpus, learners did not repeat over 92% of their interlocutors' errors.

I propose that the production of errors produces a positive result: Learners' exposure to each others' errors promotes noticing. Learners are impacted by interlocutor errors as the errors contrast with the correct language to which they are exposed. Along with the errors each learner produces, errors produced by peer interlocutors provide a plurality of candidate forms, presenting a problem that learners are generally successful in resolving. Instead of unthinkingly accepting a particular form, students must consider what is correct. Learner errors are an important part of the process of language learning. Overall, in the classroom corpus, peer interaction increases accuracy rather than reducing it, because students catch their own and each others' errors during the interactive process. The use of the L2 in interactive tasks is a learning experience that stimulates individuals to further processing after the interaction has occurred. Although it is possible that, just as with a learner's own anomalous forms, errors "picked up" from a partner may persist, no such case was found in the classroom corpus. In fact, the data show that the learners in the classroom corpus most often did not pick up errors (at least 92% of the time), but were much more likely to recognize errors as such. Although learners repeated 7.76% of their interlocutor's errors, it was much more common for the learners to follow an interlocutor error with use of the correct form or to treat the interlocutor's error (37% of cases) or to ignore the error (47% of cases). Learners appear to have a good understanding of both their interlocutor's limitations as fellow learners as well as how they can learn from each other.

CONCLUSION

Previous research has been unanimous in noting the overall benefits of peer assistance in developmentally appropriate interactive language learning tasks. Learners retain what they negotiate (Swain & Lapkin, 1998), come to collaborative solutions (Donato, 1994), and evidence improvement in their use of grammatical structures (Ohta, 2000a). The present study, which includes a database many times larger than previous studies and also follows learners longitudinally, confirms that time and time again, learners both utilize and provide developmentally appropriate assistance to their peers.

The excerpts shown in this chapter are representative examples of the facilitative effect of assisted performance. These results expand what has been shown in previous research. By working together, learners collaboratively build utterances that are a bit beyond their reach and that of the interlocutor. Assistance is responsive to the partner's need for support. Learners wait patiently for their peer interlocutors to finish their utterances, and step in to help at an appropriate time, rather than interrupting. The assistance provided is overwhelmingly helpful. The particular affordances of the listener role enable active involvement, stimulate noticing, and provide an environment where learners can stretch to reach beyond established abilities to use new language forms. Through the process of scaffolding the performance of another, learners help themselves, building bridges to proficiency as they support the production of their interlocutors. This is the key to peer assistance—that both peers benefit, the one receiving assistance and the one who reaches out to provide it. When learners help by providing a bit of a vertical construction or assisting a partner via co-construction, even if they cannot yet produce the entire utterance themselves, they are on their way to being able to do so. Research in L1 acquisition has shown that collaborative participation is a precursor of independent performance (Moerk, 1992). Assisting another with what one is also learning clearly promotes development.

Peers benefit from the opportunity these tasks give them to use and to build on their growing knowledge. In the sociocognitive theoretical framework being used to illuminate these data, the ZPD and general genetic law of development describe how development proceeds (a) as learners are assisted via interaction to do what they could not have done without appropriate support, and (b) as the language of social interaction is internalized to become a tool of thought. Learners benefit as they corporately accomplish what they cannot yet individually produce. When tasks are well designed and implemented, learners build on their knowledge to the level where they can perform with increasing independence. Table 3.9 outlines the general benefits of peer assistance. Language use provides a snapshot of development, as it is through use of the language in interaction that acquisition occurs, with internalization occurring as learners develop increasing independence in language use. In the theoretical framework used, internalization proceeds as the language of social interaction is gradually appropriated as a tool for thought. It is not accurate to say that peer interaction "causes" learning. Rather, the social interaction that occurs during L2 interactive language learning tasks constitutes learning. The metacognitive skills developed through the experience of using the L2 in real time interaction is an experience of learning that stimulates individuals to further dialogic processing in their own mental space (Donato & Lantolf, 1990; Hall, 1995a).

TABLE 3.9
The Benefits of Peer L2 Interactive Tasks

General Development	Giving and receiving assistance in and of itself promotes development as learners work on a common interactive task. Learners draw on their strengths to help one another, and use the L2 for a wider range of functions and activities than they do in teacher-fronted practice.
Vocabulary	Learners use vocabulary being learned and help each other to recall and use L2 vocabulary. Learners help each other with "word searches" and actively suggest alternative vocabulary to each other.
Pronunciation	The opportunity to use the L2 in interactive tasks helps learners to refine their pronunciation, both via self-correction and by benefiting when their partners notice their pronunciation problems.
Grammar	Through co-constructed utterances, learners corporately build utterances they cannot yet individually produce, working toward independence. Learners notice their own grammatical errors as well as the errors of others, with peer interlocutors benefiting from this process.
Interactional style	By working with a peer, learners have the opportunity to take turns and use language in ways they seldom do in teacher-fronted practice. Working together allows learners to try different types of utterances they notice the teacher using, and to learn from each other how to interact appropriately (See chapter 5 for an in-depth discussion)

The results regarding the impact of L2 errors on peer interaction are also informative. Contrary to findings of a previous laboratory study, which reported a 19%–27% incorporation rate for intermediate and advanced ESL learners working on information gap tasks in a laboratory setting (Mackey et al., 1999), in these language classes, incorporation rates were strikingly low, with most errors being treated or ignored rather than being picked up for use by the interlocutor. In the context of these form-focused tasks, rather than impede peer learning, L2 errors stimulate the learners to further language analysis as they consider which form is appropriate. Teachers monitor learner production, and errors prompt learners to actively seek the teacher's assistance in resolving problems that they cannot handle on their own. Gass (1991) summarized the notions of positive and negative evidence and their roles in L2 acquisition. *Positive evidence* consists of well-formed utterances and shows learners what is possible. *Negative evidence* consists of feedback to learners about what is not possible. Analysis of the classroom corpus indicates another source of evidence learners draw on in the language learning process—the deviant utterances of their peers, when such utterances contrast with what learners believe to be true about the L2. Conscious attention to these contrasts is also an important part of language learning processes. It is particularly interesting that learners notice and act on their peers' malformed utterances even when they, themselves, still produce the same sorts of errors. Such activity is a clear sign of development, but is more than just a signpost. The activity of noticing and collaboratively working to reformulate the deviant utterances of peers is a key part of the classroom language learning process that builds the learner's developing grammar, a process through which learner knowledge becomes more robust.

Because peer learning tasks cannot be carefully monitored by the teacher, some teachers fear that learners will not work productively during group work. In some approaches to teaching Japanese, peer interaction that is not intensely monitored by the teacher is banned in the early years of instruction due to fears that it might promote fossilization (see, e.g., Watabe, 1995, and Jorden, 1986). Contrary to teacher concerns, analysis of the classroom corpus shows that the benefits of guided peer interaction in these language focused, theme based classes far outweighed any problems that emerged. The interactive tasks realized in the activity of the targeted learners provided safe places for learners to create with the L2 in an environment in which assistance was readily available. And rather than creating a negative influence, the errors that cropped up promoted the processes of noticing and self-monitoring. As noted by Osborne and Wittrock (1983), "selective attention results in selective perception . . . we attend to and perceive *changes* in stimuli, which implies that one must have a model of the stimulation to perceive changes in it" (p. 494). Foreign language teachers can have confidence that with developmentally appropriate modeling and form-related assistance, learners will benefit from the experience of doing interactive language learning tasks. Features of task design and implementation that promote productive L2 interaction will be discussed further in chapter 6.

Questions yet to be answered in the area of assisted performance include how task and learner ability may interact to form an environment optimal for assisted performance to occur. Although most tasks and combinations of learners promoted active involvement in L2 use, this was not always the case. Not every task was productive for the learners involved. Chapter 6 specifically considers characteristics of tasks and what kinds of tasks and task implementation conditions appear to be most beneficial, with further consideration of assisted performance in relation to task type and learner variables. In addition, chapter 3 raised questions related to learner errors and the provision of corrective feedback, which are the particular topics of investigation in chapter 4.

A Learner-Centered Analysis
of Corrective Feedback as a Resource
in Foreign Language Development

Language teachers and researchers have long had an interest in the role of corrective feedback in classroom language learning. This chapter contributes to the previous literature on corrective feedback in second and foreign language classrooms by analyzing corrective feedback from a *learner-centered* perspective. This is accomplished by considering how corrective feedback functions in the different classroom settings in which the seven learners participate, including both the teacher-fronted and peer learning settings. The approach is developmental in its concern regarding how corrective feedback impacts particular learners over time. Corrective feedback is analyzed as one of the affordances available to learners in the ZPD. This chapter represents a significant departure from previous classroom-oriented work, which has placed primary focus on the behavior of teachers as providers of corrective feedback, and that has not shown how corrective feedback impacts particular learners as a lesson progresses. Much of the classroom-focused research was conducted before today's emphasis on the use of language learning tasks, when language teaching was arguably a more teacher-fronted enterprise. In many college and university foreign language classrooms today, however, teachers not only teach in a traditional sense of conveying information; teachers often work as facilitators of language learning tasks which learners do with one another. These interactive experiences form the building blocks of language development. How corrective feedback functions in both teacher-fronted and peer interactive contexts, and the roles of both teachers and learners in corrective feedback episodes have not been well investigated.

Corrective feedback is ubiquitous in language learning contexts, beginning with the L1 acquisition of children. Brown & Hanlon's (1970) often-cited claim that caretakers focused on errors that related to meaning and not to form has, in fact, been found to be an artifact of their very narrow definition of corrective feedback. Moerk's (1992) reanalysis of Brown's (1973) data found that, contrary to Brown's claim that corrective feedback was absent, almost all of the linguistic errors of Eve, the child he studied, were treated in the immediately subsequent turn. Most remarkable about the corrective feedback provided by Eve's caregivers was its smooth integration into conversation; errors of form were effectively treated without disrupting conversational flow. This typifies how corrective feedback is generally provided to children by their caregivers. In L2 language learning contexts, interest in corrective feedback has been stimulated by theory that posited that form would take care of itself given a developmentally sensitive linguistic environment (Krashen, 1985). This perspective transformed the way that many L2s were taught. Communicative language teaching held the promise of promoting SLA through learner participation in meaning-focused instructional events, in which grammatical learning would occur incidentally. Following this line of thinking, teachers worked to enrich opportunities for language learners to be exposed to comprehensible input, with immersion education programs providing what was considered an ideal language learning environment. Although learners in meaning-focused programs made impressive gains in a range of language skills, grammatical accuracy lagged beneath expectations, even in immersion programs where the best results might be expected (Harley, 1992; Swain, 1991).

Concern about raising awareness of grammatical structure while maintaining meaning-focused instruction spawned a whole research area investigating "focus on form" (see, e.g., articles in Doughty & Williams', 1998, edited volume on this topic), in immersion and L2 (primarily ESL) classrooms. Interest in corrective feedback is also evident in a flurry of recent research on the topic, including both naturalistic classroom research (Lyster, 1998; Lyster & Ranta, 1997; Ohta, 2000b; Roberts, 1995), experimental classroom research, (Doughty & Varela, 1998) and experimental research outside of the classroom setting (Mackey et al., 1999; Mackey & Philp, 1998; Oliver, 1995; Ortega & Long, 1997; Philp, 1999). This research has been most prolific in ESL and immersion classrooms, where researchers have been studying how to promote accuracy while also maintaining the gains achieved by communicative approaches to language teaching. In order to determine what instructional interventions might be effective, researchers have studied corrective feedback along with looking at how other methods of providing a language focus may enhance established meaning-focused communicative methodology. Classroom studies that have followed up differences in student performance under different instructional conditions have found that the students of teachers who more explicitly focused on troublesome language forms did better on those forms (Lightbown & Spada, 1990). Such studies also suggested that the use of grammar-focused language learning tasks may be as effective as formal instruction in promoting learner noticing of grammatical form (Fotos, 1993). Along with formal instruction and task-based instruction that provides a form-focused component, corrective feedback has drawn the attention of researchers as a way of promoting learner attention to form. Studies such as these have found that corrective feedback is effective in drawing learner attention to form in otherwise communicatively oriented classrooms (Leeman, Arteagoitia, Fridman, & Doughty, 1995; Lightbown & Spada, 1990).

There have been few focus on form studies conducted with learners of Japanese (two exceptions are Koyanagi, 1998, and Moroishi, 1998). Perhaps this is because focus on form studies have their roots in ESL and immersion classrooms where they were inspired by questions that emerged from research on meaning-focused instruction that eschewed overt teaching of grammar. Even though Japanese language teaching has also been influenced by communicative approaches to language teaching, it has remained strongly committed to form-focused instruction—what the Focus on Form literature calls "Focus on FormS." The continued use of structural syllabi in Japanese language teaching provides an opportunity to investigate the impact that this sort of focus on form has on classroom language acquisition processes.

Communicative approaches that rejected overt grammar teaching may have been more attractive to teachers of foreign languages which are typologically related to the learners' L1. English speaking learners of languages such as German or Spanish can often rely on analogies with the L1 for understanding of basic L2 syntactic and morphological structure. Approaches rejecting grammar instruction may not be as attractive to teachers of less commonly taught languages (LCTLs) or others who teach languages typologically distant from the learners' L1. Japanese language teachers in North America, even those strongly influenced by communicative approaches, have continued to rely on structurally organized syllabi, succinct linguistic explanation, and meaningful, communicatively oriented, form-focused practice to provide support for understanding and learning to use L2 structure. Compared to ESL teachers, teachers of Japanese have not tended to doubt the effectiveness of the structural syllabus. Even so, communicative approaches have had a strong influence on Japanese language teaching. In years past, form-focused practice centered around audiolingual drills. Today, while methodological approaches vary from program to program, teachers use a wider range of tools that have their origins in communicative approaches to language teaching. Along with incorporating communicative activities into existing curricula, textbooks are also starting to change. Theme-based communicative approaches are growing in popularity, and provide meaningful coherence to instruction that remains strongly form focused. The most recently published Japanese texts incorporate topical organization along with their structural syllabi (Y. Hatasa, Makino, & K. Hatasa, 1999; Makino, Y. Hatasa, & K. Hatasa, 1997; Tohsaku, 1994, 1995). Peer learning tasks in these texts promote structural and communicative practice in meaningful, topic-related contexts, with tasks such as substitution dialogues, information gap tasks, interview tasks, reporting tasks, and role play tasks. In this way, Japanese language teaching methodology has moved away from heavy reliance on structural drill. There is an increasing use of communicative drill, guided interaction, and communicative tasks. The result is that lessons in the early years of instruction maintain a structural focus while helping the learner to use the language for a real-life purpose, and to be creative in using Japanese to express the learner's own meanings.

The SLA research literature has often been occupied by the question of whether or not form-focused instructional techniques, including corrective feedback, are effective enhancements to communicative language teaching, as well as what types of corrective feedback might be useful in providing form-focused interventions. In the Japanese language instructional context, which incorporates structural syllabi and explicit grammar teaching, it is meaningless to ask how inclusion of a linguistic focus might impact learner development, because such a focus is an integral part of the methodology. It has come as no surprise to many foreign language teachers that ESL and immersion education research has found that it is effective to draw learners' attention to language form. Rather, in structurally oriented classrooms, different sorts of questions are of interest. And teachers have practical questions that differ from the questions SLA researchers may ask. Should teachers monitor and correct all errors, as recommended by some methodologists? (see Jorden & Noda, 1987; Watabe, 1995) In foreign language textbooks more influenced by communicative language teaching, where structural syllabi are accompanied by thematic and functional syllabi, a range of instructional activities in both teacher-fronted and peer interactive contexts are provided, leaving teachers to develop their own approaches to corrective feedback. For teachers using these hybrid approaches, questions about corrective feedback include concerns about how and when errors should be treated (or ignored), and questions about the extent to which corrective feedback is attended to and can be used by students in the language learning setting. In addition, teachers who feel that all errors should be treated promptly may be wary of peer learning tasks because the teacher cannot be available to treat all learner errors. One important question is how learners treat (or ignore) each other's errors during peer interaction, and whether the corrective feedback provided by peers is effective. These questions form the starting point for this chapter's investigation of the classroom corpus.

The research presented in this chapter also differs from previous studies of corrective feedback in that the approach taken to data analysis is learner centered rather than being teacher centered. Teacher-centered approaches have examined corrective feedback as something that teachers provide to learners (Faneslow, 1977). This research examined the kinds of errors teachers treat or ignore, classified corrective feedback approaches, and considered how various treatment techniques may differ in terms of promoting learner progress in learning grammatical forms. The effectiveness of particular techniques has been inferred based on whether or not learners produce a verbal response, sometimes called *uptake*, in the turn following the corrective feedback, with learner repair being the desired result (Chaudron, 1977, 1986; Lyster & Ranta, 1997; Muranoi, 1998). These previous studies, while useful, have not examined what is corrective from the learners' perspective, nor have they examined how corrective feedback is realized in the peer learning setting. Although the day-to-day reality of language lessons has changed, corrective feedback studies have not looked at the implications of these changes on the provision and use of corrective feedback. In addition, previous studies tended to limit themselves to the examination of uptake, without considering other possibilities besides immediate verbal responses to feedback. The peer learning setting introduces a whole new dimension to the area of corrective feedback, from being something provided by teachers to being something that learners potentially offer one another. And, even in the teacher-fronted setting, learner responses besides uptake need to be considered. This chapter steps into these gaps in the research literature by presenting an analysis of the classroom corpus, data that enables a focus on learners and the way corrective information is available to them in the various settings in which they participate. The classroom corpus provides an opportunity to examine the role of corrective feedback in classes that incorporate communicative approaches to teaching while maintaining a consistent structural focus. In this context, corrective feedback is one of many elements which contribute a linguistic focus. Even though instruction is generally meaning focused, it is likely that the attention of learners is never far from language form.

In this chapter, treatment of learner errors in teacher-fronted work and peer learning is examined. Learner errors, whether they are made overtly in public turns, or covertly in private turns, are considered along with utterances that function as a corrective to these errors. Corrective feedback as considered in this chapter is only possible because of learner errors, but what constitutes feedback to a particular learner is not always provided in response to learner production of an error. Rather, learners have corrective experiences as their errors are treated both intentionally and incidentally, a process that will be examined in detail along with learner responses to corrective utterances, whether those responses are overt or covert. Results of analysis show that a great deal of corrective feedback occurs outside of the traditional purview of teacher control; many corrective sequences take place during peer learning tasks. Moreover, some errors that occur in the teacher-fronted context are not treated deliberately by the teacher, but are treated incidentally through the ongoing discourse in which the learner overtly or covertly participates. In other words, utterances which have a corrective function for learners include types of utterances that previous research has not considered as corrective feedback. Here, the use of this term is broadened in order to more effectively examine the sorts of utterances that have corrective value to learners. The results of analysis underscore the role of the learner as not merely responsive, but as proactive, with the errors themselves showing the learners' developmental progress in acquiring the foreign language.

This chapter is organized as follows: After reviewing of the role of corrective feedback in language development, the learner-centered methodology used to analyze the classroom corpus is explained. A definition of corrective feedback that has been developed through the process of analyzing the corpus is presented. This learner-centered definition takes into account the varying participant roles of classroom learners as they interact in teacher-fronted and peer learning settings. Following the presentation of this definition, the different types of corrective feedback found in the corpus are presented. The bulk of the chapter considers the two most prevalent types of corrective feedback, *recasts* and *incidental recasts*.[1] Research relating to the role of recasts in L1 and L2 development is discussed, and the concept of incidental recasts introduced. Incidental recasts occur when a learner is exposed to language that contrasts with the learner's erroneous utterance, but is not in response to the learner's error (Ohta, in press-b). Examination of corrective feedback from a learner-centered perspective shows incidental recasts to be a significant modality providing corrective information. Both recasts and incidental recasts will be discussed as they function in teacher-fronted and peer learning settings. Finally, learner use of self-correction is briefly examined. The chapter concludes with a summary of findings and consideration of the impact of corrective feedback on classroom language learners.

---

[1]An earlier version of the research in this chapter related to incidental recasts appears in Ohta (2000b).

CORRECTIVE FEEDBACK IN THE L2 CLASSROOM

Corrective feedback is significant to L2 development because it provides the learner with an opportunity to reflect on the utterance and consider other possibilities. In the sociocultural view, language acquisition is a social interactive process, with the learner involved in capitalizing on affordances in the L2 classroom setting (van Lier, 2000). Affordances are available through the learner's interaction with the social and material environment. This is the foundation of internalization processes that occur through interpsychological means (chap. 1, this volume). Corrective feedback is one of the affordances of social interaction that a learner may or may not notice or act on. When corrective feedback provides the correct form, learners have the opportunity to contrast their own production with that of another. In this way, corrective feedback may stimulate hypothesis testing, giving the learner the opportunity to grapple with form-meaning relationships. Corrective feedback that does not provide the correct form may prompt learners to utilize their own resources in constructing a reformulation. In either case, corrective feedback may facilitate L2 development.

Traditionally, corrective feedback techniques have not been viewed as equally effective. Some researchers have worked to determine their effectiveness by considering (a) whether or not a technique requires the learner to reformulate for themselves and (b) if there is uptake, whether or not the learner's repair is successful. Techniques that require reformulation, such as clarification requests, have been considered potentially more effective than those that do not, namely recasts (Chaudron, 1986; Lyster, 1998; Lyster & Ranta, 1997). In this view, the learner's own reformulation is seen as an interactional modification leading to interlanguage development (Pica, 1988; Swain, 1985, 1993). In addition, immediate, overt learner response to corrective feedback in the form of uptake has been prioritized as evidence of noticing. However, this approach presents a significant problem. The present or absence of an overt oral response—uptake—is certainly easily tabulated. The problem is that although the presence of uptake is indicative of learner response to corrective feedback, it is not the only possible way that learners may respond, even if they notice and make use of the corrective feedback. The absence of an overt response does not indicate a lack of learner attention or activity. An important piece of evidence for this are results from recent studies, which have found that uptake—whether reformulation or repetition—is not necessary for corrective feedback to have an effect (Mackey & Philp, 1998; Philp, 1999). These recent studies show the positive effect of corrective feedback, even when implicit, in results that are consistent with those of L1 acquisition research. In both naturalistic and experimental research, L1 researchers found that corrective feedback promotes language development (Baker & Nelson, 1984; S. M. Camarata, Nelson, & M. N. Camarata, 1994; Moerk, 1992; Nelson, 1989; Nelson, Denninger, Bonvillian, Kaplan, & Baker, 1984; Scherer & Olswang, 1984; Uzgiris, Broome, & Kruper, 1989).

DEFINITIONS AND METHODOLOGY OF ANALYSIS

Defining "Corrective Feedback"

In this chapter, corrective feedback is defined as any utterance, produced by a teacher or learner, that either (a) initiates repair on a malformed utterance, or (b) contrasts with a learner's malformed utterance. This broad definition of corrective feedback was developed through a qualitative process of examining the transcripts. The initial working definition of corrective feedback was as a type of repair (Schegloff et al., 1977). *Repair* is a process through which trouble sources in interaction are resolved. Repair is initiated by the self or another when the trouble source is identified, and may be brought to completion by the self or another. Research literature on repair in L2 classrooms (Kasper, 1985; Markee, 2000) overlaps with work on corrective feedback but is broader in scope. Corrective feedback research traditionally looked at a narrower slice of repair phenomena, primarily focusing on other-initiated, other-repair (repair initiated and completed by the teacher), and other-initiated, self-repair (repair initiated by the teacher and completed by the student), and limiting the type of trouble sources examined. In other words, corrective feedback has been viewed as other-initiated repair. This was the starting point for developing a definition of corrective feedback. Initially, this was broadened beyond considering the teacher as the sole source of feedback. Rather, all episodes that contained both an erroneous form produced by a targeted learner and some type of corrective move were collected. In order to do this, learner utterances were examined in their sequential contexts, looking at what followed them, and taking note of whether or not what followed a learner's utterance might have a corrective function. An utterance was considered to have a corrective function if it had the potential of drawing the learner's attention to his or her own erroneous utterance. It quickly became apparent that the notion of corrective feedback as other-initiated repair did capture the nature of much of the corrective feedback in the data set, but failed to capture the corrective effect of utterances that resulted in repair or noticing but could not be considered as repair initiations. And, from a learner-centered perspective, noticing and self-repair were stimulated by both the repair initiations offered by others *and* by contrasting utterances which were not repair initiations. For example, learners experienced episodes where an erroneous utterance incidentally contrasted with the utterance of a teacher or peer who was not privy to the learner's error. These contrasting utterances could not be considered as a repair initiations, because the corrective utterance was not produced with any orientation to the erroneous utterance. However, learners who experienced these contrasts did orient to them, as evidenced by change-of-state tokens (Heritage, 1984); learners also made use of the feedback by incorporating the corrected form into subsequent utterances. The corrective potential of these contrasting utterances could not be overlooked. Discovery of these episodes and consideration of their relationships to corrective feedback, as more traditionally defined, resulted in an expanded definition of corrective feedback, which was developed through the iterative process of considering the range of utterances that potentially had corrective value from the point of view of the seven learners.

Repair may be initiated by the self or another, as well as being completed by the self or another. The corrective feedback literature, unlike the repair literature, has not examined self-initiated, self-repair. And, the definition of corrective feedback adopted for this chapter also does not include self-initiated, self-repair besides that which occurs following a contrasting utterance. Even so, I have also collected episodes of self-initiated self-repair that involved malformed utterances. These instances of self-correction are briefly considered separately from instances of corrective feedback. The ability to self-correct is indicative of noticing, and is relevant to corrective feedback processes because it shows linguistic development. Because the motor processes involved in speech are intimately connected with speech perception (Baddeley, 1990; MacKay, 1992), oral production in and of itself provides an opportunity for perception that may promote learner noticing of their own errors. Corrective feedback, in fact, does not preclude learner noticing that may have occurred even if the feedback were not provided. Self-correction allows for insight into what learners are able to notice and correct without assistance. Here, self-correction is defined as a self-initiated, self-repair that occurs in the absence of other-initiated repair or of a contrasting utterance by another speaker.

Considering Audience Design

The definition of corrective feedback adopted in this chapter, as just discussed, is broader than that of previous research. The definition incorporates the notion of repair, and also acknowledges that utterances may be corrective in function even when they are not produced in response to a learner error. This definition of corrective feedback includes awareness of who utterances are designed for, and each learner's role in a particular interaction. Previous work on corrective feedback only considered utterances that were addressed to the learner who produced the erroneous utterance, whereas my approach is based on an understanding of corrective feedback as utterances that have a potentially corrective function for the learner. Corrective utterances may occur when the learner is an *addressee*, in which case the feedback is addressed to him or her, but also occur when the learner has the participant status of *auditor* or *overhearer*, in which case the utterance is actually addressed to someone else. This understanding of the learner's roles as addressee, auditor, or overhearer, is based upon Bell's (1984) theory of audience design, which considers the impact of participant status (Goffman, 1974) on social interaction, sketching the roles of addressee, auditor, overhearer, and eavesdropper and the impact of the presence of these various participants on the speaker. Auditors and overhearers are present in the social interactive setting but are not the addressee. They differ in their potential of becoming an addressee. An auditor is a ratified participant of an interaction who is a potential addressee, but is not currently being addressed. In contrast, an overhearer is not a potential addressee. In the classroom setting, an overhearer is a classroom participant who is in a position to overhear the interaction of others, as, for example, when a learner in one group is able to overhear what happens in other nearby groups. As shown in chapter 3, learners utilize what they overhear other pairs and/or groups doing as they work on language learning tasks. An eavesdropper is a person who overhears but whose presence is not known to the participants. Members of a classroom community take on addressee, auditor, and overhearer roles. These are the roles that are relevant in this examination of corrective feedback.

Audience design is relevant to corrective feedback research for two reasons. First, speakers design their utterances not only for the addressee, but also for auditors and overhearers. Research in code-switching, for example, has confirmed the importance of auditors (Nishimura, 1997) and overhearers (Hallmon, 1998) in shaping the language choice of the speaker. In the classroom setting, teachers speak for the benefit of two different audiences—the addressee and the auditor. The addressee may be an individual, or may be the entire class. When the addressee is an individual, the teacher still keeps auditors in mind when designing an utterance. Secondly, the particular role of the learner, whether addressee, auditor, or overhearer, impacts the learner's level of attentiveness, the availability of working memory, and the learner's potential for acting on the interaction. In the teacher-fronted setting, when a teacher is talking to a particular addressee, the auditors may become addressees at any time, a factor that impacts the their level of attentiveness. This holds when learners are auditors during group work as well. As overhearers during peer learning tasks, learners may overhear what goes on in other groups and capitalize on these affordances as well. As overhearers, they are principally involved in interaction with another person, and thus have less attention available for overhearing. As a result auditors might be able to make better use of utterances addressed to others than can overhearers. Auditors may also have greater resources available in working memory than addressees, who may also be occupied with formulating a response. My definition of corrective feedback takes participation status into account by considering the corrective value of utterances that might otherwise not be seen as corrective in nature, in situations where the targeted learner is not the addressee, but is an auditor or overhearer. This definition of corrective feedback acknowledges the potential corrective function of contrasting utterances that learners are privy to in their various classroom roles of speaker, addressee, auditor, and overhearer. By analyzing these students' participation, we can better understand how teacher–student and student–student interaction impacts learners, whatever their role in classroom interaction. The analysis presented in this chapter demonstrates how including these different learner roles and settings in our understanding of corrective feedback is useful in understanding, from a learner-centered perspective, the corrective resources available to the students as they work to learn the L2.

Classifying Corrective Feedback

Episodes of corrective feedback were categorized based on characteristics of the data set as a whole. Characteristics of the setting and of persons providing corrective feedback that were found to be important in the analysis are listed in Table 4.1. In addition, categories of corrective feedback were developed based on the data set. Previous research that provided taxonomies for classifying corrective feedback episodes was used for reference.

The Consequences of Corrective Feedback

When presented with corrective feedback, learners had a range of possible responses that became evident through qualitative examination of the transcripts. First, the learner might make immediate use of the feedback, incorporating it into the subsequent turn in a repair attempt that may be fully or partially successful. This is called *uptake*. Second, without repetition or reformulation, the learner may, in the subsequent turn, show that he or she noticed the feedback by producing a change-of-state token like "oh." I call this response *noticing*. Third, whether or not there is evidence of uptake or noticing, learners might make use of the feedback later during the same

TABLE 4.1
Setting and Person Providing Feedback

The Setting	The Person Providing Feedback
Teacher-fronted or peer learning	The teacher, a classmate, or both

class period. Finally, sometimes it is not clear what a learner did with the feedback due to problems with recording quality, or when overlap renders a learner turn inaudible. Three of these possibilities, *uptake*, *noticing*, and *no uptake* were used to code the episodes. Use of corrective feedback at a later time could potentially co-occur with each of these three categories, so was not coded separately, but episodes that appeared to be related to later use of the particular item were set aside for further examination.

RESULTS

Corrective Feedback in L2 Classrooms

Because corrective feedback is examined from a learner-centered perspective, with all episodes that could potentially function as corrective feedback for each learner being examined, a wide range of episodes was collected. When corrective feedback is defined by teacher corrective moves, this limits the type and range of utterances analyzed. In contrast, adoption of a learner-centered approach draws attention to whatever may function as corrective for a particular student, illuminating a wider range of phenomena. In addition, learners who spoke more in either communicative or private speech contexts provided the analyst with a greater opportunity to observe corrective sequences. Individual differences in patterns of participation as well as differences between the lessons conducted in different classes renders many sorts of quantitative analyses of the data unproductive. For example, it is not productive to compare learner totals of different feedback types when these totals are dependent on a number of factors. These factors include differences between the particular activities going on in class that day, differences in each learner's level of overt and covert (private speech) participation in activities, whether or not peer learning tasks were used in a class, and so on. Each class session and each learner's participation in that session are unique events. Quantitative analysis is included primarily as a tool that illuminates where corrective feedback occurred and how learners responded to corrective utterances in different settings. Qualitative analysis further illuminates phenomena which occur related to corrective feedback.

Corrective sequences occurred in two major settings—the teacher-fronted setting and the peer learning setting. Both teachers and classroom learners actively provided feedback to the seven learners. Table 4.2 shows where corrective episodes occurred, whether in teacher-fronted or peer learning settings. There were 150 episodes of corrective feedback in the data. Of these episodes, just over half (79 episodes) occurred in the teacher-fronted context, whereas the other 71 episodes occurred during

TABLE 4.2
Where Did Corrective Feedback Occur?

Teacher-Fronted Setting	Peer Learning Setting
79	71

peer interaction. This is interesting because class time was not evenly divided across these settings. When the total number of learner turns, including private turns and participation in choral drill, are calculated, many more learner turns occurred in the teacher-fronted than in the peer learning setting. This means that the nature of participation in the peer learning setting allows greater opportunity for individuals to receive corrective feedback.

Table 4.3 shows who provided corrective feedback in each of these settings: the teacher, a classmate or classmates, or both the teacher and a classmate or classmates. In the teacher-fronted setting, teachers provided most of the corrective feedback. Learners seldom provided corrective feedback to other learners in the teacher-fronted setting. In contrast, the most common source of corrective feedback in the peer learning setting was a classmate. When teacher and learner both provided corrective feedback, in the teacher-fronted context, this occurred during incidental recasts, where learner and teacher utterances not addressed to the learner who made the error contrast with the linguistic error. When both the teacher and a classmate were involved in corrective feedback in the peer learning setting, this generally occurred when the classmate recruited the teacher's involvement by asking the teacher if a learner's utterance was correct or when the teacher, who was standing by, confirmed a partner's explicit correction of the targeted learner.

Types of Corrective Feedback

The types of corrective feedback found in the data set are shown in Table 4.4. It is important to note here that each "type" encompasses a diverse range of actions. Any one episode cannot be assumed to be identical to

TABLE 4.3
Providers of Corrective Feedback in
Teacher-Fronted and Peer Learning Setting

	Teacher	Classmate(s)	Both Teacher and Classmate(s)
Teacher-fronted setting	60	4	15
Peer learning setting	9	59	3
Totals	69	63	18

TABLE 4.4
Categories of Corrective Feedback Found in the Data

Recast	An utterance that reformulates a learner's erroneous utterance. Recasts may contrast with learner utterances phonologically, morphologically, syntactically, or semantically, but are based on the learner's erroneous utterance and maintain semantic contiguity with it. Recasts are immediately subsequent to the utterance.
Incidental recast	An utterance that incidentally contrasts with the learner's erroneous utterance and is not in response to it. The contrasting utterance is not based on the learner's own utterance, but incidentally functions as a recast. Incidental recasts are available to the learner by attending to classroom interaction in the role of auditor or overhearer. Incidental recasts may occur immediately subsequent to the erroneous utterance, after some delay, or occasionally in overlap with the erroneous utterance. Delayed incidental recasts may happen even when the learner is addressee, but only when the utterance is not in response to the learner's own malformed utterance, but occurs later in the interaction.
Repetition	The teacher or a classmate repeats the erroneous utterance without altering the misformation.
Prompt	The teacher or a classmate uses a partial repetition to engage the learner in a reformulation.
Explicit	The teacher or classmate clearly identifies the error, explicitly indicating that the learner's utterance is incorrect, and possibly providing a reformulation or metalinguistic information.
Re-asks	The teacher or classmate re-asks the question that yielded an incorrect response.
Answer	The teacher or classmate answers the targeted learner's question about his or her own production, providing corrective feedback at the targeted learner's request.
Confirmation question	The teacher or classmate asks a confirmation question.
Comprehension question	The teacher or classmate asks a question to clarify understanding of the targeted learner's utterance.
Multiple	The teacher or classmate uses two or more of the above strategies.

others in the same category. Corrective feedback was most strongly characterized by its flexibility and situational adaptability. These categories, therefore, are best used to understand the broad variety of ways in which linguistic errors were treated, rather than as a set of discrete types.

The two broad types of corrective feedback that occurred most frequently were recasts and incidental recasts. Of the 150 corrective feedback episodes in the data set, 44 were recasts, and 47 were incidental recasts. These two types of episodes were the most frequent in the data, with only a few episodes from each other category. These two categories each incorporate a diversity of phenomena, and are discussed in detail in the following sections, but first a brief example of each is provided. As just defined, recasts are utterances that occur in the turn immediately following a learner's erroneous utterance, which repeat the semantic content of the utterance but contrast with the learner's utterance in linguistic form. Recasts are provided by a person who is currently interacting with the learner. Excerpt 1 provides an example of how Sara's line 3 utterance is recast by the teacher in line 4:

(1) 1 T: Ja rokuban, eeto S1-san doo shita n desu ka?
              Okay number six, S1, ((ask your partner)) what
              happened?

     2 S1:   Sara-san wa doo shita n desu ka?
              Sara-san, what happened?

→   3 Sr: A:h ashi (.) ashi ni::, (.) ke::ga:: (.) oh. Ashi ni, kega
              o::, (2) o: suru n desu
              A:h I (.) injury: (.) my leg:: (.) oh. I injure ((error:
              non-past tense)) (.) my leg.

→   4 T: Kega o (.) shita n desu.
              You injured ((past tense)) (.) your leg.

     5 Sr: Oh. Shita n desu
              Oh. Injured.

                                                          (Sara, 5/22)

The contrast between recasts and incidental recasts is one that relates both to participant roles and to intentionality. In the case of a recast, the one who provides the recast heard the learner's erroneous utterance and is responding to it. What I have termed *incidental recasts* are different from recasts because even though they functionally provide a recast to the learner who attends to them, they are not provided in response to the learner's utterance, but contrast coincidentally. Even learners who are not participating in face-to-face interaction are privy to incidental recasts that contrast with covert utterances produced in private speech, or during choral responses. Incidental recasts also occur during group work when an utterance by a person in another group contrasts with the learner's own utterance. Although there are different types of incidental recasts that are discussed in detail in a subsequent section, a basic example here may serve to clarify the concept. In this example, Bryce, who participates in the teacher's interaction with a classmate via his production of a vicarious response (line 4), experiences an utterance that contrasts with his own (line 5), an incidental recast:

(2) 1 T: Denwa shite okimasu. ((writing)) (.) Denwa shite
              okimasu (.) Hoka ni wa?
              Call in advance ((writing)). Call in advance (.) And what
              else?

	2	F:	Sunakku to sarada o sunakku to sarada o shite oku
			Do ((error: word choice)) snacks and salad, snacks and
			salads in advance.
	3	T:	Sunakku to sarada o:,
			Snacks and salads ACC:, *((T prompts F to provide a*
			different verb))
→	4	B:	°°Tsukete::°°
			°°*attach*°°
→	5	F:	Oh tsukutte
			Oh make
	6	B:	°°°oku°°°
			°°°*in advance*°°°
→	7	T:	Tskutte okimasu (.)
			Make in advance (.)
	8	B:	°°°Tsukutte oku°°°
			°°°*Make in advance*°°°

(Bryce, 1/27)

The remainder of this chapter focuses on recasts and incidental recasts, with many examples of each provided.

Recasts

The positive impact of recasts on language development has been shown in a broad range of studies. L1 researchers have found recasts to be particularly salient. This salience results from the semantic and proximal contingency of recasts. This is evident from the earliest stages of language development. For example, children whose mothers imitate their babbling play make a broader range of sounds more than other infants do (Masur, 1989). This research finding confirms the salience of imitative utterances. And, recasts not only contain a redundant component, but also include something new—a contrast with the erroneous utterance in, for example, phonology, grammatical form, or information presented. Simple recasts that present one contrast were found to be powerful in explaining L1 development in Moerk's (1992) reanalysis of Brown's (1973) longitudinal data. Meltzoff and Gopnik (1989) found recasting that incorporated expansion "to be maximally interesting and useful for the children" while at the same time serving "as a frame and motivation for further exchange" (p. 37). L1 research has shown that the effectiveness of recasts results both from the salience inherent in reformulations that follow the learner's own interest, as well as from the facilitation of interaction that results from the interlocutor's production of an utterance that the learner can quickly grasp and make use of in their own subsequent production. Recasts provide a scaffold for the developing child that the child utilizes in interaction with others; this process of assisted performance builds into the child's linguistic development, as recasts are developmentally tailored to the child's growing abilities. In sum, research with children has shown that recasts provide an ideal setting for linguistic processing and growth.

Among L2 researchers, there has been disagreement concerning the potential effectiveness of recasts. Some researchers have been concerned about low uptake rates for recasts. However, uptake rates are not a good indication of whether or not learning is taking place. The best evidence for this comes from child L1 acquisition research. Recasts are the child's primary source of negative evidence, and although uptake rates are quite low, over time, recasts have been shown to be overwhelmingly effective. L2 studies are beginning to show that this may apply to the L2 learner as well. Mackey and Philp's (1998) experimental study found that recasts are noticed even if learners do not repeat them. Philp (1999), in another experimental study, also found that learners overwhelmingly noticed recasts. In addition, a classroom experimental study by Doughty and Varela (1998) found recasting treatment to be effective in an immersion science classroom where learners did not repeat the recasts. An attempt was made, however, to draw each learner's attention to the recasts through a two-step process through which the teacher first repeated the learner's error. As these results and those of other studies show, recasts have been found to have a positive impact on learner development.

The effectiveness of recasts has been attributed both to their salience and to their frequency following malformed utterances. Regarding salience, the redundancy of recasts frees the attention needed for processing the linguistic contrasts they introduce. Not only do learners focus more readily on language structure when meaning is held constant, but this meaning is inherently interesting to the learner because the learner produced the utterance in the first place. Although redundancy may seem to be a negative quality, it is not. For the one receiving the recast, the utterance is even more worthy of attention because it maintains the semantic content of the learner's own utterance. In addition, redundancy promotes the learner's focus on the linguistic contrast. VanPatten (1989) suggested that comprehension of meaning must be automatized in order for the L2 learner to analyze form. Because redundancy eases comprehension, it heightens the potential for form-based analysis. Along the same lines, L1 language disorders researchers S. M. Camarata and his colleagues (1994) found that the redundancy of recasts reduces the semantic processing load, and frees processing capacity for attention to the reformulation. This is how they account for the effectiveness of recasts. In the L2 classroom context, concerns about the possible ineffectiveness of recasts have been primarily expressed for the immersion classroom context where, except for occasional corrective feedback, many classrooms provide no linguistic focus whatsoever (Doughty & Varela, 1998; Lightbown & Spada, 1990; Lyster & Ranta, 1997).

Recasts and Their Use

Even when recasts are not immediately acted on by learners, the data suggest that, combined with other sources of information available in the classroom, recasts do have an effect on learners over time. In the context of the first- and second-year university level language classes that are the focus of attention here, recasts were provided primarily of language forms that were already the focus of instruction. The classes followed a grammatical syllabus, incorporating language practice activities with a linguistic focus, even while working to guide students to be creative in using the language to express their own meanings, and, in the first-year program, while organizing instruction around thematic units.

Table 4.5 shows how learners responded to recasts in the data set during teacher-fronted sections of the class, using the categories *uptake*, *noticing*, and *no uptake*. Unclear cases are also noted. Whether or not a learner may have made use of the feedback later in class is not noted in this table. Overall, uptake rates are high for these learners—9/24, or 42%, with the rate of uptake + noticing even higher. However, there is a lot of individual variation.[2] First, we note that over the data set, none of the individuals experienced recasts very frequently—the range extends from a low of 1 (Katie), to a high of 7 (Bryce). Although the data show that recasts are the most frequently occurring corrective feedback type (a finding consistent with previous research), and that recasts are used by these learners, when each individual's experience with recasts is considered, numbers are quite low. Class sizes range from 22 to 25 students, meaning that there are many students for the teacher to call on during teacher-fronted work, and little opportunity for each individual to interact much with the teacher in class. Learners are much more often auditors than they are addressees of the teacher in the teacher-fronted setting. The data do suggest, however, that individuals respond to the recasts differently. In the teacher-fronted setting, Candace and Sara, who experience two and three recasts, respectively, both respond by using the corrected forms in their subsequent turn, yielding 100% uptake rates. Rob, however, who experiences six recasts, only makes use of the form provided one time. And, Kuo-ming and Katie do not make use of recasts at all in the teacher-fronted setting. The effect of pooling all of these numbers shows an overall uptake rate of 42%, which is high, but which does not reflect differences in individual verbal re-

---

[2]See also Foster (1998) on individual differences in rates of negotiation in small group work.

TABLE 4.5
Responses to Recasts in Teacher-Fronted Contexts

	Uptake	Noticing	No Uptake	Unclear	Total	Uptake Total	Uptake + Noticing Total
Candace	1	1			2	1/2	2/2
Rob	1		5		6	1/6	
Sara	3				3	3/3	
Kuo-ming	0		2	1	3	0/3	
Bryce	3	1	3		7	3/7	4/7
Katie	0		1		1	0/1	
Andrea	1		1		2	1/2	
Totals	9	2	12	1	24	9/24	11/24

sponse rates. Although following individual learners yields low numbers, the results show that a generalized uptake figure for a particular group, class, or teacher is unlikely to have good validity for individual learners experiencing instruction in those classrooms.

Recasts also occurred in the peer learning setting where, rather than being provided by teachers, they were almost always provided by classmates. The numbers in Table 4.6 look quite different from those in Table 4.5. While Rob, Kuo-ming, and Katie did not utilize recasts in the teacher-fronted setting, they make use of recasts in the peer learning setting, although, again, numbers for individuals are quite low. The categories *noticing* and *unclear* are not included in this table because there were no such instances in the data. As a group, all of the recasts the first-year learners received in the peer learning setting resulted in uptake, compared to less uptake in the teacher-fronted setting. The second-year learners, Bryce, Katie and Andrea, also made more frequent use of recasts in the peer learning setting. It appears that the peer learning setting may be a place where

TABLE 4.6
Responses to Recasts in Peer Learning Setting

	Uptake	No Uptake	Total	Percent Uptake
Candace	5		5	5/5
Rob	1		1	1/1
Sara	3		3	3/3
Kuo-ming	2		2	2/2
Bryce	1		1	1/1
Katie	1	2	3	1/3
Andrea	2	3	5	2/5
Totals	15	5	20	15/20

learners are better able to make use of corrective feedback. One reason may be that the peer learning setting provides a context where the learner is working on a language learning task. In this context, recasts are more immediately relevant because they not only correct a linguistic error, but are also useful for the task at hand. In contrast, in the teacher-fronted setting, there may be no opportunity for learners to make use of the feedback.

In reviewing the 11 teacher-fronted recasts that resulted in uptake or noticing, it is evident that an opportunity for the learner to reformulate was afforded by the discourse structure. After recasts, teachers stopped speaking, and learners repeated the recasts. In addition, the recasts that were repeated all focused on a single grammatical structure or lexical item, what L1 acquisition researchers have termed *simple recasts*. Excerpt 3 (shown earlier as Excerpt 1) provides an example from Sara's class.

(3)	1	T:	Ja rokuban, eeto S1-san doo shita n desu ka?
			Okay number six, S1, ((ask your partner)) what
			happened?
	2	S1:	Sara-san wa do shita n desu ka?
			Sara-san, what happened?
→	3	Sr:	A:h ashi (.) ashi ni::, (.) ke::ga:: (.) oh. Ashi ni, kega
			o::, (2) o: suru n desu
			A:h I (.) injury: (.) my leg:: (.) oh. I injure ((error:
			non-past tense)) (.) my leg.
→	4	T:	Kega o (.) shita n desu.
			You injured ((past tense)) (.) your leg.
	5	Sr:	Oh. Shita n desu
			Oh. Injured.

(Sara, 5/22)

The line 4 recast presents one contrast—tense. In addition, the teacher stops after providing the recast, producing a slot in the discourse for the learner to respond. Sara responds in line 5 with the change-of-state token "oh" and a reformulation. Although this teacher behavior allowed learners opportunity to respond, learners did not always provide an oral response. Excerpt 4 shows an example of oral drill from Rob's class where Rob's pronunciation is recast.

(4)	1	T:	Hai ja muzukashii desu. Rob-san
			Okay it is difficult. Rob.
	2	R:	Um: muzuka<u>shii</u>katta desu?
			Um: it was difficult? ((difficult is misprounounced)).
	3	T:	Mm muzuka<u>shi</u>katta desu (.) Chan-san negative?
			Mm was difficult (.) Chan-san, the negative?

(Rob, 1/24)

Although the teacher pauses after her recast in line 3, Rob does not respond. It is possible that he did not notice the pronunciation contrast. In absence of a learner response, however, it is not possible to conclude what learners did or did not notice.

When recasts were not responded to, it was often the case that teachers did not provide a slot for a learner response (Oliver, 1995). For example, in Excerpt 5, another example from Rob's class, the teacher moves on to ask a follow-up question after her recast:

(5)   1   T: Rob-san wa donna kuruma o motte imasu ka?
               Rob, what sort of car do you have?
→   2   R: Uh ii kuruma (.) uh wa::
               Uh, good car (.) uh TOP:: *((should have used accusative marker o))*
→   3   T: Ah ii [kuruma o motte imasu ka? Ii desu ne:.=
               Ah   you have a nice car? That's nice.=
     4   Ss: [hehehehehehe
     5   T: =Ja nani iro no kuruma desu ka? Nani iro?
               =So what color is your car? What color?

                                        (Rob, 2/28)

The teacher's recast in line 3 is followed by an evaluative phrase (*Ii desu ne* 'that's good'), which functions as a transition to the line 5 question that immediately follows. Differences in discourse structure may impact, but not completely determine whether or not there is uptake.

In peer learning tasks, receiving recasts helped the learners to do the tasks better. In Excerpt 6, Andrea has asked the teacher what counter to use to count "pockets." The teacher responds in line 1. And, when Andrea incorporates the counter into her own sentence, misusing *no* in the process, the teacher recasts, and Andrea immediately incorporates the correction into her overlapping utterance. Andrea's utterance is directed to her partner, who is drawing a picture of the person Andrea is describing, making the teacher's recast immediately useful to Andrea:

(6)   1   T: Eh poketto ga hitotsu futatsu=
               Eh count pockets with "hitotsu futatsu"= ((these are Japanese counters one and two))
     2   A: =Futatsu
               =Two
     3   T: Mittsu
               Three
→   4   A: Ah mitsu no poketto ga arimasu.
               Ah three GEN *pockets* NOM *exist. ((error: genitive marker should not be used))*

			There are three pockets.	
→	5	T:	Mittsu, (.) poketto ga,	[arimasu.
			Three, (.) pockets NOM	*exist ((Teacher omits genitive marker)).*
	6	A:		[Mitsu poketto ga arimasu.
				Three pockets NOM *exist.*
				There are three pockets.

(Andrea, 5/16)

Learners also made good use of recasts provided by their peer interlocutors during pair and group work. And there are also cases where, even though just one error is recast by the peer interlocutor, the learner corrects other errors during the uptake process. An example of this is shown in Excerpt 7. Underlining is used to highlight lexical items that are corrected in the excerpt.

(7) 1 C: Atama ga <u>itari</u> toki <u>nani</u> o shimasu ka?
What ((error: mis-use of 'what')) do you do when your head hurts ((error: mis-pronunciation of 'itai' (hurts) as 'itari'))?

2 S: <u>Doo</u> shimasu ka? <u>D- doo</u> shimasu ka?
How do you do? H- how do you do? ((this is correct— Japanese uses 'how' rather than 'what' for this expression))

3 C: Atama ga <u>itai</u> toki <u>doo</u> shimasu ka?
How do you do when your head hurts? ((this is correct))

4 S: Soo desu ne. (.) Nemasu. ((laughs))
Let's see. (.) I sleep. ((laughs))

(Candace, 5/22)

Candace replaces the incorrect *nani* 'what' with *doo* 'how', just as recast by her partner in line 2. In addition, in her line 3 reformulation, Candace also self-corrects her pronunciation of *itai* 'painful'.

Finally, it is important to note that a lack of response to a recast does not mean that it does not have an effect. In the following example from Andrea's class, Andrea repeatedly misuses the word *hameru* 'to wear'. This word is used to talk about wearing rings or contact lenses, and Andrea mistakenly uses it to talk about wearing slacks. Slacks, shorts, jeans, skirts and shoes require a different verb, *haku* 'to wear'. Although this has been practiced in teacher-fronted drill, in communicative interaction, Andrea repeatedly misuses *hameru*, even though none of her partners in the peer learning setting do so. She experiences repeated recasts from peers, but exhibits no uptake. Despite this, by the end of the class, she abandons *hameru* and uses *haku*, as is appropriate. In Excerpt 8, Andrea's partner recasts the lexical item in her answer to Andrea's question. Andrea is asking yes–no questions, trying to guess what a classmate she cannot see is wearing. The relevant verbs are highlighted with underlining.

(8)   1   A: Ano: shiroi no kutsu ga::
                U::h white shoes NOM::

      2   F2: Kutsu:: ga::
                Shoe::s NOM::

      3   A: Kutsu o shiroi no kutsu o <u>hamete imasu</u> ka?
                Shoes ACC white GEN ((error)) shoes ACC wearing
                ((error: verb choice)) INT?
                Is the person wearing white shoes?

      4   F: Iie <u>haite imasen</u>. Ano:::
                No, he's not. Uh:: ((correct verb for "wear," underlined))
                (3)

      5   A: Ano: ano: kuroi no kutsu o <u>hai- hamete imasu</u> ka?
                U:h u:h black GEN ((error)) shoes ACC wea- wearing
                ((error: wrong word for "wear," underlined)) INT?
                U:h u:h is the person wearing black shoes?

      6   F: <u>Hai haite imasu</u>
                Yes, he is ((correct verb for "wear," underlined))
                                                          (Andrea, 5/16)

When the partner answers Andrea's questions, she replaces the Andrea's verb choice with *haku*, the correct verb. In English questions of this type, the verb "wear" would not be included in the answer, whereas in Japanese, the verb must be included. And, in Japanese question and/or answer activity, it is customary to answer using the same verb that was used in the question. Therefore, the partner's use of a different verb is rather remarkable, and thus likely to be noticed. Even so, Andrea does not initially seem to notice. Rather, she continues using the wrong verb. In line 5, though, it appears that Andrea may have noticed. She begins the verb by saying *hai-*, the first syllable of *haite*, which would be appropriate here. However, Andrea immediately self-corrects to the erroneous *hameru*. And, again in line 6, she experiences a recast that provides the correct verb, *haku*, correctly inflected as *haite imasu*.

Later, after responding to a partner's question that uses the correct verb, Andrea twice uses *haku* appropriately. This is shown in Excerpt 9. In line 3, Andrea uses *haku* with a great deal of hesitation, and later in the excerpt, she uses it after asking for help:

(9)   1   M2: Pantsu o haite imasu ka.
                Are you wearing pants?

      2   A: Hai. Anoo anata wa uh off-whito:: shatsu o kite
                imasu ka?

          Yes. U:h are you wearing an uh off-white:: shirt?

→   3   A: Anoo uh (.) jiinzu o::: (.) jeans? Jiinzu o ha uh::::
            <u>haite imasu</u> ka?
            U:h uh: (.) jiinzu um jeans? Are you u:::h wearing
            jeans?

→   4   A: Sorekara shiroi no kutsu ga (.) kutsu o how do you
            say it? Kutsu o::: (.2)
            And white shoes (.) shoes how do you say it for shoes? (.2)

      5   M2: Haiteimasu. haki-
            Wearing. Wear-

→   6   A: What? <u>Haite imasu</u> ka? ((laughing))
            what? Is it "haite imasu?" ((laughing))

                                   (Andrea, 5/16)

In line 3, Andrea uses *haku* appropriately for the first time. Andrea's hesitation in her response is evidence of her thought during verb selection. Her cognitive processing is evident in her first aborted attempt make a question in line 3, and then in the elongation of words and filled pause (uh::::) preceding the choice of verb when she restarts the sentence. Then, in talking about shoes in line 4, Andrea needs the verb *haku* again, and asks for help, stopping right before the verb should be provided in line 4 (after the accusative marker *o*). Her partner provides the conjugated verb in line 5, and Andrea confirms the choice in line 6.

Near the end of the class, Andrea again hesitantly uses the verb *haku* correctly on her own, as shown in Excerpt 10. In this task, instead of facing each other when asking questions as they did earlier, the teacher has the students stand back to back and guess what their partner is wearing. Therefore, some of Andrea's partner P's utterances are inaudible because the microphone is clipped to Andrea's shirt front.

(10) 1   A: Hanjiinzu o:: um oh what is it? <u>Hare- haite imasu</u>
            <u>ka?</u>
            Shorts ((error: wrong word for 'shorts')) ACC um oh what
            is it? Do you we- wear shorts?

       2   P: (   )

       3   A: Sorekara::: (.) kiroi to shiroi no kutsu g- o::: (.)
            yeah. <u>haite imasu ka?</u>
            And::: (.) are you wearing yellow and white (.) shoes?

       4   P: (   )

                                   (Andrea, 5/16)

In both lines 1 and 3, Andrea uses the verb *haku*, as is appropriate, to talk about wearing shorts and shoes. The sequence of excerpts shows how implicit negative feedback in the form of recasts, combined with other examples of use of the correct verb, function as a resource to Andrea, even though there is no explicit uptake of any of the corrective feedback. By the end of the lesson, Andrea has both stopped using *hameru*, and has begun thoughtfully using *haku*, as seen by her false start in line 1, and pausing in line 3. This example provides evidence of how learners make use of recasts, even if not immediately, and provides a note of caution for researchers and teachers not to assume that learners are unable to make use of corrective feedback when uptake or noticing is not immediately evidenced.

Incidental Recasts

An *incidental recast* occurs when the learner is privy to language of an utterance that contrasts with the misformation, but is not produced in response to it. Incidental recasts are a significant modality through which learners receive information about the well-formedness of their utterances. Previous work on corrective feedback has not noted the importance or even the existence of incidental recasts. In the corpus under examination here, 47 of the 150 corrective feedback episodes involved incidental recasts. The category, incidental recasts, is diverse, consisting of a range of corrective feedback episodes that occur most often when the learner is in the role of auditor or overhearer. Sometimes, the learner's utterance was uttered as private speech, or in a private turn such as a choral context, when the learner was one of many addressees of an utterance directed by the teacher to the whole class. Sometimes incidental recasts occurred when what was uttered in a peer learning context contrasted with an utterance of another learner in another group, or when a learner's utterance contrasted with an utterance of an interlocutor that occurred somewhat later. What incidental recasts share in common is the fact that they present contrasts that are not produced in response to a learner's malformed utterance. The incidence of incidental recasts in teacher-fronted and peer learning settings is shown in Table 4.7. Even though incidental recasts are not in response to individual learner's error, uptake in the teacher-fronted setting is rather frequent, as shown in Table 4.8. Most of these in-

TABLE 4.7
Incidental Recasts

Teacher-Fronted Setting		Peer Learning Setting	
Corrective Feedback (Total)	*Incidental Recasts*	*Corrective Feedback (Total)*	*Incidental Recasts*
79	31	71	16

TABLE 4.8
Responses to Incidental Recasts in the Teacher-Fronted Setting

	Uptake	Noticing	No Uptake	Total	Percentage Uptake	Percentage Uptake + Noticing
Candace	2	1	2	5	2/5	3/5
Rob	3		5	8	3/8	
Sara	3		3	6	3/6	
Kuo-ming	4		4	8	3/6	
Bryce	1	2	0	3	1/3	3/3
Katie				0		
Andrea			1	1	0/1	
Totals	12	3	15	31	12/31	15/31

cidental recasts (29/31) involved contrasts between the targeted learner's and the teacher's utterances. Learner responses to incidental recasts ranged from, uptake, in which learners repeated or made use of the incidental recasts in the subsequent turn, to noticing, where learners said "oh," or "ah," or otherwise indicated that they noticed the contrast. In the peer learning setting, however, uptake, as defined by repetition or reformulation in the learner's turn following the feedback, was negligible. However, the data suggest that learners do attend to and make use of incidental recasts in the peer learning setting. Here, the contrasting utterances were usually uttered by another learner (14/16), rather than by the teacher (2/16), and were often available to the targeted learner as overheard utterances that occurred in another pair or group. Because learner orientation to overheard utterances is evident in the data, these instances were also collected due to their corrective potential.

Incidental Recasts in the Teacher-Fronted Setting

The potential of incidental recasts as corrective feedback phenomena emerged in the analysis because of learners' tendencies to respond to them. Learners actively make use of language that contrasts with their own L2 production even when a contrasting utterance could not possibly have been intended by a speaker as corrective, and even when such utterances are not individually addressed to the learners who utilize them.

In the teacher-fronted setting, learners receive incidental recasts that contrast with their own *private turns*. Private turns (van Lier, 1988) are turns learners perform for themselves, either as private speech (see chap. 2) or in a choral context. In private speech, learners carve out their own interactive space, producing a response that is not adapted for a listener. These self-addressed turns are usually uttered with reduced volume when the learner is not the addressee, although learners also use private speech in formulating their own public turns. *Choral responses* are somewhat different from private speech, in that teachers license choral responses by addressing questions or prompts to the class as a whole. Choral responses are produced by students who seldom use private speech. The choral drill context provides an environment for all of the learners to orally produce responses, as learners who use private speech are prone to do anyway. Unlike the soft voices and whispers used in private speech, learners who participate in choral drills usually speak at normal or raised volume. And, choral responses are addressed to the teacher, even though the teacher cannot possibly tailor feedback to each student's choral contribution. Both choral and private speech responses provide learners with opportunities to hear their own utterances and to hear how their utterances compare with those of others, resulting in corrective episodes when errors occur. In the choral setting, most incidental recasts relate to verb conjugation or pronunciation problems, because that is what is usually being practiced. The following two examples are typical. In Excerpt 11, Candace responds in chorus as the teacher prompts students to provide the verb phrase for polite requests. The polite request the teacher prompts the students to use is structured as follows:

<u>Suupaa de ringo o</u> katte-kudasai
<u>Supermarket</u> at <u>apple ACC</u> buy-please
Please buy apples at the supermarket.

The underlined portion includes the location where buying is to occur and what is to be bought. The teacher uses this part of the sentence as a prompt, and students must supply the verb phrase, which contains the *te*-form of a verb plus *kudasai*, the imperative form of the verb *kudasaru*, an honorific verb which means "give." The resulting verb phrase constitutes a request. Because of the word order differences between Japanese and English, the teacher's prompts cannot be translated, so only a word-for-word translation showing the meanings of lexical items and the function of particles is provided for this excerpt:

(11)   1   T: Suupaa de ringo o?
                Supermarket at apple ACC?
       2   Ss: Katte ku[dasai +³
                Buy   pl[ease
       3   C: [Katte
                         Buy

---

³The symbol "+" is used in choral responses to indicate that there are various overlapping responses given. The transcribed utterance is the predominant response.

4 T: Katte kudasai. Ja gohan o
   Buy please. Okay rice ACC
5 Ss: Tabete +
   Eat
→ 6 C: Tsukurite
   Make ((error: misconjugation))
7 Ss: Tsuku:: tsuku::ru tsukutte +
   Make ((various forms uttered in conjugation attempts))
8 T: Tsukutte kudasai. Hai
   Make please. Okay.
9 C: Tsukutte
   Make ((correct))
10 T: Tsukutte kudasai
   Make please
11 Ss: Tsukutte kudas[ai
   Make   please
12 C: [Tsukutte
             Make

(Candace, 2/28)

The "+" sign in the students' choral turns in lines 2, 5, and 7, indicates that there were many overlapping and various responses. Candace's line 6 error, *tsukurite*, contrasts with correct conjugations produced subsequently both by students in line 7, and in the teacher's follow-up turn in line 8, where she prompts students to repeat, which Candace does. This situation often occurs in choral drill contexts, where the teacher's follow-up turn repeats the form being drilled. In the next example, Excerpt 12, Rob's response occurs in overlap with correct responses by other students, again followed by a teacher confirmation of the correct response. Although contrasting utterances that overlap with the learner's own error may seem to be irrelevant because one might think that speakers do not perceive utterances produced in overlap, Schegloff (in press) showed that speakers are able to perceive utterances that overlap with their own. His data show how speakers orient to utterances produced in overlap. Therefore, we cannot assume that utterances that overlap with the learner's own are not available to be noticed or utilized by the learner. Here, the teacher follows Rob's response, which occurred with the others in chorus, with her own production of the correct response. She does not prompt students to repeat her response, but Rob does so anyway in line 10:

(12) 1 T: Ja:: nihongo no kurasu wa muzukashii desu ka?
      Okay: is Japanese class difficult?
    2 Ss: [Hai muzukashii desu. +
      Yes it is difficult. +

	3	Ss:	[Iie amari muzukashikunai + ((some responses

       3   Ss: [Iie amari muzukashikunai + ((some responses contain various conjugation errors)).
No, it isn't very difficult +

→   4   R: Uh::

       5   T: Hai ja: hai muzukashii desu (.) Iie amari:,
Okay, right it is difficult. (.) No, i:t,

       6   Ss: [Muzukashikunai desu
It isn't difficult.

→   7   R: [Muzukashin desu
It is difficult ((error: negation))

       8   T: Muzukashiku arimasen or muzukashiku:: (.) nai desu (.) ii desu ne?
It isn't difficult or it isn't difficult ((the English translation does not reflect that the teacher is showing two different possibilities for adjective negation)). Okay?

       9   [Muzukashiku arimasen (.) muzukashikunai desu.
It isn't difficult (.) It isn't difficult.

→   10   R: [muzukashiku nai desu
It isn't difficult

   11   T: Ja nihongo no shukudai wa (.) taihen desu ka.
Okay is Japanese homework (.) hard?

                                      (Rob, 1/24)

In response to the teacher's question about whether Japanese class is difficult, in lines 2 and 3, students give affirmative and negative answers. Some of the negative answers contain misformed negative adjectives. Rob does not respond to the teacher's initial question, but says "Uh:::::" in line 4. The teacher repeats the affirmative answer in line 5, prompting students to produce the negative form. Here, Rob responds, in line 7, his incorrect form overlapping with the correct responses of others. His response also contrasts with the teacher's follow-up in line 8, where she repeats two possible negative conjugations. In line 10, Rob repeats a correct form.

Incidental recasts that occurred in choral contexts did not always result in learner repetition of the correct form, as shown in the Excerpt 13, taken from Kuo-ming's class:

(13) 1   T: Jaa kore wa donna sofa desu ka?
Okay what sort of sofa is this?

      2   Km: Kire[i:: (.) sofa desu
Beautiful:: (.) sofa COP ((error: particle 'na' is omitted))
A pretty sofa

      3   Ss: [Kirei na sofa desu +
Beautiful COP sofa COP +

> *A beautiful sofa ((correctly inserts 'na' after 'kirei'))*

4   T: Un soo ne, kirei na sofa desu.
             Yeah right, it's a beautiful sofa.

5   (.)

6   Km: Hehehe ((laughter))

                                      (Kuo-ming, 10/24)

Here, in response to the teacher's question about the sofa, Kuo-ming and the class respond that it is beautiful, but Kuo-ming omits the particle *na* (line 2), which is necessary when adjectival nouns like *kirei* 'beautiful' are used in the prenominal position. Other students responding do use *na* (line 3), as the teacher does in her line 4 follow-up turn. Kuo-ming, however, does not repeat the correct form.

Even when students do not repeat incidental recasts, there is evidence that learners may notice them, as evidenced by whether or not they make the same error in subsequent discourse. For example, in Excerpt 14, Candace makes repeated errors with the object marker, using *no*, the genitive marker, instead of the accusative marker *o*. Her responses, which occur in chorus, contrast with those of other students and of the teacher, as shown. First, the teacher asks students to repeat her line 1 sentence—this is where Candace's first error occurs, in line 2.

(14)   1   T: Minna de (.) Sentaa wiikurii o yomimasu.
                     Everyone (.) Center Weekly ACC read.
                     All together (.) I read the Center Weekly.

→   2   C: [Sentaa wiikurii no °mmm? yomimasu°
                     Center weekly GEN °m::? read°

    3   Ss: [Sentaa wiikurii o yomimasu +
                     Center Weekly ACC read.
                     I read the Center Weekly.

    4   T: Yomimasu (.)
                     Read (.)

    5   C: Yomimasu
                     Read

    6   T: Ii desu ne hai ja kiite kudasai,
                     Good okay so please ask ((your classmate)),

→   7   C: [°Sentaa: (.) no (.) yomimasu°
                     °Center: (.) GEN (.) read°

    8   S: [Sentaa::
                     Center::

    9   T: Wiikurii o
                     Weekly ACC

   10 S: Wiikurii o:, (.) uh (.) yomimasu ka?
                     Do you read (.) uh (.) the weekly?

11   S1:   Uh hai yomimasu.
             Uh yes, I read it.
12   T: Ah (.) y[omimasu (.)soo desu ka? (.) kiite kudasai
             Ah (.) you read it (.) really? (.) please ask.
13   C: [°°Sentaa°°
                     °°center°°
→   14   S2:   Sentaa wiikurii o yomimasu (.) ka?
             Center Weekly ACC:, (.) uh (.) read INT?
             Do you read the Center Weekly?
15   C: Iie (.) °a ^ ° Iie yomimasen
             No (.) °a ^ ° No, I don't read it.
16   T: Iie yomimasen hai kore wa:?
             No, you don't read it. Right. And this is?
17   T/Ss: Nyu:su (.) wiiku
             News (.) week

                                          (Candace, 11/27)

In these eleven lines, Candace makes the same error twice. First, she uses
no instead of *o* in the choral response context in line 2. Her choral response overlaps with the correct responses of other students who use *o*. In
line 6, the teacher tells student S to ask another student whether he or she
reads the magazine. In line 7, Candace begins to softly formulate her own
answer in private speech, repeating the particle error. As the nominated
student evidences difficulty in forming the question, the teacher prompts
him in line 9, using the correct particle, and the nominated student formulates his question correctly in line 10. Then, in line 12, after showing
interest in Student 1's (S1) answer, the teacher prompts another student,
Student 2 (S2), to ask Candace the same question. S2 forms the question
correctly, providing for Candace another correct example of particle use.
All of these utterances contrast with Candace's malformation. Whether she
notices the feedback, however, is not clear. Candace's high level of engagement in the interaction is evident from her use of private speech in
working to formulate her own responses when the teacher calls on others
(in lines 7 and 13). As the interaction continues in Excerpt 14.1, another
student, Student 3 (S3), makes the same mistake as Candace (underlined,
line 20), resulting in treatment of the error by the teacher:

(14.1)
18   T: Ii desu ne hai ja [kiite kudasai (.) S3-san
             Good okay well S3, please ask
19   C: [°nyu:su wiiku°
                                 news week
→   20   S3:   Um news weekly or Newsweek (.) um_no yomimasu?
             Um news weekly or Newsweek (.) um GEN read?
             Um do you read news weekly (.) or Newsweek?

```
21  T:   Newsweek      ((T prompts))
22  S3:  O ^ =
         ACC
23  T:   =O=
         ACC
24  S3:  =O (.) o yomimasu (.) ka?
         ACC(.) ACC read (.) INT?
25  S4:  Uh hai yomimasu
         Uh yes I read it
26  T:   Hai yomimasu ah soo desu ka?
         Yes you read it, oh really?
```

(Candace, 11/27)

In line 19, Candace's high level of engagement is clear, as she privately works on the pronunciation of "Newsweek" in Japanese. In line 20, S3 uses *no* instead of *o*, just as Candace did earlier. In line 21, the teacher prompts S3 to repeat the sentence. S3 correctly provides *o*, which the teacher repeats, and S3 repeats again, completing the sentence in line 24. The teacher's treatment of S3's error is also available to Candace, who made the same error.

All of this functions incidentally as corrective feedback for Candace. The question is, does this help Candace to learn Japanese? Let's see how Candace produces similar sentences subsequently. Later, during a peer task, the students ask and answer questions about the publications they read. And, in Excerpt 15, Candace uses the accusative particle correctly (underlined):

```
(15)  1  C:   Sentaa: (.) weekly (.) wi:: wi:: (.) sentaa (.) tai (.)
              tai::=
              Center: (.) weekly (.) wi:: wi:: (.) center (.) tai (.) tai::=
      2  S:   =Taimusu=
              Times
→     3  C:   =Taimusu? Sentaa taimusu (.) ah: o: o yomimasu (.)
              yomimasu ka?
              Times? center times (.) ah: ACC: ACC read (.) read INT?
              Times? Do you read the Center Times? ((hesitation before
              the accusative particle))
      4  S:   Hai yomimasu (3) Sentaa taimusu uh (.) o yomimasu
              ka?
              Yes, I read it. (3) Do you read the center times?
              ((hesitation before the accusative particle))
→     5  C:   Iie. (.) yomimasen. (.) Nu: York taimuzu: yomimasu.
              No. (.) I don't read it (.) I read the New York Times.
```

(Candace, 11/27)

In line 3, Candace uses the accusative particle correctly. Her cognitive process of particle selection is evident in her use of a short pause, a filled pause (ah:), and elongation and repetition of the marker *o*. Her use is effortful, but she uses the particle correctly. When her partner asks her the same question in line 4, she responds appropriately in line 5, adding that she reads the *New York Times*. In line 5 she omits the accusative marker. Again, she does not misuse the genitive marker.

The choral response context provides an opportunity for learners to produce their own answers to questions or prompts the teacher addresses to the entire class. By asking the class as a whole, the teacher legitimizes the learners' use of private turns. In this context, even though the teacher is only able to broadly monitor learner responses, not to follow up each individual's utterance, learners are privy to corrective feedback in the form of incidental recasts when their malformed utterances contrast with the correct utterances of fellow classmates or the teacher. And, even without uptake or noticing, there is evidence that learners are able to make use of incidental recasts. Corrective feedback, therefore, even if not intentionally provided, is available to the students. These episodes also show how learners may benefit from corrective feedback addressed to other learners. This will be explored further.

Private Speech and Incidental Recasts

Along with choral responses, private speech also is relevant to corrective feedback. Private speech is particularly interesting, as noted in chapter 2, because it provides us with a window on learners' cognitive processes that are part and parcel of language learning. The classroom corpus shows private speech to be relevant to corrective feedback in two ways. First, utterances produced by learners in the modality of private speech potentially contrast with the utterances of other learners or the teacher. In line 7 of Excerpt 15, we saw how Candace produced an error in her private speech, an error that contrasted with subsequent correct utterances, providing Candace with an important source of information about her production. Second, private speech data provide a view of what resources are corrective for a particular learner. Private speech reveals the utility of incidental recasts, showing how learners covertly make use of contrasting utterances.

When learners participate via private speech, their linguistic errors provide them with an opportunity to experience incidental recasts. An example is provided in Excerpt 16. The teacher asked Sara, a first-year learner who is indicated by "Sr," to ask her partner, Lee, a question about his apartment. Sara responds by asking Lee about the windows in his apartment. As Lee begins to respond, Sara participates by using private speech, and the teacher prompts Lee in constructing his answer.

(16) 1 Sr: Lee-san no:: (.) Lee-san no mado wa, (.) uh, donna mado desu ka.
             Lee, (.) what is your (.) what is your window like?

      2 L: Uh, watashi no-
             Uh, my-

→   3 Sr: ((whispers)) °mado°.
             °window°

      4 L: (.)

      5 T: Watashi no mado?
             My window?

      6 L: Watashi no mado wa?
             My window TOP?

      7 Sr: Wa?
             TOP? (topic marker wa)

      8 T: Wa.
             TOP.

      9 L: Wa,
             TOP,

     10 T: Kirei
             Beautiful

→   11 Sr: °Kirei:: mado desu.°
             °Is a beau:::tiful window°°((error: copular form 'na' should be between the adjectival noun 'kirei' and the noun 'mado'))

     12: L: (.)

     13 T: Kirei: na mado desu. Hai. Hai, watashi no mado? (.) Hai, itte kudasai
             Is a beautiful COP window. Okay. Okay, my window? (.) Okay, please repeat

     14 T/L: Watashi no mado: (.) wa kirei na mado desu.
             My window (.) is a beautiful COP window.

                                                    (Sara, 10/23)

In line 11, Sara responds to the teacher's prompt of Lee by softly producing her own vicarious response, which contains an error—she omits the marker *na*—which must be used when adjectival nouns are in prenominal position. Sara's private turn then contrasts with the teacher's completion of Lee's turn in line 13. At the teacher's prompting (line 13), Lee repeats the entire sentence (line 14). Meanwhile, all of this functions as corrective feedback for Sara. Over 100 lines later in the transcript, shown in Excerpt 17, Sara corrects her partner Mary. This excerpt, previously shown in chapter 3 as an example of assisted performance, is repeated to show how the earlier incidental recast potentially served as a resource for Sara; it provides her with a foundation from which to assist her partner.

(17) 1 Sr: Ano: sumimasen! M-san no (.) tomodachi:: (.) wa (.)
              donna: (.) donna hito: desu ka
              Um: excuse me! What (.) kind of (.) friends (.) do (.) you
              have?

      2 M: Watashi no tomodachi wa, (.) kirei to, (.) um-
              My friend is, (.) beautiful and ((error: the particle 'to'
              means 'and,' but can only be used to connect two nouns)),
              (.) um-

→   3 Sr: Kirei no hi-   [Kirei na hito I think.
              Beautiful GEN per- Beautiful COP person I think. ((error:
              genitive particle 'no' is incorrect. 'Na' is the correct
              choice))

      4 M: [Kirei na hito   Kirei na hi//to.
                                 Beautiful COP person Beautiful COP pe//rson

      5 Sr: Right.
      6 M: Soshite:,
→   7 Sr: >I'll make sure.<

                                                          (Sara, 10/23)

As Sara corrects her partner in line 3, she introduces another possibility,
the particle *no*, but self-corrects to *kirei na hito*. Sara's partner, Mary, settles
on *na*, and Sara, in line 7, says she will make sure. Sara has not yet resolved
the problem but she is focused on it. This episode provides evidence of the
utility of the incidental recasts shown in the previous episode.

When the teacher addresses another student in Excerpt 18 (shown earlier as Excerpt 2), Bryce's vicarious response is incorrect. As Bryce's answer contrasts with the correct answer given by the student addressed,
Bryce has an opportunity to revise his response. In response to the
teacher's line 1 question, F responds in line 2, using the wrong verb. In
line 3, the teacher provides F with corrective feedback by prompting her
to reformulate:

(18) 1 T: Denwa shite okimasu. ((writing)) (.) Denwa shite
              okimasu (.) Hoka ni wa?
              Call in advance ((writing)). Call in advance (.) And what
              else?

      2 F: Sunakku to sarada o sunakku to sarada o shite oku
              Do ((error: word choice)) snacks and salad, snacks and
              salads in advance.

      3 T: Sunakku to sarada o:,
              Snacks and salads ACC:, ((T prompts F to provide a
              different verb))

→   4 B: °°Tsukete::°°
              °°Attach°°

5 F: Oh tsukutte
          Oh make

6 B: °°°oku°°°
          °°°*in advance*°°°

→ 7 T: Tskutte okimasu (.)
          Make in advance (.)

8 B: °°°Tsukutte oku°°°
          °°°*Make in advance*°°°

(Bryce, 1/27)

Before F reformulates in line 5, Bryce whispers his own candidate response in line 4. His response is incorrect, and contrasts with F's correct response in line 5. Bryce correctly follows up F's self-correction by whispering the auxiliary verb *oku*. The teacher then repeats the correct verb phrase in line 7, which Bryce repeats in a whisper, in line 8. Bryce obtained corrective feedback related to his line 4 error in the form of incidental recasts by his classmate F in line 4, and by the teacher in line 7.

Private speech reveals how learners may find corrective feedback in unexpected places, and how a learner's focus of attention may be different than what the teacher might expect. In Excerpt 19, Kuo-ming's English-influenced pronunciation contrasts with the teacher's pronunciation. When he answers the teacher's line 1 question, "What is this a map of?," Kuo-ming and another student provide short answers in lines 2 and 3, saying just the place name. In line 4, the teacher prompts them to produce a complete sentence, and it is her prompt that provides an incidental recast of Kuo-ming's pronunciation of the place name. The contrasting syllables are underlined:

(19) 1 T: Doko no chizu desu ka?
             What is this a map of?

      2 Km: <u>Ca</u>pitoru [(hill) hmʃhmf hehe
             Capitol   (hill) hmʃhmf hehe ((laughter)) ((error: uses
             English pronunciation of "capitol"))

      3 M: [<u>Ca</u>pito::ru Hiru
                   Capito::l Hill ((error: uses English
             pronunciation of "capitol"))

      4 T: Un. <u>kya</u>pitoru hiru no:?
             Un. A what of Capitol Hill? ((T uses Japanese
             pronunciation 'kyapitoru'))

      5 Ss: [Chizu- <u>kya</u>pitoru hiru no chizu desu ((various
             responses))
             A map—a map of capitol hill

→ 6 Km: [°°<u>Kya</u>pitoru h[[iru°°
             °°*Capitol Hill*°° *((correct Japanese pronunciation of*
             'kyapitoru'))

7   T: [[Kyapitoru hiru no chizu desu. Un.
                          A map of Capitol Hill. Yes.
                                                    (Kuo-ming, 11/18)

Although other students respond to the teacher's elicitation by working to produce the whole sentence, Kuo-ming, instead, responds to a subtle difference between the teacher's pronunciation and his own. His soft response is only available for analysis because he wore an individual microphone. Private speech allows the researcher to discover what aspect of the interaction learners are particularly attending to. Instead of reformulating the sentence as prompted, Kuo-ming made his own use of the teacher's utterance as a source of feedback on his pronunciation.

Later in the year, a class of Kuo-ming's provides an interesting example of how errors that occur in the peer learning setting may be treated much later through delayed incidental recasts. In a peer interactive task, as Kuo-ming and his partner go over a worksheet displaying pictures of people with various maladies, Kuo-ming has difficulty with tense choice, as shown in Excerpt 20:

(20) 1   P: Doo shitan desu ka?
                 What happened?
      2   Km: Uh:: uh:: (..) do I have anything? Or is this just
                 ashi ga itain desu
                 my leg hurts.
      3   P: Ashi ni kega o shitan
                 I injured my leg ((error: copula missing))
      4   Km: Ah! Keg- ashi kega o surun desu. ((pause))
                 *Ah! I in- injure ((non-past)) my leg. ((error: tense
                 incorrect. Km does, however, include the copula omitted
                 by P in line 3))*
      5   °Ashi (..) kega o surun (.) desu:.° ((writing))
                 °I injure (..) my (.) leg°((error: tense incorrect))
      6   Hehe doo shitan desu ka?
                 Hehe what happened?
      7   P: Netsu ga:: aru n desu
                 I have a fever ((correct tense))
                                                    (Kuo-ming, 5/22)

In line 2, Kuo-ming proposes *ashi ga itain desu* 'I hurt my leg', and his partner provides the new expression they have just learned, *ashi ni kega o shita*, which means 'I've injured my leg'. When Kuo-ming repeats the expression, however, both initially and softly when writing it down, he uses the nonpast tense on the verb. Following peer activity, when the teacher goes over the worksheet with the students, as shown in Excerpt 21, another student makes the same mistake. Note Kuo-ming's line 5 response to the corrective feedback directed to S10 in line 4:

(21) 1 T: Hai ja rokuban. Kore wa doo desu ka? Eh:to ja::
                 S9-san to S10-san.
                 Yes number six. How about this? Okay uh:: S9 and S10.

       2 S9: Doo shitan desu ka?
                 What happened to you?

       3 S10: Uh ashi ni uh kega o suru n desu.
                 Uh I will hurt my leg. ((error: wrong tense))

       4 T: Ashi ni kega o [(.) shita n desu
                 I hurt my leg. ((teacher uses correct tense))

  →   5 Km: [ash ni ^ shita n (.) a:h!
                                   Hurt (.) a:h! ((Km repeats correct tense))

       6 T: (   ) ashi ni kega o shita n desu. Ne? Ashi ni kega o
                 shita
                 (   ) I hurt my leg. Right? I hurt my leg

  →   7 Km: [shita n   [de::su.
                 hurt ((past tense))

       8 T: [Past tense o tsukatte kudasai. [ii desu ka? Ashi ni kega
                 o shita n desu.
                 Please use past tense.   okay? I hurt my leg

  →   9 Km: [[°Kega o shita n°
                 °Hurt my leg°

      10 T: [[Hai ja nanaban Kim-san to Sam-san.
                 Okay well number Seven, Kim and Sam
                                                  (Kuo-ming, 5/22)

As soon as the teacher utters the verb *shita* in line 4, Kuo-ming notices the discrepancy. This is evidenced not only by his repetition of the verb, but by the change-of-state token "ah:!" that shows his attention to the contrast. This example shows how powerful incidental recasts can be, even when they are delayed. Here, Kuo-ming is not the addressee, but is an *auditor*—a ratified participant who is not currently being addressed. He continues to focus on the word *shita*, in lines 7 and 9, reducing volume to a whisper, as he works to make the form his own.

Incidental Recasts in the Peer Learning Context

In the peer learning setting, incidental recasts seldom occur in a position immediately subsequent to the learner's error, as is typical in the teacher-fronted setting. In addition, because learners may be engaged in interaction with another interlocutor, the contrasts are less likely to be noticed, as indicated by negligible uptake and noticing responses. However, there is evidence that even though learners may not audibly demonstrate their awareness, they are able to make use of what they overhear in other groups. This was shown in chapter 3 in discussion of assisted performance. In addition, the data show how learners make use of incidental recasts much later in a particular interaction. Whether or not students are able to learn from these contrasts likely depends on their ability to remember their own utterances for comparison with the utterances of others. If they do, and if they attend to the talk around them, they may be able to notice contrasting utterances and to make use of them, overtly or covertly. In one example, during pair practice, Rob repeatedly uses the topic marker *wa* where the accusative *o* should be used. In the teacher-fronted follow-up to this activity, *wa* is never used in this context, only *o*. Later, when the teacher calls on Rob, he uses *o* correctly. In this instance, it is not clear whether Rob's correct use is caused by his noticing the contrast between his own incorrect use of *wa* with the correct use of *o* by others, but it is clear that this delayed contrast was an affordance available to Rob. In a similar case shown in Excerpt 22, Kuo-ming makes a tense error, using the nonpast form instead of past form when taking about an injured finger. The first time he uses the expression, he makes this mistake. And, right after he does, a member of the pair working beside Kuo-ming's pair uses the past morpheme *ta* correctly:

(22) 1 P: Doo shita n desu ka?
              What's wrong?

→   2 Km   Ah yubi o kiru- kiru n desu. (.) °Yubi o kiru:: n
              desu.° ((writing))
              I will cu-cut my finger. (.) °I cut my finger.° ((writing))
              ((error: wrong tense—Km uses non-past instead of past
              tense))

      3   ahem (.) hehe Doo shita n desu ka?
              Ahem (.) hehe what's wrong?

      4 S1:   Doo shita n desu ka? ((neighboring pair))
              What's wrong?

      5 S2:   Yu:::::bi o ki- ki- ((neighboring pair))
              Fi:::::nger ACC cu- cu- ((verb stem of cut, repeated twice
              without any marker of tense))

→   6 S1:   kita   ((neighboring pair))
              Cut ((past marker is correct. 'kitta' is mispronounced as
              'kita' without the geminate))

                                        (Kuo-ming, 5/22)

It is not clear whether or not Kuo-ming notices the contrast between his use of *kiru* 'cut' (nonpast tense) in line 2, and S1's use of *kitta* 'cut' in line 6. Later, the teacher goes over the worksheet with the students. In Excerpt 23, she calls on Kuo-ming to do the same item in line 1, though instead of answering the question, he asks it, and works with a student who uses the correct tense in line 3:

(23) 1 T: Hai hachiban. Ja: eh:to Kuo-ming-san to S12-san
             Okay number eight. Okay uh: Kuo-ming and S12.
     2 Km: ((laugh)) doo shita n desu ka?
             ((laugh)) What happened?
     3 S12: Yubi o (..) kitta n desu
             I cut ((past tense)) my finger.
     4 T: Un yubi o kitta n desu. Kitta [kore mo past tense
             desu ne?
             Yes you cut your finger.   Cut   this also is in past tense,
             okay?
→   5 Km: [kitta n desu
                                          cut ((past tense))
                                          (Kuo-ming, 5/22)

Notice that when the teacher follows up the student's correct response (line 3) with a repetition of that response (line 4), Kuo-ming repeats the tensed verb in line 5 in a private turn. Still later, as shown in Excerpt 24, the students are guided to add another line to their dialogue. After asking "What's wrong" and telling the partner that he or she "looks pale," the partner is free to insert their own response explaining their illness or injury. As the teacher guides the students in repeating the scripted lines of the dialogue, Kuo-ming gives his own explanation of an injury in private speech, a response in which he initially uses the wrong tense, but self-corrects to the past tense form in line 7.

(24) 1 T: Doo shita n desu ka?
             What happened?
     2 Ss: [Doo shita n desu ka?
             What happened?
     3 Km: [Dohoho shitahaha n desu ka ((laughing))
             What happened ((laughing))
     4 T: Kao iro ga warui n desu ne
             You look pale!
     5 Ss: [Kao iro ga warui n desu ne
             You look pale!

6   Km: [Kao iru ga warui n desu ne:
                You look pale!
→   7   Km: °°Yubi ((laughs)) o kiru n hehe desu hehe (.) °°°kita
                n desu.°°°
                °°*I cut ((error: non-past tense)) my finger ((laughs)) (.)*
                °°°*cut*°°° *((correct: past tense. error: pronunciation of 'kita'*
                for 'kitta'))

                                    (Kuo-ming, 5/22)

These data provide a good example of how learners get feedback on their misformed utterances from many sources. A variety of episodes work together in guiding learners as they acquire the language. Katie, a second-year student, draws on a variety of resources for improving her use of a grammatical structure in a role-play task. This task is much less structured than the one from Kuo-ming's first-year class. Here, learners were instructed specifically in the instructions written on the task sheet "not to worry about grammar too much." The role play is not designed to pivot around one particular structure, but learners need a range of structures for requesting advice, making suggestions, and giving directions. As Katie works in a pair, and later in a group of four, her use of a grammatical structure for giving advice improves dramatically. Two structures are possibly involved here, structures (a) and (b), as shown:

(a) Basu no hoo ga ii desu.
     Bus GEN *side* NOM *good* COP.
     "The bus is better."
(b) Basu de shoppingu sentaa ni itta hoo ga ii desu.
     Bus by shopping center DAT *go-complete side* NOM *good* COP.
     "It is good to go to the shopping center by bus" or "I recommend you go to the shopping center by bus."

These structures are used to give advice, and both involve the word *hoo*, which means 'side' or 'direction'. The word *hoo* indicates the item that the speaker is recommending. The structure shown in (a) is a simple genitive structure, where the learner must show that the bus is better by literally saying "the 'side' of the bus is good." This expresses the opinion that the bus is the better choice. In (b), a similar suggestion is made by creating a relative clause that modifies the noun *hoo*: The phrase *basu de shoppingu sentaa ni itta* modifies the noun *hoo*, meaning it is better to go by bus. The structures are related in that both involve the basic sentence pattern *X ga ii*—"X is good." They differ in that the noun phrase in (a) is a genitive phrase, and the noun phrase in (b) involves noun modification by a relative clause.

In this class, Katie's first attempt to use one of these expressions of advice appears in group work, as shown in Excerpt 25. Here, two lines of glossing are provided—a word-for-word gloss and a more colloquial translation. The location of errors is underlined in the Japanese and the word-for-word gloss, but may not be apparent in the colloquial English translation because English lacks these particular grammatical characteristics.

(25)
→ 1 K: U::m (.) bus ^ <u>basu:: (.) no ga ii</u> to omoimasu. To monorail.
            U::m (.) bus- <u>bus:: (.) GEN NOM GOOD</u> QT think. And monorail.
            U::m (.) bus- bus)) (.) better I think. And monorail.
            ((error: should be 'basu no hoo ga ii' not 'basu no ga ii'))
    2 F: Um hm?
→ 3 K: Ah bus to monorail (2) kuruma <u>ga:: (.) desu</u> kuruma::
            Ah bus and monorail (.) car <u>NOM (.) COP</u> car::
            Ah bus and monorail (.) the car (.) is car::
                                            (Katie, 6/2)

In both lines 1 and 3, Katie is unable to use the structure (a) correctly. In line 1 she omits the word *hoo*. And, as she elaborates her statement in line 3, her attempt completely falls apart. Later in the activity, shown in Excerpt 26, Katie again omits *hoo*, this time omitting the adjective *ii* 'good' as well:

(26) 1 K: (Basu) <u>no:: ga desu</u>. (4)
            (bus) GEN NOM COP. ((error: should be 'basu no hoo ga ii desu'))
→ 2 S3: Basu no hoo ga ii desu. ((in background))
            Bus GEN hoo NOM good COP.
            The bus is better. ((this is correct))
    3 K: °°no ga:::::°°
            °°GEN NOM::::°°((error: still incorrect. Should be 'no hoo ga'))
→ 4 S4: Kuruma no hoo ga::: (.) takushii yori: (.)
            Car GEN side NOM::: (.) taxi than: (.)
            A car, rather than a taxi . . . ((this is correct))
    5 S5: Takushi de iku no: (   )
            Taxi by go COMP: (   )
            Going by taxi: (   )

6 F: Oh taxi::
7 K: Uh huh.

(Katie, 6/2)

This time, Katie is privy to the interaction of the neighboring trio, S3, S4, and S5. Right after her line 1 misformulation, S3, a student in the neighboring triad, says the same sentence Katie attempted. In private speech, Katie softly repeats her error, which then contrasts with S4's utterance in line 4. The utterances in lines 2 and 4 function as incidental recasts to Katie, an overhearer. Katie's partner, F, takes advantage of these overheard resources. As Katie's group begins to talk about taxis in line 5, F picks up the word 'taxi', using what she overheard from the neighboring group.

Later in this interaction, Katie again tries to express that the bus is faster. This time, shown in Excerpt 27, Katie uses structure (b) in line 5, making three errors with the structure. She makes a word choice error, choosing the verb *oriru* 'get off' instead of *iku* 'go'. She makes an aspectual error, failing to use the completative aspect (the morpheme *-ta*). And, she includes the genitive marker *no* between the verb and the noun *hoo*—this particle can only be used to connect two nouns. Verbs can directly modify nouns, so the particle is not used.

(27) 1 K: Basu de:: <u>oriru</u> no to: (.) uh: (.) jitensha:: (.) de
               <u>oriru</u>:: (.)
               Bus by <u>get off</u> CMP and: (.) uh: bicycle (.) by <u>get off</u>:: (.)
               Between getting off the bus, and getting off the bicycle
               ((grammar is correct, but the choice of the word 'oriru' is
               odd))

      2   oh (.) wait. no:: yori uh benri desu. (2)
               oh (.) wait. CMP:: rather uh convenient. (.)
               ((Whole utterance: Getting off the bus is more convenient
               than getting off a bicycle.))

      3   Oh man, it's so hard to remember all that. (8)
      4 F: So you said between bus?
→   5 K: Basu de oru (   ) <u>basu de oriru no hoo</u> ga (2)
               Bus by be (   ) <u>bus by get off GEN</u> side NOM (2)
               Getting off- (   ) getting off the bus is (2)

      6 T: Kuruma mo hayai shi basu mo hayai. Ii desu yo.
               It's fast to take a car or the bus. That's right.

      7   Demo sore wa (.) (   ) kuruma de itta hoo ga hayai desu.
               But that TOP (.) (   ) car by go-complete side NOM fast COP.
               But as for that (.) (   ) it's faster to go by car. ((T substitutes
               the correct verb 'iku' which means 'go' for 'oriru'))

     8   S7:   [bus is faster
     9   K: Basu de [orita::   [(.) <u>orita::</u> hoo ga ii desu.
                Bus by   [get off-complete::[(.) get off-complete:: side
                NOM good COP
                Getting off the bus is better. ((K still is using the wrong verb))
    10   T: [Kuruma de itta hoo ga hayai.
                                       car by go-complete side NOM fast
                                       It's faster to go by car.
                                                          (Katie, 6/2)

After trying (and failing) to use a comparative structure in lines 1 through 3, Katie rephrases using structure (b) in line 5, making the errors just noted. After she abandons her utterance in line 5, it contrasts incidentally with that of the teacher. The teacher is speaking to the neighboring group, and uses structure (b), as Katie attempted to. As S7, a member of the group the teacher is addressing, responds, in line 9 Katie reformulates her own sentence, producing a much improved version that is correct structurally, but still uses the wrong verb. Her utterance overlaps and incidentally contrasts with the teacher's repetition of her own utterance, shown in line 10.

Later in the class, pairs are combined to produce groups of four, and to explain their recommendations to another pair. Here, Katie again works to express that the bus is the best choice. This time, she gets it right, as shown in line 1 of Excerpt 28.

    (28)
→   1   K: Ah bus- (.) basu de (.) uh shoppingu center itta:::
                hoo ga ii desu
                Ah bus- (.) bus by (.) uh shopping center go-complete:::
                side NOM good COP
                Ah bus- (.) it's better to go to the shopping center by bus.
                ((K chooses the appropriate verb, 'iku'))
     2   M1:   Basu de?
                By bus?
     3   K: Basu to monorail de
                By bus and monorail
     4   M2:   Oh. Basu to monoreeru wa ichiban (jikan ga kakaru)
                janai desu ka?
                Oh. But don't the bus and monorail take the most time?
                                                          (Katie, 6/2)

Katie's correct formulation of the recommendation uses structure (b), and is formed with considerable effort, as shown by pauses, and elongation of the verb *itta* 'go-complete'. She uses an appropriate structure and chooses an appropriate verb. And, the two new group members, M1 and M2, ask about her recommendation.

In the peer learning setting, incidental recasts provide these learners with an important source of corrective feedback. For Kuo-ming, the incidental contrast between his own utterance and that of the neighboring pair is one of the resources he may have attended to. In the same way, Katie's misformed utterances incidentally contrast with those available to be overheard from a neighboring pair and of the teacher. Katie's performance improves until she accurately produces a difficult structure that is not the explicit focus of instruction in this class. These data show how incidental recasts may function as important sources of information to students about the correctness of their own utterances, information that may then be utilized as resources to improve their own production.

Noticing Corrective Feedback Addressed to Others

Another source of negative evidence for students is corrective feedback that is not even addressed to them, but is addressed to others. We have seen in Excerpts 14, 14.1, and 21, how Candace and Kuo-ming both utilized corrective feedback that was directed to other students, and was relevant to errors they made previously in private speech (Candace) or during peer interaction (Kuo-ming). Learners also attend to corrective feedback addressed to others that is not related to one of their own errors during the class period. For example, Candace repeats recasts that are directed to others, as shown in Excerpt 29, where she repeats adjectival noun and adjective negative constructions in line 5:

(29) 1 T: Kon shumatsu hima desu ka? Kylie-san
            This weekend are you free? Kylie
     2 K: Um (..) iie (.) um (.) uh:: (.) hima- (.) hima: (.) hima
            nai,
            Um (..) no (.) um (.) uh:: (.) not (.) not (.) not free
            ((error: wrong negator)).
     3 T: Hima ja^ arimasen
            You're not free ((T corrects form))
     4 K: Oh ja arim[asen
→   5 C: [°°hima ja^ arimasen°°
                    °°not free°°   ((C repeats correct form))
                                            Candace, 1/24

Candace whispers her own repetition of the teacher's corrective feedback, showing its salience even though it is not addressed to her. Collection and transcription of private speech data allow documentation of this phenomenon, which may apply to learners who use less private speech who may mentally attend to corrective feedback addressed to others by using inner speech.

Self-Correction

Self-correction is not corrective feedback, but is corrective in nature. In self-correction, through the process of producing an utterance in the L2, learners notice errors in their own utterances and act to repair them. There were 59 episodes involving self-correction in the data set where corrective feedback was not provided by the teacher or a peer, but where learners noticed their own linguistic errors, both initiating and completing repair. This includes self corrections by the seven learners' peer partners and, in the teacher-fronted setting, by the seven learners' classmates who publicly responded to the teacher. Many of the excerpts shown already in this book contain instances of self-correction, like Excerpt 30, which presents a portion of Excerpt 5 shown in chapter 3:

> (30) 1 Km: Um (1) um (1) suteki <u>no::</u> (.) um ske-suteki <u>na</u> sofa
> desu <u>ka?</u> (2) Desu <u>ne</u> or desu <u>k-</u> (.) haha desu
> <u>ne:,</u> (.)
> *Um (1) um (1) is it the (.) nice ((wrong particle)) um*
> *ni-nice ((correct particle)) sofa ((wrong final particle))?*
> *(.) ((re-states copula with corrected final particle and*
> *wrong final particle)) (.) ((chooses correct final particle))*
>
> 2 P: Ah donna sofa desu? (2)
> *Ah which sofa do you mean? (2)*
>
> 3 Km: Suteki na ha ((laugh)) sofa desu, hehehe (.)
> *The nice ((correct particle)) ha ((laugh)) sofa hehehe (.)*
>
> 4 P: Soo desu ka?
> *Oh really?*
>
> (Kuo-ming, 10/24)

In the first turn, Kuo-ming self-corrects the genitive *no* to the copular *na*, as well as wavering on the choice between the final particle *ne* and the question marker *ka*, finally choosing *ne* as appropriate. This is a typical example of self-correction. Self-correction occurred in teacher-fronted and peer learning contexts as shown in Table 4.9. The peer activity differs from the teacher-fronted setting in the greater amount of self-correction that occurs. Here, self-correction does not refer to all instances of repair, but only to self-initiated, self-repair of linguistic errors that occurs in absence of a contrasting utterance. Reformulations were occasionally erroneous, but were overwhelmingly correct. Sometimes, though, self-correc-

TABLE 4.9
Self Correction in the Teacher-Fronted and Peer Learning Settings

Setting	Self-Correction
Teacher-fronted setting	10
Peer learning setting	49
Totals	59

tions resulted in an error. Excerpt 31 is a good example by one of Candace's partners:

(31) 1   S: Uh (2) tsukare tsukarete iru toki (.) tsukarete iru::
                  <u>no</u> toki um (.) doo shimasu ka?
                  Uh (2) tire- when you're tired ((correct)) (.) when you:::r
                  ((incorrect insertion of the genetive particle, underlined
                  above)) tired um (.) what do you do?

                                                          Candace, 5/22

However, self-corrections overwhelmingly resulted in correct or improved forms. Of the 59 self-correction episodes, 7 resulted in a wrong form, 3 resulted in an improvement that was still not correct, and the other 48 episodes resulted in a correct form.

Self-correction was rare in the teacher-fronted setting, and half of the 10 episodes occurred in the seven learners' private turns (either private speech or choral turns) where the self-correction could not be observed by the teacher. Excerpt 32 shows one of the teacher-fronted cases (previously displayed as Excerpt 21 in chap. 3):

(32) 1   Cls: Kara-san no tsukue wa donna tsukue desu ka?
                  Kara, what is your desk like?
      2   T: Hai.
                  Right.
→   3   K: Watashi no tsukue wa (.) um, (.) <u>kirei</u> tsukue-
                  kirei:: na tsukue desu.
                  My desk is a (.) um, (.) pretty des- pre::ty desk.
                                                          (Sara, 10/23)

Most of the self-corrections found occurred during interaction with peers. Qualitative examination of the transcripts reveals that, although learners have the opportunity to create their own utterances in the teacher-fronted setting, their participation in this context is necessarily limited due to the large number of students in each class. In the peer learning context, they are freer to experiment with language and to produce their own utterances. This creation of individual utterances is evident in the self-correction that occurred. About half of the self-corrections had to do with word choice, word formation, and pronunciation (27). The rest were related to syntactic or morphological problems, such as particle choice or insertion, inflection of verbs and adjectives, question formation, noun modification, and tense/aspect. Just as self-correction in the peer learning setting occurred when learners were creating their own utterances, in the teacher-fronted setting also, self-correction tended to occur when learners were creating their own sentences rather than when they were repeating after the teacher.

SUMMARY AND DISCUSSION

A wide variety of corrective feedback episodes occurred in these foreign language classrooms; the focus of this chapter was on recasts and incidental recasts, the two types of corrective feedback that occurred most frequently. The results of this study show individual diversity in how learners respond to corrective feedback, while providing evidence that corrective feedback is a resource for learners in the process of language learning. The corrective feedback episodes involving these seven learners were almost evenly divided between teacher-fronted and peer activity settings, an interesting finding because the learners actually spent much more time in teacher-fronted practice than in the peer learning setting.

In the teacher-fronted setting, uptake rates for recasts were quite high, but there were dramatic individual differences in uptake and a wide range in how often each individual experienced recasts. Incidental recasts also occurred in the teacher-fronted setting, with a robust uptake rate, again varying widely from learner to learner. Even though incidental recasts do not require any response, learner tendency to make use of them shows the salience of the contrasts they present. When an incidental recast contrasted with a learner's production in private speech or choral drill during teacher-fronted practice, learners tended to notice the contrast and make use of the incidental recasts. The contrasts available in classroom talk constitute affordances available for the learner to utilize. Another way to think of affordances is to conceptualize them as *opportunities*—the contrasts available through recasts and incidental recasts are opportunities for the students who are ready to use them. The data provide examples of how learners take up these opportunities and incorporate correct forms into later utterances after experiencing both recasts and incidental recasts in the teacher-fronted setting.

In the peer learning setting, students also experienced corrective feedback. The uptake rate for recasts in the peer learning setting was much higher than in the teacher-fronted setting, and the recasts were almost all provided by peers, rather than the teacher. Again, however, this uptake rate does not reflect individual differences in either the number of recasts directed to each learner, or in how often the learners made use of the recasts. Compared to the teacher-fronted setting, small group or pair interaction provides a setting where learners were better able to apply what they learned from recasts. Incidental recasts in the peer learning setting presented quite a different situation. In the teacher-fronted setting, incidental recasts were available to students in a choral drill context, or when the teacher addressed another learner. These incidental recasts were available when the learner was one of many addressees (in the choral setting), or when the learner was an auditor—a potential addressee privy to the teacher's interaction with another classmate. These roles entail high levels of attentiveness, making it likely that learners will notice and use the incidental recasts. In the peer learning setting, however, incidental recasts were usually available to learners as overhearers of the language produced in the interactions of other groups or pairs working in parallel. The level of attention is arguably lower for overhearers than for auditors or addressees. Figure 4.1 graphically depicts the potential levels of attention linked to each role. The nature of particular student roles means that incidental recasts available to be overheard in the peer learning setting are arguably less salient than incidental recasts of the teacher-fronted setting, which occur when the learner is an auditor or is one addressee of many. This low level of salience is evidenced by negligible uptake. Even so, the data do provide evidence that learners in the peer learning setting make use of incidental recasts in their ongoing developmental processes. Finally, the peer learning setting also provided an environment conducive to self-correction. Although self-correction is not corrective feedback, self-correction was significant in this analysis because of its effectiveness. The prevalence of self-correction in the peer learning setting also provides further insight into the nature of the differences between the two settings, un-

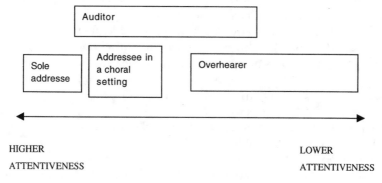

FIG. 4.1.   Potential level of attentiveness linked to particular student roles.

derscoring the opportunities the peer learning setting affords for language learners to make use of the language being learned.

Corrective Feedback—Is It Effective?

Classroom studies have prioritized the presence or absence of uptake as indicative of the effectiveness or ineffectiveness of corrective feedback. The present study shows how, even in the absence of uptake, learners benefit from corrective feedback. The findings provide additional evidence, which, along with the results of recent L2 experimental studies, shows that L2 speakers notice corrective feedback. The present analysis demonstrates that uptake is not the only way in which learners use corrective feedback. The data show how corrective feedback has an effect, over time, as learners increase in accuracy over a class period. In addition, the data show that learners have opportunities to receive corrective feedback related to their utterances that are not audible to the teacher (nor to researchers using a central microphone to collect data), in private speech and choral responses. Moreover, learners capitalize on corrective feedback addressed to their classmates, learning from their classmates' errors and how they are treated by the teacher. In the covert arena, as private speech data show us, learners are likely making better use of corrective feedback than studies have normally observed. Learners who do not produce as much private speech may still be active in noticing contrasting utterances and applying these affordances in their mental activity. The interaction that occurs in the classroom is not only between teacher and addressee, and between learner and learner, but the data suggest an abundance of inner interactive events that occur during classroom foreign language instruction.

This study shows that corrective feedback is clearly useful to classroom learners. Different types of feedback provide different opportunities for learners. The higher levels of attentiveness of learners who are addressees means that they may be more likely to notice the feedback, but learners who are offstage as auditors and overhearers, or as one of many addressees, also make use of corrective feedback, and may, because of more abundant resources in working memory, be better equipped to do so than addressees. Some students may be better able to take advantage of corrective feedback when they are out of the spotlight or unencumbered by the need to produce an utterance. In addition, the presence or absence of uptake, although it does not tell us whether or how learners are going to use corrective feedback, may tell us something about the learner's developmental level. Learners are best able to imitate what they are developmentally ready to learn.

Finally, this chapter shows the flexibility and adaptability of corrective feedback in different classroom settings with different learners. Just as each teacher and language class session is unique, each learner's participation is also unique. Results show strong individual differences. Teachers and peer partners flexibly adapt themselves to their interlocutors, transforming language learning tasks into unique activities. Corrective feedback is a varied process that is uniquely tailored to each situation as it unfolds moment by moment. The learner-centered approach taken in this study provides a step forward because it acknowledges this diversity. Longitudinal tracking of particular learners through classroom lessons allows us to see learning processes as they unfold, and to see learners making use of a range of linguistic affordances. Particular classroom techniques may not result in immediate evidence of development, but the seeds of development may become evident later in a lesson. Even when the effect of an interaction may seem to be immediately evident, that particular effect cannot be said to be caused by the particular corrective feedback episode, because a history precedes it. Corrective feedback is part of each learner's language learning history, providing resources that learners draw on in their development. Language development follows the interactive events that are its building blocks. Considering that learners find corrective value in a wide range of utterances, it makes sense to be skeptical about claims that prioritize a particular type of corrective feedback over another. Attempts to prove the superiority of a particular modality of participation over another, for example, of reformulations over repetition or imitation, may lead to an oversimplified model of SLA. Corrective feedback, in all of its complexity, is an important part of language developmental processes, not only for children, but for adult L2 learners as well.

Chapter 5

The Development of Interactional Style in the First-Year Classroom: Learning to Listen in Japanese

This chapter investigates the acquisition of interactional competence by examining how learners develop the ability to use appropriate listener responses in Japanese.[1] To effectively communicate in the L2, students must learn more than how to use vocabulary and grammatical structures appropriately. They must also learn how to interact using the language. Interaction is more than simply putting together sentences correctly. Learners must develop the ability to use the language appropriately in context, and to act as listeners as well as speakers. To listen appropriately, they must learn to use various interactional devices that show empathy, interest, and attention. Japanese language learning provides an excellent context to observe the development of interactional style because Japanese is a language rich in listener response expressions. Important listener responses include assessments, other expressions of alignment, confirmation questions, and a range of expressions that involve the final particle *ne*. These expressions are available to the learner in the interactional environment of the classroom (Ohta, 1993, 1994); though depending on the teacher and teaching approach, they may or may not be the subject of explicit classroom focus. Students experience these conversational features when the teacher acts as listener; learners are also privy to listener response expressions as peripheral participants in the teacher's interactions with other students.

---

[1]Earlier versions of this work appear as Ohta (1999), which uses data from one subject, and Ohta (in press-b), which analyzes data from two subjects.

179

Even for learners acquiring the L2 in Japan, research has shown that listener responses are difficult to acquire. Only 20% of the beginning learners studied by Matsuda (1988) used any listener responses, even though they were residing in Japan. Rather, skill in listener responses appears to be a mark of the advanced speaker. In her study of the conversation of advanced non-native pairs, Horiguchi (1990) found that most advanced speakers approached nativelike use of a wide range of listener responses.[2] Marriott (1994) found that Australian returnees from a high school year in Japan showed increased facility with backchannel responses. Like listener responses, development in the use of *ne*-marked expressions of alignment by adult learners in Japan has been found to proceed slowly for beginners, beginning with the set phrase *soo desu ne* 'that's right, isn't it', (Sawyer, 1991), and to be characterized by errors, some of which have their source in L1 transfer of epistemological concepts (Yoshimi, 1999). Researchers agree on the difficulty that second and foreign language learners have in acquiring these expressions (Ohta, 1994, in press-b; Sawyer, 1991; Siegal, 1996; Yoshimi, 1999).

The current study examines longitudinal development of listener responses among classroom foreign language learners in a foreign language setting where they encounter the language exclusively through classroom experience. Classroom learners have been shown to be sensitive to pragmatic information conveyed through classroom discourse (Ohta, 1997b, 1999), so it is reasonable to hypothesize that they might show development in the area of listener-response expressions, even if such expressions are not the focus of instruction. This chapter uses the first-year classroom data from the classroom corpus to examine how beginning learners develop the ability to use expressions that range from acknowledgement to alignment over an instructional year. The chapter first investigates the listener-response expressions available in the classroom environment. Then, the longitudinal development of four, first-year learners is analyzed. As evidenced by learner language use, results show that students are sensitive to listener responses, to expressions that are explicitly taught, as well as to more subtle response types. Students appear to be particularly responsive to instruction in use of listener responses; in addition, spontaneous use of such expressions also emerges. Results of analysis show individual variation in the extent to which students use L2 listener responses when not instructed to do so, as well as variability in the range of different expressions each student uses. Based on these results, I propose a developmental continuum of responses from *acknowledgement* to *alignment*.

---

[2]Horiguchi (1990), studied the following under the broad umbrella of listener responses: *aizuchi* (backchanneling), *ootai* (short answers), *hannoo* (assessments), *kakunin* (confirmation questions), *sakidori* (anticipatory responses), and three types of repair.

Learners begin without using any listener responses, even in English, moving toward use of expressions of acknowledgement, and finally alignment. All four learners become proficient in using acknowledgement responses, whereas only two of the four spontaneously use aligning assessments by the end of the academic year. These findings give insight into the development of interactional style among classroom learners, providing a foundation for study of how learners of other languages develop in the area of listener responses.

BEING A "GOOD LISTENER" IN JAPANESE

Three commonly occurring types of Japanese listener responses are expressions of acknowledgement, expressions of alignment, and confirmation questions. Expressions of acknowledgement show that a conversation partner is listening attentively. Aligning expressions are used by one speaker to show empathy, understanding, or concurrence with another. Alignment often takes the form of a secondary assessment. *Assessments* are verbal evaluations of experience that often contain an adjective and provide description of what the speaker is experiencing or has experienced, or, perhaps, a sympathetic evaluation of what one's interlocutor has experienced. Learners develop the ability both to do initial assessments and to show alignment—to agree with the assessments or factual descriptions expressed by their interlocutors. Listeners use *confirmation questions* to confirm their understanding of information conveyed in conversation. Like expressions of alignment, confirmation questions are also critical in the display of empathy, interest, and attention in conversation. Listener responses are common features of ordinary conversation, which are necessary for conversation to flow smoothly.

Native speakers know how to show not only that they are listening, but to show interest and empathy as appropriate. To do this, speakers use a range of expressions, including confirmation questions, assessments, repair initiations, anticipatory responses, and the backchannel responses called *aizuchi*[3] in Japanese (Horiguchi, 1990). Comparisons of listener responses between Japanese and Americans have shown the Japanese to be much more verbal in listener responses than Americans are (Maynard, 1989, 1993; Miller, 1995). One area of verbosity is in the explicit oral expression of alignment. Japanese interlocutors frequently use explicit ex-

---

[3]The Japanese term *aizuchi* is often translated in English with the broader terms *backchannel responses* or *listener responses*. Here, the term listener responses is not intended as a translation of *aizuchi*, but incorporates a broader range of expressions, including assessments and confirmation questions that, although functioning as listener responses, have generally not been included as examples of *aizuchi*.

pressions that convey alignment with the emotional tenor of their partner's talk. Strauss (1995) analyzed the listener responses of Japanese,
Korean, and American residents of Southern California who experienced
the Northridge earthquake. She found that Japanese conversationalists
verbally expressed alignment more often than either their Korean or
American counterparts. This does not mean that the American or Korean
pairs were less sympathetic or less interested, but that the interactive style
of the Japanese differed in frequency of aligning expressions, particularly
aligning assessments. Strauss (1995) provides the data shown in Excerpt 1
as an example. In the translation of the Japanese, the final particle *ne* is included without being translated.

(1)   1 Ai: Maa rosanzerusu mo sou iu- na: nanchiundaroo
                ibento no ooi tte iu ka: warui imi de
                Well, Los Angeles has been, what shall I say? Eventful,
                in a bad sense.

→   2 Hide: Ho:nto ni <u>ne</u> shizen to no tata- <u>ne</u> tatakai desu yo
                <u>ne</u>
                It's true ne. *Its like a strug-* ne *struggle against nature*
                ne

→   3 Ai: <u>Ne</u> soo desu <u>nee</u>
                ne. *Exactly* nee

       4 Hide: Demo amerika no:, seefu toka:. sono: amerikajin
                kanari borantia seeshin ga aru shi: Kanari hayaku
                hukyuu hayakatta desho
                But the American government, or well, the American
                people have a pretty good volunteer spirit and, the damage
                repair was pretty fast, right?

In the first two lines, Ai provides an assessment of life in Los Angeles, as
eventful in a negative sense. Note Hide's alignment in line 2—not only
does he agree in the beginning of his turn with *honto ni ne* 'That's true, *ne*',
but he upgrades Ai's assessment, describing life in Los Angeles as a struggle against nature. In line 3, Ai then aligns with Hide's upgrade of her assessment. Note the role of *ne* here in lines 2 and 3. Hide uses *ne* three
times in one turn, expressing alignment, and adding his own aligning assessment. In line 3, Ai uses *ne* twice in agreeing with Hide. This final particle *ne* is a critical element that expresses alignment. Hide continues in line
4, assessing how what he sees as an American propensity to volunteerism
was important in the aftermath of the earthquake.

The conversation continues in Excerpt 1.1. In line 5, Ai aligns with
Hide's line 4 assessment as follows:

(1.1)

→   5   Ai: Hayakatta shi
                 (It) was fast, and

→   6   Hide: <u>Nee</u> boku ga bikkuri shita no wa taioo ga hayai na:
                 to omotte. seefu nanka mo. n nihon no taioo ni
                 kuraberu to <u>ne</u>?
                 Nee what surprised me was, I thought that their reaction
                 was fast, and the (American) government's too, compared
                 to Japan's reaction ne?

→   7   Ai: Hayai desu yo <u>ne</u>
                 It was fast, ne?

      8   Hide: Mattaku yuushuu. ii desu yo ne
                 Completely excellent. (They are) good ne

She agrees with Hide, using the same word "fast," chosen by Hide in line 4, as well as the particle *shi*, meaning "moreover." In line 6, Hide aligns with Ai's line 5 expression of alignment, saying *Nee*, which alone functions to express alignment. Hide then builds on the theme by comparing the quick response of the Americans to his impression of responsiveness in Japan. In line 7, Ai aligns with Hide's comparison. And, in line 8, Hide upgrades Ai's agreement that Americans were *hayai* 'fast', with the extreme case formulation *mattaku yuushuu* 'completely excellent', and another nemarked assessment of American responsiveness as "good." Ai continues in line 9 of Excerpt 1.2, taking up Hide's comparison by adding the reason that responses to the earthquake are slow, and using *ne* in providing her example. Hide's response in line 10 is an emphatic "*Nnneee.*"

(1.2)   9   Ai: Ee. nihon wa nanka yosan kimeru toka itte
                 [yuujuufudan desu yo <u>ne</u>.
                 Yeah. As far as Japan is concerned, (they) say something
                 like they have to budget the costs and they can't make a
                 [decision ne

→   10   Hide: [<u>Nnneee</u>
                 Nnneee
                 (From Strauss, 1995, No. 19, emphasis added)

The overall impression of this conversation is of two people who are completely in tune with one another, who understand one another to the extent that each can build on the interlocutor's talk. Because the video recording session was the first time these two people had met, this is particularly remarkable. This sense of being "in tune" is built not only on the shared experience (which was common among Japanese, American, and Korean pairs), but in Japanese it is also built with expressions of alignment, many of which involve assessments and the affective particle *ne*. In this example from Strauss' data, a variety of expressions of alignment is evident. The line 7 assessment, *Hayai desu yo ne* 'they were fast *ne*' or 'they were fast, weren't they' is in the form of a confirmation question, which makes the interlocutor's alignment all the more expected; the sequential consequences of a question make an answer, in this case the aligning assessment in line 8, immediately expectable. Along with these overt displays of agreement and empathy, expressions that show understanding and interest, such as the use of *Ee* 'yes' in line 9 are used. The use of more neutral devices may seem less frequent due to a high frequency of aligning assessments that replace them in this affect-loaded conversation.

Based on her study, Strauss (1995) proposed a continuum of listener responses, from acknowledgement to alignment. In Fig. 5.1, I provide a graphic representation of the continuum Strauss verbally describes. Continuers usually take the form of brief tokens such as *hai*, *ee*, or *un*, all of which may be translated as 'yes'. Rather than indicating agreement, continuers usually show comprehension or acknowledgement—that the listener is foregoing the opportunity for repair (Schegloff, 1982). The same expressions that function as continuers may also show agreement, in which case they function as "agreement tokens." Because the use of agreement tokens may be ambiguous between acknowledgement and alignment, they are listed in the center of the continuum. When they actually function to show agreement, they move beyond acknowledgement toward alignment on the continuum. On the alignment end of the continuum are assessments, which more actively show the listener's concurrence with the teller's point of view. Strauss' (1995) study of interactional style also confirmed C. Goodwin and M. H. Goodwin's (1987) finding that when assessments occur in a conversation, they provide a salient environment for the expression of alignment. The production of an assessment by one interlocutor may be naturally followed by an expression of alignment by another interlocutor.

Expressions of alignment also occur when discussing facts. Conveyance of factual information creates conditions appropriate for confirmation

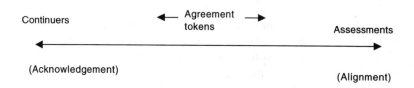

FIG. 5.1. Continuum of expressions from acknowledgement to assessment.

questions, which support the information received. These questions, which were not discussed by Strauss, would fall nearer the acknowledgement end of the of the continuum. They may show attention, surprise, empathy, or the need for additional information. Confirmation questions may also function as continuers. Prototypically, a confirmation question may be considered as part of a two-turn routine with Initiation-Response (I-R) structure, the initiation turn containing the information provided, and the response being a confirmation question marked with *ne*, as follows:

A: Provision of information
B: Confirmation question + *ne?*

This response may function to show understanding or acknowledgement. In addition, the answer to a confirmation question may also be an aligning move, functioning again as a listener response:

A: Provision of information
B: Confirmation question + *ne?*
A: Aligning response

Here, the confirmation question triggers alignment with the information expressed in the question. This results in a three-turn interactional routine. The provision of information acts as first pair part to a second-turn confirmation question, which acts as a first pair part for an expression of alignment. Excerpt 2 provides a classroom example.

(2)	1	P:	Ima nanji desu ka?
			What time is it?
	2	Sr:	Um (2) kuji?
			Um (2) Nine o'clock?
	3	P:	Kuji
			Nine o'clock.
	4	Sr:	I guess that's ten after (.)
	5	P:	Kuji:::
			Nine o'clock:::
(1)→	6	Sr:	Juppun desu.
			Ten minutes.
	7		(5)
(2)→	8	P:	Kuji juppun desu <u>ne:?</u>
			Nine-ten ne:?
(3)→	9	Sr:	Soo desu <u>ne.</u>
			Yes, that's right ne.

(Sara, 12/4)

Sara and her partner Peggy are doing a task where they ask each other the time, drawing hands on the clocks on their worksheets. This excerpt shows all three turns of the routine: provision of information, confirmation question, and expression of alignment. This conversational routine was explicitly taught in this lesson. The aligning expression, *soo desu ne*, is used for general purposes of alignment, whether with assessments or with expressions of fact. The final particle *ne* is critical in face-to-face communicative contexts for the maintenance of affective common ground in Japanese conversation (Cook, 1992).

WHAT IS *NE* AND WHY IS IT CRITICAL IN SPOKEN JAPANESE?

The final particle *ne* is frequent in ordinary Japanese conversation. Without *ne*, conversation cannot flow smoothly. *Ne* has a range of functions under the umbrella of affective common ground, or cooperative agreement in feeling (Cook, 1988, 1992). In this chapter, the use of *ne* in assessments and expressions of alignment is of primary concern.

Ne has been commonly described as a particle that elicits agreement or seeks confirmation. The use of *ne* to mark shared information has been frequently noted in the literature. Kamio (1990, 1997), explained this use of *ne* according to a theory of territories of information. In considering the status of information in terms of who has access to knowledge of what is being uttered, *ne* marks that which is accessible to both interlocutors. For example, upon meeting, it is common to mention the weather as a way of greeting. One might say to another, "*Atsui desu ne.*" A colloquial English equivalent would be "It sure is hot!," with a more literal translation being "It's hot, isn't it?" To this, the interlocutor would respond, "*Soo desu ne,*" meaning "It sure is!," or, more literally, "It is, isn't it." Here, *ne*, uttered with falling intonation, indicates not a confirmation question, but an assessment. Both interlocutors have experienced the heat, and *ne* indexes joint access to this experience. *Ne*, with rising intonation or intoned with a higher pitch, is used for confirmation questions, as shown in the previous section, to confirm information just received from one's interlocutor. In these uses of *ne*, agreement is expected because the information or experience is available to both parties. With confirmation questions, there may be a degree uncertainty on the part of the one asking, but the speaker has high expectations of an affirmative response. Substantial uncertainty would be indicated by the use of the interrogative marker *ka* rather than *ne*. In this way, *ne* is used to mark both assessments as well as statements of fact, as long as the information is in the "territory" of both interlocutors (Yoshimi, 1999). *Ne* is a critical marker in these contexts. For learners from English-speaking backgrounds, although

English has tag questions that resemble some of the functions of *ne*, the broad usage of *ne* in shared information contexts is something that must be acquired to interact naturally.

In the context of language classes, one might expect that *ne* would be used differently than in ordinary conversation. In fact, an examination of a corpus of nine first-year classes found that *ne* was, as in ordinary conversation, by far, the most frequent final particle used (Ohta 1993, 1994). The classrooms studied did evidence a frequency of *ne* much lower than that of ordinary conversation. This is an unsurprising result when we consider that *ne* is most frequent in face-to-face conversational contexts, and less frequent or absent in settings that distance the interlocutors, such as public speaking (Cook, 1992). The classroom combines a variety of speaking styles within its walls, accounting for a lower frequency of *ne*. In the next section, the classroom use of devices that indicate listener response, including those involving *ne*, is further considered.

ANALYSIS OF LISTENER RESPONSES IN THE FIRST-YEAR CLASSROOMS

Analysis of listener responses in the classes of Candace, Rob, Sara, and Kuo-ming, the four first-year learners in the classroom corpus, begins by examining how listener responses were used in their classrooms in general. This section first reviews the role of interactional routines in language learning with a focus on the *initiation/response/follow-up* (IRF) routine, which is particularly relevant to the use of listener responses. Then, the use of listener responses in the first-year classes is analyzed. This involves considering how listener responses perform as part of the regular environment of interactional routines experienced by these learners. In addition, an analysis of how teachers explicitly guided learners is presented. Finally, we examine the development of the four learners' use of listener responses over the academic year.

Listener Responses and the Interactional Routines of the Classroom

Chapter 1 provided an overview of the powerful role that interactional routines play in the language development of both naturalistic and classroom language learners. Learners acquire facility in L2 interaction through progressively expanded involvement in interactional routines, as they move from peripheral participation to more and more active involvement. Analysis of the first-year classes revealed that a variety of listener responses were regularly used in predictable contexts. In this section we

examine how listener responses are incorporated into classroom interactional routines.

The IRF Routine

The IRF routine is a major routine of foreign language classrooms (Consolo, 1996; Mehan, 1985; Ohta, 1993, 1994; Sinclair & Coulthard, 1975;
van Lier, 1988). The third turn of the IRF sequence, the follow-up turn is
particularly important as a locus for listener responses (Ohta, 1999). The
IRF routine is defined by its structure, but the turns may have different
functions. Some of these functions are shown in Table 5.1. The minimum
IRF sequence contains an initiation and response turn, with an optional
follow-up turn. The initiation turn is generally a question, but need not be.
Drill prompts, greetings, statements and/or words for student repetition,
are other examples of initiations. Initiations are first pair parts requiring a
response—examples are shown in Table 5.1. The follow-up turn, which
comes after the response turn, is where the teacher's evaluation or comment occurs. Use of the follow-up turn for evaluation (including expressions of praise such as "very good") is a hallmark of teacher talk (Mehan,
1985). However, because the third turn need not be evaluative in nature,
the term follow-up (Sinclair & Coulthard, 1975) is used here rather than
the term evaluation (Mehan, 1985). The content of the follow-up turn varies, depending on content of the response turn. Following drill or mechanical practice, a follow-up turn is likely to contain an evaluation such as
hai 'yes', or *ii desu ne* 'good/well done'. In contrast, when a referential question is used, the follow-up turn is more likely to include a comment responsive to the content of the preceding turn. Possible responses include
an indication of comprehension (such as *Mm* or *Un*, which both meaning
'uh-huh' or more extended *Aa soo desu ka* 'is that so'), or an assessment
(such as *omoshiroi desu ne::* 'how interesting'), or other content-related
comments. These sorts of responses would also be found outside of the
classroom in nonpedagogical contexts.

TABLE 5.1
Possible Content of IRF Routines

	Initiation Turn	Response Turn	Follow-Up Turn
1	Question	Answer	• Indication of comprehension (minimal)
			• Indication of comprehension (extended)
2	Drill prompt	Response	• Evaluation
			• Aligning assessment
			• Confirmation question

TABLE 5.2
Student and Teacher Participation in the
IRF in Teacher-Fronted Contexts

Turn	Percent of Turns Taken by Teachers	Percent of Turns Taken by Students
Initiation	87%	13%
Response	12%	88%
Follow-up	97%	3%

The follow-up turn of the IRF routine allows for many expressive possibilities, from evaluation, to expression of interest, to aligning assessment; it has a highly predictable structure, but the IRF's variable content means that the routine is adapted for a range of expressive situations. The IRF's predictable structure and frequent occurrence allow beginning language learners to anticipate where listener responses may occur. The flexibility and predictability of the IRF sequence work together to make it a powerful form of social interaction for L2 learners.

Classroom studies have repeatedly shown that student participation in the IRF is generally confined to the response turn—students seldom participate in initiation or follow-up turns in teacher-fronted settings (Ohta 1994, van Lier 1988). Table 5.2 shows the percentage of IRF turns occupied by students and teachers in a classroom data set that includes the first-year classes of the classroom corpus (Ohta, 1999). Table 5.2 shows that teachers took 87% of initiation and 97% of follow-up turns, with students taking the response turn 88% of the time. The turn least often used by learners was the follow-up turn, the turn where listener responses, whether expressions of acknowledgement, confirmation, alignment, or assessment, are most likely to cluster (Ohta, 1993, 1994). Teacher dominance of the follow-up turn, however, has significance for language learners because it provides an environment where learners can be repeatedly exposed to listener responses in meaningful contexts. The teachers' use of listener responses is a critical part of the interactive linguistic environment of the classroom. By looking at how teachers use the follow-up turn, the analyst can observe the interactional style that students peripherally and actively participate in as class members.

Teacher Use of Listener Responses

In the corpus, the teachers used a variety of listener response types in their interaction with individual students and with the class as a whole. Different interactional configurations provided opportunities for the learners to interact one to one with the teacher. Learners were also auditors, experienc-

TABLE 5.3
Classroom Teachers for Targeted Students

| | Teacher Pseudonyms | | |
Students	Fall	Winter	Spring
Candace	Yasuda	Yasuda	Yasuda
Rob	Yasuda	Yasuda	Jones
Kuo-ming	Kikuchi	Yasuda	Yasuda
Sara	Nakata	Nakata	Yasuda

ing the teachers' interactions with others. The auditor's role, which was introduced in chapter 4, is particularly powerful because the auditor may become a participant at any time, raising the level of attentiveness of the learner in that role above that of mere overhearer.

The four first-year learners experienced similar interactive environments. One source of continuity in the data set is that the students had teachers in common over the academic year, as shown in Table 5.3. Two of the teachers, Ms. Jones and Ms. Nakata, are non-native speakers. Ms. Yasuda and Ms. Kikuchi are native speakers. All teachers used a variety of listener responses, including using *ne* for assessments, expressions of alignment, and confirmation questions.

Excerpt 3 includes examples of a variety of follow-up turn phenomena. The teacher is asking students about their rooms, and uses the follow-up turn for acknowledgement, confirmation questions, and aligning assessments. When she learns new information about the students' rooms, she reacts to positive information with the assessment *Ii desu ne*, 'That's nice', in lines 5, 7, and 14. *Ne*, here, is uttered with falling intonation common to assessments. She also shows interest using a confirmation question in line 3, and acknowledgement expressions including *Aa soo desu ka* 'Is that right/I see' and a few of its variations in lines 9, 11 and 17. These expressions are underlined in Excerpt 3.

(3)   1 T: Rob-san no heya wa shizuka desu ka?
               Rob, is your room quiet?

        2 R: Hai shizuka desu.
               Yes, it is.

→   3 T: <u>Shizuka desu ka:</u>. Totemo shizuka?
               Oh, so it's quiet. Very quiet?

        4 R: Hai
               Yes

→   5 T: Totemo shizuka desu. <u>Ii desu ne:</u>. hai (.) Kim-san no heya wa doo desu ka?

It's very quiet. <u>How nice ne:.</u> Okay (.) Kim, what is your room like?

6 K: Hai (.) um (.) totemo shizuka desu.
Yes (.) um (.) it's very quiet.

→ 7 T: Totemo shizuka desu (.) <u>ii desu ne:.</u> hai (.) Sally-san no heya wa doo desu ka?
Very quiet (.) <u>that's nice ne.</u> Okay (.)What about your room, Sally?

8 S: Totemo:: (.) shizuka desu
It's very:: (.) quiet

→ 9 T: Totemo shizuka desu (.) <u>soo desu ka:.</u> Yanny-san no heya wa doo desu ka?
It's very quiet (.) <u>I see:.</u> Yanny, what is your room like?

·10 Y: (   ).

→ 11 T: Ara <u>soo desu ka</u> (.) hai ja akarui (.) to kiite kudasai. Allan-san (.) Greg-san ni kiite kudasai. (...) Greg-san no heya wa?
Oh, <u>is that so.</u> (.) Okay, please ask whether it is bright. Allan, (.) please ask Greg. (...) Greg, is your room . . .

12 A: Greg-san no heya wa: (.) akarui desu ka?
Greg, is your room (.) bright?

13 G: Um (.) ee (.) uh:: totemo (.) akarui desu
Um (.) yeah (.) uh:: it is very (.) bright.

→ 14 T: Ah <u>ii desu ne.</u> hai ja Clark-san (.) Wanda-san ni?
Oh <u>that's nice ne</u>. Okay well, Clark (.) ask Wanda?

15 C: (.) Um (.) Wanda-san no heya wa (.) akarui desu ka?
(.) Um (.) Wanda, is your room (.) bright?

16 W: Uh (.) Iie (.) amari (.) akaruku (.) arimasen.
Uh (.) No (.) it is (.) not very bright.

→ 17 T: <u>Ah soo desu ka?</u>
<u>Oh really?</u>

(Yasuda, 11/13)

By using a variety of listener responses, the teacher shows attentive interest in student talk. The teacher's high level of interest likely increases the salience of her responses to her student interlocutors and their classmates.

Ii desu ne is the most frequently occurring assessment produced by the teachers. This expression functions both as an assessment and as an evaluation meaning "good." These two uses of *Ii desu ne* can usually be distinguished by the intonation contour on *ne*. Above, where *Ii desu ne* functioned as an assessment, *ne* was characterized by falling intonation (transcribed with a period after *ne*). When *ne* is uttered with a higher pitch or rising intonation, *Ii desu ne* functions as a positive evaluation, with potential English translations of "good" or "that's good" or "very good." This evaluative expression is commonly used in question–answer activities or drills that rely on repetition or display questions. It is also used as a transition from one question to another, just as "good" or "okay" might be used in English to close off a line of questioning. This expression can also serve transitional and evaluative functions simultaneously. An example is shown below in Excerpt 4:

(4) 1 T: Paris. (.) wa pari. hai (.) jaa Pari:::
             Paris. (.) is "Pari." Okay (.) Okay Pari::s
     2 ss: N[nani ga arimasu ka? [
             W hat is there?
→   3 T: [ni?   [Hai ii desu ne, kore wa?
              in?   Yes good, and this?
     4 S: Chuugoku ni nani ga arimasu ka?
             What is there in China?

(Kikuchi, 11/18)

In this excerpt, the teacher works to get students to formulate the question '*Pari ni nani ga arimasu ka?*' 'What is there in Paris'? The students leave out the dative particle *ni* and the teacher prompts its inclusion. In line 3, she then uses the evaluative expression *ii desu ne* 'good', as the students complete the question. This expression serves as both evaluation and transition—the teacher moves from asking about Paris to asking about China. The use of *ne* as an evaluation is different from its use in assessments that are responsive to the content of learner utterances, and is a mark of teacher talk (Ohta 1993, 1994). The assessment, however, is arguably more salient due to the heightened mutual orientation produced through its production and utterance (C. Goodwin & M. H. Goodwin, 1987).

The informal acknowledgement *mm* or *un*, the English equivalent of which would be "uh huh" or "mm hm," is another listener response often used by teachers. In Excerpt 5, the teacher uses this minimal response in line 3 before asking a follow-up question.

(5) 1 T: Terebi o mimasu ka?
             Do you watch TV?
     2 S: Hai
             Yes
→   3 T: Mm nani o mimasu ka?
             Uh huh what do you watch?
     4 S: Nyuusu o mimasu
             I watch the news.
     5 T: Un hai nyuusu
             Uh-huh yes the news

(Yasuda, 11/27)

The teacher's brief follow-up acknowledgement, "Mm," in line 3, is immediately followed by a new initiation, a follow-up question. In line 5, the teacher again uses the follow-up turn for a listener response, the informal acknowledgement, *un* 'uh-huh' and the more formal *hai* 'yes' combined with a repetition of the student's answer "the news." These expressions appropriately display listener attention and interest. The teachers varied in how often they used the expressions *mm* and *un*, depending on the formality of the language they used in their classrooms. Ms. Yasuda and Ms. Kikuchi used these informal acknowledgement expressions frequently.

Depending on the topic of discussion, the teachers used fewer or more listener responses. One day, Ms. Yasuda asked the students about whether or not they owned cars, and about what kinds of cars they drove. In her follow-up to learner responses, she used many aligning assessments:

(6) 1 T: Anoo Jamie-san wa (.) donna kuruma o motte imasu ka?
           Um, Jamie (.) what kind of car do you have?
      2 S: Ah kuruma wa motte imasen.
           Ah I don't have a car.
  →   3 T: Ah soo desu ka? <u>Zannen desu ne:.</u>
           Is that right? <u>That's too bad ne:.</u>
      4   Kim-san wa donna kuruma o motte imasu ka?
           Kim, what kind of car do you have?
      5 K: Ii kuruma ((laughs))
           A nice car
  →   6 T: Ah ii kuruma o motte imasu ka? ((All laugh)) <u>Ii desu ne::.</u>
           Ah a you have a nice car? ((All laugh)) <u>That's nice ne::.</u>
           (Yasuda, 2/28)

Following up a students' line 2 response that he does not have a car, the teacher provides an aligning assessment in line 3 (underlined). In line 3 the teacher also displays her interest in the learner's answer through her use of *Aa soo desu ka.* When Kim, in line 5, answers that she has a nice car, the teacher's expansion in line 6 shows attentive interest. And, through her assessment (underlined), the teacher shares in the student's good fortune of having a nice car by aligning with the positive affect expressed by the student. Although the students here are not specifically guided in the use of these expressions, they are peripheral participants in routines in which listener response expressions are used by the teacher, both when they are interacting with the teacher, and when they observe the teacher's interactions with others.

Confirmation questions marked with *ne* or the question marker *ka* may also serve as listener responses. *Ne*-marked confirmation questions and the aligning responses they elicited were seen in Excerpt 2 in the context of a time-telling task. And, an example of a *ka*-marked confirmation question was shown in line 3 of Excerpt 3.

Teacher Guidance in the Use of Listener Responses

In addition to using listener responses, the teachers also provided guidance in their use. In this section, a few examples are provided that show how the teachers worked to scaffold learner participation as active listeners.

One activity that explicitly guided the use of aligning assessments was a greeting routine. Based on the weather, this routine begins with a *ne*-marked assessment of the weather in the first turn, and elicits an aligning assessment from students who are also experiencing the same weather. *Ne*, with falling intonation, marks both the initial and aligning assessments. In Japan, this sequence might be considered equivalent to the American English, "How are you → I'm fine," greeting sequence. The routine works like this: First, a person initiates the routine by commenting on the weather, making an initial *ne*-marked assessment. The initial turn varies according to how hot, cold, pleasant, or unpleasant the weather is. The interlocutor must show agreement by producing the appropriate listener response—an aligning *ne*-marked assessment. The teacher, using this routine, explicitly guides the interlocutor to use assessments. At first, students repeat parts of the routine, eventually performing their turns without prompting. In Excerpt 7, the teacher guides students in performing the first turn.

(7)   1   T: Kyoo wa donna tenki desu ka:: (.) donna tenki::?
                 What's the weather like today? (.) What's it like?
      2   Ss: Iya na (.) iya na
                 Unpleasant (.) unpleasant
      3   R: Iya na tenki.
                 Unpleasant weather.
      4   T: Iya na tenki desu (.) ne?
                 The weather is unpleasant (.) ne?
→   5   Minna de: (.) iya na tenki desu ne::.
                 All togethe:r (.) The weather is unpleasant ne::.
      6   R: [Iya na tenki desu ne::.
                 The weather is unpleasant ne::.
      7   Ss: [Iya na tenki desu ne::.
                 The weather is unpleasant ne::.

8   T: Soo desu ne::. Ame dakara, ame? Hai.
           It sure is ((unpleasant)) ne::. Because it's raining,
           raining? Right.

(Yasuda, 12/2)

After guiding students to do the first turn of the greeting (line 5), which the students do in lines 6 and 7, the teacher then provides the listener response, *soo desu ne*, in line 8. The students are observers of the teacher's listener response. The teacher's prompts to repeat the appropriate assessment, and production of the listener response portion of the routine allows the students to experience appropriate listener response activity, even though they do not produce the listener response turn.

Learners also produced the listener response portion of the routine as shown in Excerpt 8, in a different class:

(8)   1   T: Hai ja hajimema:su (.) ohayoo gozaima:::su
                Okay let's begi:n (.) good mo:::rning.
      2   Ss: Ohayoo gozaimasu
                Good morning
      3   T: Kyoo wa iya na tenki desu ne:
                The weather is unpleasant today ne:
→ 4   Ss: <u>Soo desu ne:</u>
                It is ne:
→ 5   T: Iya:: <u>soo desu ne::</u>
                Unpleasant it is ne::

(Yasuda, 11/24)

In line 4, the students respond to the teacher's line 3 *ne*-marked initiation with an aligning assessment marked with *ne*, *Soo desu ne* 'It is, isn't it'. This triggers extended assessment activity by the teacher in line 5, as the teacher aligns with the student response. The routine allows students to participate in the production of extended assessment activity. In addition to producing their own aligning assessment, the learners also participate in a process where the teacher provides an assessment that aligns with the one the students produced.

Students were also explicitly guided to use confirmation questions to follow up the provision of information. In Excerpt 9, Sara and Peggy are doing the pair time-telling task that was introduced in Excerpt 2. The excerpt begins as Sara tells the time, but Peggy does not use confirmation questions as she was instructed. The teacher interjects with a confirmation question in line 4:

(9)   1   Sr: Yooo:nju oh. yon::ju so okay yonjugo. Ah! (1)
              Yonjugofun.
              Fo::::::ur oh. For::ty so okay forty-five. Ah! (1) Forty-five
              after.

2 P: Hai hehe
         Yes hehe

3 Sr: Does it-

→ 4 T: Yonjugofun desu ne. Hai.
            Fourty five after ne. Right.

(Kikuchi, 12/4)

As Sara and Peggy continue with another question, the teacher stops the class at the point where the confirmation question would occur. This is shown in Excerpt 9.1, where the teacher reminds the students to do confirmation questions in the indicated line and beyond:

(9.1) 5 Sr: Ano sumimasen. Ima nanji desu ka?
               Uh excuse me. What time is it?

6 P: U:m (.) hachiji?
         U:m (.) eight o'clock?

7 Sr: Hachiji.
         Eight o'clock.

8 P: [Nijupun desu.
         Twenty after.

→ 9 T: [hai minasan chotto ii desu ka?
            Okay everyone, can I have your attention for a minute?

10 Sr: Ni::ju
          Twenty::

11 T: Doo yatte kaku- kakunin shimasu ka?
          How do you con- confirm?

12 Sr: Ni::::ju.
          Twenty::

13 T: Tatoeba juujigofun   [[desu ne?
          For example, 10:05   ne?

14 Sr: [hachiji nijuppun [
                                      eight twenty

15 P: ga (.) ne?
          NOM (.) ne?

→ 16 T: Hai ne o tsukatte kudasai (.) kakunin.
             Yes please use ne (.) to confirm.

17 Sr: Hachiji niju:pun desu ne?
          It's 8:20 ne?

18 P: Hai. (.) Soo desu yo
          Yes. (.) That's right yo

(Kikuchi, 12/4)

As the teacher makes her announcement, Sara is still working to repeat the time Peggy said. When the teacher asks, in lines 11 and 13, how to confirm the time, Peggy answers with *ne* in line 15. The teacher agrees, asking the class to use *ne* to confirm, which Sara then does in line 17. The teacher explicitly guides students to use *ne* for a confirmation routine.

Teachers guided students to use the listener response *Aa soo desu ka*, as shown in Excerpt 10. Rob and his partner are doing a question–answer interview task, asking each other about daily activities. As they are working, the teacher calls from across the room, reminding students to use *Aa soo desu ka* to respond to their partners' answers.

(10) 1 R: Ah shimbun:: (.) o yomimasu?
              Do you read the newspaper?

      2 D: Sorry? (.) Hai (.) o shimasu
              Sorry? (.) Yeah (.) I do. ((error: uses accusative particle without including the object. Also, should use the verb 'read', not 'do'))

      3 R: Dono: (.) yomimasu ka?
              Which (.) do you read? ((error: R uses the pre-nominal form of the question word 'which'.))

      4 D: (3) Um (3) USA Today hehe (.) o yomimasu. USA Today o: (.) o yomimasu
              (3) Um (3) I read hehe (.) USA Today. I read (.) USA Today.

→   5 T: ((from a distance)) Minasan itte kudasai yo:: aa soo desu ka::.
              Everyone please say "Oh really?"

      6 R: Ah soo desu ka::.
              Oh really?

      7 D: Koohii de- koohii o nomimasu?
              Coffee with- do you drink coffee?

                                                              (Yasuda, 11/27)

These examples show how listener responses are available to students as peripheral participants, and that teachers also provide some explicit guidance to students about how and when to do certain types of listener responses. More examples of teacher guidance will be provided in the following sections as we observe the progress of the four first-year learners during the academic year.

Student Development in the Use of Listener Responses

Analysis of the language of the teachers in this corpus reveal that peripheral participation in routines involving teacher use of listener responses is available to all of the students, and that the students received some guidance in the use of listener responses. The question addressed in the rest of chapter 5 is how the four first-year learners develop in their use of listener response expressions.

Because the IRF structure of classroom discourse restricts student use of listener responses by limiting access to the follow-up turn, the availability of listener responses in the interactive environment of the classroom does not guarantee that students will necessarily use them when they interact with the teacher during teacher-fronted classroom activities. In a previous study of the use of *ne* in beginning L2 classrooms (Ohta, 1993, 1994), I found that although teachers frequently used *ne*, students rarely used *ne* in teacher-fronted contexts. Though students may have been willing and able to try out *ne*-marked utterances, the IRF structure of classroom discourse restricted their opportunity to participate in the very turn in which these expressions most frequently occurred—the follow-up turn. Although the structure of teacher-fronted work provides ample opportunities for students to observe their teachers' use of listener responses, that same structure constrains student participation. In contrast, peer learning tasks create opportunities for students to develop interactional competence in ways that are precluded by the IRF structure of teacher-fronted work (Ohta 1995a, 1995b, 1997, 1999, 2000a, in press-a). All turns are open for the students to use. The peer learning setting, therefore, potentially provides a context in which the development of listener responses may be observed.

In fact, observation of the four learners reveals that peer learning tasks are an important locus for development of interactional style. In this setting, learners flex their linguistic muscles, not only by using the forms and vocabulary taught, but they also try out listener responses. The importance of teacher-fronted work is also evident in the peer learning context. In peer interaction, learners reap the benefits of their peripheral participation in assessment and alignment activity. Although the classroom environments of the four students were quite similar, the learners' use of listener response devices varies dramatically when on their own in interaction with peers. However, the learners follow a similar developmental sequence of listener responses from acknowledgement to alignment. Next we explore learner development of the use of listener responses.

The Four Learners

Data for two of these learners, Candace (Ohta, 1999) and Rob (Ohta, in press-b), were examined in earlier studies. Here, all four first-year learners are considered, providing a larger data set for consideration of how beginning learners develop interactional competence. Rob, Kuo-ming, Candace, and Sara all evidence growth in their language abilities and their use of listener responses.

In the process of analysis, when learners do not yet produce a type of listener response such as aligning assessments, data are analyzed for evidence of progress. For example, students cannot be expected to use aligning assessments if they do not yet use *ne* to do initial assessments. The male students, Rob and Kuo-ming, evidenced slower progress than the female students, Sara and Candace. Considering a continuum of listener responses from acknowledgement to alignment, the learners' attainment can be summarized as shown in Table 5.4. By the end of the year, all four learners spontaneously use *Aa soo desu ka* to acknowledge their interlocutor's contributions. Although the minimal expressions of acknowledgement *un, mm*, and *hai* 'uh-huh, yes' would seem quite simple to use in contrast to the longer *Aa soo desu ka* 'Is that so?/Really?', only three of the four students use these, beginning with *hai* 'yes' and moving toward use of more informal expressions *un* and *mm* 'uh-huh'. *Soo desu ne* 'it is, isn't it' is not used by any of the students to indicate alignment; it is either misused, used as a hedge, or not used at all. This result stands in striking contrast to Sawyer's (1991) finding that *soo desu ne* was the first use of *ne* mastered by the language learners he studied in Japan, a result he said was unsurprising because *soo desu ne* was "not only frequent and salient in the input, but also extremely useful" (p. 104). Although *soo desu ne* was used by the teachers in this data set, students did not adopt this listener response. Finally, two of the learners, Candace and Sara, develop the ability to use *ne*-marked assessments as listener responses. Rob never uses *ne*-marked expressions without scripting or prompting. Kuo-ming uses an assessment once, but not as a listener response. Analysis of the data shows how these learners develop in terms of using listener responses to express acknowledgement and alignment. Rob and Kuo-ming's data are considered, including analysis of episodes concerning use of the final particle *ne*. This will be followed by examination of Sara and Candace's development.

Rob and Kuo-ming

In the fall quarter, Kuo-ming and Rob rarely used listener responses, even in English. Excerpt 11 shows this lack of listener responses when Rob and his peer partner do an interview activity in the L2:

(11) 1 R: Uh: (..) supotsu wa: itt- iya- (.) supootsu wa:: shimasu (.) ka.
             Uh: (..) sports TOP *itt- iya- (.) do you do sports?*

      2 S: Iie shimasen
             No I don't

      3 R: Uh biru wa nomimasu (..)[ka?
             Do you drink beer?

TABLE 5.4
Progress in Using Listener Responses Over One Academic Year

	Responses That Acknowledge		Responses That Align	
	Un/Mm/hai 'uh-huh/yes'	Aa soo desu ka. 'Is that so?/Really?'	Soo desu ne. 'It is, isn't it'.	~desu ne. '~ isn't it'.
Rob	Uses *hai* occasionally	Uses spontaneously	Misuses	Uses only when scripted or with prompting
Kuo-ming	Uses "un" occasionally	Uses spontaneously	Does not use	Uses only when scripted or with prompting
Candace	Uses all three	Uses spontaneously	Uses as a hedge, not as a listener response	Uses assessment once Uses spontaneously
Sara	Yes	Uses spontaneously	Does not use	Uses spontaneously

4   S: [Nomimasu (.) yomimasu
    (.) uh hai ⌢ yomimasu
                                    drink (.) read
    (.) uh yes I read[4]
5   R: Hahahaha Benkyoo shimasu (.) ka?
         Hahahaha Do you (.) study?
6   S: Uh hai benkyoo shimasu,
         Uh yes I study,
7   R: Uh: (.) eiga (.) imasu (.) ekimasu
         Uh: (.) do you (.) go to (.) movies ((error: mispronounces
         verb 'go'))
8   S: Iie ikimasen
         No I don't ((S pronounces the verb 'go' correctly))
9   R: Niuuyooku Timesu o- Shiatoru taimusu yomimasu?
         Do you read the New York Times- the Seattle Times?
10 S: Uh hai yomimasu
         Uh yes I do.

                                                         (Rob 11/27)

Expressions of acknowledgement are not scripted in this activity, and the students do not use them but simply run through questions and answer in an "interrogation" style. At this level, although they have already been introduced to the expression, *Aa soo desu ka*, students do not use it. In Kuoming's first data there are not any question–answer activities analogous to that shown for Rob. In his class, pair activities focus on scripted dialogues. Excerpt 12 provides an example of a dialogue that scripts use of initial assessments and listener responses, which are difficult for learners.

(12) 1   Pf: Kirei beddo desu ne::.
                That's a beautiful bed ne::. ((Error: 'na' is omitted after
                'kirei'))
      2   Km: Hmhe dono bedo:: (.) desu ka?
                Hmhe which bed?
      3   P: Ah (2) kono atarashi beddo desu.
                Ah (2) this new bed.
      4   Km: Ah soo desu ne:,
                Oh it is ne:,
      5   hehe(.) um (1) um (1) suteki no:: (.) um ske-suteki
                na sofa desu ka? (2) Desu ne or desu k- (.) haha
                desu ne:, (.)
                hehe (.) um (1) um (1) that's a nice (.) um ni- nice sofa?
                (2) COP ne or COP INT? (.) haha COP ne? (.)

---

[4]Note the similar pronunciation of *nomimasu* 'drink' and *yomimasu* 'read' in Japanese.

> *((error: first chooses genitive particle 'no' after suteki, but*
> *self-corrects to 'na'. Also first chooses the interrogative*
> *particle rather than 'ne', but self-corrects.))*

6   Pf: Ah donna sofa desu? (2)
           Ah which sofa?
7   Km: Suteki na ha sofa desu, hehehe (.)
           It's a nice sofa hehehe (.)
8   Pf: Soo desu ka?
           Oh really?
9   Km: Soo desu. Hehahaha
           It is. Hehahaha

(Kuo-ming, 10/24)

Because the assessments and listener responses are scripted, Excerpt 12 does not tell us much about what Kuo-ming and his partner can do for themselves. The turns, including assessments, acknowledgement expressions, and aligning expressions, are all scripted (though the learners do choose what to talk about—whether sofas, or watches, or whatever), and the teacher led extensive repetition practice, including role-playing the short dialogue with the students, before having them work in pairs. Later fall quarter data may give a better indication of what Kuo-ming was able to do at the beginning of the year. Excerpt 13 reveals that Kuo-ming already demonstrates an awareness of the third turn of the IRF as a turn for his use. Here, he uses both *Aa soo desu ka* and English to show acknowledgement:

(13)   1   Km: Heh Nyuu Yoorku ni nani ga arimasu ka?
                  Heh what is there in New York?
       2   M: E:h o::h. (3) Statue of Liberty::: ga arimasu.
                  E:h o::h (3) there's the Statue of Liberty.
→   3   Km: Ah soo desu ka hahahaha.
                  Oh really hahahaha.
                  ((Lines 4–8 skipped))
       9   Km: Pa::ri (.) hn hn is that -? Paari ga nai- (.) Paari ni
                  ga nani ga arimasu ka?
                  Pa::ris (.) hn hn is that- what is there (.) what is there
                  in Paris?
      10   M: (4) Uh Eiffel uh (.) Pa:ri ni (.) Eiffel Tower ga (.)
                  arimasu.
                  (4) Uh the Eiffel uh (.) In Pa:ris (.) there's the (.)
                  Eiffel Tower.
→   11   Km: Okay. That's cool

(Kuo-ming, 11/18)

At this early stage, Kuo-ming already uses the follow-up turn as a place for listener responses, using *Aa soo desu ka* in line 3, and an English listener response in line 11. From comparing Rob's November performance with Kuo-ming's, it is clear that they are not developing at the same pace; Kuo-ming already has a greater awareness of the follow-up turn and has begun using L2 listener response expressions.

Over the year, both Rob and Kuo-ming improve in their use of expressions that show attention to the interlocutor. They increase in their use of listener responses and guidance by the teacher impacts their use of these devices. At first, Rob uses *Aa soo desu ka* only where scripted, but gradually begins using the expression on his own, using it frequently and appropriately by the end of the year. Rob never does use assessments in the data set. Kuo-ming also learns to use *Aa soo desu ka* appropriately and reduces his reliance on English listener responses. It is not until the last data collected for the year that Kuo-ming spontaneously uses a *ne* marked aligning assessment.

Using *Aa soo desu ka*

Rob's ability to show attentive listening increases dramatically over the year, as seen in the increase in his use of the expression *Aa soo desu ka*. At first, Rob uses this expression only when scripted, but he begins to use the expression spontaneously from later in the fall quarter, using it naturally and comfortably by the end of the year. In the last class transcribed for fall quarter, Rob uses *Aa soo desu ka* three times—once after being prompted by the teacher, and twice spontaneously. In Excerpt 14, part of which was shown earlier as Excerpt 10, Rob says *Aa soo desu ka* twice in an interview activity in which he is asking about his partner's daily activities:

(14) 1 R: Uh terebi o mimasu ka?
          Uh do you watch TV?
      2 D: Uh hai shimasu. Hehehe (.) hehe
          Uh yes I do. Hehehe (.) hehe
      3 R: Nani o mimasu ka?
          What do you watch?
      4 D: (4) Sports o (mimasu).
          (4) *(I watch) sports.*
  →   5 R: Ah soo desu ka? (.)Ah shimbun:: (.) o yomimasu?
          Oh really. (.) Do you (.) read the ne::wspaper?
      6 D: Sorry? (.) Hai (.) o shimasu=
          Sorry? (.) Yes (.) I do=
      7 R: =Dono: (.) yomimasu ka?
          Which (.) do you read?

	8	D:	(3) Um (3) USA Today hehe (.) o yomimasu.

        8   D: (3) Um (3) USA Today hehe (.) o yomimasu.
                 USA Today o: (.) o yomimasu
                 (3) Um (3) I read hehe (.) USA Today. I read (.)
                 USA Today.
        9   T: ((from a distance)) Minasan itte kudasai yo:: aa
                 soo desu ka::.
                 ((from a distance)) Everyone say "aa soo desu ka" okay?
  →   10 R: Ah soo desu ka::.
                 Oh really?

                                                (Rob, 11/27)

In line 5, Rob says *Aa soo desu ka* without being prompted by his teacher. In line 9, the teacher prompts the entire class to use the expression. While circulating among the students, the teacher likely noticed the absence of listener responses. By making her line 9 announcement, she shows the class her expectation that they use listener responses, and suggests *Aa soo desu ka*, an expression that they have been taught, but seldom use. As winter and spring quarters progress, Rob continues to use *Aa soo desu ka* appropriately, using the expression more and more often in response to his partner. In the fall quarter, Kuo-ming also uses *Aa soo desu ka*, as we just saw in Excerpt 13, line 3. Kuo-ming also uses *Aa soo desu ka* in the winter and spring data, but not as frequently as Rob. Both develop the ability to use this expression appropriately over the year.

Development of Kuo-ming and Rob's Use of *ne*

The use of *ne* in listener responses is necessary in a wide range of daily conversational contexts. Common *ne*-marked listener responses include the expression *soo desu ne*, which shows agreement with the interlocutor, and *ne*-marked assessments, which show agreement or alignment with the feelings expressed. In the classroom corpus, neither Kuo-ming nor Rob ever begins to use *ne* in aligning listener response expressions. Rob's only use of *ne* in an assessment is in the weather routine, which explicitly guided students in the use of assessments. Rob actively participates in the routine, producing a comment about the weather that the teacher responds to with the listener response, *soo desu ne*. Rob, however, does not use *soo desu ne* appropriately, nor does he evidence spontaneous use of assessments outside the context of this routine.

Kuo-ming and Rob do not use *ne* for aligning listener responses in the data, but this does not mean that they are not developing an ability to use *ne*. It is possible that the spontaneous use of *ne* in listener responses (where the use of *ne* is not scripted by classroom materials, or dialogues, and is not prompted by the teacher, or the focus of instruction) is something that many classroom learners do not develop in the first year of instruction. This does not mean, however, that students are not on their way to developing this ability. These students do use *ne* in scripted activities, although these activities generally do not utilize *ne* in listener responses. Through guided interaction using *ne*, students may begin to understand how to use *ne* in different situations. Kuo-ming uses *ne* most frequently in a substitution dialogue task. The dialogue is practiced first in the teacher-fronted context before peers interact with each other. The instructional point is the use of demonstratives, but the teacher also spends a good bit of time on the listener response expressions and on the difference between *Soo desu ka* and *Soo desu ne*. The dialogue practiced is as follows, with the underlined portions to be substituted with other words/phrases students want to use:

A: Ii <u>tokei</u> desu ne
    That's a nice clock ne.
B: <u>Dono</u> tokei desu ka.
    Which clock?
A: Ano <u>shizuka na</u> <u>tokei</u> desu
    That quiet clock.
B: Soo desu ne:.
    It is, ne:.

By performing this minidialogue, students got extensive practice using both initial assessments and the aligning assessment, *soo desu ne*, as already shown in Excerpt 12.

In a later class, *ne* is introduced, not for listener responses, but for confirmation questions used as a foundation for giving directions. Confirmation questions can precede provision of information by confirming a bit of information accessible to both parties that will be used to build the questioner's next turn. Although these are not listener responses, developing facility with these questions may help learners to use confirmation questions as listener responses. In Excerpt 16, the confirmation question is used in a minidialogue that involves giving directions. The structure of the conversation taught in class is shown in Excerpt 15.

(15) 1 A: Sumimasen, <u>ginkoo</u> wa doko ni arimasu ka?
             Excuse me, where is <u>the bank</u>?
      2 B: Aa <u>ginkoo</u> desu ka?
             <u>The bank</u>?
      3 A: Hai
             Yes
→   4 B: Asoko ni <u>yuubinkyoku</u> ga arimasu ne?
             Do you see <u>the post office</u> over there?
             (Literally: The post office is over there, right?)

5 A: Hai.
         Yes.

6 B: <u>Ginkoo</u> wa <u>yuubinkyoku</u> no <u>tonari</u> ni arimasu yo.
         The bank is next to the post office.

The confirmation question in line 4 functions to establish joint attention to a common referent—the post office—which is then used as a point of reference in giving directions to the bank. When Kuo-ming and his partner, Doug, do the activity shown in Excerpt 16, Kuo-ming softly repeats in private speech the confirmation question his partner uses. Kuo-ming's private speech evidences his engagement and the salience of the *ne*-marked confirmation question scripted in the activity:

(16)   1 Km: Um let's see hehe ano sumimasen.(.) gakkoo:
                 wa:: doko ni: ahh arimasu ka?
                 *Um let's see hehe um excuse me. (.) where is the
                 a:h school?*

        2 (3)
        3 D: Which one?
        4 Km: Gakkoo
                 the school
        5 D: Ah gakkoo desu ka?
                 Oh, the school?
        6 (4)
        7 Km: Heh
        8 D: Ahh (3) asoko ni (4) kisaten ga arimasu ne:.
                 Ahh (3) over there a (4) coffee shop exists ne:.
→   9 Km: °Ga arimasu ne:.° yeah (1) then
                 °NOM exists ne:.° yeah (1) then
       10 (1)
       11 D: (   ) um gakkoo wa kisaten⁵ [no (.)
                 (   ) um school TOP coffee shop   GEN
       12 Km: [no::
                                                GEN
       13 S4:   Migi gawa ni
                 Right side DAT ((on the right side))
       14 D: Migi gawa:: (.) ni arimasu yo
                 *Right side (.) DAT exists ((Complete sentence: The school
                 is to the right of the coffee shop))*
       15 Km: Okay (.) that's cool (.). Hey you can ask me one if
                 you want hehe

                                            (Kuo-ming, 11/18)

---

⁵Evident misspellings represent the learners' pronunciation. The student said "kisaten" (without the geminate), not "kissaten."

In this task, learners are not reciting the dialogue verbatim, but are free to ask the location of any of the buildings on their maps. Kuo-ming, in line 1, asks the location of the school. In line 8, Doug chooses the coffee shop as the reference point, and formulates his confirmation question. In line 9, Kuo-ming softly repeats the *ne*-marked portion of the confirmation question. Then, he works together with Doug to complete Doug's explanation of the location—Kuo-ming says *no*, the postpositional possessive marker that connects *Kissaten* 'coffee shop' with the locative expression *migi gawa ni* 'on the right side'. Kuo-ming is mapping along as Doug speaks. This functions as rehearsal for Kuo-ming's own turn. In line 15, Kuo-ming provides a listener response in English—he does not yet consistently make use of acknowledgement expressions such as *Aa soo desu ka* 'I see/Is that right?' or *Hai wakarimashita* 'I understand', which would be appropriate here.

In line 15, Kuo-ming invites Doug to ask him a location. As the activity continues in Excerpt 17, Kuo-ming uses *ne* in turn 19 to draw Doug's attention to the landmark he has selected. Kuo-ming appropriately uses the *ne*-marked confirmation question scripted, albeit with a great deal of effort. The location of the pauses evidences the cognitive effort involved in Kuo-ming's production. Before uttering *ga arimasu ne*, the part Kuo-ming previously repeated in private speech (line 9, Excerpt 16), there are two pauses as well as a filled pause.

(17) 16 D: Sure
      17 Km: Heheh
      18 D: Ano sumimasen (.) sakanaya wa (.) doku ni arimasu ka?
                Um excuse me (.)where is (.) the fish market? ((error: mispronounces 'where'))
→   19 Km: (.) Ah sakanaya desu ka:? ah (.) koko ni:: ginkoo (.) ah (.) ga arimasu ne:, heheh
                (.) Ah the fish market? ah (.) Here DAT bank (.) ah (.) NOM exists ne:, heheh
                (.) Ah the fish market? Ah (.) the bank is (.) ah (.) right here, ne:, heheh
      20 T: Hai ii::::? jaa demonstration shimashoo.
                Okay? Let's do performances.
                                                                    (Kuo-ming, 11/18)

Even though it is scripted, the use of the *ne*-marked confirmation question is not easy for Kuo-ming. It will take some time for him to learn to use *ne* spontaneously. Although this use of *ne* is not in a listener response, experiences like this one may help Kuo-ming learn to use *ne* appropriately in the listener response context as well. Kuo-ming also uses *ne* spontaneously in the data collected, but not for listener responses. In Kuo-ming's winter quarter classes, he uses *Eeto ne*, an expression used for filled pauses, analogous to "uh" or "um" in English. And in the spring quarter, Kuo-ming uses assessments three times, once using a spontaneous *ne*-marked assessment in a teacher-fronted setting. Although his assessment is not a listener response, it shows a growing ability to use *ne* to mark shared experience, as shown in line 8 of Excerpt 18.

(18) 1 T: Kono kusuri wa onaka ga itai toki ni nomimasu.
        Ii desu ka? Onaka ga itai toki ni nomimasu. Kusuri
        no namae wa seirogan to iimasu.
        This medicine is for stomach-ache. Okay? We take it for
        a stomach ache. The name of this medicine is "seirogan."

     2 Km: Se::irogan.
        ((Kuo-ming says the name of the medicine, "Seirogan"))

     3 T: Seirogan to iimasu yo.
        It is called "seirogan."

     4 Km: °Seirogan°

     5 T: Seirogan. Seirogan to iu kusuri desu ne. Chotto nioi
        o kaide kudasai.
        Seirogan. This is medicine called "seirogan." Please smell
        it. ((T holds out medicine for Kuo-ming to smell.))

     6 Km: Hm. ((Kuo-ming smells the medicine))]

     7 T: Doo desu ka?
        What do you think?

→   8 Km: Hehehehe hen desu ne.
        Hehehehe it's strange ne.

                                            (Kuo-ming, 5/22)

Here, Kuo-ming does a strikingly appropriate assessment marked with *ne*. In pair activities, however, he does not do such assessments. *Ne*-marked listener responses are, however, arguably more complex than initial assessments, because they must be tailored to the content of the interlocutor's utterance.

Another sign of progress toward the use of *ne* in listener responses and other contexts is the examination of learner errors involving *ne*. In a longitudinal study of language learners in Japan, Sawyer (1991) found that the earliest use of *ne* to develop was the expression, *Soo desu ne* 'that's right, huh; yeah; I see what you mean'. Despite its superficial resemblance to *Aa soo desu ka*, *Soo desu ne* is not similar in meaning or usage. While *Aa soo desu ka* is used for purposes of acknowledgement, or indication of comprehension, *Soo desu ne* is used to show agreement or alignment with information that is provided in the previous turn. The one who says *Soo desu ne* must have previous knowledge or access to the information provided. The teachers frequently use *Aa soo desu ka*, and expressions marked with *desu ne*, including occasional use of *Soo desu ne*. Rob's teacher, for example, uses *Aa soo desu ka* (or variations) an average of 16 times per class, uses expressions containing *desu ne* 69 times per class, and uses *Soo desu ne* an average of 4 times per class. Although Rob and his classmates seldom used *ne*, the students are frequently exposed to these expressions. Ms. Yasuda taught *Soo desu ne* as an aligning response in the weather routine. Rob is responsive, and also uses *Soo desu ne*. However, his use of the expression is always in the wrong context, in places where it would be most appropriate to use *Aa soo desu ka*. Even so, his errors are clear indications of the salience of this *ne*-marked expression to Rob, of his progress in moving toward the use of *ne* in listener response expressions, and of his growing creativity in language use. He takes a risk, and tries to speak in an appropriate way. The listener response is not scripted here—Rob uses the expression on his own. His first misuse of the expression occurs early in the academic year, shown in Excerpt 19.

(19) 1 D: Doko de hirugohan o tabemasu ka?
             Where do you eat lunch?
      2 R: Uchi de tabemasu. (.) s::- shoot. Say that agai::n.
             I eat at home. (.) s::- shoot. Say that agai::n.
      3 D: Doko de::
             Where
      4 R: Doko de hirugohan tabema:su ka?
             Where do you eat lunch?
      5 D: o tabemasu
             ACC eat.
      6 R: o tabemasu ka. Doko de hiru gohan o tabemasu ka?
             ACC eat INT. *Where do you eat lunch?*
      7 D: Uh union de: (.) gohan o tabemasu.
             Uh I eat (.) at the union.
→   8 R: Ah soo desu ne::.
             ((*mis-use of soo desu ne::.—in English, a translation
             might be "That's right, isn't it."*))

                                                          (Rob, 12/2)

Near the end of the year, Rob still makes the same error, as shown in Excerpt 20:

(20) 1 R: Oh okay. Uh otoosan no namae wa nan desu ka?
             Oh okay. Uh what is your father's name?
      2 S: Tom-san
             Tom

        3   R: Uh otoosan wa toshi um::
                  Uh and his age um::
        4   S: Yonjuu kyuu sai desu.
                  He's forty-nine.
        5   R: Hai (.) uh shigoto ga:
                  Yes (.) uh and his work is:
        6   S: retired desu
                  He's retired.
        7   R: Shigoto ga arimasu?
                  Does he have a job?
        8   S: Arimasen.
                  No.
→   9   R: A::h. Soo desu ne::.

                                                    (Rob, 4/21)

Rob's usage would be correct if he already knew the information he was asking, but he does not. He misuses *soo desu ne* for *soo desu ka* about once each class in the winter and spring quarter data, with his first error occurring in December. None of the other students do this in the data set. However, this type of error has been noted for learners more advanced than Rob. Yoshimi (1999), found that in a group of learners who had from 1 to 3½ years of instruction and had been in Japan 1 to 3 months, *Soo desu ne* was used inappropriately about one-third of the time. At this time, it is not clear to what extent the conflation of alignment and acknowledgement expressions represented by use of *Soo desu ne* in contexts appropriate for *Aa soo desu ka* is a developmental error that gradually disappears with growing proficiency, or whether it continues to be a problem for advanced learners. Further analysis of the interaction of learners at a range of proficiency levels, including learners with significant interactional experience in Japan (which Yoshimi's subjects also lacked) would help to better understand these developmental processes.

Although Rob's use of *ne* is limited to these errors with *Soo desu ne*, Rob's teacher does guide students to use assessments, not only in the weather routine, but elsewhere as well. In Excerpt 21, the teacher asks students where they plan to go for their winter break. And, in line 3, she guides them to use an aligning assessment as a listener response.

    (21) 1   T: Doko ni ikimasu ka?
                    Where are you going to go?
          2   S: Uh:: (.) California? Kariforunia ni (.) ikimasu?
                    To California? I'm going to go (.) to California?
→   3   T: Ah. Kariforunia ni ikimasu. Ii desu ne:::. (.) Minna
                    de itte kudasai. Ii desu ne::.

Oh. You're going to California. That's nice ne::. Let's all
say it. That's nice ne::.
→   4   Ss: Ii desu ne::.
That's nice ne::.

(Rob, 12/2)

Rob does not participate in repeating with his classmates, but the teacher is clearly guiding students in the appropriate use of assessments. After this episode, the teacher continues to use this assessment herself, as she asks six more students. The sixth time, the teacher again prompts students to use the assessment. This is shown in Excerpt 22 (line 3). In line 5, the students join the teacher with gusto in an exaggerated intonation, prompting a chuckle from Rob.

(22)   1   T: E::to Larry-san (.) uchi ni kaerimasu ka?
U::m Larry (.) are you going to go home?
     2   L: New York uh (.) ni
to uh (.) New York
     3   T: Nyuu Yooku ni ikimasu. Nyuu yooku ni ikimasu.
De minna de::
You're going to New York. He's going to New York.
So, all together::
     4   S: Ii
nice
     5   Ss/T   Ii desu <u>ne::</u>.
That's nice <u>ne::</u>.
→   6   R: ((chuckles))
     7   T: Nyuu Yooku ni ikimasu. Aa soo desu ka,
You're going to New York. I see,

(Rob, 12/2)

This example shows how the teacher guides the students to use assessments by prompting everyone to participate. Rob does not repeat out loud, but his laughter is evidence that he may have noticed the students' response. In this class, he only participates orally in choral assessments once—in the weather routine at the beginning of class—even though the teacher prompts use of assessments three other times. This is not because he avoids participating in chorus responses; in this class, the teacher frequently prompts repetition or response with *minna de::* 'all together' (line 3), and Rob almost always participates, except when the teacher prompts students to use or repeat assessments. This is significant because, according to child L1 acquisition researchers, what a language learner repeats is an indication of what is soon to be acquired. Moreover, child learners tend not to imitate what is outside of their ZPD, the interactional space in which assisted performance works to promote cognitive development. Rob is attentive, but cannot yet use assessments without significant assistance. Even so, in class he has opportunities to participate in assessment activities. In Excerpt 23, the teacher even uses an assessment as a listener response in individual interaction with him. The teacher goes around the room asking what students plan to do over the break, and she calls on Rob in line 1:

(23) 1 T: Hai Rob-san?
                Okay ((and what about you,)) Rob?
      2 R: Benkyoo shimasu.
                I'm going to stu::dy.
      3 T: Benkyoo shimasu. (.) Ii gakusei desu ne::.
                *You're going to stu::dy. (.) What a good student you
                are ne::.*

                                                    (Rob, 12/2)

In line 3 the teacher repeats Rob's answer prior to her assessment, an act that arguably increases the salience of the assessment by making explicit the contingent nature of her response. The salience is further enhanced by the fact that Rob is the teacher's addressee.

Kuo-ming's teacher also guides students in using *ne* by scripting confirmation questions for the students use, and explicitly guiding the students in teacher-fronted practice prior to having students interact with peers. Both Kuo-ming's and Rob's teachers work to produce environments natural for the production of *ne*-marked expressions, including listener responses.

In sum, Kuo-ming and Rob's development in the use of listener responses differs somewhat. Both improve in spontaneous use of the expression of acknowledgement *Aa soo desu ka*; Kuo-ming shows some progress in the spontaneous use of assessments.

Candace and Sara

Candace and Sara show a much clearer and more dramatic improvement in their use of listener responses. Unlike Kuo-ming and Rob, both Candace and Sara create their own opportunities to use aligning assessments during peer interactive tasks. We first examine Candace's and Sara's development in expressions of acknowledgement, particularly *Aa soo desu ka*, moving to an examination of how they developed in the area of aligning assessments. Like Kuo-ming and Rob, Candace and Sara also start the academic year with different sensitivities to listener responses. Candace's earliest interactions look much like Rob's, with no use of the follow-up turn at all. In contrast, Sara begins using listener responses from the earliest class in the data set.

Using *Aa soo desu ka*

Both Sara and Candace develop facility with the expression *Aa soo desu ka*. Candace uses the expression liberally in the winter quarter data, continuing through the rest of the year; Sara uses *Aa soo desu ka* appropriately from the fall quarter on through the rest of the year. Examples appear in the following section, where the use of *ne* in listener responses is discussed.

Using *ne* in Listener Responses

Sara does not use *ne* at all in the first fall quarter class transcribed, but uses *ne* an astonishing 20 times in the second class in the corpus. Ten of these uses occur in turns responsive to a partner's utterance. The difference between the two classes is easily accounted for by examining the nature of classroom activities. Sara's 20 uses of *ne* occur as part of a confirmation routine taught by the teacher and used by the students in a peer learning task. An example of this was shown in Excerpt 2. Lines 8 and 9 of Excerpt 2 are reproduced below:

→	8	P:	Kuji juppun desu <u>ne:?</u>
			Nine-ten, right?
→	9	Sr:	Soo desu <u>ne.</u>
			Yes, that's right.

(Sara, 12/4)

After learning the time from Sara, Peggy reconfirms with her line 8 confirmation question. Sara, in line 9, agrees by providing the aligning *ne*-marked statement. The repeated use of this routine accounts for Sara's high use of *ne*.

Sara's frequent use of *ne* in this confirmation routine is initiated by the teacher, who carefully scaffolds its use by reminding the students to do confirmations (Excerpt 2). Partway through the activity, she reminds the learners to use *ne* to confirm the time, and they begin to do so, in lines 8 and 9 just shown. In line 8, Peggy asks a confirmation question using *ne*, and Sara's line 9, *Soo desu ne* 'That's right', aligns with Peggy's request for confirmation. After the teacher's reminder, Sara and Peggy diligently incorporate confirmations into their interaction. The teacher does not leave this to chance—she guides the use of *ne* in this activity and does so later in a postlistening activity. As prework for the postlistening task shown in Excerpt 24, the teacher explicitly models use of the confirmation questions she wants students to use when they check their answers with one another in pairs:

(24) 1 T Ja kondo tonari no hito to kakunin shite kudasai.
Jikan jikan o. Tatoeba kono pataan tsukatte
Nakata-sensei wa (.) tatoeba nemasu. Eh:to (1)
Nakata-sensei wa (.) juuji (.) yonjuugofun ni nemasu
ne:? Hai minasan itte kudasai. //Nakata-sensei wa
juuji yonjuugofun ni nemasu ne::?
*Okay, next confirm with the person next to you. Confirm
the times. For example, use this pattern "Prof.[6] Nakata" (.)
for example, "goes to bed." Uh (1) Prof. Nakata (.) goes to
bed at ten (.) forty-five ne:? Okay everyone say it together.
//Prof. Nakata goes to bed at ten forty-five ne::?*

   2 Ss/Sr: Nakata-sensei wa juuji yonjuugofun ni nemasu ne::?
Prof. Nakata goes to bed at ten forty-five ne::?

   3 T: Soshite eh:: [soo desu ne.
And then uh   that's right ne.

   4 Ss/Sr: [eh: soo desu ne.
*   uh that's right ne.*

   5 T: Ja kore wa? Hai itte kudasai. Nakata-sensei wa juuji ni
nemasu ne:,
*And how about this? Please say "Prof. Nakata goes to bed
at ten, ne:,"*

   6 Ss/Sr: Nakata-sensei wa juuji ni nemasu ne:?
Prof. Nakata goes to bed at ten, ne:?

   7 T: Iie
No

   8 Ss/Sr: Iie
No

   9 S5: Nemasen
She doesn't go to bed (then)

   10 T: Juuji [yonjuugofun ni nemasu::   [yo
*She goes to bed at ten forty-five   yo ((final
particle))*

   11 Ss/Sr: [juuji yonjuugofun ni nemasu yo. [
*   She goes to bed at ten forty-five yo.*

   12 S/Sr: Yo ((final particle))

   13 T: Ja kondo tonari no hito to jikan o kakunin shite
kudasai. (1)
Okay, next confirm with your partner. (1)

---

[6]The title *sensei*, used for teachers or professors, is translated as "Prof." when it is used as a title.

14 Sr: Oh boy. I don't know if I did this right.
15 Pf: Ii desu ka? Nakata-sensei wa (..) go-ji-go-fun ni (.) uchi
          ni kaerimasu::
          Okay? Prof. Nakata (..) goes home at (.) five after five::
16 Sr: Hai soo desu ne. I'll do the next one.
          Yes, that's right ne. I'll do the next one.
17   Nakata-sensei wa ^ (1) oh juji? (.) juji (.) yon? ju: go:
          fun? ni ^ uh nemasu ne:.
          Prof. Nakata (1) um ten? (.) goes to sleep at ten fifteen ne:.
18 Pf: Hai soo desu ne, (1) Nakata-sensei wa kuji ni-ju-pun
          ni jugyoo ga
          That's right ne, (1) Prof. Nakata has class at nine twenty
          ((the Japanese sentence is missing its verb))
19 Sr: °Oh you're right. Nijupun°
                °*Twenty after*°
20 Pf: Jugyoo ga u::h (.) arimasu ne
          (At nine-twenty) she has class ne ((Here, Pf includes
          the verb))
21 Sr: Soo desu ne.
          She does ne.

(Sara, 12/4)

The teacher sets up the task so that the students understand how to do the confirmation questions. She has the learners repeat after both the initial confirmation question (line 1 and line 5), and affirmative and negative responses (line 3 and line 10). Although Peggy does not use *ne* in her first turn (line 15), both Peggy and Sara use *ne* appropriately in subsequent turns, for the initial confirmation question, and for agreeing with their partners.

Ne was used more often by the students in this class than in any other class in the corpus. Sara's frequent use of *ne* is carefully scaffolded by her teacher, a non-native speaker. In setting up tasks, the teacher made it clear to the students how to ask confirmation questions, as well as how to align with the stance expressed in the confirmation question. Other teachers used similar activities but this careful pre-task work was omitted. Consequently students in other classes did not use *ne* when they did confirmation activities with their peers. For example, another teacher uses a task that has students use *ne* to confirm answers to listening comprehension questions. The teacher tells the students to use *ne* in their confirmations, and the written instructions on the worksheet also say to use *ne*-marked confirmation questions. Excerpt 25 shows the teacher's oral instructions.

(25) 1 T: Hai ja tonari no hito to hai eh:to (confirm) o shite
              kudasai. Ne o tsukatte::, (.) Yasuda-sensei wa ^ (.)
              Ne? tomodachi to dekakemashita ne? Ne?

Okay, so confirm with the person next to you. Use "ne,"
(.) "Prof. Yasuda ne? (.) went out with a friend ne?" Ne?
(Rob 1/24, Candace 1/24)

There were two pairs miked in this particular class—one pair (Candace and her partner) uses *ne*, but the other pair (Rob and his partner) makes no attempt to do so. The teacher neither models the use of *ne*, nor does she monitor the pair that fails to use *ne*. She does not do any other consciousness-raising activities either related to using *ne* for confirmation questions. In contrast, Sara's teacher leads teacher-fronted choral practice of the *ne*-marked confirmation turns with her students *and* repeats this practice when the students have difficulty using *ne*. Sara's frequent use of *ne* in the late fall quarter may be best accounted for by her teacher's careful use of activities that scaffold use of *ne* in a developmentally appropriate way. The teacher helps her students to use *ne* in a way they could not have done without such assistance and prompting. Teacher sensitivity to student use of affective particles, coupled with appropriate support such as modeling or reminders, are important in promoting appropriate use of these particles. There are no activities involving similar levels of teacher support and or guidance in Candace's data and Candace does not use assessments or any expressions of alignment or acknowledgement in the fall quarter data.

Sara's teacher begins the 12/4 class by commenting on the weather— this is the same "weather routine" that was used by Rob and Kuo-ming's teacher. In Excerpt 26, in response to the teacher's assessment, Sara uses *ne* spontaneously in an aligning assessment.

(26) 1   Sr: Ohayoo gozaimasu
                 Good morning
      2   T: Kyoo wa iya na tenki desu ne:,
                 The weather's unpleasant today ne:,
→   3   Sr: (.) Soo desu ne.
                 (.) It is, ne.
      4   T: Ne?
                 ((Sara coughs several times. Teacher moving around the class—class hasn't started yet.))
      5   Sr: Totemo iya na tenki.
                 Very unpleasant weather.
      6   S3:   Huh?
      7   Sr: Totemo iya na tenki
                 Very unpleasant weather
      8   S3:   Hmph.

(Sara, 12/4)

Sara greets the teacher in line 1. The teacher responds with a *ne*-marked assessment about the weather, a typical greeting. Sara continues appropriately (after a pause) with the listener response *soo desu ne*, as appropriate in this routine. Sara's high level of engagement in the routine is evident—after the teacher leaves, she appropriates the teacher's words, and tells her classmate about the weather in line 5. She does not use *ne*, as would be most appropriate, but her repetition of the teacher's words shows a high level of engagement, even though the class has not begun yet.

In the winter quarter data, Sara uses *ne* spontaneously in four assessments; three of these align with her interlocutor's affective expression. Sara also uses *ne* one other time in an aligning expression. Excerpt 27 shows Sara's mastery of *Aa soo desu ka* to express appropriate interest, as well as her use of aligning assessments.

(27)   1 H: Ooraru intabyuu to shiken wa doo deshita ka?
So, how were the oral interview and the test?

2 Sr: Ah! (.) Sa:: (.) ooraru intabyuu wa: (2) mmm (.) omoshiro::katta desu. (1) U:::::m shiken wa (.) muzukashikatta desu (.) H-san wa?
Ah! (.) well (.) the oral interview was (2) mmm (.) interesting. (1) The test (.) was difficult. (.) How about you, H-san?

3 H: Ooraru intabyuu wa yokunakatta desu (kedo)
The oral interview wasn't so good (but)

4 Sr: Mm hm?

5 H: (2) de- demo:: (2) shiken wa yasashikatta desu.
(2) bu- but:: (2) the test was easy.

→   6 Sr: Soo desu ka:: ((laughs)) (3) That's the exact opposite of what I thought. Konshu:: wa (.) Konshu wa: doo:: deshita ka?
Oh really:: ((laughs)) (3) That's the exact opposite of what I thought. This week (.) how was this week?

7 H: (6) Konshu wa tai- (.) taihen deshita.
(6) This week was di- (.) difficult.

→   8 Sr: Ah, soo desu ka? Zannen desu ne::.
Oh really? That's disappointing ne::.

9 H: Sara-san wa?
How about you, Sara?

10 Sr: Hmm?

11 H: Sara-san wa?
How about you, Sara?

12 Sr: Eeehh (.) Konshu wa:: mm::: isogashikatta desu (.) °isogashikatta desu.° (2) Takusan arubaito o shimashita. (4) H-san wa?

U::m (.) this week was m:: busy (.) °it was busy° (2) I worked
a lot. (4) How about you, H-san?

13 H: Shiken to:: repooto ga takusan arimashita kara (.)
         isogashikatta desu.
         I had lots of exams and papers so (.) it was busy.

→   14 Sr: Taihen desu ne:. (.) ((laughs))
              That's tough ne:. (.) ((laughs))

15 H: Soo desu.
         Yes it is.

16 Sr: Hehe. (2) Mmmm (5) Ooraru intabyuu:: to::: shiken:
         (.) ga arimashita (.) kara, (1) takusan benkyoo
         shimashita::. (10) Demo: watashi ga^ ((while
         yawning)) ((error: 'wa' would be better)) (.) takusan
         arubaito shimashita. (3) Desu kara isogashikatta desu.
         Hehe. (2) Mmmm (5) I had the oral interview and exam
         (.) so, (1) I studied a lot. (10) But, I ((while yawning))
         (.) worked a lot. (3) That's why I was busy.

                                                          (Sara, 2/7)

Note how Sara responds to her partner in lines 6, 8, and 14. In lines 6 and
9, she uses *Soo desu ka* or *Aa soo desu ka*, both of which are appropriate expressions of interest or attentiveness. In lines 8 and 14, Sara also does
follow-up aligning assessments. This is a substantial mark of growth, although she has difficulty in distinguishing when to use *zannen* 'disappointing' and when to use *taihen* 'difficult/arduous', both of which are used for
sympathetic aligning assessments. Use of *zannen* in line 8 is inappropriate.

   In her last class in the corpus, Sara is still using *ne*-marked listener responses to show sympathy with her partner (and still confusing the words
taihen and *zannen*). This is shown in Excerpt 28:

(28) 1 Sr: Doo shita n desu ka?
               What happened?

      2 Pm: Yubi o (.) kiru n desu.
               I (.) will cut my finger ((error: tense))

      3 Sr: Hehe (..) Ah so desu ka:::, taihen desu ne::, za- ano
               zannen desu ne:::. hehehe
               Hehe (.) Oh really:::, that's awful ne::, ho- how
               disappointing ne:::.

                                                          (Sara, 5/22)

Besides using *ne* in listener responses, Sara also competently uses *ne* in
other ways. Like Kuo-ming, who uses *eeto ne* to show he is thinking, Excerpt 29 provides an example where Sara also uses *ne* for this purpose:

(29) 1 R: Kaguu::: wa, doko ni arimasu ka?
            Where is furniture?
→   2 Sr: <u>Kagu desu ne:::</u>, um:: kagu uriba wa^ >where's
            this one< oh! Rokka hahahai: ni arimasu.
            *<u>Furniture::: ne:::</u>, um:: The furniture section is^*
            >where's this one< oh! On the sixth floor hahahaha.
      3 R: Rokkai ni desu ne?
            The sixth floor, ne?
      4 Sr: Hai. Rokkai
            Yes. The sixth floor.
      5 R: Arigatoo gozaimasu
            Thank you very much
      6 S: Doo itashimashite
            You're welcome

                                                    (Sara 3/3)

Sara's use of *ne* in line 2 cannot be properly translated in English. It shows her reflection on the word, *furniture*, used in the process of trying to figure out where the furniture section is located in the department store layout depicted on her handout. Like the set phrase *Eeto ne:* 'let's see', Sara's line 2 expression functions as a hedge.

Sara's facility in using *ne* for listener responses is also evident when she provides instruction to her peer interlocutors. In Excerpt 30, Sara instructs her partner, Rita, in the use of *ne*-marked confirmation questions (line 7).

(30) 1 Sr: Um (.) Bunboogu uriba wa, (3) nanakai ni, arimasu.
            Um (.) the stationary section is, (3) on the seventh floor.
      2 R: A^ soo desu ka.
            Oh, really?
→   3 Sr: And so you confirm "nanakai desu ne,"
            And so you confirm "It's on the sixth floor, ne,"
      4 R: Arigatoo gozaimashita.
            Thank you very much.
      5 Sr: What am I supposed to say? Doo itashimashite
            What am I supposed to say? You're welcome

                                                    (Sara, 3/3)

In Sara's last recorded class, along with using *ne* in aligning listener responses, she also uses *ne* in initial assessments. In Excerpt 31, Sara tells the teacher that the person who did the worksheet drawings is a good artist. She uses a *ne*-marked initial assessment for this purpose:

(31) 1 Sr: hehe (.) hehe (.) hehehehe ((laughing at pictures))

→   2   Sr: Ii aatisuto desu ne:.
                  What a good artist ne:.
      3   T: So desu ka? watashi ga kakimashita.
                  Really? I drew that.
      4   Sr: Hehehehe So desu kaa?
                  Hehehehe oh really?
      5   T: [Hai.
                  Yes.
→   6   Sr: [Ii desu ne:::. Soo desu ka::? Hehehehe
                  It's nice ne::. Really? Hehehehe
      7   T: Arigatoo (.) mada mada desu.
                  Thanks (.) but I'm not good at it yet.
      8   Sr: Ah! Hehehehehehe
                  Ah! Hehehehehehe

                                                              (Sara, 5/22)

Here, in interaction with the teacher, Sara uses two spontaneous assessments. First, in line 2, she says that the person who drew the pictures is a good artist. Then, in line 3 she learns that the teacher drew the pictures, and in line 6, she comments that they are nice pictures. Sara uses *ne*-marked assessments for both purposes. Her assessments initiate a natural and friendly interaction, as the teacher denies her own artistic skill in line 7, to Sara's amusement.

Candace also develops in the use of listener responses from acknowledgement to alignment. Her speech at the beginning of the academic year shows a striking absence of listener responses in either Japanese or English. When she participates in pair activities in the 11/27 class, she has 20 opportunities to take a follow-up turn. In 14 of these cases, she makes no follow-up response at all. She struggles to form utterances, and is clearly focused on creating sentences and understanding what her partner says. Excerpt 32 provides an example of the lack of listener responses in one of Candace's early classes. Here, she and her partner are participating in a pair interview task. Arrows are used to mark locations where follow-up turns could potentially occur.

    (32)   1 S: Supootsu o shimasu ka?
                     Do you play sports?
           2 C: Hai ^ (.) hai shimasu.
                     Yes (.) yes I do.
→   3 S: (.)
           4 C: B- Biiru:. (.) biiru: o: (.) nomimasu ka:?
                     Do you (.) drink b- beer?
           5 S: Iie nomimasen.
                     No, I don't.

→   6 C: (.) Nihongo: benkyoo shimasu ka?
             (.) Do you study Japanese?
      7 S: Hai shimasu
             Yes, I do.
→   8 C: Hehehe
             Hehehe
      9 S: (.) Uh (.) biiru o nomimasu?
             (.) Uh (.) do you drink beer?
     10 C: Iie (.) uh (.) nomimasen
             No (.) uh (.) I don't.
→   11 S: Nihongo no benkyoo o shimasu ka?
             Do you study Japanese?
     12 C: Hai ^ (2) hai uh (.) benkyoo shimasu.
             Yes (2) yes uh (.) I do.
→   13 S: Eiga (.) ni (.) ikimasu ka?
             Do you go to movies?
     14 C: Iie (.) ikimasu (..) ikimasen.
             No (.) I go (..) I don't.
→   15 S: (.)
     16 C: Eiga:: Eiga ni (.) ikimasu ka.
             Do you go to (.) movie:: movies?
     17 S: Hai ikimasu
             Yes, I do.
→   18 C: Eiga mimasu ka?
             Do you watch movies?

                                          (Candace, 11/27)

Neither Candace nor her partner uses follow-up turns; and, there are no
listener responses. Rather, they simply ask one question after another.
The only flicker of a listener response is Candace's laughter in line 8,
which is responsive to her partner's obvious answer to Candace's obvious
question. As the year proceeds, however, Candace begins to do listener responses, first for expressions of acknowledgement, and later for alignment. Excerpt 33 provides an example where, in the winter quarter data,
Candace incorporates a listener response showing acknowledgement. The
response, *Aa soo desu ka*, is used when Candace asks her partner a question
during an interview task. Candace uses *Aa soo desu ka* to respond to her
partner's answer even though this turn is not scripted into the task.

   (33)   1 S: Nanji kan (.) benkyoo o shimashita ka?
                 How many hours did you study?
           2 C: Uh: yo ji (.) yo ji-
                 Uh: four hour (.) four hour- ((error: 'yoji' means 'four
                 o'clock', and can't be used to express duration)).

   3 S: [Aa soo desu ka::.
      Oh really.

   4 C: [Uh yo ji:: han kan gurai (.) benkyoo o shimashita.
      Uh about four hour half (.) I studied. ((error: syllables
      of 'yojikanhan' which means 'four and a half hours' are
      mixed up))

   5 S: Hai
      Yes.

   6 C: Hahahaha (.) Ah soo desu ka. uh um shumatsu: (..)
      nani o shimash- shimash- (.) nani o shimasu ka?
      Hahahaha (.) Oh really. Uh um over the weekend (..) what
      d- d- (.) what do ((error: tense)) you do?

   7 S: Ehto: (.) suupaa ni: ikimasu
      Uh (.) I go to the supermarket ((error: tense))

→ 8 C: Ah: soo desu ka?
      Oh really.

   9 S: Hai
      Yes.

   10 C: Kaimono ni ikimasu ka?
      Do you go shopping? ((error: tense))

   11 S: Iie
      No.

                 (Candace, 1/24)

Candace uses *Aa soo desu ka* appropriately in line 8; and, in line 3, her partner also uses *Aa soo desu ka* as a listener response. It is interesting to note
that Candace also uses the expression inappropriately in line 6—she over-
uses *Aa soo desu ka* as a follow-up to her own response. After she finishes
answering her partner's line 1 question in line 4, her partner uses the minimal acknowledgement response *hai* 'yes' in line 5. In line 6, after laughing, Candace says *Aa soo desu ka*. This is her only mistake with the expression in the data. Candace's overuse of *Aa soo desu ka* is evidence of how
salient it is to her.

  Two months later, in the spring quarter, Candace uses a greater variety
of follow-up turn utterances, including assessments expressing comprehension and evaluation. She uses these in Excerpt 34 after her partner
successfully connects two sentences during an oral grammar activity. For
readers who do not understand Japanese, the essence of Candace's struggle in this sentence-connection activity will not be clear from the English
translation. In Japanese, to connect two sentences involves a morphological inflection of the clause-final verb or adjective in the first clause to connect it to the second. Lexical items such as "and" cannot be used to combine two sentences into a single sentence. In order to produce English
translations, though, the word "and" was used where necessary, even

though this does not reflect the Japanese. Excerpt 34 exemplifies the point that Candace has begun to use assessments as listener responses. Here, Candace's line 13 and line 19 assessments show her appreciation of her partner's response.

(34) 1 C: Eigo ga waka- wakatte to wakatte furansugo wakarimasu?
I understand English and understand French? ((error: mis-use of the conjunction 'to', which means 'and', but is only used to connect nouns, not clauses)).

      2 T: Wakarimasen.
Don't understand.

      3 C: Ah wakarimasen. Sa:h! Oh! Wakarimasen
Ah don't understand. Sa:h! Oh! Don't understand

      4 T: Ii desu ka? To wa dame desu yo.
Okay? You can't use "to"

      5 C: Hmm.
Hmm.

      6 T: Wakatte (.) furansugo ga wakarimasen.
I understand English, (.) not French.

      7 C: Ah

      8 T: To arimasen.
There's no "to."

      9 C: Hai. Wakarimasu. (1)
Yes. I understand. (1)

      10 S: Taihen desu ne
It's difficult ne

      11 C: ((Laughs))

      12 S: (   ) wa nihonjin de (   ) no sensei desu.
(   ) is Japanese and a teacher of (   ).

→ 13 C: Mm ii desu ne. ((Laughs)) Sensei no (.) um hum (.) oko? No. Okas. No. Okosan?
Mm good ne. ((Laughs)) The teacher's oko? No okas. No. Okosan?

      14 S: Someone else's child?
Someone else's child?

      15 C: Is it okodomo? Oko oko oko. Hmmm.
Is it okodomo? Oko oko oko. Hmmm.

      16 S: Okosan I think. Yeah.
Okosan I think. Yeah.

      17 C: Just okosan? Uh thank you. Sensei no sensei- sensei no okoosan wa um (.) yas- yasete- te yasete iru? Yasete ite yasete ite? Uh totemo um chiisai desu. ((laughs)) Arigatoo.

> *Just okosan? Uh thank you. The teacher's child is um (.)*
> *thi*⌃ *thin? Thin? And very um small. ((laughs)) Thanks.*
> *((error: 'okosan' is mispronounced as 'okoosan' the second*
> *time it is used))*

    18 S: Yamada-san wa tenisu ga joozu de yakyuu wa joozu
              ja arimasen.
              Yamada-san is good at tennis, not at baseball

→   19 C: Mm ii desu ne. ((Laughs))
              Mm good ne. ((Laughs))

                                    (Candace, 4/24)

After struggling with her own answer and getting help from the teacher, Candace's partner shows appreciation for the difficulty of the task by saying *taihen desu ne* 'it's difficult, ne', in line 10. Then, her partner does the next item on the worksheet with ease. Candace shows appreciation of her partner's skill, saying *Ii desu ne* 'That's good/very good ne' in line 13. This *ne*-marked assessment praises her partner's answer. After Candace struggles with her own turn in lines 13 through 17, and her partner again connects sentences with ease in line 18, Candace again remarks *Ii desu ne* 'That's good/very good ne' in line 19. It is also interesting to see Candace's use of *"mm"* along with the *ne*-marked assessment. Her teacher often says "mm" to show acknowledgement, and Candace begins using this, even though its use has not been taught.

In the final class of the data set, Candace uses the greatest variety of listener responses. Most significantly, she uses more assessments, with a wider variety of adjectives. An example is shown in Excerpt 35. In this task, Candace and her partner are asking and answering questions about a series of pictures that show people with various injuries and ailments. Note Candace's assessment in line 4.

  (35) 1 L: Doo shita n desu ka?
              What happened?

        2 C: Ha ga itai n desu. (2) Doo shita n desu ka?
              My tooth hurts. (2) What happened?

        3 L: Uh (.) koshi ga (.) ita- itai n desu.
              Uh (.) my back (.) hur- hurts.

→   4 C: Hmmm. <u>Zannen desu ne::.</u>
              'Hmmm. That's too bad ne::.

                                      (Candace, 5/22)

Candace's assessment expresses sympathy for her partner's back pain. Although, like Sara, Candace misuses *zannen*, Candace's use of an aligning assessment that is congruent in content with her partner's talk is evidence of her growth. Along with trying out new words like *zannen* 'disappointing', Candace also continues using *Ii desu ne*. In Excerpt 36, Candace and her partner ask each other what they do when suffering various ailments. In line 5, Candace uses an aligning assessment:

(36) 1 C: Hmm. Atama ga itari toki nani o shimasu ka?
                Hmm. What do you do when you have a headache?
                ((error: adjective 'itai' is mispronounced. Also, use of
                "what" is incorrect)).

      2 S: Doo shimasu ka? D- doo shimasu ka?
                How do you do? Ho- how do you do ((Japanese uses
                "how" not "what" in this context)))

      3 C: Atama ga itai toki doo shimasu ka?
                How do you do when you have a headache ((both problems
                corrected))

      4 S: Soo desu ne. (.) Nemasu. ((laughs))
                Let me see. (.) I sleep ((laughs))

→   5 C: Hahahaha. Ii desu ne:::.
                Hahahaha. That's goo:::d ne::.

                                                        (Candace, 5/22)

After Candace asks the question (line 1), her partner first corrects her wording of the question (line 2), and Candace rephrases her question. Candace's partner pauses (line 4), and then answers the question. Candace's line 5 assessment conveys a hearty appreciation for her partner's answer, shown through the highly elongated *ne:::* and falling intonation. In the laughter they share and Candace's explicit indexing of common ground through her assessment, Candace displays a shared enjoyment of the language game that students can play as they try to choose appropriate, grammatically simple answers in class. Here, S chose the one-word, versatile, *nemasu* 'I sleep', rather than more difficult answers (such as *kusuri o nomimasu* 'take medicine') that are part of the new vocabulary for this lesson.

Candace and Sara? Rob and Kuo-ming? Who Is Typical?

In their first year of language study, Sara and Candace develop the ability to spontaneously use *Aa soo desu ka* earlier than Rob and Kuo-ming, and moved beyond them in their use of aligning assessments. Sara and Candace push beyond the question–answer structure of the pair interview tasks used in their classes. At first Candace, like Rob, does not use any listener responses. However, she gradually incorporates them appropriately in the follow-up turns, moving beyond Rob in her facility with listener responses. Sara also improves over the year, and produces the broadest range of listener-response turns. Most importantly, her listener responses are appropriately coordinated with her interlocutor's response. In contrast, Rob and Kuo-ming, although evidencing development in the use of *ne*, and ability to acknowledge their partners responses, are still primarily working within a question–answer discourse structure and do not develop the ability to spontaneously align with interlocutor responses.

In comparing Candace's and Sara's listener responses with the slower development of Kuo-ming and Rob, one wonders who might be more typical. All of these students had the same teacher part of the time, with Rob, Candace and Kuo-ming having the same teacher most of the time, as shown in Table 5.3. Candace and Rob were even in the same class for two quarters. Though classroom environments were similar, these students' progress is markedly different.

To better understand individual differences, the use of listener responses by Candace, Sara, Rob and Kuo-ming was compared with the listener responses of their various peer partners. The purpose of this comparison was to see how the progress of these four learners related to the progress being made by their peer partners. Another purpose of this analysis was to find out if the students have been influenced by their interlocutors. Did those who progressed faster have interlocutors who used more listener responses? Were the learners emulating their peer interlocutors through a process of speech accommodation? In order to address these question, I counted the use of *ne* and of the listener response *Aa soo desu ka* used by the four learners and their peer partners. Rather than counting *ne*-marked assessments, the use of *ne* by the learners was counted because Kuo-ming and Rob did not use *ne*-marked aligning listener responses.

The results of this analysis shows that in most cases the targeted learners used more of these devices than their peers did. At the same time, their use of these interactional devices is related also to that of their peer interlocutors. Table 5.5 displays these numeric results. In the table, the number of times in the corpus that a targeted learner used a device (*ne* or *Aa soo desu ka*) is shown in a ratio with the total number of times the device was used by the learner and peer interlocutors. This yields a percentage of to-

TABLE 5.5
Targeted Students' Use of *ne* and Their
Partners' Use of *ne* in Peer Learning Tasks

	Sara/Total	Candace/ Total	Rob/Total	Kuo-ming/ Total
ne	28/40 (70%)	11/20 (55%)	5/6 (83%)	10/26 (38%)
Aa soo desu ka	21/32 (67%)	10/22 (42%)	28/32 (72%)	6/8 (75%)

tal uses uttered by each of the four learners. The targeted learners, over-all, were more innovative in their language use than their interlocutors were. The results also show that there appears to be a "matching process" that occurred between the targeted learners and their peer partners. In general, targeted learners who used more of these devices worked with peers who also used more of these devices; and, those who used fewer of these devices interacted with peers who were similar. Considering *ne* and *Aa soo desu ka* separately, all of the targeted students except Kuo-ming used *ne* at least as often as their partners did. And, Kuo-ming used *ne* as often as his partners did except for in the very first class in the fall quarter, where many of the occurrences of *ne* appeared. In this class, Kuo-ming's partners used *ne* much more frequently (Kuo-ming used *ne* 3 times to his partners' 9). As the year progressed, however, Kuo-ming's use was similar to that of his partners'.

Results also show that Sara, Candace, and Kuo-ming all worked with partners who also use *ne*. Rob, however, worked with partners who virtually never used *ne*-marked expressions in the data collected. Despite Rob's own limited use of the particle, and the fact that three of the times Rob used *ne* were when he misused the expression *soo desu ne* for *Aa soo desu ka*, Rob was clearly more innovative in his language use than his partners were—83% of the uses of *ne* were by Rob. Sara also used *ne* more frequently than her partners did. Candace used *ne* slightly more often, and Kuo-ming used *ne* just as often as his partners did (except for the fall quarter). The figures for *Aa soo desu ka* reveal that all of the students worked with partners who also used the expression. Except for Candace, who used *Aa soo desu ka* bit less often than her partners did (42% of uses), the targeted students used *Aa soo desu ka* substantially more than their partners did (67% to 75% of uses). Rob worked with students who virtually never used *ne*. This may have dampened his own efforts to experiment with the particle. In contrast, Candace, Sara, and Kuo-ming's partners all use *ne* in the peer learning context. Working with other learners who also attempt to use new forms may encourage the learner's development.

Sara and Candace used *ne* for aligning listener responses. Table 5.6 considers only the use of *ne* in aligning assessments. Overall, Sara and Candace used *ne* more frequently than their peer partners did, and when only uses of *ne* in aligning expressions are considered, this difference becomes even

TABLE 5.6
Use of *ne* in Expressions of Alignment

	Candace	Candace's Partners	Sara	Sara's Partners
Uses of *ne* in expressions of alignment	9	3	23	8

more dramatic. Table 5.6 shows that Candace and Sara used many more aligning expressions than their pair-work partners did. It is possible that their development may represent a high mark for the first-year learner.

FROM ACKNOWLEDGMENT TO ALIGNMENT: PROPOSING A DEVELOPMENTAL SEQUENCE

Based on the development of these learners, a developmental sequence for acquisition of listener response expressions may be proposed. This sequence was initially proposed based only on Candace and Rob's data (Ohta, in press-b). Analysis of Sara and Kuo-ming's development is, for the most part, congruent with the proposed sequence. The sequence posits that learners first develop the ability to use expressions of acknowledgment, moving toward use of expressions of alignment. This developmental sequence is displayed in Table 5.7. In general, this developmental sequence

TABLE 5.7
From Acknowledgment to Alignment: A Proposed Developmental
Sequence for L2 (Japanese) Listener Responses

Stage 1	Students ask and answer preformulated questions. There is no use of expressions of acknowledgment or alignment, in English or in the L2, unless scripted. The follow-up turn of the IRF sequence is left unused, with speakers moving immediately, or after a pause, to a new initiation.
Stage 2	Students begin to use the follow-up turn for expressions of acknowledgment, such as repetition of L2 words and laughter.[7] Use of L2 minimal response expressions of acknowledgment such as *hai* are rare. Alignment expressions are used only where scripted.
Stage 3	Students begin to use expressions to show acknowledgment, particularly when prompted by the teacher, but occasional spontaneous use emerges also. Occasional use of the minimal response *hai* continues. Alignment expressions are used where scripted, and on a limited basis when prompted by the teacher.
Stage 4	Students use acknowledgment expressions with facility, beginning to use minimal expressions of acknowledgment beyond *hai*, such as the informal *mm* and *un*, on occasion. Alignment expressions appear when prompted by the teacher.
Stage 5	Spontaneous use of a limited range of L2 expressions of alignment emerges. Minimal response expressions occur more frequently. Expressions of alignment are still limited to those commonly used by the teacher.
Stage 6	Students appropriately use a broader range of expressions of acknowledgment. Alignment expressions are used spontaneously, with greater lexical variety tailored to conversational content.

[7]It appears that learners also begin to use the follow-up turn for repair at this stage. Horiguchi (1990) included repair in her rubric of listener-response behaviors. Examination of the development of learner-repair strategies is beyond the scope of this chapter.

TABLE 5.8
Use of *Hai, Un,* and *Mm*

	Hai	*Un*	*Mm*
Kuo-ming	Yes	Yes	Yes
Candace	Yes	Yes	Yes
Rob	Yes	No	No
Sara	Yes	No	No

appropriately represents the growth of the four learners. The learners develop at different paces, but generally follow a path from acknowledgment to alignment. Although originally proposed based on Candace and Rob's development, the only aspect of the sequence that does not jibe with the data from Sara's and Kuo-ming's classes is the expansion of minimal responses beyond the formal *hai* to the informal *mm* or *un*, proposed in Stage 4. Table 5.8 shows which minimal responses the four learners used in the classroom corpus. Candace's and Kuo-ming's data is most consistent with the proposed sequence, whereas neither Rob nor Sara use informal expressions of acknowledgement in the corpus. Candace, in particular, shows a steady development of minimal response expressions from *hai* at first, moving to use of informal expressions as well. Kuo-ming tends to mix the three expressions. It is also interesting that Sara, who became most skilled in terms of aligning expressions and who used *Aa soo desu ka* with facility, did not ever use informal minimal response expressions. More data is needed to determine the extent to which learners begin to use informal minimal responses, and how these should be handled in considering a developmental sequence from acknowledgment to alignment. It may be necessary to develop a sliding continuum for formal and informal registers, or to further consider how development of formal and informal registers relates to the development of listener responses.

Setting questions of formality aside, the developmental pace of the four learners is shown in Table 5.9. This table shows the dates of transcripts when language use consistent with each stage appeared. Both Candace and Rob begin at Stage 1 in the fall quarter (11/27 transcript). In contrast, Stage 1 is not evident in either Kuo-ming's or Sara's data. In early winter (1/24 data), Candace and Rob have both moved into Stage 2. Kuo-ming is already at Stage 2 in his earliest data set, and enters Stage 3 earlier than Candace and Rob do. In the 11/18 class, Kuo-ming is already using the follow-up turn a bit more flexibly than Rob or Candace did in their November data, only leaving one follow-up slot empty. He uses *Aa so desu ka* once, but otherwise uses English minimal responses, laughter, repetition, comments in English (like "that's cool"), and a repair initiation. He does not yet use *hai*. It appears that he is actually between Stages 1 and 2, but be-

TABLE 5.9
Progress Through Stages of Listener Response Development

	Stage 1	Stage 2	Stage 3	Stage 4	Stage 5	Stage 6
Candace	11/27*	1/24	2/28	→	4/24	
Rob	11/27	1/24	2/28	4/21		
Kuo-ming		11/18	1/30	5/22		
Sara			10/23	12/4	2/7	

*Dates indicate transcript dates.

cause of his use of *Aa soo desu ka*, Stage 2 may be more appropriate. His single use of *Aa soo desu ka* is not sufficient for Stage 3, which requires *occasional* spontaneous use. Sara's first transcript, from 10/23, places her in Stage 3, using *Aa soo desu ka* on occasion without prompting from the teacher. Sara is the only Japanese-American of the four, although she reported that the Japanese language was never used in her home. It is possible, however, that peripheral participation in interactions of elderly relatives or informal contact with Japanese people raised her awareness of L2 listener responses above that of the other three learners. Her spontaneous, appropriate use of *Aa soo desu ka* from the October data suggests experience with this expression prior to the onset of instruction in late September. Sara proceeds the most rapidly through these sequences, showing Stage 4 usage in December (12/4), and Stage 5 usage in February (2/7). She remains in Stage 5 through the rest of the year. Candace's data do not evidence Stage 4—she moves to Stage 5 two months after Stage 3. At around the same time, Candace enters Stage 5, using two alignment (*ii desu ne* and *taihen desu ne*) expressions appropriately and spontaneously; Rob enters Stage 4, and uses acknowledgement expressions with facility. Rob still does not use aligning expressions, but none were scripted for use in the activities, and the teacher did not prompt students to use them. Like Rob, Kuo-ming also remains in Stage 4 in his last data set. At the same time, Candace remains at Stage 5, but uses a slightly broader range of expressions than she did earlier, adding *zannen desu ne* to her repertoire. Here, at Stage 5, Candace has acquired the ability to show alignment with her interlocutor within the limits of her L2 vocabulary, using the affective particle *ne* appropriately for this purpose.

The four learners develop at different rates, and evidence sensitivity to different listener-response expressions. Rob's misuse of *soo desu ne* shows his awareness of this expression's potential as a listener-response expression; the other students do not use *soo desu ne* as a listener response. Rob and Sara do not show awareness of minimal response expressions beyond the formal expression *hai*, whereas Candace and Kuo-ming also use the more informal expressions *un* and *mm*. Sara and Kuo-ming evidence a more rapid start than do Rob and Candace. Kuo-ming's bilingualism (he is a native speaker of Mandarin), and Sara's potential exposure to the L2 outside of class may be factors here. None of the students advance to Stage 6 in the classroom data examined, although Sara and Candace both reach Stage 5, albeit on very different timetables. Of particular import in validating the existence of a developmental sequence of listener responses from acknowledgment to alignment is the fact that none of the students show facility with aligning expressions prior to using expressions of acknowledgment. This proposed sequence remains to be evaluated and possibly revised based on developmental studies of other learners. It is also possible that learners who learn in a second language context where they have daily interactions with native speakers outside of class might experience a different developmental sequence. Informal acknowledgement expressions would, for example, be likely to appear in the language of learners abroad more consistently than they do for classroom learners.

This study of the development of listener responses provides solid evidence that beginning learners are sensitive to pragmatic information. Learner participation in the routines of the classroom, in interaction with the teacher as addressee and auditor, and in interaction with peers, provides a range of opportunities for learners to be involved in routines involving listener responses. Materials design which encourages use of listener responses through scripting, as well as teacher involvement in prompting and explicit modeling of listener responses, builds into learner development. Learners capitalize on these experiences by using language in the peer setting that is more advanced than the language they use in teacher-fronted interaction. The learners did not evidence spontaneous use of listener-response expressions in teacher-fronted interactive contexts—the more flexible participation structure of the peer learning setting provides an environment conducive to linguistic and pragmatic experimentation and growth. In observing peer interactive data, we see evidence of development that the teacher may not see. These data show the power of classes conducted in the L2, the power of different modes of participation, and the learner innovation and growth that occurs during peer interactive tasks. Learners vary in developmental pace, but appear to follow a similar sequence of development, from acknowledgement to alignment. How the proposed sequence will be validated or adjusted based on other data remains to be seen. These findings are provocative, however, because they suggest that, as in other areas of L2 development, learners may also follow a common route of development in the area of interactional style.

Chapter 6

From Task to Activity: Relating Task Design and Implementation to Language Use in Peer Interaction

In analyzing data for the first five chapters of this book, questions in addition to those addressed in each chapter continued to emerge. In particular, when looking at learner activity as realized in the implementation of various language learning tasks, various factors emerged that appear to impact what happens during task performance. These include features of instructional style, task design, task implementation conditions, and learner orientations. This chapter is different from the five preceding it. This chapter queries the classroom corpus for information regarding how task design and implementation impact learner activity in the L2 classroom. Even for learners in the same classroom, tasks are implemented under different conditions. The "same task" is never really "the same," even for learners who are working side by side. Students come to class with different levels of preparation, exhibit different levels of engagement, and have different understandings of tasks. Individuals have their own dispositions toward language learning. Some, such as a learner's propensity to be active and involved or to avoid participation, may seem relatively stable. Other learner orientations to classroom activities may vary from day to day depending on the pressures impacting the learner. And, different groupings or pairings of students may also have an effect, depending on whether or not a peer interlocutor is engaged in the task. The inactive, uninvolved student who works with a similar peer may behave differently when paired with a highly engaged interlocutor. As Coughlan and Duff (1994) noted in their aptly titled article, "Same Task Different Activities," even under experimental conditions with a repeated task design, different learners have different understandings of identical tasks and the same individual over time may perform different activities when asked to repeat the same task at a later date.

Along with learner variation, teachers also vary. They have different sorts of training, experience, and interests. Instructional styles differ among teachers, even those who work with the same curricular materials. Teachers differ in their sensitivity to learner difficulties. They vary in how they implement tasks. Some teachers implement tasks in an incremental fashion that carefully prepares learners for peer interaction, whereas others introduce tasks more abruptly. Some teachers seem to be more accessible than others during peer work. Some teachers incorporate post-task accountability exercises, whereas others move immediately to other matters after discontinuing a task. In addition, the same teacher varies techniques from day to day. Teaching is situationally driven, tailored to the matters, materials, and time constraints at hand. All of these factors impact what happens during task implementation in a foreign language classroom.

Task design is another factor that evidences a great deal of variety. Task sheets and textbook presentations of tasks vary in their transparency to learners and in the amount of support built into task design. Some incorporate examples, schematic structures, or vocabulary for "mining," others do not. And, along with all of this variability, the classroom environment created by the interaction between the teacher and a particular group of students varies. Ask any teacher about the differences between two classes, and one learns that different classes have different personalities.

The variety of conditions and combinations of individuals, teachers, materials and tasks is dizzying. In the classroom corpus, these conditions naturally vary, and no control over any aspect of the classroom was exercised. Because of this, the data contains a range of tasks and implementation conditions. These data are useful for exploration of issues involved in the use of tasks in the foreign language classroom. Analysis of these data allow formation of inferences about how different factors impact students' language behavior during peer L2 activity. These inferences will form a foundation for future studies involving intervention, which can work more explicitly to manipulate conditions to better understand how different factors impact learners' language use in the L2 classroom.

In this chapter, I discuss observations that have emerged through the analysis of the classroom corpus. While discussing these observations, questions for further research will be raised. This chapter was developed through a process that began with the consideration of a couple of the most basic questions that face teachers or researchers interested in promoting L2 development in a classroom setting:

(1) In the classroom corpus, what task implementation and design characteristics appear to promote the sort of L2 interaction that stimulates language development?

(2) What factors seem to cause peer learning activities to fail to be spaces that promote language learning?

These questions address two sides of the same coin. What factors seem to co-occur with a productive and positive collaborative learning experience, and what factors seem to work against such an outcome? By addressing these two related questions, this chapter delves into the murky relationship between *task* (what it is that learners are asked to do in interaction with one another) and *activity* (what it is that they actually do). The goal of this chapter is not only to discuss research results, but also to think beyond the corpus in order to ask questions that are larger than the data set. This chapter raises issues that cannot be fully treated here, but provides an opportunity to address pedagogical concerns by starting with the corpus.

In order to address the two basic questions just raised, we must first review what it means for an interaction to promote language development. What does optimal interaction during peer learning activities look like? I answer this question by both summarizing findings of previous chapters as well as making inferences based on these findings. Productive peer interaction in the classroom setting is characterized by creative use of the L2 to perform tasks, active resolution of problems that emerge with use of the L2 in solving these problems via assisted performance. In optimal peer interaction, a ZPD emerges. That is, there is sufficient challenge that learners are, with peer assistance, able to move beyond their individual capabilities. In addition, optimal peer interaction in the L2 classroom occurs in the L2, with limited use of English. The interaction is not error free (error-free performance, in fact, is indicative of tasks that lack appropriate challenge, or which do not push beyond regurgitation of memorized material), nor are learners bogged down by problems. In optimal interaction, learners take risks and try new language forms, even though this means making errors and receiving assistance. Optimal interactions are characterized by a sense of "flow." There is movement and development, with learners progressing (as indicated by reduction in errors and increase in fluency and creativity), helping each other, and calling on the teacher to resolve difficulties. Previous chapters illustrated these sorts of interactions—interactions that stimulate mental activity (as seen in private speech), and assisted performance that results in gains for the learners who participate. We have also seen how adept learners are at incorporating corrective information from a range of sources. Over time, optimal interactive experiences lead to development of L2 proficiency—a larger vocabulary, more flexible repertoire of morphosyntax, and a gradually more nativelike, interactional style.

The answers to the two fundamental questions raised here cannot be provided neatly in two discrete sections, one dealing with what promotes optional interaction and one dealing with what impedes it. Rather, similar features (for example, task repetition), may be linked to both, depending on other factors. In this chapter, such complexity will not be avoided, but the goal is to provide interpretation of the complex factors that may influence what it is that learners do when they are working with peers on language learning tasks. This chapter is divided into two major sections, one dealing with the L1, and one with the L2. First, the conditions that appear to promote or discourage overreliance on L1 use in the classroom corpus is considered. Results show that although there are individual differences, L1 use is also influenced by instructional variables related to task design and implementation. Second, the chapter considers the relationship between task design, pre-task work, and language use during peer learning activity. This section of the chapter centers around a set of questions developed to query aspects of task design and implementation. These questions are pedagogical in focus—they have been designed not only in an attempt to understand the present corpus, but also to promote the development of task design and implementation strategies that might best create conditions for the L2 development of classroom learners in the early years of instruction. My hope is that the explorations in this chapter will result in a better understanding of how task and peer activity relate to one another, a matter that will be revisited in the chapter's conclusion.

LEARNER USE OF ENGLISH: THE RELATIONSHIP BETWEEN TASK DESIGN, TASK IMPLEMENTATION, AND INDIVIDUAL DIFFERENCES

The use of English by these learners of Japanese appears to be impacted by features of materials and instructional design. At the same time, there are strong individual differences. Different learners seem to have different thresholds of English use, with some using much less English and others using English much more frequently. In this section, both the aspects of task implementation that are controlled or manipulated by the teacher as well as learner propensities to use more English or to use more Japanese are considered. The use of English is related to the question of what impedes and what promotes L2 development in peer interactive tasks. What is the optimum role of English during peer tasks? What causes overreliance on the L1?

Along with the abandonment of grammar-translation method as the method of choice in foreign language teaching, and the increase in approaches that develop speaking and listening skills along with reading and writing skills, the use of English in L2 classrooms has been discouraged or prohibited. Audiolingualism focused on drill, eschewing explanation of what would come to be known behaviorally through habit-forming exercises. The direct method, which became particularly popular as a way of teaching Spanish, prohibited any use of English in the classroom. Not only does the direct method reject use of spoken English, but also of written English. Flash cards with translations, for example, are not used. Total physical response (TPR) became popular as a technique of teaching language without use of the L1. In Krashen's natural approach (Krashen & Terrell, 1983), as in the direct method, extensive use of context (and cognates) avoided teacher use of English in the classroom, although beginners were encouraged to show comprehension even in the L1 at early stages. In this way, learner utterances in English could be used as tools for the teacher to teach L2 vocabulary relevant to learner interests and needs. Today, it may be taken for granted that teachers should conduct foreign language classes primarily in the L2, although teachers have been found to vary widely in the extent to which they do so (Duff & Polio, 1990). Even so, speaking more L2 and less L1 is likely a goal of most foreign language teachers, both for themselves and their students. Some university foreign language programs have policies prohibiting the use of English in the classroom.

Although the teacher's ideal may be that learners use only the L2 to accomplish collaborative tasks, studies show that students do use the L1 to some extent. In the teacher-fronted mode of instruction, it is possible for the instructor to avoid the use of English and to prohibit students from using English. However, when peer learning tasks are introduced, the teacher gives up turn-by-turn control of learner language use. Research has suggested that L1 use may be related to task complexity. Brooks et al. (1997) studied the use of learners' L1 (English) and L2 (Spanish) in the talk of third-semester university learners of Spanish who repeated similar tasks in a laboratory setting. When a task was repeated, the learners' use of English declined and use of Spanish increased. At first, English facilitated the use of Spanish by serving as a tool for task management; the use of English diminished as task management issues were resolved. Nakaone (1999) was interested in whether Brooks et al.'s (1997) results would be found with other tasks, and conducted a smaller study in her own university level, second-year Japanese classroom. Nakaone repeated picture sequencing tasks on two consecutive days of instruction, miking two pairs of learners who worked together on both days. She found a reduction in the use of English for task management in the second sequencing task, but one pair's use of English increased dramatically as they worked to resolve a grammatical problem that emerged in the second task. The students' use of English helped them to solve the grammatical problem and to continue using the L2 to tell the story. Nakaone found, as did Brooks and his colleagues, that learners used English as a thinking tool to mediate their activity when their L2 knowledge was insufficient for that purpose. Nakaone's findings showed English to have a productive role in the learners' predominantly L2 interaction. For foreign language students, the L1 is an important element needed for thinking processes.

The following section examines how English was used by learners in an environment where teacher use of English in the classroom was rare, and where use of the L2 by students was highly valued.

Measures of English Language Use

An objective method of quantifying English language use was needed in order to examine how much English was used in various tasks. The method developed was to note which lines of transcript contained English and which did not. A percentage of transcript lines containing English was then calculated. The presence of a single word of English in a line of transcript was counted as a line containing English. In the same way, a line that was entirely in English was also counted as a line containing English. This measure of English use may overstate the use of English, because a single English language word in a line meant that the line was counted as containing English. In order to insure that the counts did not result in an unrealistic portrayal of the discourse used in any particular task, a qualitative review of each task was conducted with percentages of lines containing English for each task in mind. Lines with little English were balanced by lines containing a great deal of English. The qualitative judgment was consistent with the results of the objective measure, revealing the objective measure to be a good indication of the amount of English used. It is important to keep in mind that a figure like 30% doesn't mean that 30% of the talk was in English, but means that 30% of the transcript lines contained English.

Using this measure, the proportion of lines containing English was compared across activities for individual learners, across classes, and across learners and levels. Percentages were calculated for each task. Using the percentages for the tasks of each learner, medians were recorded. Table 6.1 shows the median percentage of transcript lines containing English for each learner,[1] along with the range across tasks for each learner and level. The amount of English used varied not only across learners, but also varied dramatically across levels. Some of the tasks used in these classes require interaction in the L2, such as interview or role play tasks, and others, such as matching tasks or worksheet answer comparison tasks, do not. Inclusion of only interactive tasks yields slightly lower medians. Although the expectation might be that English use would decrease with growing proficiency, comparison of first- and second-year medians shows that the second-year learners used a great deal more English than the first-year learners. It must be kept in mind that this second-year curriculum is not a continuation of the first year, but that a new curriculum

---

[1]English is the first language of all of the students except Kuo-ming, an immigrant from Taiwan, whose first language is Mandarin Chinese.

TABLE 6.1
Percentage of Transcript Lines Containing
English: Median and Range

First Year	Median	Range	Second Year	Median	Range
Kuo-ming	11.60%	0%–56.3%	Katie	32.70%	24.1%–83.1%
Candace	16.70%	0%–45.2%	Bryce	35.90%	20.3%–74.3%
Sara	24.60%	4.2%–48.8%	Andrea	43.20%	5.3%–82.7%
Rob	38.70%	8.3%–100%			
Average	23.60%		Average	40.85%	

was implemented at the first year. It is inappropriate to assume that the second-year group might represent a continuation of the first year. It is more appropriate to compare the two groups not as groups of potentially lower and higher proficiency, but as groups that experience different sorts of language learning tasks implemented in different ways. This, as we will see when the results of qualitative analysis are discussed in a later section, provides an interesting range of task types and implementation conditions for comparative purposes.

The function of the English used by learners was determined through development of categories as they emerged during analysis of the data. These categories were then used to examine all peer learning activity that occurred when the various tasks were implemented. For each activity, if a particular function was present, it was noted as such, yielding a list of English language functions that occurred in each activity in the corpus. For purposes of presentation, these functions are divided into "language-related functions," "task-related functions" and "other functions." The functions of English found in the transcript are shown in Table 6.2. Language related functions relate to production of the foreign language. Examples include word searches, use of English words in L2 sentences, repair, questions about the L2, explanations of the L2, resolution of spelling difficulties, requests for confirmation that an utterance was correct, and translation of words, phrases, or utterances into English. The primary task-related function is task management. This includes use of English to get a task going (for example, to figure out what to do and decide who will do what), to bring a task to a close, or to regulate a task in progress. *Visual* refers to use of English to figure out visual materials such as pictures, maps, or charts. Other functions of English that do not fall into the language-related or task-related functions include private speech, which is used to mediate the learner's cognitive processes. In addition, interactive functions such as praise, acknowledgement, self-evaluation, and content-related comments are included here. *Other conversation* refers to conversation that is semantically unrelated to the task at hand.

TABLE 6.2
Functions of English in Peer Activity in the Classroom Corpus

Language-Related Functions	Task-Related Functions	Other Functions
Word search	Task management	Private speech
Vocabulary substitution	Visual	Praise
Repair		Acknowledgement
Translation		Content-related comment
Language question		Self-evaluation
Explanation		Other conversation
Spelling		
Confirmation request		

The most common function of English was task management, which occurred in 68.2% of all tasks. Of the language-related functions, the most
commonly occurring functions were language questions (56.5%), translation (48.2%), and explanation (36.4%). Of "other" functions, acknowledgement (37.7%), content-related comments (35.3%), and private speech
(29.4%) occurred most frequently. Other conversation was comparatively
infrequent (14.1%), although this figure varied widely across levels and individual students. Comparisons between first- and second-year students are
shown in Table 6.3. These comparisons cannot be used to infer a developmental continuum, but rather to help form questions for qualitative examination of the corpus. Consistent with the finding that fewer turns of the
first-year tasks contained English as compared to second-year tasks, most of
the functions shown in Table 6.3 occurred less frequently in first-year activities than in the second-year activities. Use of English for task management,
language questions, translation, explanation, acknowledgement, and other
conversation was considerably more common in the second-year data than

TABLE 6.3
Percentage of Activities Containing English
Used for Particular Functions

Function	First Year Percentage	Second Year Percentage	Combined Percentage
Task management	59.62%	81.82%	68.24%
Language questions	48.08%	69.7%	56.41%
Translation	40.38%	60.61%	48.24%
Explanation	32.69%	42.42%	36.47%
Acknowledgement	32.69%	45.45%	37.65%
Private speech	30.77%	27.27%	29.41%
Content-related comments	38.46%	30.3%	35.29%
Other conversation	5.77%	27.3%	14.1%

in the first-year data. In the second year, more English was used for a broader range of functions. Qualitative analysis of the tasks and their implementation is used to illuminate reasons for these differences.

Understanding the Numbers: English Use in Peer Interaction

The use of the L1 for task management purposes has been noted in previous studies (Brooks et al., 1997; Nakaone, 1999) as well as here. The use of English for task management helps to explain the large gap between how much first- and second-year students used English during peer language learning tasks. Comparisons are shown in Table 6.4. As the data show, the second-year students used more English for task management than the first-year students. One reason for this emerges when the types of tasks are examined. First-year students were repeatedly asked to do similar sorts of tasks—interview and simple role-plays tasks, for example. The tasks assigned second-year students had much more complexity and variety. In addition, the first-year textbook guided teachers in the use and selection of tasks that were, in general, of appropriate difficulty. Second-year teachers, who used a textbook that did not contain any peer interactive tasks, made their own materials individually and corporately. Some of the teachers in each level were teaching with tasks for the first time. For second-year teachers, inexperience was compounded by the need to develop tasks. As a result, sometimes the teachers considerably overestimated what the learners would be able to do, and underestimated the amount of support learners would need. Some of the more complex tasks used in the second-year classes involved multiple steps that built on one another. Learners used more English to manage this complexity. For example, in multiple-step tasks, learners had to figure out the information they would need to collect for subsequent task steps, as well as who they should work with, and, perhaps, the role they were to play in different parts of the task.

TABLE 6.4
Task Management in English—Average Number of Transcript Lines Per
Task for First- and Second-Year Learners

First year	Transcript Lines With English Used for Task Management (Ave.)	Second year	Transcript Lines With English Used for Task Management (Ave.)
Kuo-ming	1.73 lines	Katie	6 lines
Sara	1 line	Andrea	3.5 lines
Candace	1.38 lines	Bryce	2.9 lines
Rob	1.75 lines		
Average	1.43 lines	Average	4 lines

English use increased when learners were not sure what to do. And, use of the L2 was reduced if learners were unable to do subsequent task steps. Similar tasks were seldom repeated. Therefore, the start-up time for second-year tasks was lengthier and involved more English use by students.

Another difference between the first- and second-year classes relates to the use of teacher-fronted instruction prior to peer learning tasks. In first-year classes, tasks were introduced as a part of theme-based, grammatically sequenced units. Pre-task instruction introduced new language to learners (whether vocabulary or morphosyntax), and the teachers consistently involved the whole class in the same kind of task in the teacher-fronted setting prior to having students work with each other. During this process, new vocabulary (often related to the theme) and structures were introduced and practiced, or previously introduced language was reviewed. In addition, teachers provided visual support to ease learner use of newly introduced inflections. This was usually done with schematic representations of a structure written on the blackboard. Along with teacher-fronted practice of tasks, teachers often led demonstrations of tasks and involved one or more students in the demonstration process. And, when a dialogue was involved, teachers built up the task incrementally, such that learners practiced bits and pieces of the dialogue before being asked to improvise during peer interaction. Because the theme was constant from day to day, learners clearly understood the topic (for example, "my town" or "housing") and developed a vocabulary that was consistently used throughout a particular unit. These practices resulted in the smooth integration of tasks into lessons. Tasks flowed logically out of teacher-fronted phases of instruction. When it was time for peers to work together, the learners usually "jumped right in" to tasks in the L2 with minimal need to use English to figure out who was to do what, what the topic was, or what they were supposed accomplish.

In contrast, tasks in the second-year classes tasks were introduced more abruptly. Tasks did not flow smoothly from the instructional phase of lessons. Rather, instruction often did not incorporate task features. One teacher explained grammatical structures without providing any modeling of how to do the tasks she introduced. After the grammar practice, she distributed worksheets and told students to do the task. Others provided lengthy L2 explanations of tasks, including verbal instructions of what to say in the L2, but did not give learners the opportunity to practice the key phrases, grammar, or vocabulary prior to doing the task. Sometimes these explanations were supplemented with written instructions in English. And, although first-year lessons generally followed a theme over a 2- to 3-week period, topics in the second year often shifted within the same lesson. As a result of these practices, in the second year, the language learning tasks were not well integrated into the lessons. In particular, lack of demonstrations, lack of consistent topics, and lack of provision for pre-task practice left students uncertain about what they were to do (as evidenced by the number of turns used for task management) and had a significant impact on the quality of L2 used by learners during peer interactive tasks.

Individual Differences in L1 Use

In addition to differences between first- and second-year task design and implementation, individual differences appear to have an impact on how much English the learners used. This will be demonstrated through a comparison of the interaction of two first-year learners. In the fall and winter quarter, Candace and Rob were enrolled in the same class, yielding several examples of how the two students and their peer interlocutors approach tasks differently. As shown in Table 6.1, Rob's peer activities, overall, contain a higher degree of English use (38.7% of transcript lines containing English), than do Candace's (16.7%). The amount of English also differs dramatically. Candace's peer interaction ranges from 0% to 45.2% of transcript lines containing English, while for Rob the range is 8.3% to 100%. Although Candace and Rob were in the same class for two quarters, experiencing the same language lessons, differences in their use of English are useful to illustrate the range of individual learner behavior, and to consider why some students frequently use English whereas others do not.

During one of the lessons in the corpus, Rob and Candace both perform a simple question–answer task. The focus of the lesson is "weekend activities." After a short quiz that tested vocabulary used to talk about daily activities, the teacher asks students questions using the expressions just tested. She asks whether they play sports, drink beer, study Japanese, watch movies, and so on. Students answer these yes–no questions in the teacher-fronted setting, and the teacher has the learners repeat each answer in chorus. For the interactive task, the teacher distributes worksheets that have pictures and vocabulary prompts written in the L2, with blanks for learners to check off the yes–no answers of three interviewees. Students are to generate their own questions using these prompts. The vocabulary on the handout is the same as that which was used in homework assignments, tested on the quiz, reviewed, and practiced. Students, then, have been given many opportunities to learn the vocabulary used. In the task, learners must use that vocabulary to ask yes–no questions about whether their interlocutor participates in the various activities that have been talked about in class. The peer task flows smoothly from the progression of classroom activities, and provides the students with an opportunity to use the L2 to formulate and ask questions of their peers. The first five of the eight items on the worksheet are reproduced in Figure 6.1. Each prompt includes both a simple drawing and a vocabulary word written in Japanese.

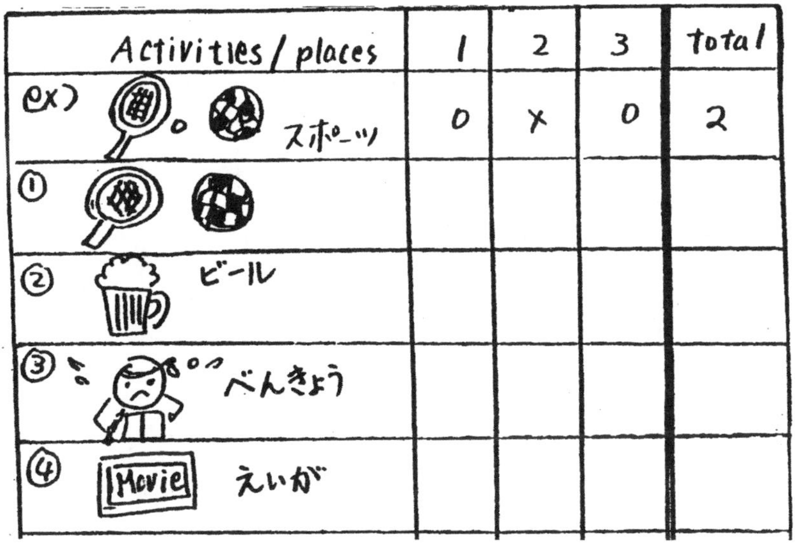

FIG. 6.1.   Interview worksheet for first-year Japanese: First five items.

In Excerpt 1, Candace and her partner, S, immediately begin in Japanese, asking and answering questions fairly smoothly.

(1) 1 C: Supo- (.) a::h (.) tenisu:: (.) tenisu:: s- tenisu o shimasu (.) ka?
          Spor- (.) a::h (.) tenni::s (.) do pl- do you play (.) tennis?

     2 S: Iie shimasen
          No I don't

     3 C: Supo:zu o- o shimasu ka?
          Do you d- play sports?

     4 S: Iie shimasen
          No I don't.

     5 C: hehehehe (.) Arigatto gozaimasu
          *hehehehe (.) thank you very much ((error: 'arigato'
          is misprounounced as 'arigatto'))*

     6 S: Supootsu o shimasu ka?
          Do you play sports?

     7 C: Hai ^ (.) hai shimasu.
          Yes (.) yes I do.

     8 S: (.)

     9 C: B- Biiru:. (.) biiru: o: (.) nomimasu ka:?
          B- bee:r. (.) do you (.) drink beer?

    10 S: Iie nomimasen.
          No I don't.

11   (.)
12   C: Nihongo: benkyoo shimasu ka?
             Do you study Japanese?
13   S: Hai shimasu
             Yes I do
14   C: Hehehe
15   (.)
16   S: Uh (.) biiru o nomimasu?
             Un (.) do you drink beer?
17   C: Iie (.) uh (.) nomimasen
             No (.) uh (.) I don't
18   S: Nihongo no benkyoo o shimasu ka?
             Do you study Japanese?
19   C: Hai^ (.) hai uh (.) benkyoo shimasu.
             Yes (.) yes uh (.) I do.

                                               (Candace, 11/27)

Candace and S take turns asking and answering questions. Their grammatical accuracy is high, as they appropriately use the verbs they are
learning in their answers. In English do–support allows the generic answers "yes, I do" and "no, I don't" regardless of what verb is used, but in
Japanese the learners must use the verbs in both their questions and their
answers. They make a few errors in pronunciation. The lack of other sorts
of errors does not mean the task is easy for them—the frequent pauses in
the interaction show the high level of effort involved. Neither learner uses
any English. Without using English, they manage turn shifts—Candace
asks a couple of questions first, with her partner then asking questions
also, until both ask and answer all of the questions. When Rob and his
partner Harry work on the same task in the same classroom, they use English much more often (underlined), as shown in Excerpt 2.

(2)   1 R: Supo:tsu wa: shimasu ka?
                Do you play sports?
       2 H: Um say iie
                Um say no
       3 R: Hehehe biru no- (.) hehe nomimasu (.) biru: (.) o^
                nomimasu (.) //ka?
                Hehehe do you dr- (.) hehe drink (.) bee: (.) do you drink
                beer? ((error: 'biiru' is misprounounced as 'biru'))
       4 H: Sure (.) umm[hahaha hai nomimasu
                Sure (.) umm   hahaha yes I do.
       5 R: [hahahah
       6 R: Uhh I have no idea what number three is

```
 7  H:  You:: put on a headband and sweat
 8  R:  Hahahah do ya?
 9  H:  I don't know what that is
10  R:  Ben- benkyoo?
        Stu- study?
11  H:  That's study isn't it (.) benkyoo?
12  R:  Benkyoo shimasu ka?
        Do you study?
13  H:  Uh (.) iie (.)benkyoo[ (.) shimasen
        Uh (.) iie (.) I don't (.) study
14  R:                      [Hai
                             yes
15      Movie (.) uh no ei: (.) eiga (.) mimasu ka?
        Movie (.) uh no mo: (.) do you watch movies?
16  H:  Hai ei- eiga (.) mimasu ka (wait. mimasu.)
        Yes I watch (.) mo- movies (wait. I watch.) ((error: mis-use
        of interrogative particle 'ka' with a statement))
17  R:  Nu: what is that (2) Sentoraru (2) ai:: (.) what is that (.)
        number 5 (.) Times?
18  H:  I think it's [times (.) tae:ma
19  R:               [But it's ta: (.) here's ah (.)
20      Sentoraru taimasu (.) taimusu (.) to yomimasu (.) ka?
        Do you read (.) the Central Times (.) Times? ((error: particle
        'to' used instead of the accusative 'o'))
```
                                                           (Rob, 11/27)

In line 6, Rob initiates use of English, asking about number three (see Fig. 6.1). Harry responds by giving a literal description of the picture. In Japan, students studying hard for exams are often represented as wearing a cloth sweatband over their brow. American learners would be unlikely make the connection between this representation and the concept of studying, except that the character shown is sweating over a book, and the noun *benkyoo* 'studying' is written next to the picture. Harry's literal description, "put on a headband and sweat," is followed by Rob's laughter. In line 10, Rob finally reads the accompanying vocabulary word, and they move on. The picture depicting studying may have also have confused Candace—she paused in line 11 of Excerpt 1. She might have paused to consider the picture and read the word *benkyoo*, but the pause could also result from a subtle negotiation of who should take the next turn. In line 17 of Excerpt 2, Rob uses English again—first starting to say "New York," reading the English title of the newspaper, and then working to decode the Japanese for "Central Times." Rob uses English to ask his partner how to read the word and as he sounds out the L2 text. In contrast, Candace and her partner use much less English, as shown in Excerpt 3:

(3)   1   C: Sentoraru: (.) <u>weekly</u> (.) wi:: wi:: (.) sentoraru (.) tai
(.) tai::=
Central: (.) weekly (.) wi:: wi:: (.) central (.) ti (.) ti::

      2   S: =Taimusu=
=Times=

      3   C: =Taimusu? Sentoraru taimusu (.) ah: o: o yomimasu
(.) yomimasu ka?
=Times? Do you read ah read (.) the (.) Central Times?

      4   S: Hai yomimasu (3) Sentoraru Taimusu uh (.) o
yomimasu ka?
Yes I do (3) do you (.) read the Central Times?

      5   C: Iie. (.) yomimasen. (.) <u>New</u> <u>York</u> Taimuzu:
yomimasu.
No. (.) I don't. (.) I read the New York Times.

                                              (Candace, 11/27)

In line 1, after reading *sentoraru* 'central', Candace says "weekly," filling in
the name of a local entertainment weekly, as she guesses what might come
next. She works with the syllable "wi," but then abandons the word
"weekly" and sounds out what is written, beginning the word *taimusu*
'times' by repeating the syllable *'tai'*. As she repeats *"tai,"* lengthening the
vowel, S chimes in with the word *taimusu* in line 2, and Candace immediately adopts the word for her own use in line 3. Candace and her partner
resolve the problem by using a minimum of English—the only English
word they use is "weekly." Instead, they use the strategies of waiting and
coconstruction. Candace's partner waits through several pauses as Candace works to formulate her sentence and she chimes in with the word
taimusu, which Candace quickly adopts. All of this is accomplished in Japanese, the L2.

  Candace and Rob also differ in the amount of English used for content-
related comments and unrelated conversation. In Candace and her partners' talk, English language comments do not develop into continued conversation in English. However, Rob and his partner's English language
comments tend to develop into conversations, as shown in Excerpt 4.

(4)   1   R: Mars Attacks wa omoshiroi desu ka?
Is Mars Attacks interesting?

      2   S: (.) Mada wakarimasen.
(.) I don't know yet.

      3   R: (.) Yomimasen desu ka. (.) or no- mimasen
(.) You don't read it? (.) or no- don't see ((error—tense))

      4   S: Mimasen?
Don't see? ((error—tense))

> 5 R: Mimasen. <u>Did not see it</u> ((error—'mimasen' means
>   'don't see'))
>   (.)
> 6 R: Ghost of Mississippi wa omoshiku arimasen
>   *Ghost of Mississippi isn't interesting. ((error: pronunciation*
>   *of 'omoshiroku' as 'omoshiku'))*
> 7 S: Ahh soo desu ka? hehehe <u>It wasn't very good?</u>
>   *Oh really? hehehe It wasn't very good?*
> 8 R: <u>I thought it was going to be but it wasn't.</u>
> 9 S: <u>What's it about?</u>
> 10 R: <u>Um Medgar Evars, assassination.</u>
> 11 S: Um (.) eiga (.) eigo wa (.) muzukashii desu
>   *Um (.) movie- (.) English (.) is difficult.*
>   *((error—pronunciation of movie 'eiga' as 'eigo', which*
>   *means 'English'))*
>
>   (Rob, 1/27)

Rob's partner's line 7 question in English, "it wasn't very good?," a content-related question, prompts continued conversation in English. Candace and her partners also make content-related comments and questions in English. They do this much less often than Rob. In addition, conversations in English do not develop from their English language comments. Excerpt 5 provides an example where Candace's partner asks about a vocabulary word:

> (5) 1 L: Eh, donna kuruma o motte imasu ka?
>   *Eh, what kind of car do you have?*
>   2 C: ((laughs)) Chiisai furui (.) kuruma uh kuruma o
>   motte imasu.
>   *((laughs)) I have a small old (.) car uh car.*
>   3 L: <u>What is</u> kuruma?
>   4 C: Kuruma? Um, <u>car.</u>
>   5 L: Oh, chiiisai? <u>Oh you?</u>
>   6 C: <u>I know it</u> ((laughs)) Motte imasen.
>   *I know it ((laughs)) I don't have a car.*
>
>   (Candace, 2/28)

In line 3, Candace's partner Lisa uses English to ask a vocabulary question, and Candace provides the English translation in line 4. As Lisa works to understand Candace's question, repeating *chiisai* 'small', in line 5, she asks, "Oh you?" And, Candace answers in a combination of English and the L2. Candace then immediately asks Lisa another question in the L2.

Comparing Candace and Rob's use of English, Rob uses more English both to solve Japanese language problems and for conversation, which develops from content-related comments in English. In addition, compared to Candace and her partners, Rob and his various partners are much more voluble in English. Table 6.5 compares percentages of lines containing English for identical tasks done by Rob and Candace. Candace and Rob both chose their own partners; the teacher did not assign pairings for any of the tasks. Rob and his partners used 8.3% to 60% more lines containing English than Candace and her partners. I tried to determine whether Rob and Candace influenced their partners to use more or less English by looking at the direction of code switching, and whether either was more or less likely to switch to English or to maintain a switch than the partners. However, I was unable to find any pattern. Rather, it appears that learners choose to work with students who have a similar orientation toward peer learning tasks. Candace and her peers tended to avoid English; they only used English when they were truly stymied or for brief comments. In contrast, Rob and his partner used English much more freely. As a result, they used less Japanese.

Even with the same classroom conditions, students vary in orientation toward peer learning tasks. In the same classroom with the same teacher and what appear to be the same learning conditions, we can see how learners differ. One important factor may be how learners view the classroom language learning enterprise. In the language program where these data were collected, the teachers and language program discourage (but do not strictly prohibit) the use of English. Even so, students may or may not buy in to the idea that the foreign language classroom is a place where they should use the L2 as much as possible. Candace, an experienced language learner, used English when necessary to resolve a problem or provide or obtain an explanation, but actively worked to keep interaction in the L2. Rob, on the other hand, both used more English and was less engaged in L2 interactive tasks. The comparison of Rob and Candace's use of English reveals that we must take care before assuming that a particular example of classroom language use is caused by instructional practices rather than

TABLE 6.5
Percentage of Lines Containing Any English:
Same Interactive Tasks Done by Candace and Rob

Task Number	Date	Rob	Candace	Difference
1	11/27	36	6.3	+29.7%
2	1/24	8.3	0	+8.3%
3	1/24	20	9.1	+10.9%
4	2/28	63	23	+40%
5	2/28	100	40	+60%
6	2/28	60	45	+15%
7	2/28	45	29	+16%

TABLE 6.6
Percentage of Lines Containing English in Candace
and Rob's Tasks: Re-ordered From the Lowest to
Highest Percentage of English Use in Rob's Tasks

Task #	Date	Rob	Candace
2	1/24	8.3	0
3	1/24	20	9.1
1	11/27	36	6.3
4	2/28	63	23
7	2/28	45	29
6	2/28	60	45
5	2/28	100	40

individual differences. This being said, the data also show that instructional practices, including task design and implementation features, impact how learners use language in the classroom. Table 6.5 showed difference between the groups. However, as Table 6.6 shows, if we reorder Table 6.5 beginning with the tasks where students used the least English, listing the tasks according to the amount of English used, the tasks fall into nearly the same order for both Rob and Candace. As shown in Table 6.6, with the exception of tasks 1 and 3, and 5 and 6, which are reversed for Candace, the order is congruent. This comparison nicely illustrates an important point. Although there are strong individual differences, Candace and Rob's L1 use is not haphazard, nor is it idiosyncratic. Instructional variables related to task design and implementation influence how much English the students use in these tasks. And, English is not the only area of language use impacted by instructional design. The way the L2 is used—and therefore learned—by students in the classroom is also influenced by instructional design.

TASK TYPE, PRE-TASK INSTRUCTION, AND QUALITY OF L2 USE

Factors that influence the use of English also influence the quality of L2 language use during peer interactive tasks. Analysis of the classroom corpus does not produce definitive answers, but suggests a set of questions that can be asked about peer interactive tasks and their potential benefits for beginning language learners. Based on observations made during the process of analyzing the data set, a set of questions was developed. These questions are useful for a couple of purposes. First, they may guide a retrospective examination of peer discourse during language learning tasks.

Second, as they are tested on this and other data sets; what is learned from these questions can be used in developing more effective language learning tasks. Through this process, these questions can be tested and adapted. Some questions address positive features of tasks that, in the present corpus, produced good results. Other questions address task features that, in the present corpus, were linked with learner discourse that was less productive. In this chapter, I mentioned that differences in L1 use across the two program levels are likely due to factors related to instructional design rather than to the level of the learners. Reflecting on these differences inspired some of the questions. My goal in developing these questions was to produce a tool that might illuminate factors that contributed to the success or failure of particular tasks. Here, *success* is defined as:

(1) A high rate of L2 participation with limited L1 use for task management, to provide a needed vehicle for thought (in private speech or to work out linguistic problems), or for occasional vocabulary substitution.

(2) Use of L2 vocabulary and structures appropriate for the task.

(3) Learner support of each other in sustaining meaningful L2 interaction.

A fourth mark of success permeates these three items:

(4) In successful peer interaction, there is a high level of learner engagement.

Engagement is a positive orientation toward peer interaction and language learning as indicated by a high level of involvement in L2 use, and evidence of sustained effort during peer learning tasks. This fourth feature is prerequisite to the other three—without sustained learner engagement, no peer interactive task can be successful. And, as is shown, learner engagement is impacted by how tasks are designed and implemented.

As just discussed, these questions are presented as a retrospective tool to deepen understanding of learner discourse and the relationship between task design, implementation and learner activity in the classroom. There is another potential application for these questions. To the extent that they are found to be insightful as tested with the classroom corpus and other data sets, these questions can be used as a prospective tool that may be used prior to task implementation to consider what might transpire, and to help teachers in planning lessons and designing tasks for beginning language learners. Applied to tasks in advance, the questions may help with understanding potential strengths and weaknesses of a particular task by anticipating how the task might impact peer interaction. The questions are designed so that a "yes" answer indicates that a task may promote meaningful and useful L2 use that will stimulate language development. A "no" answer flags features that may possibly make a task less productive. The questions allow consideration of whether or not a particular task may benefit from adjustments that may make it a more effective teaching and/or learning tool.

I begin here by listing the questions in Table 6.7, followed by discussing each question with additional comments and examples provided. For the analyst examining the learner discourse, the questions provide a beginning in understanding how the design of a task and its implementation may shape learner discourse. The questions are ordered so that a teacher considering the potential of a task might be able to consider the possible effects of a task. The first five questions relate to task design, matters that

TABLE 6.7
Interactive Tasks for Beginning Learners:
Questions for Task Analysis and Evaluation

---

(1) Is the task meaningful? Is there a consistent theme or topic that motivates task selection and provides coherence across lessons?

(2) Do learners need to interact in the L2 in order to accomplish the task?

(3) If a task incorporates repetition, is the repetition meaningful or useful from the learners' perspective?

(4) Does the task allow for creativity and innovation appropriate for the learners' developmental levels? If scripting is used, does pre-task guidance prepare learners to innovate by adding turns or adjusting content, rather than simply using the script as a dialogue to be read or regurgitated? And, if scripting is used, is the dialogue an appropriate length?

(5) Does the task or pre-task work provide appropriate guidance as to discourse structure, so that learners have the opportunity to develop conversational style?

(6) Does the teacher manipulate pairings of students as appropriate to optimize learner participation and performance?

(7) Does pre-task instruction and/or practice include sufficient opportunity for learners to access the forms and vocabulary that are needed for the task so that the learners will, with cooperative effort, be able to use these meaningfully when doing the task? Or, is provision made to provide linguistic guidance during the task or between repetitions?

(8) Are learners familiar with the task type? If not, is a demonstration included?

(9) If tasks build on one another such that a subsequent task cannot be done unless a previous task has been successfully completed, are checking mechanisms in place to insure that learners can productively proceed to the next phase?

(10) Is there provision for learners to get help from the teacher as well as from supporting materials?

(11) Is the level of support provided appropriate for the learners, so that the task presents a reasonable, stimulating challenge with learners able to resolve problems and use the L2 with an acceptable level of accuracy? Is support withdrawn as appropriate?

(12) Does post-task follow-up provide learners with an opportunity to resolve questions and problems that occurred during the task?

(13) Is homework used to optimize post-task review and pre-task preparation?

---

may be decided by a teacher in the planning phase before the task is ever used in the classroom, although their effects may not be discovered by the analyst until implementation of the task by learners is underway. Question 6 through question 9 query aspects of task design that are realized in the implementation of tasks. Question 10 and question 11 consider the level of support available. The last two questions, 12 and 13, ask about post-task follow-up.

Task Design

> (1) Is the task meaningful? Is there a consistent theme or topic that motivates task selection and provides coherence across lessons?

The first question addresses the meaningfulness of tasks, and their place in a thematically coherent organization of lessons. "Meaningful," here is broader in meaning than the word "communicative" has become in the language teaching world. The word "communicative" has often been used to mean "information exchange." Whether or not a task contains information exchange is not a very well-rounded measure of a task. In nonpedagogical interaction, much talk does not, in fact, involve information exchange. We repeatedly tell each other the same stories, or complain about the same problems. We participate in conversational rituals that have nothing to do with information exchange, but have everything to do with human interaction. In the same way, information exchange is but one aspect of language learning tasks. In the classroom corpus, there are tasks that involve information exchange and tasks that do not, but both have the potential to be meaningful or unmeaningful. Here, "meaningful" first refers to whether or not a learner needs to be able to understand the partner's utterance in order to respond. Dialogue recitation, in these terms, is not meaningful, because the learner need not understand in order to build a response. The response may simply be triggered by the hearing of the previous utterance, with the response also being uttered without cognizance of its meaning. Meaningfulness, therefore, refers to the extent to which the learner is dependent on an understanding of the previous utterance in order to proceed further. Secondly, meaningfulness also relates to the extent to which the task is interesting learners. Information exchange tasks, when done with a pressure for task completion or for their own sake, may not be very interesting to learners. Meaningful tasks are also interesting. Whether or not a task is interesting relates to its appropriateness for a particular group of learners based on their ages, language proficiency, and need for the L2. Sometimes a task that appears uninteresting—a task, for example, that lays out known information to be manipulated—might be interesting because doing the task in a foreign language is fun and challenging. A task that might be boring or mundane to a high level speaker might be very interesting to a beginner. Particular tasks or task types may also lose their meaningfulness with overuse. Meaningfulness as a measure of a task is both objective (in the sense of assessing whether learners need to understand the interlocutor's utterance in order to proceed) and subjective (in the sense of surmising whether or not a task will be interesting for a particular group of learners).

> (2) Do learners need to interact in the L2 in order to accomplish the task?

The classroom corpus contains some tasks that learners were able to accomplish with minimal use of the L2. Based on an analysis of these tasks, it appears that if the L2 is not needed to accomplish a task, learners will be much more likely to use the L1. The best example of this from the corpus is a matching task, where groups of four learners are given slips of paper with sentences on them that they are to connect using *kara* 'so' or *kedo* 'but'. When doing the task, the learners use the L2 only for reading sentences aloud. Most of the talk involves translating the sentences and talking about which should be joined. This result is unsurprising because these beginning level students do not know the language needed to manage the task in the L2. As they start in Excerpt 6, much of the language involves reading the slips of paper aloud in Japanese, with some English for task management:

(6)   1 Z: Ga owarimas:en des[hita
              But I didn't finish.
       2 F: [Teepu o kaimashita:: (.)
                                       I bought a tape::
       3 Z: Paate hehehe °(   )°
              Party hehehe   °(   )° ((error pronunciation))
       4 F: Shuumatsu wa tomodachi: ga kimashita
              This weekend my friends came.
       5 G: Shuumatsu wa
              This weekend
       6 F: Weekend
       7 Z: Takkusa:n (.) takusan what the heck does
              [that mean?
              "Takkusa:n" (.) "takusan" what the heck does that mean?
       8 F: [How about this one?
       9 G: (Zenzen)
              (Absolutely)

10	F:	Shuumatsu tomodachi ga kimashita kara benkyoo

10   F: Shuumatsu tomodachi ga kimashita kara benkyoo
          shimasen deshita (.)
          This weekend my friends came so I didn't study (.)
11   Do we have'ta like write it in or just know? (.) just know
          ( ) that's a "kara" (('kara' means 'so'))
12   G: The "kara*'s*" over here [but the
13   F: ["Kara's" over here and
          the "ga" (('ga' means 'but')) is over there
14   Z: Gohon o tabemas:u ah o tsukurimas:hita (.)
          I ea:t ah I made: rice (.) ((error: mispronounces 'rice'.
          Self-correction: replaces 'eat' with 'made'))
15   F: Depaato ga tanoshikatta desu
          The department store was fun
16   Z: Toshokan de: benkyoo shimashita
          I studied at the library
17   F: Toshokan de benkyoo shimashita study at the library
          I studied at the library study at the library
18   Z: Ah huh (.) I have no idea
19   F: Oh
20   Z: Takusan
          A lot
21   F: Where's that "isogashii?" (('isogashii' means 'busy'))
          Do you have an "isogashii?"
22   Z: No
23   G: What is takusan?
24   F: A lot

                                              (Kuo-ming, 1/30)

As the task continues, talk shifts from reading L2 sentences aloud and con-
necting them, to translating L2 sentences into English and using English
to manage the matching task. This is shown in Excerpt 7.

(7)   1   G: Kyoo: (.) kyoo shiken (.) shiken ga arimashita:
               Today: (.) today there was (.) a test:
      2   F: Kara
               So
      3   G: Kara: ah eiga ni ikimasen [deshita
               so: ah I didn't go to the movies
      4   Z: [What about - haha wait
               here's [ah here's ahh
      5   F: [What was it? Kyoo (   ) ah
                      What was it? Today (   ) ah
      6   Z: Studying in the:: [toshokan de
               Studying in the:: in the library

```
 7  F:                              [oh (    ) have a test but
 8  G:   No yesterday I had a test so I didn't go [to the movie
 9  Z:                                            [Oh
10  F:   "Kyoo wa" is today
11  Z:   desh::
         wa::s
12  G:   Isn't that (     )
13  F:   "Kinoo" is yesterday
14  G:   [Oh I was thinking (    )
15  Z:   [(    ) toshokan de benkyoo shimasu
         (     ) I will study at the library
16  F:   So
17  Z:   Bi - the test
18  F:   Oh ok toshokan [de benkyoo shimas:h:ita: ga
         Oh ok I studied      at the library but
19  G:                  [Oh yeah that works that still works
20  Z:   Where's the test?
21  F:   Ei - eiga ni
         Mo- to the movies
22  Z:   But then there's - (      ) take out that with this? 'kay
         where's the test?
23  F:   Test is right here
24  Z:   Oh that's the test
25  F:   Oh no I'm sorry test is (.) right here
26  Z:   Ok stick those together
                                            (Kuo-ming, 1/30)
```

As they continue, they realize that all of their sentences use *kara* 'so', but none of them use *ga* 'but'. In line 1 of Excerpt 8, F prompts them to work to make sentences with *ga*.

```
(8)   1  F:   We need a "ga" we're not - //we
      2  Z:   Oh none of 'em has a "ga" awh man hehe
      3  F:   No it doesn't hafta we just hafta wait a minute kinoo
              wa hima deshita:
              No it doesn't hafta we just hafta wait a minute 'yesterday
              I was free:'
      4  Z:   Kara:
              So:
      5       (5)
      6  F:   "Ga"::: (.) here's a good "ga". (.) ano
      7  Z:   Hehehehe
      8  F:   I don't know
      9  Z:   (        ) yeah "ga's" um
```

10 F: Gotta have some "ga's" we don't [have
11 Z: [Hehahahaha
12 F: Gohan go- ah where's that oh gohan o tsukurimashita:
          Rice ri- ah where's that oh "I made rice:"
                                            (Kuo-ming, 1/30)

In this matching task, Japanese is used for reading aloud, and English is used for the problem solving interaction. The value of this task depends on the teacher's goals for the lesson. In this setting where the classroom is the only place for students to interact in the L2, overuse of tasks that can be accomplished in English would take away learner opportunities to use the language being learned. In the corpus, these sorts of tasks did not occur often. And, certainly they may work toward L2 learning goals such as strengthening metalinguistic knowledge or reading skills. Even so, one wonders whether class time might be more effectively used if students did the reading and matching part of the task at home, and brought their *kara* 'so' and *ga* 'but' sentences to class to be used in a different task. Or, whether a reading–matching task, done at home, could serve to help learners understand the conjunctions, which could then be incorporated into a different interactive task. Any type of task that can be done without speaking the L2 is prone to this problem.

---

(3) If a task incorporates repetition, is the repetition meaningful or useful from the learners' perspective?

How repetition is used in a task and the level to which that repetition is useful or meaningful to students is asked in the third question. Repetition has been shown to be a useful task feature by Brooks et al. (1997) and Nakaone (1999), because it frees learners from the need for as much English for task management in subsequent tasks. On the other hand, repetition also has the potential of eroding interest in a task, thereby making a task less meaningful to learners. In the classroom corpus, task repetition was, in many cases, both useful and meaningful to students, but in other cases the monotony of repetition appeared to wear students down, and to erode the quality of L2 used. In repeated tasks, some students began to use telescopic language, or to use English to do the tasks more quickly. Excerpts 9 and 10 provide an example of this from one of Bryce's classes. For the task, each learner was given a magazine picture. The assignment is for learners to ask each other yes–no question until they guess one item being worn in a classmate's magazine picture. After obtaining a "yes" answer, the learner is to ask the fictional name of the person in the picture. Then, the learner can move on to ask someone else. Basically, the task is a guessing

TABLE 6.8
Verbs Meaning "Wear" in Japanese

Japanese Lexical Item	Verb Meaning	Body Location	Typical Clothing Items
Kiru	Wear	Torso	Shirt, blouse, dress
Haku	Wear	Lower body	Slacks, shoes, skirt
Kaburu	Wear	Head	Hat, head-scarf

game—learners must ask yes–no questions until they get a "yes" answer. At first, the learners ask each other questions using the various verbs meaning "wear," which are lexical items introduced in the current chapter. Japanese has a range of verbs meaning wear that are used for items worn on different parts of the body, shown in Table 6.8. Besides the verbs listed in Table 6.8, there are other verbs that are used depending on the manner in which items are worn, such as *maku* 'wind, roll' for scarves, or *hameru* 'slide on' for things such as contact lenses and rings, and *kakeru* 'hang' for eyeglasses. The verb *suru* 'do' is used for a range of accessories such as belts, necklaces, and watches. When beginning the task, one of several that use the various verbs, the learners at first use these verbs when asking about items that might be worn in the pictures. In Excerpt 9, Bryce appropriately uses two of these verbs:

(9) 1 B: Yubiwa o: ah hame- yubi o hameteiru- imasu ka hameteimasu ka?
Is she wea- um a ri- do you wear a ri- is she wearing a finger? ((error: 'yubiwa, literally 'finger-ring', is pronounced without its last syllable)).

2 M: Iie
No

3 B: Iie, u::::m (.) ah suutsu o sh-sh- kiteimasu ka?
No, u:::m (.) ah is she sh- sh- wearing a suit?

4 J: Hai kiteimasu.
Yes, she is.

5 B: Dore desu ka?
Which is it?

6 J: Carrie-san desu.
It's "Carrie."

(Bryce, 5/16)

After asking a few people, the interaction between Bryce and his interlocutors becomes strikingly abbreviated, what Skehan (1998) called a "lexicalized" style of interaction. Excerpt 10 shows how Bryce and his partner, Pf, do the task just by saying the names of clothing items:

(10)   1   B: A:h nekuresu?
                  A:h necklace? ((error: nekkuresu pronounced 'nekuresu)).
       2   Pf: Iie.
                  No.
       3   B: Nekutai?
                  Necktie?
       4   Pf: Iie
                  No
       5   B: Yubiwa?
                  Ring?
       6   Pf: Huh?
       7   B: Ring?
       8   Pf: Iie.
                  No.

                                                        (Bryce, 5/16)

The communicative goal of the task—to guess an item being worn in the picture—remains. However, many repetitions of the task with different interlocutors has eroded the value of the task for practicing the various verbs meaning "wear." All that is left is the goal of getting through the task by finding a "yes" answer.

Another side effect of repeated tasks are learners who take the instructions very literally and limit their participation to the number of times they are told to repeat the task. If there is more class time available, some learners appear to remain engaged in repeating the task more times; others stop abruptly after the requisite number of repetitions. Excerpt 11 shows the last few turns of an interview task with Rob. The students were instructed to ask three people. After Rob answers his third partner's last question, he stops, whereas others in the class spend a few more minutes doing their interviews

(11)   1   S2:   Uh kyoodai ga nannin imasu ka?
                  Uh how many brothers and sisters do you have?
       2   R: Uh futo- uh fu:ta:ri: (.) ga imasu. Uh
                  Uh I have tw- two (.) Uh ((error: particle 'ga'))
       3   S2:   Ah soo desu ka. Ii desu ne:.
                  Oh really. That's ni:ce.
       4   R: Hehe so much for that.

                                                        (Rob, 4/21)

Rob sums up his attitude in line 4—he has done what was required and goes no further.

Furthermore, what the teacher may believe is the same task may, when repeated, become a different activity altogether (Coughlan & Duff, 1994). In the following decision-making task, learners are to orally list what they should do to prepare for a hypothetical camping trip. Then, the teacher regroups learners and has them repeat the task. Excerpt 12 shows what happens when the task is repeated, and Andrea is again asked what she will do to prepare for the hypothetical trip:

(12)	1	S2:	Nani o shite okimasu ka?
			What will you do in advance to prepare?
	2	A2:	Uh? Watakushi desu ka?
			Uh? Me?
	3	S:	Hai.
			yes.
	4	A:	Um (.) u::m (.) tentu o sooji:: (.) shite (.) okimasu. Is that right?
			Um (.) u::m) (.) clean (.) the (.) tent (.) Is that right?
			((error: 'tento' mispronounced as 'tentu'))
	5	S:	Uhh hoka ni wa?
			U:h other than that?
	6	A:	Hoka ni wa::. ((other than that)) uh. u::h (.) I don't know. It's just whatever you're going to do //in advance?
	7	S:	Yeah whatever you do.
	8	A:	Uumm.
	9	A:	I don't know.
→	10	A:	I feel like we're repeating what we were just saying before? I mean it's weird.

(Andrea, 2/5)

Even though Andrea contributed to generating ideas in her previous group, she seems to be uncertain when the task is repeated. She suggests cleaning the tent in line 4. Finally, in line 10, she comments that what they are doing seems odd because it is "repeating what we were just saying before." Repetition did not serve to make the interaction more meaningful for Andrea.

---

(4) Does the task allow for creativity and innovation appropriate for the learners' developmental levels? If scripting is used, does pre-task guidance prepare learners to innovate by adding turns or adjusting content, rather than simply using the script as a dialogue to be read or regurgitated? And, if scripting is used, is the dialogue an appropriate length?

> (5) Does the task or pre-task work provide appropriate guidance as
> to discourse structure, so that learners have the opportunity to
> develop conversational style?

Question 4, regards creativity and innovation and Question 5 concerns
guidance in discourse structure. Both are related to the question about
repetition. The data show that learners become quite engaged in tasks
that allow them leeway to use their own ideas. If the repeated version of
the task in Andrea's class had involved expansion, or incorporated something new and different, the freshness and meaningfulness of the interaction might have been maintained. In Excerpts 8 and 9, the nature of the
learners' activity changes dramatically from early repetitions to late repetitions. At first, the questions are meaningful to learners. The task is interesting and seems to present a challenge, as evidenced by learners having
occasional difficulty with verb choice, something the learners help each
other with. Later, the usefulness of the task for language practice erodes
away. Because both interviewer and interviewee know the nature of the
questions that are to be asked, it is no longer necessary to devote cognitive
effort to selecting and using the verbs. As an alternative, if the task sheet
could have guided students to adjust the nature of the task in subsequent
rounds from a yes–no guessing game into, say, a descriptive task or some
other kind of task, this process of abbreviation may not have not occurred.
In such a task, verb usage would not have been superfluous but would have
been integral to completing the task.

In the classroom corpus, learners were highly engaged in tasks in which
they had some influence. Dialogue practice, which may be a rote and
meaningless activity, came alive when a short dialogue was built up
through teacher-fronted practice for a task involving asking and answering questions about a map. In this task, the dialogue was not recited.
Learners needed to adjust the content of each utterance to situations they
chose. Thus, the task was meaningful—the learners needed to understand
each other in order to participate. The dialogue was transformed as learners exercised their volition in choosing what to discuss.

Guidance in discourse structure means helping students not only to
make statements or to ask questions, but to include listener response turns
when appropriate. Some teachers used task repetition as an opportunity
to teach discourse structure. In one example, the teacher reminded learners to use listener responses. Such guidance transformed the task into yet
another activity, as learners added their own listener response turns, creatively and meaningfully using the L2. As shown in the analysis in chapter
5 of how learners developed in their use of listener responses, at first,
learners were unable to use such responses. But as they became more adept at working with L2 structure and vocabulary, they were able to focus

more on other aspects of their L2 production, including sociolinguistic aspects. When giving students a chance to do the same task again, teachers can use the opportunity to provide additional guidance to help learners expand their roles and participate in the interaction in a more sophisticated way. Through this process, the same task again becomes transformed to another different and meaningful activity.

Implementation of Tasks

> (6) Does the teacher manipulate pairings of students as appropriate to optimize learner participation and performance?

Question 6 concerns how learners are paired for peer learning tasks. In the classroom corpus, the teachers rarely had learners change partners, and never assigned particular students to work together. As shown in the comparison of Candace and Rob's interaction with their partners, it appears that learners follow the old adage, "water seeks its own level." They tend to work with others who have a similar level of commitment to the classroom language learning enterprise, or who share an understanding of their role as learners. Although this is terrific for committed learners, those with less interest may drag each other down. Less committed learners may benefit from the opportunity to interact with a peer whose greater degree of preparation and engagement may stimulate more effort. Previous research has shown how engaged learners with stronger or weaker L2 skills can work together with positive results. Studies of peer interaction have not examined how less engaged learners might benefit from working with learners who have a higher level of engagement. Nor have studies examined how such pairings might impact the more engaged learner. If it were possible to stimulate the less involved learner without eroding the quality of the interaction for the more committed peer, such pairings would be valuable. Strategies that elevate student commitment to the classroom language learning enterprise may have a strong impact on L2 development. How learner pairings impact L2 discourse remains to be examined in future studies.

> (7) Does pre-task instruction and or practice include sufficient opportunity for learners to access the forms and vocabulary that are needed for the task so that the learners will, with cooperative effort, be able to use these meaningfully when doing the task? Or, is provision made to provide linguistic guidance during the task or between repetitions?

(8) Are learners familiar with the task type? If not, is a demonstration included?

(9) If tasks build on one another such that a subsequent task cannot be done unless a previous task has been successfully completed, are checking mechanisms in place to insure that learners can productively proceed to the next phase?

Questions 7, 8, and 9 inquire about pre-task instruction and checking mechanisms. These questions concern the teacher's role in creating an environment that encourages productive interaction by learners in peer tasks. The classroom corpus contains many examples showing the effects of pre-task instruction and practice. Negative outcomes that are related to an absence of these are also evident in the data. When pre-task work is done effectively, tasks emerge smoothly with little need for learners to use English for task management, and learners move seamlessly into productive L2 use. Excerpt 13 shows a first year interview task that involves asking classmates what foods and drinks they like. The task flows smoothly from pre-task, teacher-fronted question–answer work:

(13) 1 T: Ne, ano::, Walt-san wa donna nomimono ga suki desu ka?
              Well um:, Walt, what sort of drinks do you like?
       2 W: Koocha (.) koocha ga suki desu.
              Tea (.) I like tea.
       3 T: Ah: soo desu ka? Ii desu ne, (.) Ja, chotto ^
              paatonaa ni kiite kudasai? Donna nomimono ga suki desu ka? Soshite donna tabemono ga suki desu ka? (.) Hai.
              Oh really? That's good, (.) Okay, take a moment to ask your partner? What sort of drinks do you like? And what sort of foods do you like? (.) Okay.
       4 O: Hannah-san wa donna tabemono ga suki desu ka? (3) Piza?
              Hannah, what sorts of food do you like? (3) Pizza?
       5 H: Huh. Hai (.) piza::[: (.) piza:: ga:: suki desu.
              Huh. Yes (.) pizza:: (.) I like pizza
       6 O: [hehehe
       7 H: Sara-san wa?
              What about you Sara?

                                                    (Sara, 2/7)

The teacher's question in line 1 is the last of several questions she asks in the pre-task practice period. Lines 1 to 4 show a smooth transition between teacher-fronted practice, the teacher's request that the students interview each other, and Sara and her partner's commencement of the interview. In contrast, when there is insufficient pre-task work, things can become unproductive rather quickly. Learners may not understand how to do an unfamiliar task (question 7). Or multilayered tasks may lack necessary checking mechanisms (question 8). Things can fall apart for the learners when they are procedurally or linguistically unprepared for tasks. In the classroom corpus, there are examples that illustrate both points. There are task that learners had difficulty doing because of a lack of pre-task demonstration or practice. There are also multistep tasks in which students needed to have properly completed an earlier step in order to do the next step of the task, but where the teacher did not check to see if the learners were able to do so. In these cases, although the teacher continued the lesson, little productive interaction may have occurred for the learners involved. Excerpt 14 illustrates both points. First, there is no demonstration or pre-task practice of what learners are to do, and one learner in the pair does not understand the task. In addition, to do the task, learners need to have correctly completed a previous step. The teacher has read a listening passage three times and students have selected answers to multiple choice questions while listening. The task is for learners to confirm their answers with each other by using *ne*, a final particle that here functions like a tag question. The teacher does not demonstrate what she wants them to do, nor does she have a pair demonstrate, but learners are expected to understand the task based on her oral explanation in the L2. In Japanese, confirmation questions are quite simple to form by adding *ne* to a statement and using rising intonation. In Excerpt 14, the difference between confirmation questions and ordinary *ka*-marked questions seems to be a problem for William, Candace's partner. In addition, the learners are not prepared to handle what might transpire if their answers do not match. As beginning learners in their fourth month of the first-year course, without pre-task preparation they simply cannot handle the linguistic demands of such a possibility. This excerpt begins with the teacher's instructions in line 1. Then, the learners begin the task with William asking an ordinary question rather than a question using the tag *ne*. Candace tries to set things right, but then the matter is complicated by the possibility that her partner may not have understood the listening passage:

(14) 1 T: Ii desu ka? (5) Hai ja tonari no hito to hai eh:to
              (confirm) o shite kudasai. Ne o tsukatte::, (.)
              Yasuda-sensei wa ^ (.) Ne? tomodachi to
              dekakemashita ne? Ne?

> *Okay? (5) So with the person next to you, please confirm*
> *your answers. Use 'ne' ((tag question)) and (.) Prof.*
> *Yasuda (.) went out with her friends, ne? ne?*

2 W: Yasuda-san wa um (.) s:: (.) sooji o shimashita ka?
      Did Yasuda-san um (.) s:: (.) clean? ((error: student uses
      'san' instead of 'sensei' to as a title for the teacher))

3 C: Uh mooichido itte kudasai?
      Uh would you say that again?

4 W: Yasuda-san wa (.) um uh sooji o sooji o shimashita
      shimashita ne.
      Yasuda-san (.) um uh clean um cleaned, ne.

5 C: Sooji o (.) Oh I think she means (1) like (.) uh ichi?
      Cleaned (.) Oh I think she means (1) like (.) uh number
      one?

6   Yasuda-san wa:: (.) Yasuda-san to tomodachi to
      dekakemashita n- (.) Un dekakemashita ne. Right.
      and then like dekakemashita dekakemashita yo
      "Yasuda-san (.) went out with her friends n- ne." Right.
      ((Error: use of connector 'to' instead of topic marker 'wa'))
      And then like "Yes, she went out with her friends."

7 W: Iie
      No.

8 C: Iie?
      No?

9 W: Um I don't know

                                                    (Candace, 1/24)

From this point, further confusion ensues. This interactive task is built on
a couple of assumptions by the teacher—that learners understood the listening passage and that they were able to understand her instructions. In
fact, neither pair who was miked in this particular class—Candace's pair or
Rob's pair—do what they were instructed to do. Like Candace's partner,
Rob and his partner did not appear to have understood the listening passage. They spoke in English about the content of the passage, and did not
ever form a confirmation question. The teacher, meanwhile, seemed to
have no idea that students were having difficulty with the listening passage. She did not do any follow-up checking or review between the listening comprehension task (where learners selected multiple-choice answers
from a worksheet) and the interactive confirmation task.

This task combines a listening task with an interactive task. Other
multistep tasks build one interactive task on the results of another. In a
second-year class, after not quite figuring out the first part of the task, a
learner had difficulty participating productively in the next two task steps.

The teacher was not accessible, and the students seemed rather unconcerned about what transpired in their group role-play task. Lack of teacher checking between stages of multilayered interactive tasks results in some learners not being able to productively participate, because each step was dependent on earlier work. For low level learners, some kind of accountability or checking mechanism is necessary. With effective troubleshooting mechanisms in place, students are more productive during peer learning tasks.

Considering Available Support

> (10) Is there provision for learners to get help during task implementation from the teacher as well as from supporting materials?
>
> (11) Is the level of support provided appropriate for the learners, so that the task presents a reasonable, stimulating challenge with learners able to resolve problems and use the L2 with an acceptable level of accuracy? Is support withdrawn as appropriate?

Question 10 and question 11 consider the level of support available—whether the teacher is accessible to assist students (question 10) and whether the level of support is such that the learners are appropriately challenged by a task (question 11). The teacher's role was touched on in the previous paragraph, when considering how teacher checking mechanisms need to be built into task design. Question 10 refers to the teacher's general availability to learners. In the classroom corpus, rather than having a dampening effect on student interaction, teacher availability and intervention enhances the effectiveness of tasks. In first-year classes, the accessibility of the teacher was evident in how often learners beckoned the teacher to assist with trouble spots. In the second year, where teachers were less accessible, the students tended to get bogged down more often. Teacher accessibility relates to physical proximity—learners asked for assistance as the teacher came near. The data show that when teachers were accessible, learners included them in their collaborative activity to resolve problems they could not resolve among themselves. The teacher served as an important source of support, and teacher intervention was quite helpful. When teachers helped to resolve problems, learners proceeded with confidence. Accessible teachers gave students an avenue of assisting their partners as well. Excerpt 15 provides an example. The students are discussing what they would do if they had different ailments. Candace asks her partner for help in line 4 because she is not sure how to say *arukanai* 'don't walk'.

(15)   1 S: Ashi ga (.) uh ashi ni (.) kega o:^ sh- shita: toki ga
                  doo shimasu ka?
                  What would(.) you do if you hu- hurt (.) your leg?
                  ((error: particle 'ga'))

        2 C: Um um hon o:: yomimasu. Hehehe.
                  Um um read a book. Hehehe.

        3 S: Soo desu ka?
                  Oh really?

→   4 C: How would we say we don't walk? (.) A::rukunai? (.)
                  Arukunai. I don't walk? You know 'cause you said if
                  I had a leg injury? Arukunai? ((error: incorrect
                  pronunciation of 'arukanai' (doesn't walk)
                  as 'arukunai'))

        5 S: Aruku arimasu aruku nai hai arukunai
                  ((S confirms C's incorrect conjugation))

        6 C: Hmm

→   7 S: Arukanai ((S corrects arukunai to arukanai))

→   8 C: Arukanai?   ((C requests confirmation.))

        9 S: Aru<u>ka</u>nai.   ((S confirms))

→   10 T: Arukanai.   ((T confirms))

       11 C: Ah thank you. Arukanai. Hmm .hh (.) Ka^ kase o
                  hiku: (.) um (.) kaze o hiku (.) toki doo shimasu ka?
                  Ah thank you. Arukanai. Hmm .hh (.) what do you do (.)
                  um (.) when you will have a cold? ((self-correction: 'kaze'
                  first misprounounced as 'kase.' Error: tense))
                                                    (Candace, 5/22)

In line 4, Candace asks how to say "don't walk," and then answers her own question by saying *arukunai*. This contains a conjugation error—it should be pronounced *aru<u>ka</u>nai*, not *aru<u>ku</u>nai*. In line 5, her partner confirms her incorrect choice. As Candace considers this in line 6, saying "Hmm," her partner corrects the error in line 7. Candace repeats with question intonation in line 8. In line 9, the partner repeats again, emphasizing the corrected syllable. The teacher confirms this choice. The students successfully solved the problem on their own as the teacher stood by, observing this process, and confirming their correct choice. This help was effective. Later in the same class, Candace says *arukunai* in teacher-fronted practice, but immediately self-corrects to *arukanai*.

Students asked questions about their partners' difficulties, as shown in chapter 3 on assisted performance and chapter 4 on corrective feedback. These chapters gave examples where learners, noticing discrepancies between their peer's performance and their own idea of how the L2 should be formed, ask for the teacher to help. The corpus also contains counter-examples that show how things go wrong when teachers are not accessible. The corpus shows that students do have difficulties that may not be anticipated by teachers, no matter how clear things may seem to the teacher. The teachers who most effectively implemented tasks were available to students and checked on progress in a helpful manner. Teacher involvement also functions as an accountability measure, helping students to be more responsible in their use of peer learning time. In classes where teachers were not available, unrelated conversation in English occurred more frequently during peer learning time.

Post-task Follow-Up

(12) Does post-task follow up provide learners with an opportunity to resolve questions and problems that occurred during the task?

(13) Is homework used to optimize post-task review and pre-task preparation?

Post-task follow-up is an important feature of task design and implementation. In the classroom corpus, learners took good advantage of post-task opportunities to resolve questions or problems that were raised during peer learning tasks. Post-task follow-up also provides an accountability measure—learners must do the task in order to successfully participate. Table 6.9 documents the occurrence of post-task follow-up in the 85 interactive tasks in the corpus. Follow-up was provided by the teacher, by a subsequent task, or was not provided, as shown. In the first year, 82.4% of all interactive tasks included teacher-led follow-up work. Sometimes there was no follow-up, usually when class ended just as a task was discontinued. Other times, the teacher immediately moved to new material. In the first-year classes, interactive tasks were never built on one another such that one interactive task served as follow-up for another. In the second-year classes, a lower percentage, 55.9% of interactive tasks, were followed up by the teacher. These teachers occasionally used one interactive task to follow

TABLE 6.9
Post-task Follow-Up

	Follow-Up Provided by the Teacher	Follow-Up Provided by the Next Task	No Follow-Up	Totals
First year	42 (82.4%)	0 (0%)	9 (17.6%)	51
Second year	19 (55.9%)	5 (14.7%)	10 (29.4%)	34
Totals	61 (71.7%)	5 (5.9%)	19 (22.4%)	85

up another, a strategy absent from the first-year data. As discussed in the previous section, this strategy did not appear to be very effective because learners were left to their own devices to work out the tasks without sufficient support. Perhaps if a teacher-checking mechanism had been used, these subsequent tasks may have been more effective. This task feature might be more productive for higher level learners who have larger vocabularies and solid intermediate to advanced proficiency.

Question 13 asks about homework, something that was not collected or analyzed as a part of this longitudinal study. However, it makes sense that when homework is used for pre-task practice or preparation, it may have a positive effect on peer interaction. Homework may also be productively used for post-task review or expansion. How homework functions in foreign language development remains to be examined in future studies.

CONCLUSION

Through its investigation of some questions related to classroom learning, this final chapter underscored what previous chapters showed. Not only is there a relationship between language learning tasks and the peer activity that is realized as learners do tasks, but each participant in the classroom enterprise has an important role to play. In this chapter, we see how tasks that promoted L2 interaction were designed so that learners had to interact in the foreign language in order to do the tasks. However, many more factors impact the nature of learner activity. This chapter shows the importance of the individual differences acknowledged implicitly in previous chapters. Different learners do the same tasks differently because of their own interests, abilities, and understandings of tasks. This chapter asked questions that previous chapters have not—about how teachers impact classroom learning processes through the selection, design, and introduction of tasks to students. How the teacher prepares the learners for a particular task has a major impact on what transpires in peer interaction. Although the earlier chapters focused on learners themselves, in this chapter we see that language learning is not just about learner activity, but language learning is about the activity of teachers and materials developers as well.

Previous chapters developed a strongly student-centered perspective on the classroom learning enterprise. This chapter brings the teacher back into focus as the one who orchestrates the classroom learning situation. Analysis shows that beginners need a great deal of support in order to be successful at peer learning tasks. Some of the support they need comes from peers, but much also comes from task design and implementation, support provided by teachers. This support involves integrating tasks into lessons so that they logically flow from the instructional sequence. It is not sufficient for a teacher to simply tell beginning students how to do a task, or what form and/or vocabulary they should use. Rather, productive peer interaction was characterized by a great deal of pre-task work. Teachers involved students in pre-task instruction so that they had the opportunity to use new vocabulary and forms prior to doing tasks. And, they led interactive demonstrations of tasks to be accomplished. These strategies equipped learners for productive use of the L2 to accomplish the tasks.

Although current teaching methodology has idealized communicative tasks as the goal of instruction, these students in the first 2 years of Japanese language learning still have a rather fragile grip on their L2 resources. They are dependent on teachers to provide structuring and preparation for tasks in order for them to participate productively. In addition, although earlier chapters showed the resourcefulness of students in helping themselves and solving their own problems, this resourcefulness does not make the teacher superfluous. Tasks which were not appropriately tuned to the learners' developmental level were not successful. In addition, teacher intervention, as well as the teacher's availability to be invited to intervene, are important factors that influence learner–learner interaction. Peer interactive tasks were not as successful when teachers were not available to intervene. Although it is naturally the goal of teachers to help students to become independent users of the L2, internalization is a gradual process, and learners benefit from teacher participation and intervention in their interaction with peers.

Investigation of how learners use English during peer interactive tasks underscores the impact of contextual and learner variables on task performance. People use language as a cognitive tool (Vygotsky, 1987). In peer interaction, the extent to which learners rely on English partly depends on the clarity of the task and how smoothly it is integrated into the lesson, as well as whether the task is developmentally appropriate. Though Rob used more English than Candace, the two learners consistently used more or less English for the same tasks. This shows that English use is related to features of task design and implementation. Comparison of the two students also shows the importance of differences in the orientations of individual learners. Individual differences are an important area for future research.

Analysis of how learners and teachers interact in these classes raises awareness of the various factors that impact student activity in the classroom. This is important because language proficiency develops through a process of internalizing the language of social interaction. Further studies are necessary to better understand how this occurs. In terms of considering the relationship of task and activity with L2 development, there is a variety of promising research, both recently published and under development. Studies that manipulate task features are needed in order to better understand how task and activity are related.

With this final chapter, this book draws to a close. The research reported here shows the importance of the classroom setting for language learning, and how L2 developmental processes are about much more than curriculum and teaching, but are centrally about what learners do in their interface with the affordances of the classroom setting. The research reported here shows the richness and variety of L2 learning processes realized; examination of learning processes as they occur in a particular social interactive setting reveals their complexity. This complexity, however, can be understood in a principled way through use of a sociocognitive theoretical framework, which considers the relationship between the individual, his or her participant roles, and the social setting. The framework used allows the learner's engagement with the affordances of the language learning setting to come into view. Analysis of private speech provides evidence of the high level of mental activity of learners as they engage with the L2 in the classroom. This data also gives us a glimpse of internalization processes as realized in a social interactive setting. The construct of the ZPD and its role in internalization shows that what is important is not just tasks, but tasks that provide a developmentally appropriate challenge combined with the availability of developmentally sensitive support. The collaborative process of assisted performance that occurs in the ZPD serves to individualize tasks to learners' individual needs as they work to express and comprehend L2 meanings.

This book demonstrated how learners individualize the learning space by acting on affordances particular to their own needs. This occurs not only when learners work with peers but also in the teacher-fronted setting. Learner errors and the contrasts that result from them, whether occurring in the form of recasts addressed to the learner by a teacher or peer, or incidental recasts that happen to co-occur, provide students with corrective feedback, an important affordance of the classroom setting. Learners have different opportunities in different participant roles. Considering the impact of these roles on the learners' developmental experience is clearly important. In addition, findings show that these learners did not tend to "pick up" the errors of their peers, but rather the production of errors in these form-focused classes produced contrasts that learners could capitalize on in hypothesis testing processes. These findings underscore the need to take a learner centered view in considering the role of learner errors and the linguistic contrasts that learners experience through their own activity.

Related to these different participant roles, from addressee to auditor to overhearer, is learner opportunity to experience a range of interactional routines in the classroom space, and to develop interactional competence through engagement with the L2 setting. The four first-year learners showed a sequential process of growth in their interactional competence as considered through observation of Japanese listener response expressions. This study confirms the sensitivity of learners to pragmatic information available in the L2 classroom as evidenced by their processes of acquiring interactional competence.

Finally, further longitudinal studies of classroom SLA are needed, along with other longitudinal studies that investigate situated L2 development. By understanding the development of individuals as they use the L2 in their daily lives, we gain insights into learning processes that cannot be gained through other methods. Future studies of situated L2 learning will be useful to increase our understanding of these processes and of how different sorts of interactive settings provide different opportunities for L2 learning to occur. Results of these studies, like the results of the study reported in this book, will find ready application in the hands of teachers, material developers, and others who are in the business of creating environments that promote L2 development.

This study provided a learner centered view of classroom SLA processes, showing the richness and individuality of the classroom learning processes of seven learners. Each approach taken to SLA research has the strength of bringing particular phenomena into clearer focus for the researcher hoping to understand and explain SLA processes. The sociocognitive framework used here provided the opportunity to take a learner centered view of classroom interactional events. This perspective is an important one as SLA researchers work to understand the interface between learners and different types of L2 interactive settings, and how the affordances of this interface are acted on by learners as they develop L2 proficiency.

References

Ahmed, M. K. (1994). Speaking as cognitive regulation: A Vygotskian perspective on dialogic communication. In J. P. Lantolf & G. Appel (Eds.), *Vygotskian approaches to second language research* (pp. 157–172). Norwood, NJ: Ablex.

Appel, G., & Lantolf, J. P. (1994). Speaking as mediation: A study of L1 and L2 text recall tasks. *Modern Language Journal, 78,* 437–452.

Baars, B. J. (1997). *In the theater of consciousness.* New York: Oxford University Press.

Baddeley, A. (1990). The effects of irrelevant speech on immediate free recall. *Bulletin of the Psychonomic Society, 28*(6), 540–542.

Baker, N., & Nelson, K. (1984). Recasting and related conversational techniques for triggering syntactic advances by young children. *First Language, 5,* 3–22.

Behrend, D. A., Rosengren, K. S., & Perlmutter, M. (1988). A new look at children's private speech: The effects of age, task difficulty, and parent presence. *International Journal of Behavioral Development, 12,* 305–320.

Bell, A. (1984). Language style as audience design. *Language in Society, 13,* 135–204.

Bellack, A., Kliebard, H., Human, R., & Smith, F. (1966). *The language of the classroom.* New York: Teachers College Press.

Berk, L. E. (1986). Relationship of elementary school children's private speech to behavioral accompaniment to task, attention, and task performance. *Developmental Psychology, 22*(5), 671–680.

Berk, L. E. (1992). Children's private speech: An overview of theory and the status of research. In L. E. Berk & R. M. Diaz (Eds.), *Private speech: From social interaction to self-regulation* (pp. 17–53). Hillsdale, NJ: Lawrence Erlbaum Associates.

Berk, L. E., & Garvin, R. A. (1984). Development of private speech among low-income Appalachian children. *Developmental Psychology, 20,* 271–286.

Bivens, J. A., & Berk, L. E. (1990). A longitudinal study of the development of elementary children's private speech. *Merrill-Palmer Quarterly, 36*(4), 443–463.

Bjorkland, D. F. (1987). A note on neonatal imitation. *Developmental Review, 7,* 86–92.

Brooks, F. (1992a). Spanish III learners talking to one another through a jigsaw task. *Canadian Modern Language Review, 48,* 696–717.

Brooks, F. (1992b). Communicative competence and the conversation course: A social interaction perspective. *Linguistics and Education, 4*, 219–246.

Brooks, F., Donato, R., & McGlone, J. V. (1997). When are they going to say "it" right? Understanding talk during pair-work activity. *Foreign Language Annals, 30*(4), 524–539.

Brown, R. (1973). *A first language*. Cambridge, MA: Harvard University Press.

Brown, R., & Hanlon, C. (1970). Derivational complexity and order of acquisition in child speech. In J. R. Hayes (Ed.), *Cognition and the development of language* (pp. 11–53). New York: John Wiley & Sons.

Camarata, S. M., Nelson, K. E., & Camarata, M. N. (1994). Comparison of conversational recasting and imitative procedures for training grammatical structures in children with specific language impairment. *Journal of Speech and Hearing Research, 37*, 1414–1423.

Cazden, C. B. (1976). Play with language and meta-linguistic awareness: One dimension of language experience. In J. S. Bruner, A. Jolly, & K. Sylva (Eds.), *Play: Its role in development and evolution* (pp. 603–608). New York: Basic Books.

Chaudron, C. (1977). A descriptive model of discourse in the corrective treatment of learners' errors. *Language Learning, 27*, 29–46.

Chaudron, C. (1986). Teachers' priorities in correcting learners' errors in French immersion classes. In R. Day (Ed.), *Talking to learn* (pp. 64–84). Rowley, MA: Newbury House.

Clancy, P. M. (1985). The acquisition of Japanese. In D. I. Slobin (Ed.), *The crosslinguistic study of language acquisition, volume I: The data* (pp. 373–524). Hillsdale, NJ: Lawrence Erlbaum Associates.

Consolo, D. A. (1996). Classroom interaction and the status of student speech in EFL lessons. Unpublished manuscript, State University of Campinas, Brazil.

Cook, H. M. (1988). Sentential particles in Japanese conversation: A study of indexicality. Unpublished doctoral dissertation, University of Southern California, Los Angeles, CA.

Cook, H. M. (1992). Meanings of non-referential indexes: A case study of the Japanese sentence-final particle *ne*. *Text, 12*(4), 507–539.

Coughlan, P. (1995). Conversations with Vovo: A case study of child second language acquisition and loss from a socio-cultural perspective. *Issues in Applied Linguistics, 6*(2), 123–136.

Coughlan, P., & Duff, P. (1994). Same task, different activities: Analysis of SLA task from an activity theory perspective. In J. P. Lantolf & G. Appel (Eds.), *Vygotskian approaches to second language research* (pp. 173–193). Norwood, NJ: Ablex.

Diaz, R. M. (1992). Methodological concerns in the study of private speech. In L. E. Berk & R. M. Diaz (Eds.), *Private speech: From social interaction to self-regulation* (pp. 55–81). Hillsdale, NJ: Lawrence Erlbaum Associates.

DiCamilla, F., & Lantolf, J. P. (1994). The linguistic analysis of private writing. *Language Sciences, 16*(3/4), 347–369.

DiNitto, R. (in press). Can collaboration be unsuccessful? A sociocultural analysis of classroom setting and Japanese L2 performance in group tasks. *Journal of the Association of Teachers of Japanese*.

Donato, R. (1988). Beyond group: A psycholinguistic rationale for collectivity in second language learning. Unpublished doctoral dissertation, University of Delaware.

Donato, R. (1994). Collective scaffolding in second language learning. In J. P. Lantolf & G. Appel (Eds.), *Vygotskian approaches to second language research* (pp. 33–56). Norwood, NJ: Ablex.

Donato, R., & Lantolf, J. P. (1990). The dialogic origins of L2 monitoring. In L. Bouton & Y. Kachru (Eds.), *Pragmatics and language learning*, volume 1 (pp. 83–97). Urbana-Champaign, IL: University of Illinois.

Doughty, C., & Varela, E. (1998). Communicative focus on form. In C. Doughty & J. Williams (Eds.), *Focus on form in classroom second language acquisition* (pp. 114–138). Cambridge, MA: Cambridge University Press.

Doughty, C., & Williams, J. (Eds.). (1998). *Focus on form in classroom second language acquisition*. Cambridge, MA: Cambridge University Press.

Duff, P. A., & Polio, C. G. (1990). How much foreign language is there in the foreign language classroom? *Modern Language Journal, 74*, 154–166.

Dunn, W., & Lantolf, J. P. (1997). The zone of proximal development and i + 1: Incommensurable constructs, incommensurable discourses. Unpublished manuscript, Cornell University, Ithaca, NY.

English, H. B., & English, A. C. (1958). *A comprehensive dictionary of psychological and psychoanalytical terms*. New York: David McKay Company, Inc.

Faneslow, J. (1977). The treatment of error in oral work. *Foreign Language Annals, 10*, 583–593.

Foster, P. (1998). A classroom perspective on the negotiation of meaning. *Applied Linguistics, 19*(1), 1–23.

Fotos, S. S. (1993). Consciousness raising and noticing through focus on form: Grammar task performance versus formal instruction. *Applied Linguistics, 14*(4), 385–407.

Frauenglass, M., & Diaz, R. M. (1985). Self-regulatory functions of children's private speech: A critical analysis of recent challenges to Vygotsky's theory. *Developmental Psychology, 21*, 357–364.

Frawley, W., & Lantolf, J. P. (1984). Speaking and self-order: A critique of orthodox L2 research. *Studies in Second Language Acquisition, 6*, 143–215.

Frawley, W., & Lantolf, J. P. (1985). Second language discourse: A Vygotskyan perspective. *Applied Linguistics, 6*, 19–44.

Frawley, W., & Lantolf, J. P. (1986). Private speech and self-regulation: A commentary on Frauenglass and Diaz. *Developmental Psychology, 22*, 706–708.

Fuson, K. C. (1979). The development of self-regulating aspects of speech: A review. In G. Zivin (Ed.), *The development of self-regulation through private speech* (pp. 135–217). New York: Wiley.

Gass, S. M. (1991). Grammar instruction, selective attention and learning processes. In R. Phillipson, E. Kellerman, L. Selinker, M. Sharwood Smith, & M. Swain (Eds.), *Foreign/second language pedagogy research: A commemorative volume for Claus Faerch* (pp. 134–141). Philadelphia, PA: Multilingual Matters.

Gass, S. M. (1997). *Input, interaction, and the second language learner*. Mahwah, NJ: Lawrence Erlbaum Associates.

Goffman, E. (1974). *Frame analysis: An essay on the organization of experience*. Cambridge, MA: Harvard University Press.

Goodwin, C. (1979). The interactive construction of a sentence in natural conversation. In G. Psathas (Ed.), *Everyday language: Studies in ethnomethodology*. New York: Irvington Publishers.

Goodwin, C., & Goodwin, M. H. (1987). Concurrent operations on talk: Notes on the interactive organization of assessments. *IPRA Papers in Pragmatics, 1*(1), pp. 1–54.

Guerrero, M. C. M. de (1994). Form and functions of inner speech in adult second language learning. In J. P. Lantolf & G. Appel (Eds.), *Vygotskian approaches to second language research* (pp. 83–116). Norwood, NJ: Ablex.

Gupta, P., & MacWhinney, B. (1995). Is the articulatory loop articulatory or auditory? Reexamining the effects of concurrent articulation on immediate serial recall. *Journal of Memory and Language, 34*, 63–88.

Hall, J. K. (1995a). (Re)creating our wolds with words: A sociohistorical perspective of face-to-face interaction. *Applied Linguistics, 16*, 206–232.

Hall, J. K. (1995b). Aw, man, where you goin?: Classroom interaction and the development of L2 interactional competence. *Issues in Applied Linguistics, 5*, 37–62.

Hall, J. K., & Brooks, F. B. (1995). Interactive practices, L2 interactional competence and SLL/A in classrooms: An integrative theoretical framework. Unpublished manuscript, University of Georgia, Athens.

Hallmon, J. E. (1998). Style-shifting from hyoojungo to Osaka-ben. Term paper, University of Washington, Seattle, WA. ERIC data base # ED 432 154.

Harley, B. (1992). Patterns of second language development in French immersion. *Journal of French Language Studies, 2*(2), 159–183.

Hatasa, Y., Makino, S., & Hatasa, K. (1999). *Nakama, volume II*. Boston, MA: Houghton-Mifflin.

Heritage, J. (1984). A change-of-state token and aspects of its sequential placement. In J. M. Atkinson & J. Heritage (Eds.), *Structures of social action: Studies in conversation analysis* (pp. 299–345). Cambridge, MA: Cambridge University Press.

Horiguchi, S. (1990). Jookyuu nihongo gakushuusha no taiwa ni okeru kikite toshite no gengo koodoo [Listening behavior in the conversations of advanced learners of Japanese]. *Nihongo Kyooiku, 71*, 16–32.

Jefferson, G. (1986). Notes on 'latency' in overlap onset. *Human Studies, 9*(2–3), 153–183.

Johnson, K. E. (1995). *Understanding communication in second language classrooms*. New York: Cambridge University Press.

John-Steiner, V. (1992). Private speech among adults. In L. E. Berk & R. M. Diaz (Eds.), *Private speech: From social interaction to self-regulation* (pp. 285–296). Hillsdale, NJ: Lawrence Erlbaum Associates.

Jorden, E. H., & Noda, M. (1987). *Japanese, the spoken language, volumes I–III*. New Haven, CT: Yale University Press.

Jorden, E. H. (1986). On teaching nihongo. *Japan Quarterly, 33*(2), 139–147.

Kamio, A. (1990). *Joohoo no nawabari-riron: Gengo no kinooteki bunseki [The theory of territory of information: A functional analysis of language]*. Tokyo: Taishuukan Shoten.

Kamio, A. (1997). *Territory of information*. Amsterdam: John Benjamins.

Kanagy, R. (1995). Developmental sequences in learning Japanese: A look at negation. *Issues in Applied Linguistics, 5*(2), 255–277.

Kanagy, R. (in press). Developmental sequences, second language acquisition, and Japanese language pedagogy. In H. Nara (Ed.), *Advances in Japanese language pedagogy*. Columbus, OH: National Foreign Language Center, Ohio State University.

Kasper, G. (1985). Repair in foreign language teaching. *Studies in Second Language Acquisition, 7*, 200–215.

Kohlberg, L., Yaeger, J., & Hjertholm, E. (1968). Private speech: Four studies and a review of theories. *Child Development, 39*, 691–736.

Koyanagi, K. (1998). The effects of focus-on-form tasks on the acquisition of a Japanese conditional "to": Input, output, and task-essentialness. Unpublished doctoral dissertation, Georgetown University, Washington, DC.

Kramsch, C. (1992). The dialogic emergence of culture in the language classroom. In J. E. Alatis (Ed.), *Georgetown University Round Table on Languages and Linguistics, 1992* (pp. 465–488). Baltimore, MD: GURT.

Krashen, S. D. (1985). *The input hypothesis: Issues and implications*. New York: Longman.

Krashen, S. D., & Terrell, T. O. (1983). *The natural approach: Language acquisition in the classroom*. New York: Pergamon Press.

Kuczaj, S. A. (1983). *Crib speech and language play*. New York: Springer-Verlag.

Lantolf, J. P. (1994). Sociocultural theory and second language learning. *The Modern Language Journal, 78*, 418–20.

Lantolf, J. P. (1997). The function of language play in the acquisition of L2 Spanish. In W. R. Glass & A. T. Perez-Leroux (Eds.), *Contemporary perspectives on the acquisition of Spanish*. Somerville, MA: Cascadilla Press.

Lantolf, J. P., & Ahmed, M. (1989). Psycholinguistic perspectives on interlanguage variation: A Vygotskyan analysis. In S. Gass, C. Madden, D. Preston, & L. Selinker (Eds.), *Variation in second language acquisition, I: Discourse and pragmatics* (pp. 93–108). Philadelphia, PA: Multilingual Matters.

Lantolf, J. P., & Aljaafreh, A. (1996). Second language learning in the zone of proximal development: A revolutionary experience. *International Journal of Educational Research, 23*, 619–632.

Lantolf, J. P., & Appel, G. (Eds.). (1994). *Vygotskian approaches to second language research.* Norwood, NJ: Ablex.

Lantolf, J. P., & Frawley, W. (1985). On communication strategies: A functional perspective. *Rassegna Italiana Di Linguistica Applicata Estratto Dal, 2–3.*

Lave, J., & Wenger, E. (1991). *Situated learning: Legitimate peripheral participation.* New York: Cambridge University Press.

Leeman, J., Arteagoitia, I., Fridman, B., & Doughty, C. (1995). Integrating attention to form with meaning: Focus on form in content-based Spanish instruction. In R. Schmidt (Ed.), *Attention and awareness in foreign language learning* (pp. 217–258). Honolulu: University of Hawaii Press.

Levinson, S. C. (1983). *Pragmatics.* Cambridge, MA: Cambridge University Press.

Lightbown, P. M., & Spada, N. (1990). Focus-on-form and corrective feedback in communicative language teaching: Effects on second language learning. *Studies in Second Language Acquisition, 12*, 429–448.

Long, M. H., & Crookes, G. (1992). Three approaches to task-based syllabus design. *TESOL Quarterly, 26*(1), 27–56.

Long, M. H., & Robinson, P. (1998). Focus on form: Theory, research and practice. In C. Doughty & J. Williams (Eds.), *Focus on form in classroom second language acquisition* (pp. 15–41). Cambridge, MA: Cambridge University Press.

Luria, A. R. (1973). *The working brain.* New York: Basic Books.

Luria, A. R. (1982). *Language and cognition.* New York: John Wiley & Sons.

Lyster, R. (1998). Recasts, repetition, and ambiguity in L2 classroom discourse. *Studies in Second Language Acquisition, 20*, 51–81.

Lyster, R., & Ranta, L. (1997). Corrective feedback and learner uptake: Negotiation of form in communicative classrooms. *Studies in Second Language Acquisition, 19*, 37–66.

MacKay, D. G. (1992). Constraints on theories of inner speech. In D. Reisberg (Ed.), *Auditory imagery* (pp. 121–149). Hillsdale, NJ: Lawrence Erlbaum Associates.

Mackey, A., & Philp, J. (1998). Conversational interaction and second language development. Recasts, responses, and red herrings? *Modern Language Journal, 82*(3), 338–356.

Mackey, A., McDonough, K., & Kim, Y. (1999, March). NNS/NNS interaction: Feedback and input incorporation. Paper presented at the Annual Conference of the American Association for Applied Linguistics, Stamford, CT.

Makino, S., Hatasa, Y., & Hatasa, K. (1997). *Nakama, Volume I.* Boston, MA: Houghton-Mifflin.

Markee, N. (1995). Teachers' answers to students' questions: Problematizing the issue of meaning making. *Issues in Applied Linguistics, 5*, 63–92.

Markee, N. (2000). *Conversation analysis.* Mahwah, NJ: Lawrence Erlbaum Associates.

Marriott, H. (1994). Acquiring sociolinguistic competence: Australian secondary students in Japan. *Journal of Asian Pacific Communication, 4*(4), 167–192.

Masur, E. F. (1989). Individual and dyadic patterns of imitation: Cognitive and social aspects. In G. E. Speidel & K. E. Nelson (Eds.), *The many faces of imitation in language learning* (pp. 53–72). New York: Springer-Verlag.

Matsuda, Y. (1988). *Taiwa no nihongo kyooiku—aizuchi ni kanrenshite [Teaching Japanese conversation: Aizuchi].* Nihongogaku, 7(13), 59–66.

Maynard, S. (1989). *Japanese conversation: Self-contextualization through structure and interactional management.* Norwood, NJ: Ablex.

Maynard, S. (1993). *Discourse modality: Subjectivity, emotion, and voice in the Japanese language.* Philadelphia, PA: John Benjamins.

McCafferty, S. G. (1992). The use of private speech by adult second language learners: A cross-cultural study. *Modern Language Journal, 76*, 179–189.

McCafferty, S. G. (1994a). The use of private speech by adult ESL learners at different levels of proficiency. In J. P. Lantolf & G. Appel (Eds.), *Vygotskian approaches to second language research* (pp. 117–34). Norwood, NJ: Ablex.

McCafferty, S. G. (1994b). Adult second language learners' use of private speech: A review of studies. *Modern Language Journal, 78*(4), 421–436.

McHoul, A. W. (1978). The organization of turns at formal talk in the classroom. *Language in Society, 7*, 183–213.

Mehan, H. (1985). The structure of classroom discourse. In T. A. Van Dijk (Ed.), *Handbook of discourse analysis, volume 3: Discourse and dialogue* (pp. 119–131). London: Academic Press.

Meltzoff, A. N., & Gopnik, A. (1989). On linking nonverbal imitation, representation, and language learning in the first two years of life. In G. E. Speidel & K. E. Nelson (Eds.), *The many faces of imitation in language learning* (pp. 23–52). New York: Springer Verlag.

Miller, L. (1995). Verbal listening behavior in conversations between Japanese and Americans. In J. Bommaert & J. Verschueren (Eds.), *The pragmatics of intercultural and international communication* (pp. 111–130). Amsterdam: John Benjamins.

Moerk, E. L. (1992). *A first language taught and learned.* Baltimore, MD: Paul H. Brookes Publishing Company.

Moroishi, M. (1998). Explicit vs. implicit learning: The case of acquisition of the Japanese conjectural auxiliaries. Unpublished doctoral dissertation, Georgetown University, Washington, DC.

Muranoi, H. (1998, March). Corrective recasts and JSL learners' modification of interlanguage systems. Paper presented at the Third Pacific Second Language Forum, Aoyama Gakuin University, Tokyo, Japan.

Nakaone, T. (1999). L1 use in task-based language learning: A socio-cognitive approach. Term paper, University of Washington, Seattle, WA.

Nelson, K. (1986). *Event knowledge: Structure and function in development.* Hillsdale, NJ: Lawrence Erlbaum Associates.

Nelson, K. E. (1989). Strategies for first language teaching. In M. Rice & and R. L. Schiefelbusch (Eds.), *The teachability of language* (pp. 263–310). Baltimore, MD: Paul H. Brookes Publishing.

Nelson, K. E., Denninger, M., Bonvillian, J., Kaplan, B., & Baker, N. (1984). Maternal input adjustments and non-adjustments as related to children's linguistic advances and the language acquisition theories. In A. Pelligrini & T. Yawkey (Eds.), *The development of oral and written languages: Readings in developmental and applied linguistics.* Norwood, NJ: Ablex.

Nishimura, M. (1997). *Japanese/English code-switching: Syntax and pragmatics.* New York: Peter Lang.

Ochs, E. (1988). *Culture and language development: Language acquisition and language socialization in a Samoan village.* New York: Cambridge University Press.

Ohta, A. S. (1993). Activity, affect and stance: Sentential particles in the discourse of the Japanese as a foreign language classroom. Doctoral dissertation, University of California, Los Angeles. (University Microfilms International No. 9411371)

Ohta, A. S. (1994). Socializing the expression of affect: An overview of affective particle use in the Japanese as a foreign language classroom. *Issues in Applied Linguistics, 5*, 303–25.

Ohta, A. S. (1995a). Applying sociocultural theory to an analysis of learner discourse: Learner–learner collaborative interaction in the zone of proximal development. *Issues in Applied Linguistics, 6*, 93–121.

Ohta, A. S. (1995b). The impact of teacher stance on the use of affective particles in classroom narratives. In H. Nara & M. Noda (Eds.), *Proceedings of the 1995 ATJ Conference on Literature, Language and Pedagogy* (pp. 163–172). Middlebury, VT: Association of Teachers of Japanese.

Ohta, A. S. (1997a, July). *Classroom SLA and pair work*. Paper presented at the Linguistics Society of America Linguistics Institute, Applying Applied Linguistics Workshop, Cornell University, Ithaca, NY.

Ohta, A. S. (1997b). The development of pragmatic competence in learner-learner classroom interaction. In L. Bouton (Ed.), *Pragmatics and Language Learning, Volume 8* (pp. 223–242). Urbana-Champaign, IL: University of Illinois.

Ohta, A. S. (1998, March). The role of language play in the acquisition of foreign language by adult learners: Evidence from the classroom. Paper presented at the American Association of Applied Linguistics Annual Conference, Seattle, Washington.

Ohta, A. S. (1999). Interactional routines and the socialization of interactional style in adult learners of Japanese. *Journal of Pragmatics, 31*, 1493–1512.

Ohta, A. S. (2000a). Re-thinking interaction in SLA: Developmentally appropriate assistance in the zone of proximal development and the acquisition of L2 grammar. In J. P. Lantolf (Ed.), *Sociocultural theory and second language learning* (pp. 51–78). New York: Oxford University Press.

Ohta, A. S. (2000b). Re-thinking recasts: A learner-centered examination of corrective feedback in the Japanese language classroom. In J. K. Hall & L. Verplaeste (Eds.), *The construction of second and foreign language learning through classroom interaction* (pp. 47–71). Mahwah, NJ: Lawrence Erlbaum Associates.

Ohta, A. S. (in press-a). Japanese second language acquisition in the classroom: What the voices of teachers and students tell us about the process of learning Japanese. In H. Nara (Ed.), *Advances in Japanese Language Pedagogy*. Columbus, OH: National Foreign Language Center, Ohio State University.

Ohta, A. S. (in press-b). From acknowledgement to alignment: A longitudinal study of the development of expressions of alignment by two classroom learners of Japanese. In K. Rose & G. Kasper (Eds.), *Pragmatics in Language Teaching*. New York: Cambridge University Press.

Oliver, R. (1995). Negative feedback in child NS–NNS conversation. *Studies in Second Language Acquisition, 18*, 459–481.

Olsher, D. (1999, March). Collaborative completions: An interactional resource for scaffolding in language learner discourse. Paper presented at the 1999 Annual Conference of the American Association for Applied Linguistics, Stamford, Connecticut.

Olszewski, P. (1987). Individual differences in preschool children's production of verbal fantasy play. *Merrill Palmer Quarterly, 33*, 69–86.

O'Malley, J. M., Chamot, A. U., Stewner-Manzanares, G., Kupper, L., & Russo, R. P. (1985). Learning strategy used by beginning and intermediate students. *Language Learning: A Journal of Applied Linguistics, 35*, 21–46.

Ortega, L., & Long, M. H. (1997). The effects of models and recasts on the acquisition of object topicalization and adverb placement in L2 Spanish. *Spanish Applied Linguistics, 1*, 65–86.

Osborne, R. J., & Wittrock, M. C. (1983). Learning science: A generative process. *Science Education, 67*, 489–508.

Pashler, H. E. (1998). *The psychology of attention*. Cambridge, MA: MIT Press.

Peck, S. (1980). Language play in child second language acquisition. In D. Larsen-Freeman (Ed.), *Discourse analysis and second language research* (pp. 154–164). Rowley, MA: Newbury House.

Peters, A. M. (1985). Language segmentation: Operating principles for the perception and analysis of language. In D. I. Slobin (Ed.), *The Crosslinguistic Study of Language Acquisition Volume 2, Theoretical Issues* (pp. 1029–1068). Hillsdale, NJ: Lawrence Erlbaum Associates.

Peters, A. M., & Boggs, S. T. (1986). Interactional routines as cultural influences upon language acquisition. In B. Schieffelin & E. Ochs (Eds.), *Language socialization across cultures* (pp. 80–96). New York: Cambridge University Press.

Philp, J. (1999, March). Constraints on "noticing the gap": A study of NNS' apperception of recasts in NS–NNS interaction. Paper presented at the 1999 Annual Conference of the American Association for Applied Linguistics, Stamford, Connecticut.

Piaget, J. (1962). *The language and thought of the child*. Cleveland, OH: Meridian. (Original work published 1923)

Pica, T. (1988). Interlanguage adjustments as an outcome of NS–NNS interaction. *Language Learning, 38*, 471–493.

Platt, E. (1995). Challenges to the input/output model in second language acquisition. *Sunshine State TESOL Journal*, 1–12.

Porter, P. A. (1986). How learners talk to each other: Input and interaction in task-centered discussions. In R. R. Day (Ed.), *Talking to learn* (pp. 200–222). Rowley, MA: Newbury House.

Ramsey, R. M. G. (1980). Language-learning approach styles of adult multilinguals and successful language learners. *Annals of the New York Academy of Sciences, 345*, 73–96.

Reiss, M. (1985). The good language learner: Another look. *The Canadian Modern Language Review, 41*(3), 511–523.

Reynolds, P. C. (1976). Play, language and human evolution. In J. S. Bruner, A. Jolly, & K. Sylva (Eds.), *Play: Its role in development and evolution* (pp. 621–635). New York: Basic Books.

Roberts, M. (1995). Awareness and the efficacy of error correction. In R. Schmidt (Ed.), *Attention and awareness in foreign language learning* (pp. 163–182). Honolulu: University of Hawaii, Second Language Teaching and Curriculum Center.

Roebuck, R. (1998). *Reading and recall in L1 and L2: A sociocultural approach*. Norwood, NJ: Ablex.

Rubin, J. (1981). Study of cognitive processes in second language learning. *Applied Linguistics, 2*(2), 117–131.

Rubin, K. H. (1979). The impact of the natural setting on private speech. In G. Zivin (Ed.), *The development of self-regulation through private speech* (pp. 265–294). New York: Wiley.

Sacks, H., Schegloff, E. A., & Jefferson, G. (1974). A simplest systematics for the organization of turn-taking for conversation. *Language, 50*(4), 696–735.

Samuda, V. (in press). Guiding relationships between form and meaning during task performance: The role of the teacher. In M. Bygate, P. Skehan, & M. Swain (Eds.), *Researching pedagogic tasks: Second language learning, teaching and assessment*. London: Pearson.

Saville-Troike, M. (1988). Private speech: Evidence for second language learning strategies during the 'silent' period. *Child Language, 15*, 567–590.

Sawyer, M. (1991). The development of pragmatics in Japanese as a second language: The particle *ne*. In G. Kasper (Ed.), *Pragmatics of Japanese as a native and target language* (pp. 83–125). Honolulu: University of Hawaii.

Schegloff, E. A. (1982). Discourse as an interactional achievement: Some uses of "UH-HUH" and other things that come between sentences. In D. Tannen (Ed.), *Georgetown University Round Table on Languages and Linguistics, Analyzing discourse: Text and talk* (pp. 71–93). Washington DC: Georgetown University Press.

Schegloff, E. A. (in press). Overlapping talk and the organization of turn-taking for conversation. *Language in Society, 29*(1).

Schegloff, E., Jefferson, G., & Sacks, H. (1977). The preference for self-correction in the organization of repair in conversation. *Language, 53*, 361–382.

Scherer, N., & Olswang, L. (1984). Role of mothers' expansions in children's language production. *Journal of Speech and Hearing Research, 27*, 387–396.

Schieffelin, B. B. (1990). *The give and take of everyday life: Language socialization of Kaluli children*. New York: Cambridge University Press.

Schieffelin, B., & Ochs, E. (Eds.). (1986). *Language socialization across cultures*. Cambridge, MA: Cambridge University Press.

Schmidt, R. (1990). The role of consciousness in second language acquisition. *Applied Linguistics, 11*, 129–158.

Siegal, M. (1996). The role of learner subjectivity in second language sociolinguistic competence: Western women learning Japanese. *Applied Linguistics, 17*(3), 356–382.

Sinclair, J. M., & Coulthard, R. M. (1975). *Towards an analysis of discourse: The English used by teachers and pupils*. London: Oxford University Press.

Skehan, P. (1996). A framework for the implementation of task-based instruction. *Applied Linguistics, 17*, 38–62.

Skehan, P. (1998). Processing perspectives on second language development and performance. Plenary address, Annual Conference of the American Association for Applied Linguistics, Seattle, WA.

Smith, D. J., Reisberg, D., & Wilson, M. (1992). Subvocalization and auditory imagery: Interactions between the inner ear and inner voice. In D. Reisberg (Ed.), *Auditory imagery* (pp. 95–119). Hillsdale, NJ: Lawrence Erlbaum Associates.

Smolucha, F. (1992). Social origins of private speech in pretend play. In L. E. Berk & R. M. Diaz (Eds.), *Private speech: From social interaction to self-regulation* (pp. 123–141). Hillsdale, NJ: Lawrence Erlbaum Associates.

Snow, C. E., Perlmann, R., & Nathan, D. (1987). Why routines are different: Toward a multiple-factors model of the relation between input and language acquisition. In K. E. Nelson (Ed.), *Children's language, volume 6* (pp. 65–97). Hillsdale, NJ: Lawrence Erlbaum Associates.

Strauss, S. (1995). Assessments as a window to socio-linguistic research: The case of Japanese, Korean, and (American) English. In M. Tokunaga (Ed.), *Gengo-henyoo ni kan-suru taikeiteki kenkyuu oyobi sono Nihongo kyoiku e no ooyoo [Systematic study of language variation with applications for Japanese foreign language education]* (pp. 177–91). Tokyo: Kanda University of Foreign Studies.

Swain, M. (1985). Communicative competence: Some roles of comprehensible input and comprehensible output in its development. In S. Gass & C. Madden (Eds.), *Input in second language acquisition* (pp. 235–256). Rowley, MA: Newbury House.

Swain, M. (1991). French immersion and its offshoots: Getting two for one. In B. F. Freed (Ed.), *Foreign language acquisition research and the classroom* (pp. 91–103). Lexington, MA: D. C. Heath.

Swain, M. (1993). The output hypothesis: Just speaking and writing aren't enough. *The Canadian Modern Language Review, 50*(1), 158–164.

Swain, M. (1997). Collaborative dialogue: Its contribution to second language learning. *Revista Canaria de Estudios Ingleses, 34*, 115–132.

Swain, M., & Lapkin, S. (1998). Interaction and second language learning: Two adolescent French immersion students working together. *Modern Language Journal, 82*, 320–337.

Tarone, E., & Liu, G. (1995). Situational context, variation and SLA theory. In G. Cook & B. Seidlhofer (Eds.), *Principle and practice in applied linguistics: Studies in honour of H. G. Widdowson* (pp. 107–124). Oxford: Oxford University Press.

Tharp, R. G., & Gallimore, R. (1991). *Rousing minds to life: Teaching, learning, and schooling in social context*. New York: Cambridge University Press.

Tohsaku, Y. (1994). *Yookoso!: An invitation to contemporary Japanese*. New York: McGraw-Hill.

Tohsaku, Y. (1995). *Yookoso!: Continuing with contemporary Japanese*. New York: McGraw-Hill.

Uzgiris, I. C., Broome, S., & Kruper, J. C. (1989). Imitations in mother–child conversations: A focus on the mother. In G. E. Speidel & K. E. Nelson (Eds.), *The many faces of imitation in language learning* (pp. 91–120). New York: Springer Verlag.

van Lier, L. (1988). *The classroom and the language learner: Ethnography and second language classroom research*. New York: Longman.

van Lier, L. (1996). *Interaction in the language curriculum: Awareness, autonomy, and authenticity.* New York: Longman.

van Lier, L. (2000). From input to affordance: Social-interactive learning from an ecological perspective. In J. P. Lantolf (Ed.), *Sociocultural theory and second language learning.* New York: Oxford University Press.

VanPatten, B. (1989). Can learners attend to form and content while processing input? *Hispania, 72,* 409–417.

Vygotsky, L. S. (1978). *Mind in Society: The development of higher psychological processes.* Cambridge, MA: Harvard University Press.

Vygotsky, L. S. (1981). The genesis of higher mental functions. In J. V. Wertsch (Ed.), *The concept of activity in Soviet psychology* (pp. 147–188). Armonk, NY: Sharpe.

Vygotsky, L. S. (1987). Thinking and speech. In R. W. Rieber & A. S. Carton (Eds.), *The collected works of L. S. Vygotsky, volume 1.* New York: Plenum Press.

Watabe, M. (1995, April). Japanese language teaching without teaching context: Are we producing *onchi* learners?. Conference keynote address at Shaping the Next Generation: National Strategic Assessment of Japanese Language Education, University of Maryland at College Park.

Weir, R. H. (1962). *Language in the crib.* The Hague: Mouton.

Weir, R. H. (1976). Playing with language. In J. S. Bruner, A. Jolly, & K. Sylva (Eds.), *Play: Its role in development and evolution* (pp. 609–620). New York: Basic Books.

Wertsch, J. V. (1985). *Vygotsky and the social formation of mind.* Cambridge, MA: Harvard University Press.

Wong Fillmore, L. (1989). Teachability and second language acquisition. In M. Rice & R. L. Schiefelbusch (Eds.), *The teachability of language* (pp. 311–332). Baltimore, MD: Paul H. Brookes Publishing.

Wood, D., Bruner, J., & Ross, G. (1976). The role of tutoring in problem-solving. *Journal of Child Psychology and Psychiatry and Allied Disciplines, 17,* 89–100.

Yoshimi, D. R. (1999). L1 socialization as a variable in the use of *ne* by L2 learners of Japanese. *Journal of Pragmatics, 31,* 1513–1525.

Zivin, G. (1979). Removing common confusions about egocentric speech, private speech, and self-regulation. In G. Zivin (Ed.), *The development of self-regulation through private speech* (pp. 13–49). New York: Wiley.

Appendix

TRANSCRIPTION CONVENTIONS

[	Indicates overlap with portion in the next turn that is similarly bracketed.
[[	Indicates overlap with portion in the next turn that is similarly bracketed. Used when the single bracket is used in the previous line/turn so that there will not be confusion regarding what brackets correspond to.
→	Line to be discussed in the text.
___	Portion of special note to the current analysis is underlined.
CAPS	Small caps in the discourse are used to show the speaker's emphasis.
?	Rising intonation.
,	Slight rise in intonation.
.	Falling intonation.
(( ))	Comments enclosed in double parentheses.
:	Elongation of a syllable.
(.)	Brief pause.
(..) (...)	Longer pauses.
(#)	Timed pause.
-	False start.
° °	Reduced volume—soft voice.
°° °°	Reduced volume—whispered.
°°° °°°	Reduced volume—very soft whisper, with consonant sounds articulated and certain vowel sounds difficult to determine.

T: The teacher in the particular excerpt; the identity of "T" may differ across excerpts.

S1:, S2: Unidentified student.

^ Glottal stop.

> < Spoken more quickly.

ABBREVIATIONS USED TO GLOSS JAPANESE

ACC	Accusative case marker.
NOM	Nominative marker.
TOP	Topic marker.
DAT	Dative marker.
GEN	Genitive marker.
INT	Interrogative marker.
adv	Adverbial affix.
CMP	Complementizer.
CONJ	Conjunction.
COP	Copula.
nom	Nominalizer.

Author Index

A

Ahmed, M. K., 3, 34
Aljaafreh, A., 10
Appel, G., 3, 15, 34
Arteagoitia, I., 130

B

Baars, B. J., 76
Baddeley, A., 67, 136
Baker, N., 135
Behrend, D. A., 31
Bell, A., 104, 137
Bellack, A., 28
Berk, L. E., 14, 17, 31
Bivens, J. A., 14, 17
Bjorklund, D. F., 5
Boggs, S. T., 6
Bonvillian, B., 5, 135
Brooks, F. B., 3, 6, 8, 10, 34, 74, 75, 236, 240, 256
Brown, R., 129, 143
Bruner, J., 6

C

Camarata, M. N., 135, 144
Camarata, S. M., 135, 144
Cazden, C. B., 31

Chamot, A. U., 35, 40
Chaudron, C., 132, 134
Clancy, P. M., 123
Consolo, D. A., 8, 188
Cook, H. M., 186, 187
Coughlan, P., 3, 232, 259
Coulthard, R. M., 28, 188
Crookes, G., 22

D

Denninger, M., 135
Diaz, R. M., 17
DiCamilla, F., 3
Donato, R., 3, 10, 34, 74, 75, 76, 124, 125, 236, 240, 256
Doughty, C., 129, 130, 144, 145
Duff, W., 3, 232, 236, 259
Dunn, W., 3

E

English, A. C., 68
English, H. B., 68

F

Faneslow, J., 132
Fotos, S. S., 130

Frauenglass, M., 17
Frawley, W., 14, 17, 34
Fridman, B., 130
Fuson, K. C., 17

G

Gallimore, R., 9, 73
Garvin, R. A., 14, 31
Gass, S. M., 33, 78, 126
Goffman, E., 104, 137
Goodwin, C., 78, 184, 192
Goodwin, M. H., 184, 192
Gopnik, A., 143
Guerrero, M., 3
Gupta, P., 67

H

Hall, J. K., 3, 6, 8, 125
Hallmon, J. E., 137
Hanlon, C., 129
Harley, B., 129
Hatasa, K., 131
Hatasa, Y., 131
Heritage, J., 136
Hjertholm, E., 31
Horiguchi, S., 180, 181
Human, R., 28

J

Jefferson, G., 78, 79, 135, 155
Johnson, K. E., 5
John-Steiner, V., 14, 34
Jorden, E. H., 127, 131

K

Kamio, A., 186
Kanagy, R., 123
Kaplan, B., 135
Kasper, G., 135
Kim, Y., 113, 114, 116, 126, 129
Kliebard, H., 28
Kohlberg, L., 31
Koyanagi, K., 130
Kramsch, C., 3
Krashen, S. D., 32, 129, 236
Kuczaj, S. A., 15, 32, 33, 54

Kupper, L., 35, 40

L

Lantolf, J. P., 3, 10, 14, 15, 17, 34, 36, 68,
   69, 74, 125
Lapkin, S., 3, 10, 113, 116–117, 124
Lave, J., 6, 41
Leeman, J., 130
Levinson, S. C., 78
Lightbown, P. M., 130, 145
Long, M. H., 22, 129
Lui, G., 3
Luria, A. R., 4, 18, 19, 68
Lyster, R., 129, 132, 134, 145

M

MacKay, D. G., 20, 67, 68, 136
Mackey, A., 113, 114, 116, 126, 129, 134,
   144
MacWhinney, B., 67
Makino, S., 131
Markee, N., 28, 135
Marriott, H., 180
Masur, E. F., 143
Matsuda, Y., 180
Maynard, S., 181
McCafferty, S. G., 14, 34
McDonough, K., 113, 114, 116, 126, 129
McGlone, J. V., 34, 236, 240, 256,
Mehan, H., 28,188
Meltzoff, A. N., 143
Miller, L., 181
Moerk, E. L., 92, 125, 129, 135, 143
Moroishi, M., 130
Muranoi, H., 132

N

Nakaone, T., 236, 240, 256
Nathan, D., 5
Nelson, K. E., 5, 135, 144
Nishimura, M., 137
Noda, M., 131

O

Ochs, E., 5
Ohta, A. S., 3, 6, 8, 9, 10, 12, 14, 17, 28,
   74, 75, 76, 124, 129, 133, 179,
   180, 187, 188, 189, 192, 198, 228

Oliver, R., 129, 148
Olszewski, P., 17, 70
O'Malley, J. M., 35, 40
Ortega, L., 129
Osborne, R. J., 76, 127

P

Pashler, H. E., 76
Peck, S., 32, 33, 65
Perlmann, R., 5
Perlmutter, M., 31
Peters, A. M., 6, 70
Philp, J., 129, 134, 144
Piaget, J., 13
Pica, T., 134
Platt, E., 3
Polio, C. G., 236
Porter, P. A., 113

R

Ramsey, R. M. G., 34, 35, 39
Ranta, L., 129, 132, 134, 145
Reisberg, D., 20
Reiss, M., 35, 36, 39, 40, 68
Reynolds, P. C., 69
Roberts, M., 129
Robinson, P., 22
Rosengren, K. S., 31
Ross, G., 6
Rubin, J., 35, 40
Rubin, K. H., 17
Russo, R. P., 35

S

Sacks, H., 78, 79, 135, 155
Saville-Troike, M., 12, 17, 32, 33, 54, 65, 69
Sawyer, M., 180, 199, 208
Schegloff, E. A., 78, 79, 135, 155, 184
Schieffelin, B. B., 5
Schmidt, R., 50, 79
Siegal, M., 180
Sinclair, J. M., 28, 188
Skehan, P., 22

Smith, D. J., 20
Smith, F., 28
Smolucha, F., 15, 31, 38
Snow, C. E., 5
Spada, N., 130, 145
Stewner-Manzanares, G., 35, 40
Strauss, S., 182, 184
Swain, M., 3, 10, 47, 113, 116, 117, 124, 129, 134

T

Tarone, E., 3
Terrell, T. O., 236
Tharp, R. G., 9, 73
Tosaku, Y., 131

V

van Lier, L., 3, 5, 14, 39, 71, 134, 153, 188, 189
VanPatten, B., 144
Varela, E., 129, 144, 145
Vygotsky, L. S., 6, 9, 10, 13, 17, 18, 73, 76, 90, 269

W

Watabe, M., 127, 131
Weir, R. H., 12, 17, 32, 33
Wenger, E., 6, 41
Wertsch, J. V., 6, 10, 13, 18, 74
Williams, J., 129
Wilson, M., 20
Wittrock, M. C., 76, 127
Wood, D., 6, 9

Y

Yaeger, J., 31
Yoshimi, D. R., 180, 186, 210

Z

Zivin, G., 17

Subject Index

A

Aa soo desu ka, 182–187, 190, 197, 199–204, 208–210, 213, 217–218, 221–222, 225–227, 229–230

Acknowledgement, 181–186, 190, 199–201, 208, 212, 221–222, 228–231

Active learning, 41, 50–64, 66, 71–72

Active listening, 77–79

Activity, 232–268
  effect of task design and implementation on activity, 250–261
  learner L1 use during activities, 235–249
  relationship between task and activity, 232–234, 268
  see also Peer interactive tasks

Addressee, 137–138
  see also Participant roles

Agreement tokens, 184–185
  see also Listener responses

Aizuchi, see Listener responses

Affordances, 3, 31, 71, 76, 128, 134, 142, 175
  as opportunities, 175
  corrective feedback as affordances, 128, 134
  in ecological model of SLA, 71

in private speech, 31
  see also Ecological model of SLA

Alignment, 181–190, 193–195, 199–204, 208–212, 216–221, 224–231
  aligning assessments, 181–182, 184, 188–190, 193–195, 199, 210, 212, 216–218, 224–227

Articulatory processes, 67–68

Asking for one's partner, 100–102

Assessments, 181–187, 190–195, 199–204, 208–212, 216–225
  see also Alignment

Assimilation/expansion processes, 19, 70–71

Assisted performance, 6, 9–11, 73–127, 194–197
  and interactive routines in classroom, 6
  enabling function of listener's role, 76–77, 79
  differential knowledge, role of, 76
  language acquisition as assisted performance, 9–13
  peer assistance, 88–124
    asking for one's partner, 100–102
    correcting linguistic errors, 96–100
    explaining, 102–103
    exposure to errors of peers, 113–124
    language play, 106–112

overhearing, 104–106
prompting and co-construction,
    91–96
waiting, 89–91
working memory and selective at-
    tention, 75–88
projection, role of, 78
teacher guidance in use of listener re-
    sponses, 194–197
see also Corrective feedback
Attention, 75–88
active listening, 77–79
joint attention, 81
selective attention, 75–88
see also Participant roles
Audience design, 136–138
see also Participant roles
Audio-video recording procedure, 25
Auditor, 137, 189–190
see also Participant roles
Auditory processes, 67

B

Backchannel responses, *see* Listener re-
    sponses
Beginning learners, production demands
    for, 77
see also Working memory

C

Checking mechanisms during interactive
    tasks, 261–265
Child language learners, 12–14, 18,
    31–33, 69–70, 125, 129,
    143–144
first language acquisition, 12–14, 18,
    31–32, 125,129, 143–144
corrective feedback, 129, 143–144
error similarity to adult second
    language learners, 125
inner speech, development of, 18
private speech, 12–14, 31–32
second language acquisition,
    31–33, 69–70
Choral responses, incidental recasts dur-
    ing, 154–160
Classroom, 3–4, 6–9, 37–127, 134–271
corrective feedback in second lan-
    guage classrooms, 134–178

audience design, 136–138
types of corrective feedback,
    140–172
interactional style in first-year class-
    room, development of,
    179–231
initiation/response/follow-up rou-
    tine, 188
student development in use of lis-
    tener responses, 197–228
teacher guidance in use of listener
    responses, 194–197
teacher use of listener responses,
    189–194
language learning in classroom con-
    text, 3–4
peer interactive tasks, 6–9, 73–127,
    232–271
assisted performance, 73–127
exposure to errors of peers,
    116–117
interactional routines in the class-
    room, 6–9
task design and implementation,
    232–271
use of English during peer interac-
    tive tasks, 235–249
private speech in foreign language
    classroom, 37–72
active learning, 71–72
assimilation/expansion processes,
    70–71
hypothesis testing, 69
individual differences in participa-
    tion, 68
simulative mode of functioning,
    private speech as, 69–70
structure of classroom events and
    private speech, 66
types of private speech in class-
    room data, 39–64, 67–68
Classroom participation, *see* Participa-
    tion, classroom
Co-construction, 78, 88–89, 91–96
Communicative language teaching, 22,
    129–132, 252, 269
Comparison of utterances, 48–51, 69
Completion of utterances, 50–54, 65–66
Confirmation questions, 141, 181,
    185–187, 190, 194–197,
    205–207, 213–219
Continuers, 184–185

see also Listener responses
Conversation, 28, 75–88, 179–231,
    260–261
  conversation analysis,28
  discourse structure of interactive
    tasks, 260–261
  peer interaction as conversational
    process, 75–88
  use of listener responses in conversa-
    tion, 179–231
  see also Social interaction
Correction, *see* Corrective feedback,
    Self-correction
Corrective feedback, 73–178
  classifying corrective feedback,
    138–139
  consequences of corrective feedback
    138–139
  definition, 135
  influence of learner errors on other
    learners 113–124
  impact of audience design and partic-
    ipant roles, 136–138
  importance of longitudinal data,
    177–178
  lack of uptake, 149–152
  learner-centered analysis, 128, 133,
    135–136
    definitions and methodology of
      analysis, 135–139
    results, 139–178
  longitudinal data, importance of,
    177–178
  peer interactive tasks and assisted
    learning, 73–127
  self-correction, 90, 115, 136, 173–175
  types of corrective feedback, 140–172
    correcting linguistic errors, 96–100
    explaining, 102–103
    incidental recasts, 152–172
    language play, 106–112
    next turn repair initiators (NTRI),
      96–99
    noticing corrective feedback ad-
      dressed to others,
      172–173
    prompting and co-construction,
      91–96
    recasts, 98–99, 143–152
  uptake, 132, 134, 138, 144–152,
    152–169, 175–177

Creativity in peer interactive tasks,
    259–261
Cultural values and concepts, 6–9, 73,
    134, 179–187
  general genetic law of cultural devel-
    opment, 10, 73
  interactional routines and cultural
    concepts, 6–9
  listener responses in Japanese, impor-
    tance of, 179–187
  sociocultural view of language acquisi-
    tion, 134

D

Data analysis, 2, 4–5, 21, 28, 30–31,
    37–39, 128–178, 180, 187, 226,
    237–240
  English language use, measures of,
    237–240
  learner development as part of func-
    tional system, analysis of 2,
    4–5, 21
  learner-centered analysis of corrective
    feedback, 128–178
  listener responses, longitudinal devel-
    opment of, 180, 187, 226
  methods of discourse and conversa-
    tion analysis, 28
  private speech as acquisition-in-pro-
    cess, 30–31, 37–39
Data collection, 21–28
  audio-video recording procedure, 25
  learner volunteers in study, 23–24
  teachers involved in data collection
    sessions, 24–25
  transcription of data, 26
Developmental sequence for listener re-
    sponses, 228–231
Direct method, 235–236
Discourse structure of interactive tasks,
    260–261

E

Eavesdropper, 137
Ecological model of SLA, 2–3, 71
Egocentric speech, 13
  see also Private speech
Engagement, 3, 31–32, 41, 55, 59, 65,
    71, 138–139, 206, 217, 250,
    261

importance in second language learning, 3, 31, 71
in peer interactive tasks, 250, 261
private speech as evidence of engagement, 31–32, 41, 55, 59, 65, 138–139, 206
repetition, 55, 59
vicarious responses, 41, 65
in teacher-fronted interactive routines, 217
English, use by second language learners during interactive tasks, 235–249
functions of English, 238–240
individual differences in use of English during interactive tasks, 242–249
measures of English language use, 237–242
Error correction, *see* Corrective feedback
Errors, 96–100, 113–124
exposure to errors of peers, 113–124
linguistic errors, correction of, 96–100
see also Corrective feedback, Self-correction, Self-repair
Evaluation, 181, 188, 191–192
Expansion processes, *see* Assimilation/expansion processes
Expert–novice interaction, 75–77, 87
Explaining, 102–103
External speech, relationship to private speech, 15, 18–19

F

First language use, *see* English
First language acquisition, *see* Child language learners
Focus on form, *see* Form-focused instruction
Form-focused instruction, 129–131, 235
Formulaic language, s*ee* Interactional routines
Functional systems, 4–5, 10, 21

G

General genetic law of cultural development, 10, 73, 125
Grammatical form, *see* Form-focused instruction

Group activity, *see* Social interaction, Peer interactive tasks

H

Hypothesis testing, 30, 46–54, 65, 69, 134
Ii desu ne, 190–192

I

Imitation, role in language comprehension, 16–17, 20, 143
Immersion education programs, 129–131, 144–145
Incidental recasts, 133, 141–143, 152–172, 175–176
definition, 141, 152
relationship to private speech, 160–165
Individual differences in language learning, 38–39, 68, 178, 225–269
differences in learner activities when doing same task, 232–235
effectiveness of corrective feedback, 178
first language use during interactive tasks, 242–249, 268–269
listener responses, use of, 225–228
oral rehearsal, 68
private speech, variability across individuals, 38–39, 68
Initiation/response/follow-up routine, 6, 8–9, 188–189, 198, 228
Inner rehearsal, *see* Mental rehearsal
Inner speech, 2, 15–21
development of inner speech, 2, 18–21
relationship to private speech, 15–17
see also Internalization
Innovation in peer interactive tasks, 259–261
Interaction, *see* Social interaction, Peer interactive tasks
Interactional routines, 5–9, 185, 187–189
Interactive tasks, *see* Peer interactive tasks
Internalization, 1–29, 73–74, 125
foreign language development as dynamic internalization process, 1–29

development of inner speech, 18–21
internalization of social interaction, 11–18
role of private speech in internalization, 12–14
peer interactive tasks and internalization, 73–74, 125
Interpsychological plane of linguistic functioning, 10, 18–19, 48, 67, 71, 73, 134
Interpsychological speech, *see* Social interaction
Intrapsychological plane of linguistic functioning, 10, 19, 47, 67, 71, 73
IRF routine, *see* Initiation/ response/ follow-up routine

J

Japanese, 22–23, 26–27, 41, 43, 54–55, 58, 62, 81–83, 93, 96, 106–107, 115, 130–131, 179–231
adjectival forms, 58, 62, 93, 96, 106–107
affective particles, 115, 186, 204–212, 213–225, 226–7, 230
see also Ii desu ne, Ne, Soo desu ne
affixes, rehearsal of, 54–55
confirmation questions, 181, 185–186
English translations of excerpts and examples, 26–27
desiderative form, 43
interactional style and listener responses, 179–231
analysis of listener responses in first-year classrooms, 187–228
proposed developmental sequence in use of listener responses, 228–231
role of listener responses in Japanese conversation, 181–186
locative expressions, 41
past form, 43
question forms vs. statements, 81–83
teaching methodology, 22–23, 130–131

meaning- v. form-focused instruction, 130–131
task-based instruction, 22–23
types of learner errors, 115

L

Language manipulation, *see* Manipulation of language
Language play, *see* Manipulation of language, Private speech
Learner-centered approach, 30, 72, 128–178
analysis of corrective feedback, 128–178
learner-centered student activity, 30, 72
Learner volunteers used in study, 23–24
Learning strategies and private speech, 34–36
Listener responses, 179–231, 260–261
analysis of listener responses in first-year classrooms, 187–228
initiation/response/follow-up routine, 188–189
student development in the use of listener responses, 197–228
teacher use of listener responses, 189–194
developmental sequence in use of listener responses, 228–231
teacher guidance in use of listener responses, 194–197, 260–261
types of listener responses in Japanese, 181–187
see also Acknowledgement, Agreement tokens, Alignment, Assessments, *Ii desu ne, Soo desu ne*
Listening, active, 77–79

M

Manipulation of language, 15–20, 31–33, 36, 61–65, 69–72, 106–112
during peer interactive tasks, 106–112

language play and private speech, 15–20, 31–32, 36, 61–65, 69–72
definitions and functions of private speech, 15–18
as evidence of analysis, 20
in foreign language classroom, 61–65, 69–72
studies of adult language learners, 36
studies of children learning first language, 31–32
studies of children learning second language, 32–33
see also Private speech
Meaning-focused instruction, 129–131
Meaningfulness of tasks, 252–253, 256–260
Mechanisms of assistance, *see* Assisted performance
Memory, effect of oral rehearsal on, 35, 67
see also Working memory
Mental rehearsal, 15–17, 20, 35–36, 67–68
inner speech, relationship to, 20
oral rehearsal, relationship to, 67–68
private speech, relationship to, 15–17, 35–36
see also Inner speech
Microgenesis, 10, 74
Motor skills, 20, 68

N

Ne, 182–187, 190, 194, 198–199, 204–212, 213–225, 227, 230
Next turn repair initiation, 96–99
Noticing, 50, 69–70, 78–83, 87, 97, 124–178
active listening during peer interaction, 78–83, 87, 125–127
corrective feedback, response to, 128–178
corrective feedback addressed to others, 172–173
definition, 138
incidental recasts, noticing of, 153, 155, 160, 165–167
recasts, noticing of, 144–152
self-correction, 173–175

exposure to errors of peers and noticing, 124
private speech and noticing, 50, 69–70
Novice–expert interaction, 75–77, 87
NTRIs, *see* Next turn repair initiators

O

Object regulation, 13
Oral rehearsal, 18–19, 33–36, 41–69, 70–72
active learning and oral rehearsal, 71–72
assimilation/expansion processes, 70–71
child second-language learners, 33
hypothesis testing, 69
individual differences in oral rehearsal, 68
inner speech development, 18–19
learning strategy studies, 35–36
manipulation, 61–65
of grammatical forms, 54–55, 58
of words and expressions, 56–58, 60
relationship to mental rehearsal, 67–68
repetition, 54–61, 64–65
role in language learning, 67–68
vicarious response, 41–54
Other regulation, 13, 73
Overhearing, 104–106, 137–138, 141, 152–153, 166, 170–172, 176–177
overhearers, learners' role as, 137–138, 141, 152–153, 166, 170–172, 176–177
as resource for learner performance, 104–106

P

Pair activity, *see* Peer interactive tasks
Participation, classroom, 3–4, 6–9, 41, 50–64, 66, 71–72, 77–79, 136–138, 179, 187–190, 193, 197–198
active participation, 41, 50–64, 66, 71–72, 77–79
active listening, 77–79

private speech, 41, 50–64, 66,
71–72
in context of classroom persons and
artifacts, 3–4
in initiation, response, and follow-up
routine, 188–189, 198
in interactional routines, 6–9
peripheral participation, 179, 187,
190, 193, 197–198
Participant roles, 136–138, 142, 176–177,
189–190
Pedagogical approach of language classes
studied, 22–23
Peer interactive tasks, 8–11, 22–23,
46–47, 66, 73–124, 89–103,
104–112, 124–178, 198–271
activity, relationship to task, 234
assisted performance in peer interactive tasks, 9–11, 88–112
asking for one's partner, 100–102
assistance with linguistic errors,
96–100
explaining, 102–103
language acquisition as assisted
performance, 9–11
language play, 106–112
overhearing, 104–106
prompting and co-construction,
91–96
waiting, 89–90
benefits of peer interactive tasks,
124–127
corrective feedback during peer interactive tasks, 128, 131–133,
139–140, 146–153, 165–178
incidental recasts, 165–172, 176
recasts, 146–152, 175–176
exposure to errors of peers, 113–124
language program and pedagogical
approach of study, 22–23
listener response development during
peer interactive tasks,
198–231
peer learning, theoretical basis of,
73–75
private speech during interactive
tasks, 46–47, 66
self-correction during peer interactive
tasks, 173–175, 176–177
task design and implementation,
232–271
creativity and innovation, 259–261

degree of interaction in second
language, 253–256
familiarity with task type, 262
first language use in peer interactions, 235–249
guidance in discourse structure,
260–261
meaningfulness of tasks, 252–253,
256–260
need to use the L2, 253–256
optimal peer interactions, 234–235
pairings of learners, 261
post-task follow-up, 267–268
pre-task instruction and checking
mechanisms, 261–265
repetition, 256–260
support availability, 265–267
teacher-fronted instruction prior
to interactive tasks,
241–242
working memory and selective attention in peer interaction,
75–88
see also Social interaction, Assisted
performance
Post-task activities, 267–268
Pre-task activities, 241–242, 249–251,
260–265
and quality of L2 use, 249–250
impact on learner L1 use, 241–242
Private speech, 11–21, 30–72, 79–81,
84–85, 108, 118–119, 139, 142,
152–153, 160–172, 175, 177,
206, 238–239
classroom foreign language acquisition, role in, 30–72, 79–81,
84–85, 108, 118–119, 206
active learning, evidence of,
71–72, 79–81, 84–85,
108, 118–119, 206
assimilation/expansion processes
and private speech,
70–71
classroom events, impact on private speech of, 66
data used in study, 37–38
frequency of private speech in
classroom, 38–39
hypothesis testing, 69
individual differences in participation, 68
manipulation, 61–65

oral rehearsal, 67–68
previous research, 31–36
repetition, 54–61, 65
simulative mode of functioning,
        private speech as, 69–70
student awareness of private
        speech, 40–41
vicarious response, 39–54, 65
corrective feedback and private
        speech, 139, 142, 152–153,
        160–172, 175, 177
definitions, 14–17, 38
first language use in peer interactive
        tasks, 238–239
functions of private speech, 17–18
inner speech, relationship to, 18–21
internalization, role of private speech
        in, 11–14
Private turns, 39–40, 66, 140, 152–153,
        160, 174
Process vs. product, 3
Projection, 78–79, 81, 83–87, 92
Prompting, 88–89, 91–96, 141
Pronunciation, 106–112

R

Recasts, 98–99, 133–134, 141–152,
        175–176
    see also Corrective feedback, Inciden-
        tal recasts, Uptake
Regulation, 13, 17–18, 31, 34, 73–74
    movement from other regulation to
        self-regulation, 13, 73–74
    regulatory function of private speech,
        13, 17–18, 31, 34
Repair, 79, 83–83, 89, 96–100, 103, 132,
        134–136, 138, 173, 239
    corrective feedback and repair, 132,
        134–136, 138
    by listener in peer interaction, 79,
        83–84, 89
    next turn repair initiation, 89,
        96–100, 103
    self-repair, 135–136, 173
    use of first language for repair, 239
    see also Self-correction
Repetition, 5, 17, 31–35, 40, 46, 54–68,
        70–71, 120–124, 134, 138, 141,
        153, 156–159, 165, 167, 172,

188, 192–193, 202, 211, 217,
        227, 251, 256–250
    and corrective feedback, 134, 138,
        141, 153, 156–159, 165,
        167, 172
    repetition as evidence of uptake,
        134, 138, 153, 156–159,
        165, 167, 172
    repetition as type of corrective
        feedback, 141
assimilation/expansion processes,
        70–71
children, studies of, 31–33
in development of interactional style,
        188, 192–193, 202, 211 217,
        227
functional system, part of, 5
interlocutor error, repetition of,
        120–124
learning strategies, studies of, 35
manipulation, 61–64
    oral rehearsal, 67–68
    of grammatical forms, 54–55, 58
    of words and expressions, 56–58, 60
use in private speech, 17, 31–35, 40,
        46, 54–68, 70–71, 172
use in peer interactive tasks, 251,
        256–260

S

Scaffolding, see Assisted performance
Scripting, 212, 231, 251
Selective attention in peer interaction,
        75–88, 127
Self-correction, 90, 115, 136 126,
        173–177
    see also Self-repair
Self-monitoring, 35, 127
    see also Self-correction, Self-repair
Self-regulation, 13, 17, 73
Self-repair, 135–136, 173
Simulative mode of functioning, 69–70
Social interaction, 1–29, 30, 33, 47–48,
        65, 69, 73–127, 134–138,
        179–231
    corrective feedback as affordance of
        social interaction, 134–135
    development of interactional style by
        first-year students of Japa-
        nese, 179–231

hypothesis testing, 30, 33, 47–48, 65, 69
initiation/response/follow-up routine, 188–189, 198, 228
language acquisition through social interaction, 1–29
interactional routines and language acquisition, 5–9
internalization of social interaction, 11–21
learner and social/interactive environment, 2–5
sociocognitive perspective, 21–28
participant status, impact on social interaction, 136–138
peer interactive tasks and assisted performance, 9–11, 73–127
assisted performance during interactive tasks, 88–112
exposure to errors of peers, 113–123
peer learning, theoretical basis of, 73–75
working memory and selective attention, 75–88
see also Peer interactive tasks, Assisted performance
Social speech, transformation into private speech, 15–17
Socialization in the classroom, see Interactional routines
Sociocognitive perspective of language acquisition, 21
Soo desu ne, 195, 199, 204–205, 208–210, 217, 230
Subvocalization, 20, 68
Successful learners, private speech and, 35–36, 39
Support, see Peer interactive tasks, Assisted performance

T

Task, see Peer interactive tasks
Task-based language instruction, 22–23
see also Peer interactive tasks
Teacher-fronted setting, 7–8, 39, 51–66, 107–108, 119, 121–122, 128, 131–133, 139–140, 145–149, 152–160, 173–175, 188–198, 210–217, 236, 241–268
corrective feedback in teacher-fronted setting, 128, 131–133, 139–140, 145–149, 152–160, 175
audience design, 137–138
incidental recasts, 152–160
recasts, 145–149
error correction after peer interaction, 119, 121–122
interactional routines in teacher-fronted setting, 7–8
language play in teacher-fronted setting, 107–108
listener response expressions, 188–198, 210–217
initiation/response/follow-up routine, 188–189, 198
student development in the use of listener responses, 197–198
teacher guidance in use of listener responses, 194–197, 210–217
teacher use of listener responses, 189–194
peer interactive tasks, relationship to, 241–268
post-task follow-up, 267–268
pre-task instruction, 241–242, 249–251, 260–265
support during tasks, 265–267
private speech in teacher-fronted settings, 39, 51–66, 119
application to social speech, 72
frequency, 39, 66
manipulation, 61–65
repetition, 54–61, 65, 119
vicarious response, 39–54, 65
self-correction in teacher-fronted setting, 173–175
use of first language, 236
see also Teachers, Teaching methodology
Teachers, 24–25, 233, 260–270
role of teachers in peer interactive tasks, 233, 260–270
importance to peer interactive tasks, 260–270
variation in teaching styles, effect of, 233
teachers involved in data collection sessions, 24–25

see also Teacher-fronted settings,
        Teaching methodology
Teaching methodology, 129–131,
        232–271
    meaning- v. form-focused instruction,
        129–131
    task design and implementation,
        232–271
        creativity and innovation, 259–261
        degree of interaction in second
            language, 253–256
        effect on use of first language by
            learners, 235–249
        guidance in discourse structure,
            260–261
        meaningfulness of tasks, 252–253
        pairings of learners, 261
        post-task follow-up, 267–268
        pre-task instruction and checking
            mechanisms, 261–265
        repetition, 256–260
        support availability, 265–267
    see also Teacher-fronted settings,
        Teachers
Total physical response, 235–236
TPR, *see* Total physical response
Transcription methodology and conven-
        tions, 26–27, 282
Translation of excerpts and examples
        used in study, 26–27

U

Unsuccessful learners and private
        speech, 35
Uptake 132, 134, 138, 144–152,
        152–169, 175–177
    corrective feedback and uptake, 132,
        134, 138, 144–152,
        152–169, 175–177
    definition, 138
    impact of participant roles, 176–177
    incidental recasts, 152–153, 160,
        175–176

lack of uptake, 149–152
recasts, 144–152, 175–176

V

Vertical construction, 88, 95
    see also Co-construction
Vicarious response, 17, 39–54, 64–65, 71
    as evidence of assimilation/expansion
        processes, 71
    definition, 17, 39
    private speech and vicarious response,
        39–54, 64–65
    rehearsal prior to social interaction,
        42–48

W

Waiting, 88–91
Working memory, 75–85, 137–138
    and selective attention in peer inter-
        action, 75–85
    effect of audience design on working
        memory, 137–138

Z

Zone of proximal development, 9–11, 34,
        46–48, 73–76, 90, 125, 128,
        212, 234
    corrective feedback as affordance of
        ZPD, 128
    definition, 9
    definition for classroom SLA, 9
    peer interaction in the ZPD, 9–11,
        73–76, 90, 125, 234
    private speech as snapshot of ZPD,
        34, 46–48
    repetition in ZPD, 212
ZPD, *see* Zone of proximal development